I'LL STOP TOMORROW

I'LL STOP TOMORROW

Barbara Tamasi

Paraclete Press
Orleans, Massachusetts

(The facts related in this book are all true. A few of the names have been changed to protect the privacy of the individuals involved.)

Copyright © 1982 by BARBARA TAMASI
Library of Congress Catalog Card Number: 82-80405
ISBN: 0-941478-03-3
All Rights Reserved
Published by Paraclete Press
Printed in the United States of America

Forward

To read this book is an emotional experience, for Barbara Tamasi has not spared or protected herself at all in the telling of her story. This book is a trip through hell — a graphic, no-holds-barred tour through the twisting labyrinth of a young woman's mental and emotional torture and suffering, tormenting fears, the bondage of sin and degradation that is alcoholism, and the terrible suicidal despair that is its inevitable fruit.

And yet this is one of the few modern stories of human self-destruction that has a genuinely happy ending! For Barbara Tamasi finds salvation, deliverance, and healing, in the form of a real and personal encounter with Jesus Christ, whom she finds has the power to utterly and totally transform her life, giving her an entirely new existence.

Writing this brief foreward is especially meaningful to me, for I had the privilege of sharing what God was doing in Barbara's life (and that of her husband Ray) as their pastor here on Cape Cod for a period of years, following their coming to Jesus. Barbara is a very genuine and open person, with a real love for Jesus. And I watched her grow emotionally and spiritually, as she continued to wrestle with herself and strove to go on with Jesus, in His plan for her life. For Barbara, as for anyone who is serious about following Jesus Christ, this has meant gut-wrenching honesty — letting the Holy Spirit ferret out all those little tricks of self-deception which are present in all of us, but which are so subtle and so destructive.

There may be those who will conclude that Barbara Tamasi has been much too open about herself — that she has told too many of the "gory details" of her sin and self-destruction. Yet there is a crying need in American society today for someone to tell *from a Christian perspective,* the true story of a life redeemed from the horrors of alcoholism, and to tell it in such a way that the weight of alcoholism's degradation is truly conveyed to the reader. This is what Barbara has been willing to do.

Alcoholism is one of the most devastating forces in American life. Ten million Americans are addicted to alcohol, and another twenty million are dangerously close to it. The number of Americans who use alcohol has doubled in the last 25 years, and one quarter of all accidental deaths and one half of all traffic fatalities are directly related to alcohol abuse! The National Council on Drug Abuse estimates that alcoholism costs our nation $40 billion per year!

Yet alcoholism is not confined only to people who are not "born-again" Christians. There are many, many pastors and church members alike who have drinking problems that are far more serious than they are admitting to themselves or anyone else. My experience as a pastor and as a traveling preacher and teacher has convinced me that there are hundreds of thousands of church-goers who are under the illusion that they are "social" drinkers, who "occasionally take a drink or two," and who have no idea of the hold alcohol has on their lives. And there are countless others whose lives are being directly or indirectly affected by alcohol, through the drinking of their spouse, or parent, or brother or sister. There is hardly a teaching or preaching mission for me anywhere in America, that someone (usually a distraught wife or mother) doesn't come to me, asking counseling help about how to handle the hideous problems that are exploding in the family, because of someone's drinking.

This book is definitely must reading for anyone whose drinking is creeping beyond the "social" stage, but it is also an important book for all Christians to read — not only because this is such an exciting account of how Jesus Christ can change a hopelessly fouled-up life, but also because of the importance of understanding the reality of what has become one of the biggest problems in modern America.

In the final analysis, the power of this book is the honesty and reality of the testimony contained in it: the awful darkness of sin and death into which Barbara's rebellion against God led her, and the overwhelming healing power of the love that same God mercifully showered down upon her in the person of His Son, Jesus Christ.

Peter Marshall
Cape Cod, 1982

1

The sunlight cast a thousand dancing stars across the blue rippled sea. As each wave broke and foamed ashore, I watched with tears running down my face. The white sand stretched for miles along the shimmering Costa del Sol. Sitting in our Volkswagen camper with the side door swung open, I turned to look at all the new hotels and motels. Surely there were many more than when we honeymooned here two years before. The recent additions lacked design, warmth and atmosphere — garish moneymakers, I thought, cheapening one of southern Spain's most romantic vacation spots.

The reconciliation I was hoping for between Raymond and myself hadn't happened. I had so counted on our recapturing the romance we had originally found here. Letting my mind drift back to those happy times, I was soon lost in dreams of fantasy. But then I was jolted awake to harsh reality by the memory of Ray's words that very morning: "Barbara, it's over! I can't go on any longer like this! It's tearing me apart, and you, too. I love you, Princess, and God knows I've tried to make it work, but it's too much for us. Perhaps apart we'll each have a chance; together we're both being destroyed."

In two years' time, not only had the Costa del Sol deteriorated. So had I.

All my hopes for the future, for my own recovery, for life itself, were over. I knew, without a shadow of a doubt, that I did not want to go on living, not without Raymond. All the emotional security I had ever had was in him. I thought back to my reply, that morning. "Oh, Ray!" I had sobbed. "Don't leave me! I'll stop tomorrow, I promise! I'll ease off today, and —"

But he just shook his head. "It's no use, Barbara. There have been a thousand tomorrows, and they all end up like today. No, it's over!" he shouted, and then, more quietly, "Today is Friday; we'll hang on until Wednesday, to straighten out the details of luggage and tickets and the camper. But that's it."

I knew it was final. I felt alone, empty and cold — and dry, all over my body. I craved a drink. It was that time again — two hours had passed since my last, and my master was calling me.

I made my way out of the camper. Legs wobbling, hands shaking, I went looking for the nearest bar, and there were many. Inside a brand-new hotel lobby, I asked the desk clerk for the cocktail lounge. My head turned, as I followed his finger in the direction of a dimly-lit, blue room. The walls were blue, the ceiling was blue, and there were blue lights casting deeper blue shadows on the walls. The lounge was empty; there wasn't even a bartender present. Looking at my watch, it was not surprising; it was only ten o'clock in the morning. All the tourists were either on the beach this beautiful morning, or seeing the sights.

"I wish I could be normal and do everyday things," I muttered to myself. There was a small bell on the bar. "Run!" came the thought. "Now is your chance. Don't ring the bell, don't!" As I sat on the bar stool, staring at the bell that could summon relief, however temporary, I saw a chance to leave this place, and all the places like it that I had been to and was headed for. What if, with all my will, I broke through the chains, by turning around and running back to the camper as fast as I could, back to Raymond?

What if I somehow managed to stay sober for this entire day? And then tomorrow, and the day after, and the day after that? Perhaps Ray would forgive me, before the plane took me to New York. Surely he *would* forgive me, if I proved I really meant it. Right now, in spite of all the gut-wrenching misery and fear, I could start my life over. All I had to do was rotate the stool I was sitting on, get up and start walking. Do it, do it!

I shook my head. Who did I think I was kidding? I had tormented myself with this game too often. I reached out and smacked the bell hard with the palm of my hand.

As I waited, I could feel myself being engulfed by the blue loneliness in this room. Afraid to look at the blue walls that were changing shape, I focused on the door, hoping that the bartender would hurry up and come before these walls actually crept up and over me, making me one with this room.

I was reminded of those weird mirrors in the fun house at Coney Island. I could remember the hideous shapes I took on, as I stood in front of them when I was a little girl running through the amusement park, not listening to Peepa's or Uncle Leo's voices far behind me: "Bobbie, wait, wait, don't run so fast!"

But I didn't listen. I kept on going, until I suddenly stopped short in front of one of those mirrors. Terrified by what I saw, I screamed, "Peepa! Uncle Leo! Hurry! Come and get me!" I thought the mirror might somehow become long enough to touch me and make me one with it, devouring me.

The blue walls were getting closer now, and I wanted to scream. Again I slammed the bell hard. If there *was* a choice to be made five minutes or ten minutes ago, I had lost it now. I had to have a drink, or I'd go insane. "Uh, Madam." I jumped; it was the desk clerk. "Sorry to keep you waiting, but our bartender doesn't come in until later. May I get you something?"

"A brandy and a beer, please." I looked down at my hand, which was shaking, as I checked my supply of pesetas. "What difference does it make what I have," I muttered to myself. "There'll never be enough of anything to satisfy me. I always have to go back for more and more. And when I've drunk enough to get my mind and body back to where I can get up from this bar stool and walk out of here without screaming, by the time I get to the end of the block, I'll have to look for another bar and another drink."

I threw the brandy down. It was harsh stuff, and it burned my throat. It had been too long since my first few drinks early this morning. There wasn't enough alcohol in my system, and I began to feel sick. My stomach was empty, and I knew I'd be throwing up bile within minutes, unless I was able to keep the next few drinks down. As quickly as I could, I drank the glass of cold beer in front of me. It soothed my throat. I motioned for the clerk to bring another round of the same, and in a whisper added, "Please make it quick; I'm in a hurry."

Signals went out to the extremities of my body that help had arrived. As the warmth began to expand rapidly from my middle, the tremor in my hands lessened, and my breathing deepened. I relaxed; I could cope again. I could even drink the second beer without gulping it, and now I could go and purchase the pills.

Paying the bill, I left, and as though I was being led, I made my way out and up the street. People were smiling, shopping, and laughing on their way to the beach. Grimly, I turned into the local pharmacy. Not stopping to think if I needed a prescription, I asked the pharmacist for some 25-milligram Libriums.

"I have only ten milligrams, madam."

"That will be fine. I'll take as large a bottle as you can give me. I'm going to be traveling through Europe for the next three months, maybe longer. I don't want to be bothered having to stop in each country to find a doctor just to have a prescription refilled."

"Madam, you don't have to explain. I'll give you as large a bottle as you want. How will a fifty be?"

"Great! I mean, that's fine. That'll get me through the rest of this trip."

"Is there anything else I can get for you?"

"Yes," I said, straining to remember the different drugs I knew about. "Uh, I used to take some rather large red and grey capsules for stomach pain. Would you by any chance know what they are?"

"Of course; Darvon."

Like a little kid who was about to be given a large bag of penny candy, I beamed. "Yes, that's the name. Will I need a prescription for those?"

"No, not here."

"Okay, what's the largest quantity I can buy?"

"I'm sorry, but I can't sell more than fifty of them at a time."

"Oh, that's all right. I'll take them."

With the two bottles of pills rattling in my handbag as I walked out, I felt prepared. Yet still I fantasized about coaxing Ray into giving me one more chance. Tears filled my eyes, and quiet sobs wracked me, as I realized that that was all it was: fantasy. It was too late.

"Why drag the torture out until next Wednesday?" I muttered to myself, oblivious of the sidewalk passers-by. "Why not end it all now? But what if . . . ? if nothing! There have been too many if's." I looked at my watch, startled as usual at how much time had passed. I had to get back to the camper soon, if I wanted to be with Ray and the gang that night. But first I needed to fortify myself for the evening. I had to stop these awful shakes, had to function.

Death, dead, die — the words kept running through the back of my mind, taunting me. I felt cold and shivered, though the sun was beating down now, hot on the pavement.

Looking into each bar that I passed, I seemed to see them for the first time as they really were — not romantic, charming and full of atmosphere, but dark and dingy and dirty. Smiles that I had thought were warm and genuine now appeared as though they were taped at the corners of the mouths of men whose eyes roamed over me. My heart began pounding wildly. It felt irregular, my legs were rubbery, unable to support me, and my face began tightening up. Every noise, every honk in traffic, became intensified. My head echoed eerie voices and laughter. I hugged my arms to my body, as they began to flail. The sun's heat penetrated my entire being, and I felt as though I was on fire. As if I were on a desert, running for water, I darted into the next bar. It was afternoon now, and men were swarming at the bar, where glasses of red and white wine, already poured, were lined up. Working my way to the front, oblivious to those around me, I tried to pick up a glass but my hands were trembling too much. Spilling the wine, I tilted the glass slightly towards me and bent down to drink it. I finished one, two, three. And then, feeling the good warmth inside, I began to feel alive again. Life was flowing through my veins, and I could once again look up, breathe, function. Opening my purse, I put some money on the bar.

Ten or fifteen glasses of wine later, I emerged from the bar full of confidence, smiling, and as though I hadn't a care in the world. Joining with the flow of people, I sauntered down the crowded late-afternoon streets, and back to the beach where we were camping in our van. The sun was low on the horizon, and everything was bathed in liquid gold, which corresponded exactly to how I felt inside.

But as I spotted Raymond, sitting in the door of the camper, his arms folded and his head hanging low, the reality of what was happening to us hit hard. Oh, my God, no! Don't let this happen!

"Ray! Ray!" I sobbed, running and stumbling towards him. "I love you, I've always loved you, please, please don't leave me! I'll do anything, I'll try again, we'll get help, please, *please* . . ." Raymond looked up. His hazel eyes in the long, narrow face had lost their sparkle, as they gazed at me.

"You're drunk again, Barbara. Get out of my sight."

Stunned, I knew then that Raymond really intended to carry out every word of what he had said. Sensing the end of our marriage and for me, my life, I staggered across the street, in the direction of the hotel bar I frequented the most. "Oh, Ray," I mumbled, "if you only knew what hell this is, and how much you mean to me." I found a seat at the bar. "Oh, my God, Ma, Mommy, help me! Somebody, please, please help me." I thought then of my grandfather, to whom I had always turned for solace as a little girl. Up until he died, I had felt closer to him than to anyone else in the world. "Peepa," I whispered to him, "it's all over. I want to be with you and Meema now." I felt for the pills in my purse. Dark, moving shadows filtered into the room. Looking at the reflection of the bleary-eyed woman in the mirror behind the bottles, and then at my watch, I realized that it was after six. All around me were Spaniards who had stopped off for a drink on their way home. "If only I could be like them, ordering my first drink of the day," I murmured, trying in vain to remember how much beer, wine and brandy I had consumed. I lifted my head, and stared back at the woman with the bloated face in the mirror. I made myself slow down. I didn't have to gulp my wine; I had all the time in the world. Ray didn't want me back.

Outside in the early evening, the shadows were rapidly growing longer. Inside, it seemed like a dark shadow was looming ahead — very dark and very soon. My mind was settling into a grim resolve. But before it did, it suddenly seemed important to try to see where the darkness had begun. Sipping my wine with my head hung low, my long dark hair straggling around my face, I began to remember what it was like growing up in Borough Park, Brooklyn.

Our family occupied the second floor apartment of a house on 46th Street, between 14th and 15th Avenues. All the houses were close together, separated by little alleys, and it wasn't at all unusual for more than one family to live in a house. In fact, the sharing of homes and meals by other relatives or boarders was the accepted thing. Ours was a Jewish neighborhood, with a synagogue within walking distance, no matter where you lived.

In our particular apartment on the second floor, there were seven of us, living in five and a half rooms. My mother and I shared the same bedroom until I was six years old, and "Ginsey" died. Ginsey was the old widow whom Meema, my mother's mother, had felt sorry for and taken in as a boarder. When I was moved into her bedroom, I liked having a room of my own, but I did not like being alone in the dark.

My mother always stood erect and so seemed taller than her five-foot-six. Fairly slim, with her long, dark hair neatly pulled back into a well-coiffed chignon, she was elegant-looking, and her elongated face, high cheekbones, and long, straight nose added to her distinctive look. Her deep-set eyes, a family trademark, were a sparkling olive green. Dark, tailored clothes and conservative suits with wide-brim, black and navy picture hats, slightly tilted to one side, added to the sophisticated look she seemed so proud of.

She never entered a room or walked down a street unnoticed. In fact, when one added her fluency in Swedish, and her having lived abroad for more than eight years, married to a Swede, there was no one living in Borough Park with a comparable background.

Her father, Jacob Ginsbourg (who later changed his name to Bourg), had been a well-known voice teacher. Associating with artists and musically creative people, he, like Mother, had looked down on the mundane lives of the "ordinary" people of Borough Park. Mother felt significantly superior to her surroundings and had a job that bore out this conviction — selling precious stones and jewelry at the chic Georg Jensen showroom in mid-Manhattan.

I idolized Mother and couldn't wait for her to come home from work at the end of each day. From a distance, I could see her picture hat coming. Almost with awe, I would run down the sidewalk to meet her and fall into her arms. She was special — aloof and untouchable — yet she let me hold her hand as we walked the long block. The neighbors sitting on their stoops stared at us and whispered, but I didn't care.

With Meema and Peepa, everything was dependably constant, and the love was the same, too. Unlike Mother, they did not have mercurial mood changes. Mother was still suffering the aftereffects of her stormy marriage to my father in Sweden, and the war in Europe. Since her divorce became final in 1945, and I was born in 1941, I suspected that she still hoped that there might be a reconciliation. The decision she made, to move back home to Brooklyn after I was born, was a hard one. To go back, after having been away from home and from the entire life-style of her family for nine years, was something she did not want to do. But on the other hand, there was me now, and Mother was afraid of responsibility.

So home Mother went, and yet, with her heart so divided about where she was, it didn't take much to throw her into one of her frequent temper tantrums. I always found excuses for her: there were so many people living together, and we were all so different. And with each tension-packed scene that erupted in our household, there were always warm tears and embraces afterwards, when the storm was over and everyone had settled down. There was, too, the reward of freshly-packed ice cream that Uncle Leo Karl would go out and buy for us all. We would all sit in the kitchen, our favorite gathering place at any hour of the night or day — Meema, Peepa, Mother, Uncle Leo and I — finishing every drop of our ice cream and listening to the radio.

Sometimes we would go into the living room, where I would snuggle up on Peepa's lap, as he sat in his big arm chair that no one else ever dared sit in. After we got a TV, we would sit glued to our favorite programs — "Arthur Godfrey's Talent Scouts," "I Remember Mama," and "The Milton Berle Show."

As the evening drew to a close, Uncle Leo went off to sleep on the glass-enclosed porch that doubled as his bedroom. When it was cold, it was really cold on that porch, and Uncle Leo pulled the covers way up over his head. Meema would finish puttering around in the kitchen, kiss me goodnight, and go to her and Peepa's bedroom. Meema's sister, Aunt Rose, slept on a couch in the foyer or telephone room, as it was called, in between the living room and Meema and Peepa's room. I kissed Mother goodnight in the kitchen, and Peepa would tuck me in. After singing me one of his favorite old Russian songs, he began telling me a bedtime story, as he had done every night that I could remember. I loved Peepa so; his soft white hair, always neatly parted and combed, framed his handsome face.

"Peepa, wake up! Don't fall asleep now. Tell me one more story, just one more, please!"

"All right, Mamashena, all right. Your Peepa will tell you about when he was a little boy going to school in Russia." And he would pause to remember. "The winters, Mamashena, were very long and very, very cold. When I got up, it was always still dark outside."

"But Peepa, why did you get up so early? Weren't you afraid of the dark?"

"Oh no, my baby. I had to get up early, because I had to walk miles in the snow."

"Peepa, how high did the snow come on you?"

"Oh," he replied solemnly, his eyes dancing, "way up to my waist."

Taking his hand in mine, I asked, "And your hands? They must have been frozen!"

He nodded. "They were so red and cold, they hurt."

Kissing the hand, I said, "I love you, Peepa. They don't hurt any more, do they?" Smiling and shaking his head, he got up to leave and join Meema in their room, and I fell off to sleep.

How I loved Peepa and everything about him! His gentleness in caring for me was evident in everything he said and did. He was my refuge from the world outside, and the balm for all my hurts. I played with him and Meema more than any of my friends my own age. He was my hope, always there to strengthen and take care of me, forever.

Standing a plump five-foot-one, Meema was a good match for him. She mingled with everyone in the neighborhood, and there wasn't a person who didn't come to love her warm, humorous, compassionate ways. I loved Meema, adored her, and was the apple of her eye.

Meema ran the house and kept all the aunts, uncles and cousins united as a family. But just as her enthusiasm rubbed off on anyone around her, her sadness, too, rubbed off, though it was seldom in evidence. We had barely enough money to get along on in those days, and Meema was a professional worrier. Would Peepa's little furniture store bring in enough money for food that week? Often Meema hid various delicacies around the house, not wanting everything to disappear in one or two days. She had her secret hiding places, and when Mother and Uncle Leo stealthily raided the icebox in the middle of the night, they couldn't outsmart Meema, no matter how hard they tried.

But for all her ability to get her way, she could not run Mother's life; no one could. Many times Meema's heart grieved over her eldest daughter's mistakes. How badly she had wanted her Harriet to marry Clement, a good local Jewish doctor, but Mother eloped with Per Scheutz, a Swede, and a gentile as well. That broke Meema's heart and caused a mother-daughter split that had lasted until they were once again under the one roof. Meema opened her heart as well as her arms to Mother, and Mother ran to her, with all her hurt and rejection. For she was looking for love and acceptance, as well as a home to raise me in.

In our neighborhood, I used to wonder about all the men in black clothes I used to see whenever Meema took me visiting in the neighborhood. There were quite a few Orthodox Jews in Borough Park. They kept kosher homes, ate with separate dishes, and didn't answer the telephone or carry a purse or ride anywhere on Saturday. For Saturday was the Sabbath, and we all knew it, even if we didn't know what it meant. For those who wore black, attendance at Temple all day Saturday was a must. And aside from those in long black robes and wide-brimmed black hats, there were others who wore clothes with yarmulkahs.

A cantor chanting was often heard in the distance, as the men continually bowed their heads in prayer. There was much singing, and sometimes some wailing and weeping, too. Often I slipped in and out of Temple, just to see what was going on. I loved to be there when the service was over, and there would be tasty delicacies for the taking on various buffet tables set up downstairs in a fellowship room — mohn cake (cake with poppy seeds), sponge cake, home-made cookies and Halvah candy. I used to fill my little grocery bag full, if I could, and people laughed and thought me cute.

There were, of course, many reformed Jews, whose religious observances were modified, and many like ourselves who kept no laws, no fasts, and no formal customs. Indeed on occasions, Peepa even smuggled bacon into the house! Yet still, I could feel the pride of being Jewish emanating from Meema and Peepa. And more than a few Jewish customs were traditional in our home, too, like Friday night being set aside for delicious homemade chicken soup with matzoh balls, followed by gefilte fish and roast chicken or flanken (boiled beef with horseradish).

Meema prepared our Friday night feasts, and Peepa often helped by washing the dishes, once in a while breaking one as he scurried about. Meema would hold her head and scream in a high, shrill voice, "Karl, Karl, my good dishes!" They fought loudly, cried together and laughed together. They were friends, and enjoyed being with each other. And I, who could always feel their love, spent as much time with them as I could. Perfectly free to let their emotions show, they were absolutely *real* and stood undivided, as one.

Saturday was my favorite day. Alone with Meema and Peepa, I had coffee cake and light coffee with sugar cubes dunked in a tall glass — my favorite breakfast. When Uncle Leo finally got out of bed after many rousings from Meema and me, he, Peepa and I would go to the furniture store, while Meema remained home to clean up and perhaps visit some of her women friends. There were times I went with Meema from house to house, eating cakes and drinking tea, but what I loved the most about Saturday was having lunch at the store. All of Peepa's cronies came in, and Peepa went to the local delicatessen and came back with warm rye bread with caraway seeds, hot pastrami, corned beef, knishes, kosher pickles, cole slaw and Dr. Brown's celery, black cherry and cream sodas. Seated around Peepa, all nine or ten of us would eat, laughing and talking until everything was finished. When Uncle Leo took over the store for the afternoon, Peepa and I left for the movies.

Either the Loew's, the Borough Park or the Windsor would have a double-feature we hadn't seen. From two until five o'clock we would sit watching cartoons, news, previews, and two movies, laughing together, or Peepa holding my hand in the scary parts. It seemed that, no matter what the film, there was always something to cry about, and if the movie was really sad, like "The Al Jolson Story," we both cried.

On high holy days like Yom Kippur, I went to Temple, with either Meema or my friends. Depending on the Temple, we sat either upstairs with the women or to one side of a large hall. I was always very excited and felt good in the beginning of the service, although I didn't understand a word of Hebrew or Yiddish. But after a while, I became tired of standing up and sitting down so many times, and couldn't wait to leave. I watched the men, especially the rabbi and the older ones, as they prayed, bending back and forth. They would sing, lifting their hands up to the sky. When the prayer of Kaddish came, prayers for the dead, I knew the service was close to the end. Even those who weren't religious at all stood for Kaddish, and although Meema didn't sing or pray or stand much through the service, she stood for Kaddish. I privately believed that she actually came only for that part of the service.

There was a smell in synagogue, one that I couldn't associate with any other place. It was old, like opening a closet door that has all old clothes inside, no mothballs and no odors, just age. It didn't matter what temple I went into, it was always there.

Saturday over with, I looked forward to Sunday, as that was the day Aunt Mary and Uncle Leo Sheirr came to visit from Flatbush. I always wondered what kind of hat Aunt Mary would wear. It was a standing joke for us to say, "Meema, do you think Mary will have a feathered hat, or a sequined one? Or will it look like a bird's nest?"

Aunt Mary always brought me a little present and made a big

fuss over her "Pussycat." Uncle Leo Sheirr didn't show his feelings like Mary, but I never doubted his affection for me. Unlike Mother, Aunt Mary had a turned-up pug nose. Her personality, too, was different from her sister's — more outgoing and talkative. She either complemented or clashed with Mother. Some Sundays were complementary, but others turned into a great big clash. Whichever it was, I was always in the middle, hearing and seeing all.

Nevertheless, I was happy, very happy. And the night that the whole family gathered together for one of Meema's Passover (Pesach) dinners called the Seder, was the most special memory of my young childhood. Meema used her special china and silverware, and all week long she prepared different traditional dishes that befitted this festive occasion, commemorating Israel's dramatic deliverance from enslavement in Egypt.

Mother looked almost regal with her black crepe dress and Georg Jensen jewelry. Uncle Leo Sheirr was handsome in his new dark silk suit and tie, seated next to Aunt Mary, who wore a shimmering lamé dress. Even Uncle Leo Karl had taken the time to trim his new mustache. Meema was in the kitchen. Her apron covered part of her bright pink-and-white print dress. She was precious, and I beamed at her very presence; rarely did she get so dressed up. But Peepa, naturally, was the handsomest man that walked the earth. His white hair was parted and combed in place. His suit, shirt and tie were impeccable.

I felt proud of my family. Seated on a piano bench, encircled by everyone I loved, I looked down at my small glass of Manischewitz wine. As we all raised our glasses to our lips, I tasted for the first time something strong, sweet and very delicious. Intending to return my glass to the table, I held on to it instead. Tilting my head back, I swallowed every drop, except for the last. That one I held and savored as long as I could. Moments later a warm sensation flowed down my arms, legs and feet, and making its way back, rested in my stomach. What a feeling! Such warmth and sweetness. "Meema, can I please have some more of that?" I asked, pointing to the crystal wine decanter.

"No, no more for you, Mamashena." And for the briefest of

moments her smile vanished, and a look of grave concern flashed across her face. In that instant, she looked as though she wasn't even with us, remembering something dark and brooding from the past.

But dinner was well under way, and excitement and chaos echoed from the kitchen and through the hall to the living room, as Peepa carried in bowls full of hot soup. Usually, about the time we were finishing our last piece of apple strudel, Aunt Mary spilled her wine, a yearly ritual she always managed to do, as Uncle Leo Karl began clowning around. As we laughed, he became funnier and funnier, almost zany. Leaving the table, he disappeared somewhere in the house and returned with a cane in his hand, and an old, worn hat that he tilted. Impersonations of Charlie Chaplin, old drunks, and almost anything he could think of, began the show. Later, we took and watched home movies. Uncle Leo was the master of ceremonies and the star. His audience delighted in his every gesture.

Bittersweet memories, followed by tears welling up in Meema's light blue eyes, drew the evening to a close. Sitting on Peepa's lap, my head resting on his shoulder, I listened to Meema say: "When I'm gone, children, I want you all to stick close, stay together."

Aunt Mary and Mother abruptly interrupted: "No, Mama, don't talk like that. We couldn't live without you!"

2

As loved and secure as I felt at home, outside, with my friends on the block, I felt uncomfortable, gawky. Ellen Weissberg was my closest friend. She lived several houses down from us, and I spent most of my time there. She was shorter and chubbier than I, but her close-cropped curly hair always looked neat. Her parents owned their own home, even though they let out the second and third floors. And since Ellen's father was a butcher, they ate meat often. I frequently hung around their kitchen at mealtimes, hoping to be invited to stay for dinner. It was always more fun to eat at someone else's house.

I tried to please Ellen, to be accepted by her, and I let her boss me around. And when Ellen's older sister teased me about my skinny legs and long hair, saying things like: "Bobbie, you'd better have all your hair cut off, or you'll get bugs in it, and they'll never come out," I sat on the front stoop of their house and cried.

My schoolmates teased me, too, about my last name, Scheutz, and who and where my father was. The teasing intensified all that year in the second grade at P.S. 64. It hurt, as it was meant to.

Content with second place, or any place that Ellen would allow me to have when we played together, I tried desperately to win her approval, as well as her sister's. But no matter how hard I tried, I seemed to fall short of that goal. Giving in to bitter feelings of revenge, I finally exploded one hot summer's day. Most of the time we played at Ellen's house, but on this particular day she agreed to come and play with me at my house. Eagerly I forewarned Meema, and there were special cakes and cookies for us on the kitchen table with glasses of cold milk. But Ellen took one step into our hallway and turned around. "I'm going home, Bobbie. I don't want to play at your house. I don't like it here."

"No, no, you can't! You said you'd play here. I *always* go to your house!" But Ellen continued to walk down the alley, and I ran out into the small back yard behind our house. There on the ground I spotted an old leather strap. In a rage, I took the strap and ran after her. She was halfway to the street. Grabbing her by the arm and screaming "I hate you! I hate you!" I hit her hard across the back with the strap. She shrieked in pain and ran home, screaming. Dropping the strap, I just stood there, filled with panic about what I had done.

After I told Mother what had happened, Ellen's mother came running over to our house, furious at me and our whole family. Mother decided to take me to see a child psychiatrist. He asked me some questions and talked to me, then told my mother not to worry. "I wouldn't be overly concerned, Mrs. Scheutz. She's a normal child and children show their feelings and hatreds towards one another more freely than we do!"

It wasn't long before I began to cling to Meema and Peepa, even visiting them at the store during my lunch hour. Nor was the third grade any improvement over the second. I got by with my homework, with help from Uncle Leo Karl. But questions like "What does your father do, Barbara?" and "What? You've never even *seen* your father?" made me demand an answer.

"Mother, where *is* my father? Who is he, and why doesn't he want me?" But my mother always managed to pacify me for the moment or distract me, without ever really answering my question. She let slip bits of information, mere fragments that I grabbed on to, hoping somehow to get enough pieces to put the puzzle together. One of the pieces was the "war". Mother had told me that after the war broke out, she longed to return to America to Meema and her father.

"Mother," I asked then, "you mean Peepa, don't you? Why didn't you say his name?"

She looked at me solemnly. "Barbara, there is something I've been meaning to talk to you about, to tell you. . . ." But I cut her off completely, suddenly sensing that I did not want to hear one word of what she intended to tell me.

"Never mind, Mommy, we'll talk some other time. I want to go now," and I ran off.

Kneeling on the sofa on our glass-enclosed porch, I looked out the window and began to let my mind drift off into fantasy about my father coming back here for me and my mother. Even though it had been four years since the war was over, I hoped and almost believed that it was taking him all this time to get his affairs settled in Sweden, before he could actually come and stay with us all. And when he did, then I would become whole. I would run to Ellen's house first and tell her the news, and then to school and tell all my classmates and teachers. I would be like everybody else, and most important, I would finally know that my father did care about me, and that I wasn't abandoned.

My chain of thought was interrupted by the ring of the telephone. Lifting my head from the corner of the couch, I could see Meema through the glass door, talking on the telephone. I opened the door and went out to her.

"Meema, Meema," I whispered, "hurry up, please. Don't talk any more on the telphone."

Meema said a few more words and then hung up. "Mamashena, what's the matter?"

"Meema, there's something I want to ask you."

"Yes, my darling?"

"Meema, Mommy was telling me that it was because of the war that she and my father separated. She also told me that she wanted to come home to you, but when she said it, she said to Meema and her father. Why didn't she say Peepa?" Meema's smile left her face as I continued. "And I remember now that when Uncle Duddy came home from the service, he called you Mama and Karl. Why do he and Uncle Leo call Peepa Karl, instead of Daddy or Father?"

Meema's face was frozen now. "Let's go in the kitchen and have some strudel I made."

"No, Meema, I don't want strudel now. Aunt Mary and Aunt Shirley also call Peepa Karl, instead of Father. Why?" But Meema refused to answer, saying that she had to talk to my mother about something.

The next day was Sunday, and Aunt Mary and Uncle Leo Sheirr had come to visit, as they usually did. Mother called me into the kitchen, which for once was empty.

"Barbara, I have something I've wanted to tell you for a long time," my mother said in a soft but firm voice. Sensing that I was not going to like what I was about to hear and instantly recalling my conversation with Meema on the porch the day before, I drew back.

"I don't want to hear it, Mommy."

"Barbara, you will just have to listen: Peepa is not your real grandfather."

"What are you saying, Mommy? Peepa is here. He's alive!"

"Barbara, child, you've got to know the truth. Your real grandfather, Jacob Bourg, was a very special and important person. He was a great artist and teacher of voice." Seeing me recoil in shock, Mother nonetheless continued. "I know how good Peepa has been to you and how much you love him, but —"

I glared back at Mother and screamed: *"Nooo!* You don't know what he means to me, and how much I love him. None of you know. He and Meema are my life. I have no father, but I've Peepa, and he's all mine, all mine. And don't you tell me that he's not — not my blood." Hot tears filled my eyes, and I ran the length of the apartment to the bathroom, locking myself inside. I knelt beside the bathtub, my knees pressed against the cold tile floor. Agonizing sobs and pain came from deep inside me. I paid no attention to the banging on the door, until I heard my Meema's voice, faint and choking with tears: "Bobbilla, come on out, *please.* It's true, but it doesn't matter. No one can ever take your Peepa's place. The blood means nothing, nothing. He loves you with all his heart. Come out, now."

Immediately I got to my feet and opened the door. Hugging Meema for a quick moment, I ran to Peepa who was slumped over in his big chair, sobbing and blowing his nose into a big white handkerchief, the kind he always carried in his pocket. I climbed onto his lap and pressed my cheek against his. Rubbing my face hard against his whiskers so that I wouldn't feel the hurt inside my heart and the knot in my stomach, I said nothing, but just cried. Peepa held me and rocked me back and forth, until both of us were worn out from crying.

Gradually more facts unfolded that year that I was eight. I found out that Meema had had three husbands, not two, and that Aunt Shirley and Uncle Duddy were both children from her second husband, Nathan. But in my eyes, that only made things worse, because now none of the children were from Peepa. I drew closer to him than ever, determined to make up to him all the love that had never been his.

I was nine years old and in the fourth grade. It was a beautiful, sunny winter's afternoon. My books tucked under my arm, I swung around our house, and standing in the alley below the kitchen window I yelled up: "Meema? I'm home! Can you throw me down a salami sandwich and a pickle?"

Usually Meema responded right away. Waiting to see her smiling face, I called again: "Meema? Meema, where are you?" Still no response. Puzzled, I walked out of the alley, around the front of the house and up the other side alley, to the side door. Running up the stairs, two steps at a time, I stopped short before our landing. Strange voices were coming from our apartment, and the door was ajar. More hesitantly now, I climbed the last stairs, one at a time.

Meema was in the doorway, tears streaming down her face. Just then, I heard an ambulance siren. As I took one step into our doorway, I turned, looking through the living room, into the hall. Peepa was lying there on the kind of stretcher that takes people to hospitals. Men in white uniforms were hurrying him past me. "Wait,

wait! What happened, Peepa?" I rushed to his side. His eyes were wet and bloodshot. He was tightly bound in blankets, and I couldn't get to his hand. They wouldn't stop, so that I could kiss him, or anything.

"I love you, Mamashena," he barely whispered. "Remember, your Peepa loves you."

"He's had a heart attack, a serious one," a voice said from somewhere.

I paced the streets outside Maimonides Hospital in Borough Park. Too young to visit, I took long walks with Uncle Leo Sheirr, who did his best to cheer me up. "He's going to live, Bobbie," and he was right. Peepa recovered, and after all his friends and relatives had paid their respects, Meema and Peepa and I had our very own reunion, just the three of us.

We three were closer than ever after that. The following summer, we had our first vacation together. I was nine years old, and we went to a kosher resort in Spring Valley, New Jersey. Once again, I was the only child in the entire place, surrounded by grandparents from Brooklyn, Manhattan and the Bronx. We had all our meals together in one large dining hall. The food was fantastic! There was everything from potato latkes to flanken, and we ate and ate and ate. At night, I partook of all the activities that Meema and Peepa did, like playing bingo and attending the local talent show. In fact, it was at that Friday night talent show that I made my onstage debut. At Peepa's coaxing (although he didn't have to coax too much), I got up and walked out in front of the lights. The man at the piano called out: "What are you going to do, little girl?"

"I'm going to sing! I'm going to sing 'I'll Be Loving You Always.' Can you play that for me?"

"Sure, what key?"

"I don't know." So he picked one, and I sang the whole song slightly off the key he picked. I didn't care; I loved being up there in front of three hundred people, even though I had eyes only for Peepa, who sat there "qvelling" at his little girl. When I had finished, I had the nerve to sing another: 'True Love,' and the piano player tried to find my key. When I had finally finished, I stood there, blushing in embarrassment. Only one person in the audience was applauding, and that was Peepa. He was standing up and calling out "Bravo, bravo!"

Later that night, after all my tears of humiliation had been wiped away by Peepa's big white handkerchief, I asked him why the people hadn't liked me. He laughed and said: "Mamashena, these people don't know a star when they see one. But I know a shining star when I see one, and one day, my little Bobbilla, when you are a big, big girl and a mommy, like your mommy, everyone will notice you and see that you shine. It won't be like it is on the block. You won't be hurt like you have been."

With my eyes half-closed, but still basking in the secure love of my grandfather, I asked: "Are you sure, Peepa, are you sure? Sometimes I feel that Ellen and her mother don't even want me around their house. And I seem to be different from my classmates, too. I can't seem to get them to like me, no matter how hard I try."

The white-haired head nodded slowly. "Shhh, don't say that. I tell you, Mamashena, one day you will shine so brightly that everyone will want to be around you, and especially those that never did."

"Oh, Peepa, where will you be? Will you be with me when I'm grown up?" Before Peepa answered me, he took out his handkerchief and blew his nose. I knew his eyes were all filled with tears when he said: "I will always be with you. I will never leave you, my Bobbilla."

3

School was less than endurable that year. Everything I already disliked about myself became exaggerated. Catching my reflection in the storefront windows, my shoulders seemed completely rounded, compared to other girls' straight backs. I spent most of the school day fantasizing about coming home to Meema and Peepa at three o'clock, or going to Coney Island with the family, instead of concentrating on the work to be done at the moment. I had no set time to do my homework, nor did I want one. Lack of self-discipline and parental discipline, and poor study habits set the tone for my years ahead as a student, or rather as a non-student.

Mother did work on my diction and pronunciation — constantly. She was not going to tolerate a Brooklyn accent under any circumstances, or my biting my fingernails, for that matter. But there, it was will against will, and none of the medicines and mustard applied to my cuticles worked. Mother did not give up, however, in her determination to make me a lady. We had a piano in the foyer that nobody played, and so she insisted that I have private lessons. She procured a teacher who would come to the house twice a week to teach me how to play. After all, *somebody* had to take after her father, "Giacomo" Bourg (Jacob Ginsbourg). After the fourth lesson, I had given up ever mastering the piano, and even the teacher shook her head in dismay. But Mother persevered for three more agonizing months, before she finally allowed the lessons to cease.

In the meantime, the feelings of inadequacy that I was developing in the so-called "outside world" were becoming increasingly pronounced. I developed a hacking, nervous cough related to the rapid heartbeat recently discovered by our doctor. I was given a box of lozenges and sucked one after another, day after day, until the cough left. But long after it was gone, I continued taking the lozenges; in fact, I found it almost impossible to break the habit.

That summer, I turned ten and in September started the fifth grade. Uncle Leo Karl was no longer around to do my homework, in return for one of my chocolate cupcakes. He had gotten married to Aunt Gerie, December 23, 1951, and moved out of our apartment. Things and events seemed to be moving and changing at great speed, as years of stability were now disrupted by sudden waves. And they were building, harbingers of a typhoon. It broke the day Mother announced to me we had to leave Brooklyn.

"Barbara," she said softly, "I've thought about this for a long time, and this is what I feel is best for us to do. There is more to life and the world than Brooklyn, and I want you exposed to it all. We'll have two places, one in New York, and here, too, on weekends — "

"No, no! Don't take me away from Meema and Peepa! I don't want to leave or live without them! Please, please, Mommy, I beg you, don't!" I gulped for air. "I'll be good, I promise. I'll do anything, but don't separate us." I collapsed to the floor, sobbing and pleading until I could cry no more.

But my mother's mind was made up.

The days that led up to our departure were simply blanked from my mind. When the dread time finally arrived, and the black limousine that was to take us to Manhattan pulled up in front of our house, I sobbed hysterically. Pleading for the last time to be left where I was, I clung first to Meema and then to Peepa, and I saw the ache, pain and heartbreak in their eyes, too.

"Mama, help me. Please!" my mother's voice called to Meema in controlled desperation.

"What can I do!" Meema said, her own voice breaking. "Mamashena," she whispered to me, "your mommy loves you so much, you mean everything in this whole world to her. Go with her; I will always love you. You will come here on weekends and stay with us." Looking at Peepa, with his head down, sitting in his big armchair, I got down on my knees and begged him to hide me somewhere in a secret place. His face, his handsome face, was wet with tears. In that moment, I sensed they couldn't take any more pain, and nor could I.

As though in a daze, I walked down our steps, touching the side walls as if I wouldn't feel their rough cracks any more. It was so bright outside, the sun burned my teary eyes.

I walked up the alley to the waiting limousine. As I began to get in, I heard a young girl's voice say, "Goodbye, Bobbie." Turning, I saw Ellen and her mother waving goodbye to me. Biting my lip as hard as I could, I too raised my hand and waved goodbye.

Mother slid in next to me, while the driver put our bags in the trunk. She waved out the window calling, "Mama, Mama, I love you, I'll call you later." As the car began to pull away, tears once again welled up inside me. Seeing that I was pulling and tearing at my cuticles, Mother took my hand. "Everything will work out, you'll see. This big, beautiful hotel we're moving to is right on Broadway and 91st Street. We have a furnished suite, and a closet for a kitchenette. It's cozy; you'll love it. I know some people who live there. One man in particular has helped me a lot, Kopav Kagen. He's a fine cantor, one of the best in New York. I can't wait for you to meet him! And there are theaters, movies, museums, restaurants, so much for you to do and see. You'll see — you won't believe how much more there is to life than you'd ever find around here."

Jerking my hand away, I pushed down the tears and moved as far into the corner by the window as possible. For the rest of the trip, I was silent.

The Hotel Greystone was indeed impressive, with its large circular lobby and two restaurants. One was the main dining room; the other, a bar and coffee shop. It looked as if I was about the only child in the place. Apparently the residents were mostly older, retired couples, widows and divorcees. Our apartment was at the end of a long corridor, had two rooms, and was not really set up for permanent use, but Mother was determined to make it that way. She cooked in our small kitchenette and washed the dishes in the bathroom adjacent to the bedroom, doing her best to make things comfortable and ease my grief. But nothing helped.

Watching the walls at night from my twin bed next to Mother's, I could see shadows and flickering lights as the cars passed down below on Broadway. There were beeps and sirens, and sometimes loud talking, laughing and an occasional scream. I tossed and turned and focused on the flickering lights, counting the cars as they passed. Thinking of Meema and Peepa was too painful. I couldn't cry any more, but I hated those sounds, the chaotic life of the city, and especially the groups or cliques that gathered every morning and evening in the hotel lobby to gossip about the latest news. As we were new, we must have been a hot item, especially since Mother was a close friend of Cantor Kopav.

Stark's restaurant across the street on Broadway was a favorite of everyone's at any time, and we all gathered there. Nor was there another place that could match their hamburgers. So eating out became a favorite pastime, fill-in and escape.

Mother began introducing me, in rather quick succession, to the Metropolitan Museum of Art, the Museum of Modern Art, the Hayden Planetarium — and the Palm Court at the well-known and elegant Plaza Hotel. I was lonely, and so, it would seem, was Mother. I felt misplaced, stranded and uprooted. And now all Mother's own insecurities, guilt and emotions were surfacing, too, and my grandparents weren't there to shield me or act as a buffer. We fought. There were scenes, tears, and "I'm sorry, I love you," from both of us.

But my heart was in only one place, and that is all that I lived for each long week. It was a long subway ride from the 91st Street station to Times Square and then over to Borough Park. Often I became nauseated, and Mother would have to take me off the train and out on to the platform, where she held my head while I threw up, hopefully into a trash barrel.

One particular weekend in the spring of 1952, Meema was

seriously ill. She had been in bed with pleurisy, and I actually watched her grow worse and worse. By nightfall, the doctor was called. Confused and frightened, I watched him working hard, feverishly hooking up a jar of blood that was connected to a narrow tube and needle in her arm. The doctor's shirtsleeves were rolled up, his white shirt was open at the throat and his forehead was beaded with perspiration.

Uncle Leo Karl stood on one side of Meema's bed with Aunt Gerie beside him. They were nervously silent. Uncle Leo kept twisting his mouth, tears in his eyes. Peepa was at the head of Meema's bed, holding her left hand in his, every once in a while leaning towards her to brush her forehead. Mother was silent. She did whatever the doctor told her to do, and that was enough to keep her busy. Hurrying from the kitchen to the bedroom, she brought the doctor freshly sterilized needles that she had just boiled, taking back the used ones to resterilize.

"What's happening? This can't be happening!" My stomach turned, knots formed, one on top of another, until it felt as though they had reached my chest, and I could barely breathe. Filled with anxiety, I began to tremble.

Meema, seeing the look of growing panic on my face, took her left hand away from Peepa's and slowly raised it to wave to me. "Mamashena," she mouthed the word, but no sound came out.

My eyes welled up with tears that began to stream down my face. "Meema, everything's going to be okay. Meema, I love you, I . . ." I tried so hard not to lose control, but my body was not about to listen to my instructions; it trembled and shook with fear, and my heart poured forth sobs of sorrow like a wide open faucet. I felt compelled to run as far and as fast as I could. Turning, I hurried through the living room, to the stairway opposite the kitchen where I could hear my mother crying, as she continued to boil needles in every pot she could find. Afraid that she might hear me, I tiptoed down the first flight of stairs and then ran the rest of the way, until I was outside in the alley.

It was dark, except for the light of the moon and the streetlamps. Continuing to run, gasping for breath, I suddenly thought of Aunt Mary and Uncle Leo Sheirr. In all the commotion, no one had called them. They had to be told. I turned and ran midway down the block to Ellen's house. There was a boy my age there who was crippled from polio. I knew I could go to his parents' apartment and they would help me.

Climbing the stairs two at a time, I finally got to the top and banged on their door. Mrs. Gellar could see that I wasn't even able to talk, yet she seemed to know intuitively what had happened to me. When I pointed to her telephone, she smiled and nodded her head, yes, saying, "Bobbie, I'm so sorry. It's Meema, isn't it?" But those words were so painful to hear that I couldn't answer her or look at her again.

Aunt Mary's line was busy. I hung up the phone, waited about two seconds, then dialed again. Still busy. I left and ran down the stairs and out into the night again. I had to go home. Meema's face was before me. I couldn't leave her now, and I had to reach Aunt Mary and Uncle Leo.

Nothing had changed, when I returned. Uncle Leo's twitch had grown worse. His face looked almost contorted with pain as he stood by Meema's bedside watching her grow still weaker, and the doctor work harder and harder by the moment, giving her more blood, injections, taking her pulse, listening to her heart, doing everything he could think of, to try to save her life. I stayed by the telephone dialing Aunt Mary's number until I finally got through.

"Hello, pussycat," she said cheerfully, "what a nice surprise! How are you?"

"Aunt Mary, Meema is sick, awful sick! You'd better come over right now."

There was a silence, and then, "What? Oh, no! What's happening?" Accepting that I had no answer, she said, "I'll be right there," and hung up.

All the lights in the house were on. Amidst the tumult, I continued to stand in the doorway of the bedroom. I looked down at Meema in bed, and her eyes briefly met mine. As pale and listless as she was, that little winsome smile of hers and those soft blue eyes twinkled for a moment. Nodding as if to say, "It's all right, Mamashena," she raised her left hand.

"Meema," I cried out, choking with tears, as someone nearby

grabbed me by the arm and whisked me away from the doorway and down the hall, and then downstairs to the landlord's apartment. I stayed there, until I heard a loud, shrill scream. Running upstairs, I saw Aunt Mary lying on the floor. "She's fainted; get some cold water," Mother said, as she continued back to Meema's room. But Mary revived and got to her feet, to join the rest of the family at Meema's bedside. I was again taken downstairs to the landlord, until once again I heard loud screams. These were from the whole family, and they were wails.

I covered my face with both my hands, as if our house had been struck by a bomb and I was waiting for my body to be blown apart. Nothing happened. . . and then the longest silence ensued. Quietly, I walked back upstairs. The door was wide open, and all I could hear were the muffled sounds of weeping. I walked into the living room in a daze. Peepa was in his big chair, wringing his hands together, crying like a baby and calling, "Mama, Mama, don't leave me."

Against my will, the doctor escorted me out of the living room. "Barbara, I know how upset you are, and how much you loved your grandmother. I tried to save her. I did all I could, but she died." He gave me two pills from the black bag he carried, and brought me back to my family.

Sometime that night, I walked down the stairs of my only home, feeling the cracked walls for the last time. Uncle Leo Karl and Aunt Gerie took Peepa back to their apartment and Mother and me to the subway station. It was a long, lonely, cold subway ride to Manhattan.

Spring passed into summer, and one rainy Saturday morning, while Mother was out shopping, I sat by the window, staring out through the streaks of rain. Once I had been as secure as a little kitten snuggled in someone's lap. But that lap was gone now. Everyone had gone their separate ways; our family was dispersed. The only home I had ever known and loved was no longer even a visiting place. Meema, the foundation and core of our family, was dead.

Peepa had moved to Florida. Tears rolling down my cheeks, I had held his hand as Mother and I waited in Penn Station with him for the train that would take him south. After several attempts at remaining in Brooklyn, he had decided to give the furniture store completely to Leo and let his daughter Eva take care of him. The climate and accommodations would be easier for him to live with. Through my tears, I saw a small room with a bright red sign over the door: *Recordings, 35¢.*

"Peepa, Peepa, come on, let's have your voice recorded. I want to be able to hear you talk to me, when you're gone. I'll keep your record and play it forever and ever."

We went in. "What do you want me to say, Bobbilla?"

"Anything, anything at all."

We stood side by side in the small room waiting for the red light to come on, which would signal Peepa to speak. At the signal, he said: "I love you, Mamashena, with all my heart." And then he paused.

"Go on, Peepa," I whispered, "don't stop; you have more time."

"I love you, Mamashena, with all my heart," he repeated. "I love your mommy, too." Looking at me, he asked, "What do I do now?"

I thought hard. "Sing, Peepa, sing." Looking at me again with his soft blue eyes all filled up, he began to sing an old favorite Russian song of his, one that he often sang me to sleep with.

When we were through, and the record was in my hands, I held it tightly.

"Gate #11 is now open for Washington, Virginia, North and South Carolina, Georgia, Florida . . . ." The sepulchral tones echoed through the cavernous station, and a traffic jam of people quickly formed, getting up and scurrying every which way to get their last-minute magazine, candy bar or pack of cigarettes, and then dash for Gate 11.

"Oh, Peepa," I cried, holding him around the waist, "write to me often, and if you can't write, tell Eva to write for you. I love you with all my heart, and I will see you soon. You'll come back here for me, or I will come to Florida when I can, I swear it. I swear to God, we will not be separated. Goodbye, goodbye, Peepa," and I sobbed as he held me tight, then kissed my mother on the cheek, and I turned to join the crowd going down to the platform. He turned back once to wave, and brushed a tear from his own eye. Then he was gone through portal 11, and down the stairs to where the train was waiting.

I think from that moment, there was hate mixed with the love I had for my mother.

From that moment on, I lived as though my whole body ached. Aware of joy and laughter on my classmates' faces, I cried out inside, "It's not fair!"

I suppose what kept me going was my mother. I felt sorry for her, because she, too, was hurting. Her loneliness and mine drew us together like a vacuum. She had her way of escaping the unbearable pains of life, and I was developing mine.

I felt like the misfit of the entire class, that year in the sixth grade. The same group of cliquey girls that had been in my class the previous year were again with me. The other girls were free and sure about themselves and there didn't seem to be anything I could do to gain their approval. I wanted to stand up straight and tall, but after a few attempts at self-discipline, I gave up. I wanted to stop biting my fingernails down to the quick, but I didn't. I wanted to be able to laugh, but I just couldn't.

Time after time, I would stand on the edge of a group, listening to a conversation, hoping for a moment to say something and become a participant, but that moment never came. And inevitably, when and if I finally did speak, an awkward silence would follow. Sometimes they would then shrug, or someone would say, "Do you know what she's talking about?"

Stripped of every ounce of confidence, I nonetheless continued to stand on the sidelines, interrupting conversations and begging to be accepted. I never took the hint and walked away, with the result that I turned my classmates off all the more, because I threw myself at them.

Often, when my teacher gave instructions for homework, I ignored her completely. Staring off into space, I would fantasize about yesterday and tomorrow, but never was I where I was supposed to be, in the present. I hated that year and everything that was happening to me, but I didn't do a thing to change any of it. Every time I attempted to do my homework in the afternoon, I fell asleep. And after dinner, I either sat in the hotel lobby, watching the people go by, or I watched TV. Since I never denied myself the escapes that took the place of my homework, I became convinced that I lacked the power of sustained concentration and was even moderately stupid.

Tagging along with one of my class's cliques after school, I followed them to the Five-and-Ten at 92nd Street and Broadway. It was a beautiful sunny day; everyone on the street looked especially happy as they met people, ran errands, or just strolled along looking in store windows. The store was crowded. There was nothing I wanted to buy, and I didn't have any money in my pocket, anyway. Seeing one of our group take a candy bar and quickly put it in her jacket pocket, I gasped and stepped back. Watching her hasten her steps as she headed for the front door, I sensed a rush of excitement rise within me.

As this excitement built, and my heart began to beat faster, I walked down the aisle and stopped next to the candy counter. Not looking down, to my right or left, but feeling the candy bars with my left hand, I grabbed one, then two, and put them in my pocket. My heartbeat echoed in my ears like a drum beating steady and fast. With eyes focused on the light outside the big glass doors, I made my way out to the street. Turning left towards 93rd Street, I began to run.

Suddenly, I heard a man's voice yell out, "Hey you, little girl, stop! Stop, you hear me!" Although my legs became rubbery from fear, my mind was fixed on getting back to the schoolyard, and I did. Breathless, I entered the courtyard. The girls were huddled together, eating their candy bars. "Look," I said, "look at what I've got," and I pulled the two candy bars out of my pocket.

"Wow, Barbara, we didn't know you had it in you! Terrific! Come, join us."

I had done something I had never done before, nor had ever thought of doing. But it bought me a measure of approval and acceptance, and I liked the feeling of at long last belonging somewhere. But then I thought of Mother, and how she would react, and I cringed. Mother was about the most honest person I had ever known. She hated lying, especially stealing. *Stealing* — that word was so awful! I didn't do that, not really, I rationalized. What do a couple of candy bars cost? And anyway, the store could afford them more than I. Plus it was exciting, and, as well as lonely, I was bored and miserable, living in a cruel and unfair world.

I didn't steal anything else for a long time, but I often remembered the incident and the feelings I had had, especially the excitement. For one brief but exhilarating experience, I was taken out of and away from me. And anything that would enable me to forget or escape from me held a fascination and an irresistible lure.

Shortly after I turned twelve, on July 1st, 1953, Peepa came back from Florida for the summer. This time, Uncle Leo Karl got him a room in a boarding house near his and Gerie's apartment in Borough Park. The furniture store was just one block away and Peepa went there for the day and chatted with all his old cronies as they passed by. Mother and I saw him on weekends, and it was a perfect arrangement for him. My spirits lifted.

At Joan of Arc Junior High, however, it was even harder for me to get "in". The group in my class that drew their own circle were kids from upper-middle-class Jewish homes. The only other girl who came from divorced parents had her father visiting on weekends and lived in a luxurious apartment on Central Park West. She was also very pretty and popular. Boys had begun to flock around, asking her to the movies on Saturday afternoons. The other girls lived either on West End Avenue or Riverside Drive. Broadway, apparently, was losing its residential appeal.

Everyone knew everything about everyone else and what their fathers did. They all had money, and it showed; our two-room suite where we washed the dishes in the bathroom was beginning to look shabby to me. I didn't have my own room, or any place of my own to work at, like a desk — things that the other girls spoke of as necessities. So now I had another excuse for not doing my homework.

Every afternoon, I counted the minutes until I could go home and flop on my bed. *Sleep* — I wanted to nap, with the warm sunlight coming through the window, soothing and comforting me. Yet there was always homework to be done. In my mind, I would promise myself that I would do it later, after dinner. But then after dinner, I found myself jumping up and going down to the lobby. There I would pore over the news stand, talk to the bellboys, elevator operators and desk clerks. I even developed my first adolescent crush on the fair-haired Scandinavian desk clerk who was twice my age.

Sometimes I would take a walk, or coax Mother into taking me to Stark's for an ice cream soda — anything to avoid sitting down quietly, alone with me.

Because of the emotions and the pain that would inevitably follow, all memories of my home in Borough Park, of the family's dispersion, Meema's death, the total destruction of my foundation and security as a child had to be rigorously avoided. And so, convinced that I would be unable to concentrate on my homework, let alone finish it, I rarely attempted doing it. "No more pain, no more failure," I promised myself. "There has to be a way to escape from it."

It wasn't long before I found that way. The months passed slowly, once the cold of winter had set in, and Peepa had returned once again to Florida. It was the Christmas shopping season, and the Palm Court at the Plaza Hotel was breathtakingly beautiful — filled with elegant, smartly-dressed people, seated at small tables, drinking tea or cocktails with pastries or hors d'oeuvres. The word elegant was not in my vocabulary, nor had it been. I'd heard Mother use it in relation to her own life abroad and about the city, but for me that word had no meaning — until now. These people looked happy and comfortable, and they were smiling. I was none of those things and felt uncomfortable.

Eyeing Mother's martini, yet turned off by the strong odor of the gin, I pointed to another drink at a nearby table.

"What's that, Mother?" I queried, noting the attractiveness of the luscious fruit in it.

"Barbara, don't point," she replied, keeping her voice low. "I've told you, it's not ladylike."

"Okay, okay, but what is it?"

"A whiskey sour."

"I want one. Please can I have one?"

"What? You're too young, you're only twelve years old."

"I know, but I'm mature for my age; you've said so yourself. You can order it for yourself and just give me sips now and then."

"Well. . . since this is your first time here, and it is the holiday season, and we are all alone, I'll order one. But don't expect me to do this again!"

It was delicious! Smooth and fruity, the whiskey sour made me feel important, and as much a part of this large circle of people as anyone else. And there was one other feature: at the finish of my drink, there was a feeling of warmth in the pit of my stomach. Like an expanding circle, it gradually grew larger until my entire stomach felt warm inside. Even the ever-present knots of anxiety were gone. I felt so good! This was different from the pounding excitement of stealing candy bars, but it too catapulted me away from myself.

Basking in the glow I was feeling, I noticed that all unhappy thoughts had vanished. I could hear the strolling violins play, lulling all my bruises to sleep. I asked the guitarist if he knew "Far Away Places," Peepa's favorite American song. I listened without crying, knowing inside that this experience made the impossible possible. Emotionally and physically, an answer to pain was tucked away somewhere inside me.

4

A year had passed. It was the fall of 1954, and Peepa had left again for Florida for the winter. I wrote to him often and dreamed about a day when somehow everything would change, and we'd be together again for good. After the new year, it was time to think about high school. I watched with envy the girls and boys who seemed to know exactly where they were going. There were three specialized schools in Manhattan that just about every junior high school student wanted to go to. The High School of Music and Art had a regular liberal arts program, plus three extra hours every day of either music or art, depending upon what your major was. An entrance exam was required, and while I loved painting, I never dreamed of applying. Mother, however, dreamed of it for me. After all, her father had been a well-known voice teacher, and if I wasn't going to follow him in music, perhaps my talent lay in art.

"Try, try, try, Barbara! You might just get in. It won't hurt to at least try. I'm going to enroll you in the Art Students' League. It's one of the finest schools in New York, and you'll have four months there before the exam."

That exam! Well, there was another "special" school I could apply to — Performing Arts, with a major in dramatic art. In the end, I decided to go ahead and apply to both schools. Meanwhile, Mother enrolled me in the Art Students' League on West 57th

Street, and every Saturday morning from 9 a.m. to 12 noon, for the next four months, I drew figures in charcoal from live models and did still lifes, with some painting towards the end of the course.

"Do it again! It's not right here, here and everywhere," my instructor would comment. Again and again, I listened to her instructions and tried to follow her artistic eye. And all this time, I was supposed to be preparing an art portfolio. I kept putting it off, rationalizing that I wouldn't get into the school anyhow. But as the time for my interview and test drew close, I knew I had to pull something together, so the night before, I painted until the wee hours of the morning. My portfolio was sloppy, rushed and barely held the requisite material. Since there was no doubt that I was going to be rejected, I was completely relaxed for the interview and the art exam.

While I was awaiting the results at M & A, I auditioned at Performing Arts as Scarlett O'Hara from "Gone with the Wind," and also as Beth, dying in "Little Women."

"Miss Scheutz," the admissions teacher summarized after these two shaky performances, "I am not quite sure about you. Perhaps you might come back again for another try, when you're not quite so nervous."

Seated along with everyone else in our large auditorium, I awaited the results from M & A, watching the thrilled and happy faces of those who got in and the forlorn teary ones of those who didn't. I resolved that, whatever happened, I was not going to cry. The names were being called alphabetically, and they were getting close to the S's.

"Barbara Anne Scheutz," the man up front called my name, and I raised my hand so that he could see I was present. "Accepted."

"What? What did he say?" I could barely get the words out of my mouth. Classmates around me were slapping me on the back and congratulating me. "Great, Scheutzy! I never thought you'd make it," one of them commented.

"There must be some mistake; I don't believe it!" And after the list had been gone through, I ran up front and asked: "Sir, please check my name again; you said I was accepted and that can't be." I gave him my name and he thumbed through the pages.

Finding it, he shook his head and smiled. "Congratulations, young lady; you have been accepted by one of New York's finest schools."

My hands were at my mouth, my eyes teary, as I ran up the aisle, half crying and half laughing.

"Mother! Wait till I tell Mother!" Heading for the pay phone, I knew this was the biggest and best surprise since I left Borough Park. "Oh, Peepa, you will be so proud of me! I must write to you right away, or send you a telegram." For once, I had something really good to tell Peepa. And tonight, Mother and I will call Aunt Mary and Uncle Leo Scheirr, Uncle Leo Karl and Aunt Gerie, Shirley and Morty and Duddy and Edith in Washington.

As the excitement built, doubt entered my mind, clouding my joy. They had made a mistake; as soon as the teachers got to know me and had time to evaluate my work, I would be rejected. And that rejection would be worse. Maybe I'll just call Mother, and let it go at that.

Mother was ecstatic about the news, and that night we went out to dinner to celebrate. Even Kopav, her special friend, gave me a gift. I felt as though I was floating on a big, white, feathery cloud, that soared to its highest height when Peepa returned late that June. I stood at the 91st Street station on Broadway, watching everyone come up the stairs, so that I could be sure to spot Peepa and meet him half-way. And when I saw his white hair, parted on one side and neatly combed, I didn't wait to make sure it was he.

"Peepa," I screamed, at the top of the stairs, and ran down, pushing through the crowds of people who were also coming up.

"Oh, Peepa, Peepa, how I've missed you! You're here, I can hardly believe it, and you're going to be with us all weekend. This is going to be the most special weekend of my life!"

It was a special weekend, too. I was graduating from Joan of Arc, and I was going to attend my very first prom and wear a formal. I was also going out on my very first date with a boy whom I'd had a crush on for months. He had never batted an eyelash at me, and I was stunned when he invited me to the prom. On Saturday morning, after having my favorite breakfast with Peepa and Mother, lox and cream cheese on bagels, white fish and pickled herring, I went to the beauty parlor.

That was my first disappointment for that day. I came home looking like Orphan Annie. Later that night, even before turning the corner with my date, to wave goodbye to Peepa and Mother, who stood at the doorway beaming, I was informed that the reason he had asked me was because the girl of his choice was already taken, and everybody else had a date. Awkward and ill at ease, I sat on the sidelines as I watched him dance with all the other girls. Trying hard not to cry, I concentrated on going home and being with Peepa.

Peepa and Mother were waiting up for me, naturally.

"Tell me, my little Bobbilla, did you have a wonderful time tonight, dancing all the dances? I bet all the other boys were jealous that they didn't have you as their date!"

"Yes, Peepa, I had a marvelous time. I was the most popular girl there. Oh, you would have been so proud of me." I couldn't bear to tell Peepa and Mother the truth. It would hurt them too much. But later that evening, after we all had glasses of tea and apple strudel, I nestled my shoulder against Peepa's on the couch, and began pouring my heart out to him.

"Peepa, I don't think I'm at all pretty. Boys don't take to me the way they do to some of the other girls in my class, and it hurts!"

"What? Why, that's crazy! You *are* beautiful, the most beautiful! I swear it. I know beauty when I see it, and your Peepa does not lie. Mamashena, these silly little boys don't even know what they're looking at. One day, you will meet the most wonderful boy, and he will think you are beautiful and love you just the way you are, like I do." Peepa's blue eyes became cloudy with tears, and he put both his arms around me.

Feeling more at ease and a little sleepy, I looked up at him and said, "Oh, Peepa, I hope it's true. I get so lonely sometimes. I don't have you here, and I don't have Meema any more. I don't have a father or any brothers or sisters and Mommy gets so upset at times."

Mother was in the bathroom washing dishes. Taking his big white handkerchief out from his pocket, he wiped his eyes and blew his nose, but the tears kept welling up, just the same.

"Remember, Mamashena, your Mommy loves you with all her heart. She is raising you all alone, and that isn't easy. If only I was younger and healthier, I'd be here to help. But you will always be my shining star; don't ever forget it!"

"Peepa, do you know why my father doesn't want me?"

"Harriet," Peepa called out to Mother in the bathroom, "let's all have one more piece of apple strudel before we go to bed."

Peepa left for Florida early that fall, right after Labor Day, and I entered my freshman year at M & A. A whole new dimension of life opened up for me — socially, that is; as far as schoolwork was concerned, my poor study habits had not changed. During the summer, I had gotten friendly with a boy who lived across the street from Mother and me — Tommy O'Brien. He was my second date. It was a Friday night and Tommy was going to pick me up in half an hour. Pacing the bedroom floor, I now wished that I had never said yes to Tommy. There didn't seem to be any way to relax my stomach. Hardly part of our "Jewish clique", Tommy was Irish Catholic with sandy hair and blue eyes. It was his narrow turned-up nose that initially caught my attention. I was flattered when he approached me for a date, especially when he suggested going downtown in a taxi to the Capitol Theatre; that was far more impressive than a local movie.

I had watched my friends accept dates for a dance, a walk, or the local theater, but, except for an occasional creep, none of the boys paid any attention to me in school. Still quite awkward-looking at age fourteen, with skinny legs and long, straggly hair, I was round-shouldered, and the more self-conscious I felt upon entering a room, the more I stooped over. My nerves were taut. The more I thought about my entire situation, the more I feared breaking down into tears.

I felt anger rise within me and screamed inside at the unfairness of my life, and what had been taken from me. And now I dreaded this date, and didn't possibly see how I could keep it. Quickly I asked the hotel operator to get me Manhattan information. But I didn't know Tommy's father's first name, nor exactly where they lived, and there were too many O'Briens in New York to check them all. I decided then to go downstairs and meet him. I'd pretend to be sick and tell him that I couldn't reach him. He'd just have to understand. But then, what if he asked me to go out tomorrow or the day after, or next week? What could I do?

Earlier that afternoon, Mother and I had fought, and I wasn't able to let go of my reactions to her, either. Sitting on the edge of my bed, I looked through the door leading to the living room and hallway. The closet, our "kitchenette," was open. My gaze traveled around until it rested on Mother's large brown bottle, half-filled with a dark liquid. I remembered the warm glow that had relaxed my stomach, that time at the Plaza.

Suddenly I felt a surge of desire to have that feeling back again. That was the answer! That would take away these awful stomach knots and relieve my anxiety. Perhaps if I drank from that bottle, I would even be able to keep my date with Tommy.

Anticipation took over, and I went quickly into the kitchenette. Closing the door from the inside, as quickly as I could I unscrewed the top and lifted the bottle to my lips. The first swallow burned my mouth and throat. I held my nose tightly, and drank as much as I could without stopping. Coming up for air and fighting to keep the last mouthful down, I drank still more. After finishing half of what had been in the bottle and feeling a slight sensation go through my body, I finally stopped.

Mother was lying on top of her bed, asleep. I tiptoed to the bathroom and filled a glass with water. Back in the kitchenette, I carefully poured the water into the bottle until it reached approximately the level it had been at originally. Screwing back the top and leaving the door ajar the way it had been, I ran to the bathroom and brushed my teeth. Opening some perfume that was on a shelf, I gargled with it and then swallowed.

Now I was ready to go downstairs and meet Tommy O'Brien.

Every knot in my stomach was completely gone. All anxious and angry thoughts left. My face felt flushed and my entire body began to pulsate with this liquid that was quickly traveling through every vein, right down to my toes and fingertips. I felt warm, glowing and good. Comfortable with myself for the first time, I took in every moment of this beautiful euphoria that was bathing me. The same gossipy, stodgy, fat and skinny people came in and went out of the Hotel Greystone. I greeted everyone whom I thought of as a grump with a big smile. I even began opening doors for people, as though I was the doorman. "Everything is glorious! What a way to live! I have found the answer, thank God!" Talking aloud to myself now, I said: "Tommy, hurry up!"

Looking handsome with his hair neatly combed and wearing a suit and tie, Tommy waved a sheepish hello as he walked up the street. I started down the block to meet him half-way. From that moment on, I never stopped smiling.

"Are you sunburned, Barbara?" he asked.

"No, I just had a little glass of wine. It's good for your blood, lots of iron."

Stepping out into the middle of the street, he hailed a taxi. The ride down Broadway was one big blur. Noises, beeps, lights and neon signs buzzed through my mind, creating a jumble of sounds and visions. People walking and crossing the street looked disjointed. At first, my body felt on fire and then my head; it seemed as though I was ablaze.

"Open the window, please, it's so hot in here."

"Hot? It's not hot outside!" came the sharp retort of the cabdriver. But he opened the window. Trying to breathe, I stuck my head out, taking in large gulps of air.

At last we pulled up in front of the majestic Capitol Theatre, its marquee aglow. But how would I ever get up out of the cab?

"Tommy, help me, please; I'm not feeling too well."

Tommy quickly paid the driver and gave me his arm. Sensing that something was very different about me, he asked, "What's wrong?"

"I drank more than one glass, and it wasn't wine. I don't know what it was, but it was brown, and very strong." And with that, I stumbled out of the taxi, and fell on the sidewalk. Pulling myself up by grabbing Tommy's pants, I stood, but not too tall. Wobbly, slumped and reeling, I made my way into the theater. It was so dark! The balcony? How would I ever get up there?

"Hang on, you'll get there, Barbara." Somehow, stumbling over feet and falling on top of people who were seated, we managed to get two seats together by the balcony railing. Moments later, the movie screen started spinning.

"*Hey!* What's the matter here?" I yelled out. People turned their heads in my direction, as I suddenly clapped my hands over my mouth. It wouldn't have mattered where my hands were, or if I'd had a bucket. I started throwing up and couldn't stop, all over myself and Tommy and the people below us. How we got out of there is a disjointed nightmare, but to his everlasting credit, Tommy stuck by me through it all and got me home.

Tommy held me up against the door of our apartment. He knocked several times softly, while I kept falling down and banging on the door.

"Mother, hurry up and answer the door!"

"What have you done to my daughter?" my mother shrieked when she saw the condition Tommy brought me home in. It didn't matter what poor Tommy tried to say; he was the culprit! I could have died and felt as if I was going to. Needless to say, Tommy was tremendously relieved to say goodnight, and never asked me out again.

The next morning, I had momentarily forgotten the horrors of the night before.

"Oh, my head! What happened? I feel so awful!" Barely able to get out of bed, I was glad it was Saturday, and there wasn't any school. And this time I made it to the bathroom before I threw up again. Sitting on the cold tile floor in front of the toilet, I swore up and down that anyone who drank was nuts. "I'll never, *never,* do this again," I moaned, shaking my head. "Oh, my head, my stomach, I feel so awful. I swear to God, Mother, I'll never drink that stuff again!" Mother didn't say very much that morning, but she was sympathetic as she went about preparing my breakfast, hoping that I would eat something.

It wasn't long before I became part of a local group of boys and girls who met at each other's homes, went to movies, and down to Greenwich Village to hear poetry and guitar playing, and occasionally drank port wine when there weren't any parents around. The first occasion that involved wine came about a month after my bout at the Capitol Theatre. I was first in line and all too eager to get my slug out of the bottle. Completely forgotten was the misery I had gone through, and my promise never to touch alcohol again. All I recalled were those moments of warm, glowing euphoria before I became ill. I savored each memory and was excitedly drawn to the stuff that would take me away from myself again.

As we all sat round in a circle on the floor in one of the boys' rooms, passing the bottle, I noticed that my friends Iris and Lynn stopped after two turns. Not me; I kept up with the boys, going round and round, until I felt that electric warmth again, going through my entire being. Feeling completely free to talk, laugh and joke around, I became more than just part of the group. I was funny, zany, and sensed everyone's approval — except for Lynn. Lynn was the only person there who wasn't Jewish. She lived on New York's fashionable upper East Side, and came from a home that had been torn apart by alcohol abuse. She had confided her emotional insecurities to me as she had watched alcohol destroy her home.

Now, alarmed at my sudden compulsion to have more and more I even suggested that we get another bottle — Lynn took me aside and said, "Bobbie, watch it; you'll get sick. I'm worried about you."

"I'm okay; I'm just having fun. Your attitude about drinking is just too uptight. C'mon, loosen up and have some wine." But Lynn couldn't be persuaded to drink any more. Her beautiful, clear blue eyes looked cold as she detached herself from me.

As time wore on that afternoon, and 5:30 approached, we knew we had better break up, and get to our respective homes for dinner. Trying to get up from the floor, I lost my balance and toppled backwards onto a couch. I turned to one side and leaned on my elbows, trying to get up once more, only to fall back again and again. Oh, no — quickly putting my hand to my mouth, I began to throw up.

"Help me, someone; I'm sick!" But everyone hastily gathered up their belongings and left — except for Lynn. She put her arms around me, lifting me up and leaning me on her side. Walking me to the bathroom, she held one hand on my aching head, as I threw up again and again. Once more, I promised never to touch the stuff again.

That spring of 1956, Iris, Lynn and I were a threesome, but it was Lynn to whom I felt the closest. We had one big thing in common: we knew what it was to really hurt inside. Iris was someone I tried to live up to, and like my friend Ellen in Borough Park, she drew my envy. It seemed that everything about her, the entire way she and her family lived, was right and proper. And there were no loopholes — none that could be seen anyway. She had everything: a mother *and* a father, two sets of grandparents, an orthodox Jewish home, membership at a local temple, high grades in school, money, and an attractive boyfriend. At Iris's, I felt as though I were a puppy dog, watching through a window and hoping to be brought in.

Somewhere along the way, I had developed an understanding or compassion for "grown-up" problems — probably because I had lived through so many, and because my mother was now treating me more as a confidant than a daughter. Whatever the reason, my girlfriends' parents often confided their emotional hurts to me. "Barbara, it's so easy to talk to you; you're so grown up for your age." Actually, I was emotionally immature for my age, unable to cope with my daily routine or the insecurities that went along with adolescence. But I had heard grown-up conversation for most of my life, had participated in it and even offered advice, and conflict was never hidden in either my grandparents' home or now. Thus, I often found myself in the middle of other people's dilemmas, and since this brought me friends and proved to be another acknowledgment, I gravitated to those situations.

I envied both Lynn and Iris. Lynn, regal-looking with long blond hair brushed back, was almost a carbon copy of Grace Kelly. Iris was short and dark, with sparkling brown eyes. It was her warm, bubbly personality that made her popular. I was in the middle, not anywhere near as popular as either one of them, but gradually becoming each girl's best friend. For Iris, her cries of woe centered around her romantic problems and parental discipline. For Lynn, it was more serious. There were romantic problems, too, boys she had to chase away, and the usual trouble with schoolwork, but most serious was her home life. I became each girl's confidant, but my heart reached out to Lynn, who, in spite of her aloofness, became as close as a sister.

Our freshman year was over that June of 1956, and in July both Lynn and I turned fifteen. As often as we could, we met at Times Square, then took the subway to Coney Island. Both of us loved the water, especially the ocean.

"Lynn, you know what I wish more than anything in the whole world?" I asked, one lazy, sun-drenched afternoon.

"What, Bobbie?"

"That I won't be stuck in the city all my life, and that someday I could live near the beach."

"Yeah, me too." She stretched on the sand. "It's awful having to travel for an hour and a half each way by subway to get here."

After a full day of sunbathing, going in the water, and sharing our dreams and hopes about the future, we toured the boardwalk. Nathan's hotdog stand was a must. They made the best kosher frankfurters and knishes in the world. Saving our last 15¢ for the subway ride home, we went on every ride we could.

"Lynn, let's really get daring today and go on the 'Cyclone' (the largest roller-coaster). And after that we can go on the parachute jump!"

"Are you nuts?"

"No, c'mon, it'll be exciting, you'll see!"

"Bobbie, I'll go on the parachute jump, but not on the Cyclone."

"Hey," I said, as we walked in the direction of the Cyclone, "I've got a great idea! Let's see if we can get some beer at a stand."

"Beer? Now? It's afternoon; besides, we're only fifteen, and I hate beer."

"Well, I'm going to try. You don't have to like the stuff; it's what it does to you. For one thing, it'll take away your fear of the Cyclone."

"I don't know about the fear, but I do know what it does to you. Don't you remember how sick you were? You said you would never drink again, and that I shouldn't let you."

"That was a long time ago. I just drank too much, too fast, then. It'll be different this time."

Steering Lynn in the direction of one of the stands that sold draft beer, I casually walked up and said, "May I please have a stein of light or dark beer, whichever you have more of?"

"How old are you, young lady?"

"Oh," I laughed that he would even ask, "I'm nineteen."

"Yeah? Well, let's see your identification."

After trying several stands and getting nowhere, I gave up. No matter, tomorrow was Saturday, and we were going to a party, where I could drink anything I wanted. Excited just thinking about it, I fantasized about the many different kinds of drinks there would be, and what I might have. A Manhattan was known to be strong, but it was appealing, with the maraschino cherry in it. A cocktail was so sophisticated-looking, holding it in one hand with a cigarette in the other, and lipstick marks around the glass and cigarette. That was who and where I wanted to be — confidence seeping into me as each new drink was poured, able then to be with anyone and cope with anything. I would be equipped with armor to fight this hard, cruel world. A fleeting memory passed through my mind of the last time, and the time before that with Tommy, but I dismissed it, assuring myself "I'll stop at three next time."

Without telling Lynn of my intentions, I somehow got her to believe that the Cyclone roller-coaster was a funhouse. The entrance to the ride was designed in such a way that the high peaks of the tracks and the sudden descents were well hidden. But when the small, two-seated car we were in began to climb up and up and up, click-click-click, until we were overlooking all of Coney Island, Lynn let out a scream and fainted. For the rest of that tumultuous ride I held on to her and gripped the metal bar in front of me.

When the ride was finally over, and Lynn had revived, I had no desire to go on any more rides. But Lynn felt differently; insisting on getting even with me, she made me go on the parachute jump with her. Until that moment, I was totally unaware of my fear of heights. The instant of recognition came when I looked directly down as we hit the top. Seized with dizziness and a mindless terror, as we suddenly started falling, I squeezed my eyes shut, shrieked and held on to the support wires as tightly as I could, until we stopped at ground level with a loud bang.

"Whew, that was awful!" I moaned, afraid that I was about to throw up. "Ohh, Lynn, I'll never go up there again!"

Lynn looked at me, serious for a moment.

"Bobbie, you said you'd never drink again, either."

"That's different," I replied, shrugging it off, "c'mon." But as we left, I wondered. *Was* it so different? I knew there was no question about the parachute. I hated it; it made me sick. But so did the drinking. No! The drinking was different; it had to be!

"Lynn, I am going to learn how to drink like a lady, I swear it; you'll see."

The remainder of that summer I spent in Washington, D.C., staying with Uncle Duddy and Aunt Edith, and then Aunt Shirley and Uncle Morty. They all had children, and since I was the oldest of all the cousins, they looked up to me and gave me a special place, making me feel important, something totally foreign to me at home and in school. After Meema's death and the break-up of our home in Borough Park, I had made short trips to Washington on school vacations and during the summer, because I felt the love and sense of security there that I had once known. Mother had now taken a job with B. Altman's in their stationery department, and with Kopav just a few floors above us in the hotel, I knew she had someone close by.

In the fall of 1956, my sophomore year at Music and Art, I was encouraged by my art teachers to think about making art my future, and because of that encouragement, I paid attention in class and was elated when, for the first time ever, I received the grade of 90. But my other classes — English, math, biology, geography and phys. ed. were sources of sheer frustration. I found it hard to concentrate, and whenever I became confused about anything, I just gave up, never pushing through until I understood a problem and solved it. I blamed this scholastic failure on my mother, of course, for she continued to cast all her burdens and grievances, and there were many, on me.

I looked forward to the weekends, when Lynn and I toured the Greenwich Village coffee houses, and began dating. It wasn't long before I once again felt like the odd-ball I was, at my eighth grade prom. I felt like a floundering idiot unless I was out with someone older than myself and alcoholic beverages were served. And so I just assumed that boys my own age were immature. I had never really lived much within my own peer group, but rather, vicariously, through the burdens, anxieties, illnesses and loneliness of the adults around me. When I had the opportunity to learn how to swim or iceskate or ride a bike or play volley-ball, or anything socially sporty that most of the girls my age did, I stayed well in the background, afraid that I would be humiliated. Nor was I interested in spectator sports — football, basketball, baseball, hockey — after making one half-hearted attempt at each. It soon became automatic for me to give up even before I started, at anything I didn't know, and naturally at age fifteen, there was much I didn't know.

But I didn't give up on drinking. That, I was going to learn to master, and I did. At Friday night fraternity parties at NYU and Columbia University, I was now able to drink beer, highballs, or whatever, throughout the evening. I felt at home with the rest of the guys and joined in on any conversation — actually believing that with a few drinks under my belt, my IQ suddenly became higher and I was more intelligent.

I didn't know it at the time, but I was beginning to depend on something else to enable me to function socially, and feel self-confident. Occasionally I would overdo it, but the times that I became intoxicated and sick to my stomach were spaced and limited. And although my own peer group wasn't behaving in the same fashion, there were plenty of others who were.

If Mother spoke to me about the time, or the condition in which I came home on a Friday or Saturday night, I turned on her with a vengeance, continuing in the vindictive, "you'll pay" attitude with which I had chug-a-lugged from her bottle of whiskey the night of my date with Tommy. I had said: "I'll show you," and I did. I still blamed her for taking me, dragging me, out of the only home and solid foundation that I had known. In fact, I had nurtured and held on to enough hate to last me a lifetime. I showed Mother little compassion, becoming her judge and jury whenever she herself drank too much. My tongue had become a nasty weapon which I used to get back at her: "Who are *you* to tell *me* what to do? Leave me alone and let me go to hell; I hate you and I always will!"

Often I threw Mother into guilt, slamming out of the apartment late at night and walking up and down Broadway, crying. When I was all cried out, I'd come back, fall into her arms, not knowing why I ever behaved that way, and plead with her to forgive me. I swore up and down that tomorrow would be different. And when Mother filled her own loneliness with the same source of escape that I had found, she too would swear up and down afterwards that tomorrow would be different.

"I'll never drink again, Barbara, I promise. It's just that I'm so lonely. You can't understand what it's like raising a child alone without a husband all these years, and I hope you never have to, but maybe when you're grown up, you'll know what I'm going through. Please, have patience with me."

But I had no patience, and always left our suite, slamming the door behind me, running through the lobby past the desk clerk and elevator operators with tears streaming down my face. I didn't have patience, and I didn't understand. All I knew was that I should be loyal and quiet, not divulging a thing, and run, run, until the storm was over. I ran to my friend Iris's apartment, a few blocks away, trying to nestle in the comfort of their family's wholeness. But always late at night, I would toss and turn, groaning and aching as I remembered yesterday, and hated today and was fearful of tomorrow.

The New Year, 1957, saw us once again alone together, like almost every holiday I ever knew. At midnight, at the movie theater on 83rd Street and Broadway, we watched couples embrace — families, mothers, fathers and children — jumping up and down with joy, shouting, "Happy New Year!" while we sat quietly in our seats, each trying not to show the other that we were crying and breaking inside, again.

5

On July 1st, 1957, my sixteenth birthday, Mother gave me a beautiful, "sweet-sixteen" party at the St. Moritz Hotel on Central Park South — champagne, lunch and lovely gifts with a group of friends from Music and Art. This was the first time I had belonged to any group at all, and it was a new, satisfying experience. Lynn and Iris were still my closest friends, however, and we went to Coney Island together often. I planned to spend the last two weeks of July and some of August in Washington with my relatives, but the week before I was due to leave, Mother nervously announced that she was going to Florida to see Peepa and wanted me to go with her.

"But Mother, why? That doesn't make any sense. Go to Florida in July and August?"

"Barbara, I have something to tell you; come and sit down," and her words were soft but serious, as she sat on the end of my bed.

"What is it?" I asked, remaining standing, already sensing the gravity of what was coming next.

"Peepa is sick, and I am making plans to go to Florida to visit him. I would like you to come with me. We could still try to make it a vacation and have a good time. I thought I'd make reservations at the Fontainebleau in Miami Beach."

"Peepa, sick? How sick? What's wrong?"

"Barbara, Peepa has cancer."

I didn't answer Mother; I didn't hear it, yet I heard it.

"No, no, no!" I cried. My back began to stiffen, and I felt a sharp, burning pain across it, as if I'd been struck by a bolt of lightning. I grabbed the bedpost with the palm of my hand, leaning down and moving around so that I could sit down. Then I remembered Peepa holding me on his lap in his big easy chair. I began to sob, flooded by memories of Peepa telling me bedtime stories, taking me to the movies on Saturday afternoons, our lunches together at the store with all the men in the neighborhood, hot corned beef sandwiches, and kosher pickles, and on and on. As I reflected on his warm, handsome, smiling face, I saw him as he lay on the stretcher when he was stricken with his heart attack.

"But Mother," I sobbed, "Peepa was sick before and he got better. Can't he get better again? How bad is he?"

She paused for a moment before replying. "When I talked to Eva, she told me that he was failing fast."

"Ooh!" As if all the blood in my body had suddenly drained to my feet, I felt weak and cold and clammy. Peepa had always been my refuge from pain, my shield. Now he was in pain; it was he who was suffering. I wanted to run to him and beg him to help me, yet it was *he* who needed help now. Every muscle in my body tightened up; I clenched my fist and pounded the bed: "Mother, I can't go with you. Please try to understand, I just can't!"

But she couldn't understand. "What do you mean, you can't go? You have to go; he's expecting to see you, to have you with him at the —"

"No!" I shouted, tears choking my words. "I love him more than life itself, but I can't face it." I buried my head in the bedspread. "Oh God, oh God, I want to run, to hide in some secret place until this nightmare is over, and when I wake up, it will have just been a dream, and Peepa will be here with me again."

Mother stroked my head. "Oh my baby, Mamashena, I know what you must be feeling. I love Peepa, too. I have to go; nobody else in the family is going down there. You can't let me go all alone!"

"Oh Mother, please, leave me alone. I can't. I'm sorry, I'm sorry!" Getting up from my bed, I ran into the bathroom, slamming the door and locking it. Running the water as hard as I could,

I fell to my knees beside the bathtub and banged on it, sobbing hysterically: "I can't, I can't, I can't! Oh God, don't let this happen."

When I was all cried out and worn out with grief, I unlocked the door. Mother was lying face down on her bed, her head in her pillow, and she too was crying, "It's so unfair, so unfair!"

Mother and I were waiting in Pennsylvania Station for our trains: hers was going to Florida, mine to Washington. Filled with guilt and despair, I leaned towards the window in my seat, pressing my nose up against it. That way no one could see me crying. I moaned whenever Peepa's face was before me, and it was, most of the time now. I just couldn't face it, or even think about it any more. I thought perhaps I could have managed going there to be with Peepa, if only there was something to enable me to get through the pain, the suffering. But there wasn't. I couldn't even go on the way I was, to Washington.

"What am I going to do?" I moaned. Then, as I reached in my handbag for a cigarette, I noticed a waiter carrying some drinks on a tray. Like a magnet, my gaze was drawn to the cool, wet rim of the glass that spelled relief. Would I dare order a drink on this train, at sixteen? Well, maybe just maybe, I could pass for eighteen. Without giving it another thought, I summoned the waiter: "I'd like to order a drink, if I may."

"Why certainly, ma'am, what would you like?"

I didn't know what I wanted, but I didn't want to waste a moment, lest he change his mind, and I knew I had better order a stiff one, in case he decided I shouldn't have a second. Someone else might tell him to check my ID.

"I'll have an extra dry martini, please." That was the strongest drink I could think of, and besides, it had always done the job for Mother.

Two martinis after that, the train pulled into Washington. My eyes were bone dry, and I was able to think — or not think — about anything. *I had control of my mind!* Uncle Duddy was waiting for me, as I walked the long platform to meet him. My mouth was filled with perfume I'd rubbed inside it, so that he couldn't smell the gin. I was glad to see Uncle Duddy, and to be with him and Edith and the children. At both his house and Shirley and Morty's, I felt as if I was one of their own children, instead of a niece. They loved me, and cared about me. I knew it.

The first two weeks of my stay, I was constantly busy, either with my cousins, doing lots of different things, or with the neighbors next door, or dating. For by this time, I had developed a small group of my own friends in the area and had even had several dates. I came home late, after everyone was in bed, carrying my shoes and trying not to sway too much.

One morning, as I was brushing my teeth in the bathroom, I heard the telephone ring. After a few minutes, I thought I heard Aunt Edith say, "Oh, no, that's too bad." Dropping my toothbrush and leaving the water running, I ran the length of the hall to the kitchen and stood in the doorway. My heart began to pound as I became aware that the topic of conversation was Peepa. I bit my lips as I waited, not sure of what Edith was going to say, but sure that whatever it was, it was grim. And then, when I got on the phone, I didn't know whether it was my mother or Uncle Leo Karl. All I knew was that Peepa had died.

I took the train back to New York City with Uncle Duddy very early the next morning. He was a comfort on the trip, his quiet assurance was steady, but for me there were no tears, just fear. I was afraid of seeing Peepa's body in the funeral home and at the funeral. My stomach was tied up in knots, and the ache in my back never left.

There was no way I could go through that and ultimately accept it. I had to reject Peepa's death and what it meant. As each horror-filled thought about what was to come came to mind, I stiffened up, breathed deeply and tried to focus on something else, anything else.

At the funeral home, I saw my mother and Aunt Mary in black;

the whole family was there, Uncle Leo, Gerie, Shirley and Morty, but I felt as though it was just Peepa and I alone in that small room. At the entrance, I could see a long coffin at one end of the room. Peepa's daughter Eva was bent over it, sobbing, "Papa, Papa!" Slowly I walked towards the coffin, vaguely remembering Uncle Leo coming up to me and brushing my cheek with his hand, saying:

"Little Bobbie Shaftoe," his voice was whimpering. "Peepa loved you so much. You were his whole life."

When I reached the coffin, Eva had stepped back, and I was alone with Peepa. Looking down, I closed my eyes and held my stomach. Then I looked. "Oooh," I groaned. This wasn't my Peepa; it didn't look like him. He was a mere shadow of the handsome, robust man I had known — so thin, so pale, so old.

Then I heard Eva crying loudly again behind me: "He died such a horrible death. It was a nightmare! He was so afraid to die, poor Papa, and in his last breath he screamed out in pain and fear, 'I don't want to die!' "

When I heard those words, I became dizzy and light-headed, and fell backwards. Mother cried out: "Somebody, quick, she's fainting!" Uncle Duddy caught me and sat me upright in a chair. Someone else put my head between my legs, and my mother put a bottle of strong smelling salts under my nose.

"I'm okay, I'm okay, Mother," but from that moment on, I blocked out the entire funeral.

The days, weeks and months that followed were a blur. One thing I knew: I wasn't able ever to relive or even think about the times with Peepa again. And the few moments I allowed myself to peek back into the warmth of our life and love together, I was overwhelmed with grief. It was as though I was nearing the edge of a precipice — automatically, I stepped back.

Peepa died on August 16, 1957. That September I began my junior year at Music and Art High School. Mother had left B. Altman's to take a break for several months, while I continued to escape and run. In a whirlwind, I made the rounds of every place I could at my age in Greenwich Village. Usually with a small group I knew from school, or people I had met at a party or at Friday night fraternity, I didn't give a damn about my grades, or school, and yet dreaded what was coming, the college boards the next semester. On Friday night, January 3, 1958, I went bowling with Lynn, whom I had not seen lately and was anxious to spend some time with. She was about the only person I knew who really understood what I felt inside, and neither of us talked about it. Lynn was going through her own hell at that time, and I wanted to be of some help to her, if only to distract her from the reality of her life. Bowling had become something we both enjoyed, and it served as a good release for our pent-up problems and emotions. But on this particular night, Lynn seemed unusually preoccupied and worried.

"What's wrong, Lynn? You seem really upset."

She looked at me, with no attempt to hide her anxiety.

"I'm worried about Mother. Since she and Dad have separated, it's been awful. She's going up to the apartment tonight, to get some things and see him. Barbara, I'm afraid for her. In fact, I think I ought to leave here now and go meet her there!"

"No, Lynn, don't do that; don't get involved, please! But if you do go, I'll go with you."

"No, you won't! I'm not going to let you go through one of those awful scenes, too."

"I'm hardly a stranger to scenes, you know," I replied gently.

"Never mind, I won't go. C'mon, it's your turn to bowl."

Lynn's mother had been a sober alcoholic for three years, and Lynn was proud of her mother's recovery, especially since she had attempted suicide several times, once by jumping off the bridge in East New York. Lynn's father had been the editor of a well-known magazine that had gone bankrupt, and he couldn't handle that. He began lashing out at everyone and everything around him. Lynn's mother left him for her own survival, taking Lynn with her. They had been living in Greenwich Village with Lynn's older sister and her husband.

As we took turns bowling, and chatting with people we knew, I could feel the fear I saw in Lynn's eyes. "Lynn, why don't you spend the night at my house? Tomorrow is Saturday, and we can do something together."

"No, thanks, Bobbie; I want to get home. In fact, I think I'd like to leave right now."

"Okay, let's go."

It was 10:30 p.m. as I watched Lynn disappear down the subway stairs at 86th and Broadway. Calling after her, I said, "I'll call you tomorrow!" My toes felt numb from walking just three blocks, and I couldn't wait to get home. Mother had the teakettle on when I arrived and I snuggled up in bed with a cup of hot tea, and listened to some soft music on the radio.

"Mom, would you mind turning the light out? You can leave the radio on, if you want to, but I'm just beat!"

Mother turned off the light and said goodnight.

Sound asleep that night, I heard my mother's insistent voice, and my mind tried to weave it into the dream I was having. But it didn't work.

"Barbara, Barbara! Wake up, take the phone, it's for you. And it's urgent!"

Half asleep, I could barely hear her. Reaching for the receiver, my head still on the pillow, I mumbled, "Hello? Who is this? It must be the middle of the night."

Frantically, a boy's voice said: "Hurry, get up; it's Linc." I tried to concentrate; Linc was Lynn's steady boyfriend.

"I've got horrible news," he choked. "Lynn's parents are dead! Both were killed instantly. Get dressed and get down to Lynn's now! She needs you!"

I hung up the phone, and sat on the edge of the bed, not moving. Mother tried to ask me what had happened, but I was barely able to tell her what Linc said to me. I threw some clothes on and raced down the stairs to the hotel lobby, stopping short as I saw the headlines on the news stand: EX-EDITOR KILLS WIFE AND SELF IN TAXI CAB, along with a photo of the bodies on the front page.

When I got to Lynn's sister's apartment, Lynn was sitting with her head in her hands, unable to speak. I was told that when she heard the news from her sister, she had gone into shock and lost her voice. A close friend added that it was a hysterical reaction, and that her voice would return. After kissing her on the forehead and holding her for a few moments, my tears wetting her face, I took a seat opposite Lynn, and sat with everyone else in the room, in silence, except for the times when someone said: "Does anyone want something to eat? A cup of coffee?"

Everything in me wanted to say or do something to break the silence, to be of some help, to do anything to help Lynn and her sister, but all I could do was dry my eyes and sit there hour after hour, wringing my hands along with everyone else, and thinking about the present and the past, and why I was alive. What was life for and worth? "Nothing!" I mumbled to myself. "I might as well be dead. I don't live, anyway; I just exist!"

My last year at M & A was filled with busyness and excitement. In our varsity show, I played the part of a shy, coquettish young student in love with her English teacher. The teacher, naturally, was twice the student's age. She was looking for a father. Made up to look as attractive as possible, my long hair beautifully draped around my shoulders, I wore a low V-neck black jersey, a tight tweed skirt, white bobby socks and white bucks.

On opening night, the auditorium was packed, and I was all butterflies. "How in hell did I ever let myself get into this situation, Lynn?" I groaned behind stage. "I can't go on! I won't make it! I'll pass out or forget my lines and just stare off into space."

"No, you won't, Scheutzy, relax. When you're out there, you'll be fine. This is a natural for you; you know what a great ham you are." Yes, I was a ham, but in comfortable surroundings, not on stage in front of several hundred strangers! Twenty minutes before curtain time, I was pacing around and around in a circle.

Suddenly my eye caught a fellow in our class with a pint of whiskey in his hand. With my eye on that bottle as though it had cast a spell on me, I ran towards it. A flashback of the half-filled bottle of whiskey in our kitchenette before my date with Tommy raced through my mind. But I dismissed it — life, air to breathe, was just a few feet away. Again I reached for that reviving liquid that would fill my veins and stimulate my dull brain with new life.

"Excuse me, but could you possibly spare some of your whiskey? I'm going on stage in a moment and I'm very nervous."

"Sure, go ahead," he smiled, "take all you want."

An open invitation! I put the bottle to my lips.

"Bobbie! No, don't!" Lynn called out. Ignoring her, I guzzled as much as I dared to, without appearing too, too greedy. Handing back the bottle to my new friend, I grinned from ear to ear. "Saved, in the nick of time! Thank God for that bottle being here!"

Warmth soon filled me. I walked on stage and took my seat with confidence. I *was* the girl I played. Freed up to use every feminine wile, I drew this English teacher to me. I also drew the entire audience, and at the end I won a standing ovation. I couldn't believe it! I couldn't believe this was actually happening, that that thunderous applause was for me. But, oh, I loved it and wanted it to cascade forever! And I also knew what had made it possible for me to play the part.

Not only did this exciting breakthrough bring me the acceptance, acclamation and approval I had craved for so long, but that night I discovered I had a fantastic tolerance for liquor. I maintained a tremendous high, without getting ill, at the party afterwards. "You see, Lynn? I've learned how to master this stuff and drink like a lady. See that girl over there? She's making a fool of herself; she's drunk. But not me. I can drink without getting sick, and I'm perfectly charming and ladylike." Lynn didn't answer me. "Well, Lynn, aren't I?"

"I suppose so, Scheutzy; go ahead and have fun — it's your party!"

6

On July 1, 1959 I turned eighteen. I was now of legal age to drink anywhere, and to become anything or anyone I wanted. A young woman now, I no longer thought of myself as a teenager, and I quickly began to try to look years older than my age. I wore dark clothes, mostly black and charcoal grey, believing those colors to be subdued, sophisticated, and quietly sultry. In addition, my first real job at the head office of an international oil company at Rockefeller Center provided a glamorous setting and opened the way into the kind of life style I wanted. The executive world that surrounded me on the 38th floor was what I had seen at the Hotel Claridge in Atlantic City and everything I had imagined Mother's life to be like when she lived with my father in Sweden. It was also a perfect fit with the Palm Court at the Plaza Hotel.

My rather simple job, that summer, was that of mailgirl, delivering mail from desk to desk, department to department, and it gave me an almost instant opportunity to get to know everyone. Even those behind closed doors occasionally came out. And when they did, I was often around. If I received a nice big executive smile, it meant approval. Naturally, I smiled back. I learned a lot about smiles, looks, and where to be at the right time.

There were broad smiles, letting someone know you were happy and liked them. There were pensive, wrinkled-brow looks, with just a hint of a smile, letting someone know you were sizing them up, perhaps interested. And there were sad, puppy-dog, droopy-eyed looks, with half-smiles that said, "Won't somebody please feel sorry for me and give me a home?" I never stopped to think about what to give whom; I seemed to know intuitively. The last smile was reserved for men twice my age, father-figure types who wanted to play the father to little girls, comforting and helping them, especially if they were helpless and lost. I was, and they did, through snatches of conversation, boxes of candy or an occasional invitation to lunch, always with someone else along, of course.

Iris and I drifted apart. Her whole interest was centered on preparing for Skidmore College that fall, and everything that that life was going to bring her. I was jealous of her new white convertible that her parents had given her, and the beautiful wardrobe she was able to buy. Lynn was also preparing to leave — for college in Alabama. I didn't want her to go. I loved her, and she was the main stabilizing influence in my life. Whenever we'd meet that July at the Ad Lib cocktail lounge on 47th Street and Madison Avenue, a place frequented by young singles, I could never quite bring myself to order my third martini in front of her. She had a holy hatred for the stuff that had killed both her parents and left her homeless. She already knew more of suffering, and surviving, than I.

When Lynn left that summer, I became fast friends with Annette, the receptionist and my immediate supervisor. Fifteen years older than I and divorced, she found an all-too-eager confidante and drinking companion in me. Annette was sophisticated, beautiful and, most important, she drank. Although she came from a middleclass Italian family, she changed her last name, striving for the same type of life that Mother always talked about, and which was gradually becoming a goal for me also. Annette shopped at the finest stores on Fifth Avenue, wearing clothes well beyond what she could afford. Her attitude towards most of the other women at work, and they were all aware of it, was that of superiority. She believed they were jealous of her, and they were. She had won the smiles and approval of practically every executive in the company, in London as well as New York. Since I was her friend, I soon began to win that same kind of approval, and did I like it!

I rarely thought about NYU, or what it was going to be like in the fall to go to college. I had taken the job to pay for some of my tuition and the clothes I would need, but the money I made seemed to slip out of my fingers almost as fast as I earned it. Cocktails at the Rainbow Room, the English Grill, the Weston Hotel, Longchamps, Top of the Six's, and so on, took precedence.

I enjoyed my job. It was easy — a new game, and an important one. I never took my time delivering mail and messages from floor to floor; on the contrary, I acquired a reputation for being speedy and alert. I rushed down hallways, took the stairs instead of waiting for the elevator, and managed to work my way up to the front of the line at the Post Office.

One morning in August, in my usual hurry, I turned a corner without looking, and bumped headlong into someone's chest. My mail flew everywhere, but I didn't notice; I was looking into the blue eyes of a handsome, just-my-type boy carrying a package. Even his nose was turned up and short. "Sorry," I mumbled, stooping to pick up the scattered mail. "It was my fault; I never look where I'm going."

"Neither do I," he chuckled, bending down to help me. "You're the mailgirl for this floor?"

"Yes, do you work in the mail department? I've never seen you before."

"I was just hired yesterday. What's your name?"

"Barbara — um, Barbara Scheutz."

"I'm Jack Riley. Hi."

"Hi." I became flustered from ear to ear. Hoping he wouldn't notice how red my face was, I bowed my head, concentrating on retrieving the last of my mail. But it seemed that, with each few pieces I picked up, I dropped another. "You don't have to stay here and help me, honestly," I said, flustered. "You'd better get back."

"I want to, though."

"Oh!" Now I couldn't wait for all the mail to get picked up.

"Thanks, thanks a lot. Sorry I bumped you, I mean, bumped into you."

"That's okay; I didn't mind at all," and he gave me one of those big, full, acceptance smiles. My heart was pounding as he walked away.

The rest of that day, and that night as well, I spent thinking about Jack. I couldn't wait to see him again. The next morning I asked Annette if she had any "By hand" for the 35th floor, where the mailroom was.

"No, nothing, but I do have one for 41."

Sighing, I took the package and pressed the button for the elevator. It was 9:30, and as the elevator door opened, crowds were still coming in. Suddenly a tall, blond figure stepped off; my heart leaped as I recognized Jack. He tried to smile, but people were walking and moving every which way, making it difficult for him to stand still. As the elevator cleared, and I stood motionless, a man I had been waiting with asked, "Aren't you going up?"

Jerking my head, I realized he was speaking to me. To my amazement, I found myself saying: "Uh, I made a mistake. Go ahead; I'll get another elevator later." Annette looked up from her reception desk just as Jack motioned me to follow him to the other end of the corridor. I felt as though my heart could surely be heard the length of the floor. "Hey, Barbara," he said quietly, "how would you like to meet me at the Down Under at 5:30 tonight, if you're free?"

"Yes, gee, that would be fine. Yup, I'm free; I get off at five."

"Oh, I wouldn't want you to hang around for half an hour waiting for me." Instantly regretting that I had ever added that bit of information, I quickly told him I had to get a birthday card for my mother. "Great! See you later."

Of course, I smiled to myself, as I watched him go around the corner, my mother's birthday was in November, and this was August. I spent the rest of that day in and out of the ladies' room, combing and rearranging my hair. I delivered my mail, rushed back to my cubby hole, sat on my chair and thought about Jack. He was sweet, he was gentle, he was well-mannered, he must have a good heart and come from a good home. He wasn't Jewish, he was about three years older than I, and — well, he was just perfect for me. I was in love with him; I had to be! Once that was decided, I envisioned many dates, going steady, wearing his "pin," getting engaged and then married. I could just see myself, walking down a long aisle in my wedding gown — when the dumbwaiter buzzed. What? Was it 4:30 already? I took my cables and steno work off, sorted them and sped through the halls, skipping and singing. Done at 4:45, I spent the next fifteen minutes putting on fresh make-up and refixing my hair for the twenty-third time.

Annette watched me flitting around like a butterfly, and said finally, "Barbara, what's with you today?"

"Annette, I've met Prince Charming. I'm in love. Do you remember that blond boy you saw me talking to?"

"You mean that mail boy?"

I winced at the way she said "mail-boy;" to me, he seemed more than that. "Well, I have a date with him tonight, at the Down Under for drinks at 5:30."

"I see. Well, listen, Barbara: take it easy. He's young and looks very Catholic, so don't drink too much." I was startled; that was the first time Annette had ever cautioned me about drinking too much. I had not realized that she was aware of how much I did drink. She's just jealous, I said to myself, as I walked away, annoyed with her. She's probably afraid she'll lose a drinking companion herself if I begin to date Jack.

But once I was downstairs, I suddenly became extremely nervous. I had no birthday card to buy, and a whole half-hour to wait. I'd better have a drink before I meet him, I thought, so that I'll be relaxed and confident. I'll slip into the bar at the English Grill; after all, I can't go to the Down Under twice. But all the company's executives go to the English Grill; how can I walk in alone? Oh, well, I can't worry about that now; I'll just have to do it.

Walking into the English Grill wasn't as bad as I thought. I ordered a martini, but before I could finish it, another one was standing in front of me. Looking up, I saw Mr. Armstrong, who raised his glass in my direction. "I'm sorry, sir," I said, "but I'm just about to leave."

"Don't call me sir; it's Tommy to you." He must have started drinking early; about three o'clock would be my guess. Or maybe he never went back after lunch.

And speaking of time, it was five twenty-eight! Just time to go to the ladies' room, gargle some perfume, and be five minutes late, as planned. I smiled and left the martini behind. I carried a toothbrush and toothpaste now, and as I brushed my teeth, I felt so free, so relaxed and really looking forward to something for a change. Oh, I hope this works, I really hope it does!

It was obvious that Jack was as taken with me as I was with him. Not wanting anything to spoil this potential, new relationship, I didn't dare order a martini. Instead, I said, "A daiquiri, please, and not too strong."

Jack and I began to date regularly. It was happening; we were in love. For once, something was going my way. Often I would have a drink or two before a date, but even those times became fewer and fewer. I wanted only to be with him. Going to NYU now, and seeing Jack on weekends made me feel like any other girl. My time was well taken up, and I even attempted doing homework. It was glorious; I talked about Jack to everyone. And they all answered the same way: "Barbara, take it easy. It's only been a couple of months, this is your first real romance, and you're only eighteen. Besides, you'd better keep in mind that he's Catholic, Irish Catholic, and you're Jewish."

"Who cares? I'm not that Jewish. I don't gravitate to Jewish people, nor do they to me."

"What about Jack's family? Do you know anything about them?"

"No, but I will."

October — Central Park looked so colorful, with the gold, brown and red leaves rustling under our feet. Autumn was a great time to be in the city. Hand in hand, we kicked the leaves as we walked, skipped and ran through the park. Pulling Jack back, I asked him abruptly: "What are your parents like? Can I meet them sometime?"

He stopped short and turned. He looked at me, then lowered his head and said, "My parents are deaf mutes. They've always been that way, and we all communicate in sign language. My older brother is a priest. Until last year, I was going to become one, too. I took time out to think and see if that's what I really wanted to be, then I met you, and all that's changed."

I was stunned. His answers came much faster than I expected. Too much faster — I didn't want to hear all that. Unable to reply, my throat dry, I tried desperately not to show my reaction. "Oh, that's not the worst thing in the world. I mean, it doesn't matter, Jack; you said they were born that way. Um, could it be hereditary?" I wanted to kick myself; it all came out wrong — what a mess I was making! Why couldn't I keep my big mouth shut? I could see Jack trying to maintain his pride, but his eyes were downcast.

"Jack, listen: it doesn't matter! I don't care! Look at me: I'm Jewish," as if being Jewish were a malady. "My parents are divorced; I've never seen my father. But we're in love; and that can overcome everything." I began to talk faster and faster, trying to beat back the reality of what was starting to happen.

Jack interrupted me: "Barbara, I was going to tell you tonight, anyhow. Look, we're having a farewell dinner for my brother at the Top of the Six's next Wednesday night. He's sailing for Africa to do missionary work. I want you to come and meet my family. Will you?"

"Of course! I can hardly wait. What's missionary work? How will I talk to them? Do you think they'll like me?"

He just laughed at all my questions tumbling out and gave me a big hug. "I'm not worried; how could they help but like you?"

I spent the rest of that week shopping for a dress that looked "Catholic." It had to be just the right length, high neck with buttons and very subdued. Mother could sense my anxiety, but I did not tell her, nor Annette nor anyone else, what I had discovered about Jack's family. I dismissed it completely; it was just a minor problem. After all, we were in love, and that was all that mattered.

Wednesday night finally came, and at the entrance to the elegant restaurant so far above the streets of Manhattan, my feet felt as though they were sinking into the plush, thick red carpeting. We looked across the crowded dining room for Jack's family. "There they are!" he exclaimed, pointing to a rather sedate group of people gathered around a rectangular table. When I came face to face with Jack's parents, I was astonished to see that they were old. They must have been every bit of seventy. We all exchanged greetings. Jack's brother, tall, light-haired and steely-looking in his priestly attire, got up to shake my hand. I noticed he was drinking a cocktail. With an inner sigh of relief, I knew that someone would be around soon, to take my drink order. There wasn't much conversation; everyone but me spoke in sign language. I tried to keep smiling, all the while looking sweet and demure.

Later, at the farewell party on the ship that his brother was sailing on, Jack opened two bottles of champagne, and as he poured some into his mother's glass, I caught a glimpse of her pointing her finger at me, as she signed to Jack.

"What was she saying?" I later asked him.

"Uh, nothing really; just that she knew you were Jewish," Jack murmured, suddenly looking and sounding awkward.

Had something gone wrong? Oh, it must be my imagination. But when Jack took me home that night, he was quieter than usual. "I'm sorry, Barbara, but I'm really tired, and it's late," he said, turning to leave. "I'll call you during the week."

It *was* very late, and we had had a good deal to drink, both at the restaurant and then later on the ship. Gee, I wondered, knocking on the door as Jack walked down the long corridor towards the elevator, did I drink too much tonight? Did Jack's parents notice how much I drank? Or was it that I was Jewish? Something seemed different, all of a sudden.

Mother was waiting up for me, eager to know how the evening went. Lying in my bed, next to hers, I began to tell her all about Jack's family.

"Oh, my God, Barbara! All those extra problems! What if their muteness is hereditary? And a priest in the family yet..."

Four days later, Jack still hadn't called. We usually spoke to each other every night; something must be wrong. Finally, I couldn't stand it any longer, and called him. His voice was cold and distant: "Barbara, this has been a hard week for me. I've been doing some serious thinking, and I've come to a decision. I was going to call you later and ask to see you one more time."

"What are you talking about, one more time?"

"Barbara, we have to stop seeing each other," he said firmly. "It will never work out for us."

"But this is ridiculous! I don't believe you; I *won't* believe you." I refused to talk about it further. "When are we seeing each other again?" I asked, dismissing everything he had previously said.

"Tomorrow afternoon. I'll meet you at Cromwell's, at 5." Cromwell's? The drugstore didn't serve cocktails; what was wrong with him? He must be having trouble and doesn't think I'll understand.

Taking my arm the next afternoon, Jack led me outside and hastily hailed a cab. Giving the name of a restaurant on Second Avenue, we got in. Neither of us spoke. Half-way through my first Rob Roy, Jack looked me squarely in the eyes and told me that he was never going to see me again. I kept shaking my head, and he repeated the same thing in different ways, until it began to sink in.

"Please, Jack, don't do this! What's happened? Why, why, why?"

He was a different person, cool and aloof. "Do you want another drink, Barbara?"

"Yes, yes, I do! And no, I don't want to eat anything!" We hardly spoke after that, except for my periodic, "Do you think in time you'll change your mind?" Jack shook his head. I sat there, crying and drinking one Rob Roy after another. "Do you think we're too different? I mean, the fact that you're Catholic and I'm Jewish?"

"We are different, very different and come from opposite backgrounds, but I don't know for sure if that's it. I was up most of the night before making this decision. It wasn't easy, but I know I have to stop seeing you."

"Is it your parents? Do they object?"

"It doesn't matter what it is." Jack's vague reply frustrated and angered me. I drank faster than he had ever seen me, and I didn't care how many drinks I ordered, either. There was no point in holding back or pretending any longer. What was the use? And I hurt too damn much inside. But I could see him recoil, as I became drunker and drunker within that hour. How I didn't want him to see that, yet I couldn't stop drinking. The pain in my heart, as it was breaking apart, was more than I could endure.

It was a long cab-ride home, the only noise being the clicking of the meter. As we walked down the long hotel corridor to our apartment, I kept hoping he would somehow change his mind, finding it as hard to say goodbye as I did.

He bent down to kiss me goodnight, and my heart leaped. He's changed his mind, or he wouldn't want to kiss me goodnight! But after a quick kiss, he said, "Goodbye, Barbara; good luck to you."

"Please," I sobbed, "please don't say goodbye. Can't we just wait a while and then see each other in a week or two, or even three. Oh please, please, Jack, don't go through with this!" But he turned quickly and walked up the corridor. I stood there motionless, looking at him, until he was out of sight. Then I sank down to my knees and sobbed, beating the floor with my fist.

Mother jerked the door open. "Barbara! What's the matter?" Trying to verbalize how I felt threw me into a state of hysteria. Inside the apartment, Mother tried to calm me. "It's probably for the best. You'll meet someone else; we'll take a trip somewhere. You'll forget him."

But then her own grief for me overwhelmed her. "Oh my God, my baby."

Unable to get a grip on my emotions, I took a long walk on Riverside Drive to calm down. I kept wishing I was dead. But I wasn't dead, and I couldn't bear the pain inside, so I did what had already become the natural thing for me: I looked for a place to drink.

Walking back from Riverside Drive and up Broadway from 79th Street, my teeth chattered, I felt so cold. A few old leaves scuttled up the sidewalk ahead of me. It was November now, November 13, 1959, and I was at the midpoint of this school semester. Just the thought of having to go back to school that week and concentrate on work, pretending to go on living as though nothing had happened, angered and embittered me. "No, no, I won't do it," I said, shivering as I walked hastily up Broadway, peering into bar after bar, hoping to find one that looked fairly safe for me to go into alone at this late hour.

Finally I decided to head back to the Greystone and go into the bar there. What did it matter who thought what about me? I'll be dead drunk anyway, by the time I get home. It won't be as far to walk from the lobby. There was no one in the hotel bar except the bartender. I went inside and drank until I could barely walk.

The rest of that week, I stayed home from school and wandered around the streets of Manhattan during the day and Greenwich Village at night. I talked to no one, refused to eat, and drank whenever I could. Mother was frantic. "You are all I have, please, please, you must pull yourself out of this. You're young; the whole world is ahead of you. I know you will meet someone eventually who will give you the love and security you need."

"I doubt it, Mother. Nothing ever works out for me. Some people just aren't lucky; I suppose they're born that way."

"Don't talk like that! You'll will it on yourself."

"Iris and Lynn and I. I believe that of the three of us, I am the one who is doomed."

"Come, my lilla van, let me tell your cards; let's see what they say."

"Oh, those blasted cards!" I shouted, but she got the deck, and we sat down at the kitchen table. My mother first laid the queen of clubs face up on the table. That was supposed to be me. Then she cut the cards, which were actually half of a deck, as not all the cards were used. She made three small piles, the middle pile face down on the card representing me, with the two other piles on either side. The first outer pile that she turned over had the ace of clubs facing us. Since it was upside down, it meant disappointment. The first card on the middle pile was the ace of spades, also upside down. That was the worst card you could have fall on your card in the entire deck, if it was in reversed position. The third stack that Mother turned over showed the ace of diamonds. Mother clapped her hands to her mouth and muttered: "There must be some mistake; I'll do it over."

"There's no mistake, Mother," I said solemnly. "There it is: the worst tragedy, the greatest heartbreak and the most desolate life imaginable awaits me." And for once my mother was utterly speechless.

I went back to school and finished that semester, barely passing. My mind was always everywhere but where it was supposed to be, and I wanted it that way. I made no attempt to concentrate on what I was doing, becoming more and more defiant and more and more dependent on the weekends — the fraternity parties and visits to local cafes, bistros and clubs. It was there that I could get the stuff that lifted me out of the tight, dark ball of hopelessness that I was becoming. But anyone looking at me wouldn't have known how I ached inside. And some places, like the German Rathskeller on Second Avenue, a place where college students hung out, made me believe that I was like any other coed, drinking beer and having fun on a Friday night. But I wasn't like the other girls. They had two, maybe three steins of beer at the most, while I drank eight in an evening, and sometimes even ten.

Christmas and New Year's, 1960, came and went. Lynn remained in Alabama and Iris came home for the holidays. We were further apart in lifestyle than ever now. She did well in school. Her grades were high, and she had met someone at a nearby college and had gotten pinned. Iris's boyfriends were always steady. She was showered with Christmas gifts and good feelings about herself and where she was going. I too received gifts; Mother always made sure she had lots of presents for me, and Aunt Mary always met us for cocktails before Christmas in downtown Manhattan and gave me a generous present. But Aunt Mary always went home to Uncle Leo Sheirr; and Aunt Shirley and Uncle Duddy and Uncle Leo Karl all had their own families which were complete. Mother and I were alone and incomplete.

That January, I left NYU, as I had planned. My friendship with Annette had continued from the preceding summer, and she was able to get me my old job back, working directly under her. As to bumping into Jack, I didn't have to worry about that; he had left his job and enlisted in the service. There was a part of me, though, that still wanted a connection with the campus life at NYU. To me, it meant a large degree of self-worth and respectability. Also, I wanted to prove to myself and to those around me at work that I was still trying to get ahead. So, I continued on at the school of Commerce in Greenwich Village on Tuesday and Thursday evenings from 6 to 10 p.m., taking eight credits. Mother, who had quit her job at Georg Jensen for a while, decided to join me in the evenings, taking a course in psychology on the same evenings that I went.

The new semester had barely begun when Iris, who was home from Skidmore for a weekend, called me up in the afternoon. Sensing the urgency in Iris' voice, I had run the four blocks to her apartment house, after she asked me to come right over. Her mother was in the kitchen, when their maid opened the door. It was odd, I thought, that she didn't turn to greet me; she had always been so warm and hospitable. But with her back to me, standing over the sink, she said in a monotone: "Iris is in her room."

Iris met me in the hallway and motioned for me to come in. She looked expressionless when she said: "I have awful news, Barbara: Lincoln is dead."

"What? No, don't tell me that!"

Iris went on to tell me how he died, sounding almost stern as she related the events leading up to Linc's death. He had complained of dizziness and exhaustion. His gums were soft and bled easily. At the school infirmary, where they immediately took a blood sample, he was told he had mono and had to go to Mt. Sinai Hospital in New York for treatment. However, they knew that he had leukemia. Growing steadily worse each day, Linc died the following Friday. The only person he wanted near him was Lynn.

"Iris, have you told Lynn?"

"No, I haven't. I think you should. You're closer to her now than I am. Get a grip on yourself and call her."

Turning away from Iris, I ran down the hall crying, "No, no, this can't be happening!" With my hands over my face, I sobbed more and more, as pictures and memories of Linc, Lynn and I, and Lynn's parents' horrible death, all came before me, making it harder and harder for me to get a grip on myself. By the time I reached 91st Street, I had gone through all the deaths of all the people that meant something to me. I continued seeing the pictures and feeling the emotions I felt at the time of each death, and then Peepa, and that was the worst. I couldn't, wouldn't recall the loss when he died. How could I go on living with the main part of me gone? And that part was my rock core foundation.

And now Linc — what a purposeless end to such a beginning. Death was sick, evil, perverse. It had no purpose. Life had no purpose. Everything was based on luck. We were all puppets on a string, existing day by day, doing our part for nothing, nothing. Well, I was going to break my string. I was not going to play the part any more, only to end up the same way — disillusioned, frightened and dead. And I was never going to think about God again, ever. I would never go into a synagogue again. Why should I go where I would be reminded of the dirt that was heaped on Peepa's and Meema's coffins? And I was not going to Linc's funeral!

7

In the days that followed, I did my best to cheer Lynn up, but I was having my own emotional problems with what happened. I went over and over what little I knew of Linc's death. I looked for symptoms of leukemia in myself. Whenever I became ill, I was convinced that I, too, was going to end this way. Afraid of life and petrified of death, I didn't know which was worse: the existence or the end. Everything was extreme; I knew no middle ground. There was no level plane to think or rest on. I had to erase my mind, or I would go insane! My skin had begun to crawl with itchy hives. Sometimes my entire body felt as though it was on fire.

It was only when I drank that I felt released from both mind and body.

For the next six months, until July when I turned nineteen, I threw myself completely into my job, and what went with it. I became Annette's go-for. I cocktailed more frequently with her and also watched a relationship bloom between her and the president of the American division of the company. He left his wife, and he and Annette were married. Since I was there, I became an occasional third in their relationship. Avenues began to open up for me, executive avenues. I was invited to some of the nicest restaurants in New York, and all the time I developed my skills at drinking, smoking, and in the course of it, discerning other people's problems.

I received a promotion to the job of receptionist in the advertising department on the 34th floor. The manager of that department had taken a liking to me. He gave me gifts at Christmas time and told me that I was like the daughter he never had. And in my own fantasy, I pretended that he was my father, and I lived with him and his family in Tuxedo Park, New York. Whether I did my work or didn't do it, I knew I had his approval and I felt secure in my job.

In the beginning, I tried my hardest to do well at my work. The receptionist part of it was a cinch. I had no trouble smiling and being sociable, especially after a long martini lunch that enabled me to be anything to anyone. Often I was the listening partner to someone from our office or out of town, even as far as London. I listened about how competitive and hard their jobs were, how much they had to travel, and how cold and uncompassionate their wives were. Often I sat across from some man in his forties or fifties, who would recount how different his life would be, if only he'd married a girl like me. I laughed and told him how grateful he should be for his wife and work at his marriage, but inside, I ate it up. It went down like honey, soothing the many hurts and ego-deflating experiences I'd had thus far, especially the one with Jack.

On weekends, Mother and I frequented Spring Lake, New Jersey. Not only had the bars and cocktail lounges on New York's East Side become the "in" places to go, so had the Jersey shore. Young and old singles from New York crammed into the club cars each Friday night after work, hoping that this weekend would be the one where they would meet the man or woman of their dreams. For the girl like me who still wanted to find a husband to love and have for herself, it wasn't easy. Girls of all sizes and shapes were now clamoring at the fashionable hotel bars, looking for husbands. Men, too, were at the bars, but not looking for wives. They wanted, as I often heard whenever I sat opposite a man who let me in on his secret, someone with whom they could have a "meaningful relationship" — which meant a relationship with no strings attached. Of course if, during a period of time (and none of them ever specified how long that might be), the relationship still held together with the same fiery passion with which it had begun, not to mention the friendship, the mutual interests and the girl's culinary skills and brains, then, possibly, marriage might be considered.

It was on a balmy Friday night in August, when I was nineteen, that I sat across from such a man at the Allaire Hotel. His name was Roy Kiley and he was an attorney from New York. He was thirty-two and a bachelor. Since his name was Kiley and I went where Jews weren't, I assumed he was Irish Catholic. He drove Mother and me back to Manhattan that weekend, and I had my first of many dates with him, that Sunday evening.

Roy was very different from Jack. He was hard and tough in his manner, always late in calling and picking me up for a date. Half the time, he never did pick me up at the hotel. I usually met him at a restaurant or bar or his small studio apartment by Kips Bay Plaza, in the east thirties. But I sensed a stability about Roy and as I became more and more infatuated with him, I also became dependent upon him. He was older than Jack and had a profession. He also had a close-knit family that I became very fond of. I felt their warmth and acceptance of me, too, and so when I discovered that Roy's name had been changed to Kiley, and that he was actually Jewish, I wasn't at all upset. Perhaps the old adage I'd heard, "Jewish men make the best husbands and fathers," was true after all. Maybe at last I would find what I had had back in Borough Park, the family, home and feeling of tradition that was so important to me. And Roy's parents and his sister Ellie, who became an almost instant friend of mine, wanted to see Roy settle down, too. With each date, I became more hopeful; indeed, bells of eagerness were ringing in my own ears.

I continued on at NYU in the evenings until in January of 1961, I left completely. I tried to forget the fact that, just a short time ago, I had wanted a college education and was willing to work for it. Now I was willing to give it up, just like that, because I simply didn't feel like working and studying any more. I wanted every evening free for Roy, the new man in my life, and I pinned every hope I had on him.

That first month out of school, just about every hope but one was shattered. Roy would never see me on a steady basis. I could never count on him at all. Our dates were so sporadic that I rarely knew when I was seeing him, except maybe for an hour or so beforehand. The only hope I had left was that maybe, in time, I would grow on him, and that he would come to love me.

"Jewish men like to eat, and they like good food," Annette had often told me, so one afternoon I called Aunt Mary up where she worked and asked her to meet me at five o'clock and tell me how to cook something good and simple. We met at the Cattleman restaurant on 46th Street for cocktails and tons of yummy hors d'oeuvres. Aunt Mary told me over and over again how to prepare chicken paprika. After my second Manhattan, I decided to call Roy and ask him if I could come over and cook dinner for him.

"Sure, that sounds like a great idea. Come on over." Rushing to the supermarket, I bought two chickens, onions, paprika, oil, garlic and some other groceries. With both arms full of bundles and bubbling with enthusiasm, I took the Second Avenue bus down to 30th Street. When I got off the bus, however, I began to feel a little queasy. The excitement had worn off, and I began to wonder what in the world I had gotten myself into. Nervousness set in, but not for long; I knew the instant remedy, and so I walked around until I found a decent cocktail lounge to go into and have a drink before going up to Roy's apartment.

Later, I entered his small, dark studio room like a bolt of lightning. Eagerly I unloaded my packages and began to prepare dinner.

"Hey, would you like a drink? With all that work ahead of you, you're gonna need something to get you going."

"Sure, I'd love one. I haven't had anything all day."

I had two drinks that Roy poured for me and then sneaked another one from the kitchen cupboard when he wasn't looking. This was fun! And maybe it was the answer for our relationship. Perhaps if I play house long enough, he'll see that I'm a real homemaking type and marry me after all. . . .

Up until this point, I had clung to the belief that a girl should keep her distance to a point and not begin cooking for a man or going to his apartment, and so on, until they were engaged. I had been raised with this idea, and any girl who did otherwise was loose, and a man would soon lose interest in a loose girl.

But now, in 1961, it seemed to me that things were beginning to change. Men and women were living together more openly; in fact, it was being advocated so that couples would know exactly what they were getting into before deciding to spend their lifetimes together. But I was barely twenty and that seemed awfully young to me, and my mother's words about holding back still echoed in my ears, so for the next two years I limited the houseplaying to cooking an occasional meal at Roy's apartment.

In the fall of 1961, I persuaded Mother to move from the Hotel Greystone. The neighborhood had deteriorated terribly. Iris had moved to the East side, and I wondered if my change of address might help in my relationship with Roy. He often made snide comments about where we lived. I grew to loathe the Greystone and was completely fed up with hotel living. I finally made it so miserable for Mother that she agreed to leave what she felt was her home.

"Barbara, everyone in this hotel knows us and looks after us. I'm afraid that we'll be lost in a new place on the East Side. In the hotel, there are so many services, and it's so easy, and. . . ."

As Mother went on and on, I broke in, saying: "This hotel is on the downgrade. As far as the lobby is concerned, they're a bunch of *yentas*, minding everybody's business but their own."

"Barbara! You're turning into a snob!"

"That's a riot! Me, a snob! Yes, that's exactly what I am turning into. And you can blame yourself for that, too."

New Year's Eve, 1962, Mother and I were in our small two-room apartment with a closet-sized kitchen again, only now we were on Park Avenue. As usual, we were together, alone. The move from the West Side to the East Side had done nothing to change my relationship with Roy, which continued to be stormy, sporadic and confusing. Nevertheless, I convinced myself that I was very much in love with him and was intent on maintaining patience, no matter how long it took.

Mother wasn't working during the time that we lived at 1040 Park Avenue. The apartment was dark and drab. The doorman and the whole building exuded stuffiness, not to mention the entire block. We often walked east on 86th Street, where everything was much livelier, on Lexington and Third Avenues. There were cafes and German Brauhauses. Mother and I frequently had dinner in these places and after several steins of dark beer, we stayed for the dancing and show. We did anything we could to fill in the lonely hours in the evening during the week and the long, lonely Sundays. Mother was restless and worried, not sure where to go with her own life, and I was equally, if not more, confused.

It was obvious to me after living at this place for a year that Roy was not one bit closer to proposing marriage to me. I had done all I could do to show him that I really cared for him. But I was afraid to commit myself emotionally and physically. In the short time that I had known Jack, I had been blown apart. And although I felt as though I had the approval of Roy's family, I was never sure of him.

My relatives and friends, particularly Lynn, who was back from Alabama now and working in the city, and Annette, advised me to break up with him completely. "You're only going to get hurt, Bobbie. You deserve better than Roy. He's deliberately toying with your emotions, and that's cruel." Lynn and I began meeting once or twice weekly for drinks after work. She took a small room in an apartment for women run by the Salvation Army, and had a good job. She also began dating a boy named Larry, whom she had met before she went away to Alabama. They soon became serious about each other. Iris was also thinking about marriage. But as far as I was concerned, nothing was going my way.

Another empty New Year's Eve passed, with Mother and me alone, and in March of 1963, Lynn, I and another girl from work decided to take a two-week vacation to Miami Beach. I hardly ever went anywhere without Mother. But I wanted to prove to myself that I could get away from everyone and everything, if I had to. Primarily, I wanted to shake Roy up. I wanted him to worry about me while I was gone, the way Larry worried about Lynn. She was besieged with letters, cards, a telegram and phone calls. She finally cut her trip short and returned home after one week. I never heard once from Roy, not one word.

I hated Miami Beach, but I was there, and I wanted to forget my life, and the rat-race existence I was caught up in. So, every day, every night, I drank, either with this other girl at a cocktail lounge, or out with a group of guys we met somewhere, or all by myself in the guest house. I drank the day we flew home and was dead drunk by the time we landed in New York. I literally fell into Mother's arms. All in all, that trip did nothing for me, except to put me deeper into debt and give me a good taste of what it was like to drink every day for two whole weeks. I swore up and down to myself and Mother that I would never drink like that again.

It was spring, 1963, I was twenty-one and a half years old, and I was absolutely miserable. Mother and I fought a great deal now. The move to elegant, tree-lined Park Avenue had not done at all for us what I was so sure it was going to. When our fights became intolerable scenes late at night, I would slam out the door and run towards Lexington and Third, where I always found some bar to hide in for a couple of hours until things quieted down at home. Often I would come home at midnight or one in the morning, to find Mother sound asleep. Food would be everywhere, burned pots, garlic, onions and cans of tomatoes filled our small all-in-one closet kitchen.

During this time, I was given another promotion, also in the advertising department. I panicked. It was no longer the soft, plush job of receptionist. It involved learning something about the advertising trade and sitting in the back where everyone else was, instead of all by myself out front. In the back, I would be seen by everyone, and I would have to work. And looking at my track record thus far, I expected to fail and eventually be fired. Influence would only work so long. On the other hand, I couldn't very well refuse the promotion, so I took the job, scared to death. I even began taking a course at typing school which my boss, the same advertising manager, paid for. He even got me a stenotype machine, and I enrolled in school for stenotyping, too. Often he would say: "Barbara, you have got to get prepared for life. You have to be able to support yourself properly. If you should ever leave this company, you can always make an excellent salary working in a court room with a stenotype machine, or anywhere else, for that matter. Please take advantage of this offer." I thought about it and decided to take the machine and go to school, but for different reasons. Since Roy was a lawyer and needed a competent secretary, perhaps he would see an even greater benefit in having a wife who could type for him and take fast steno.

As it turned out, I barely learned to type and gave up on the steno machine after two months, returning it to my boss.

That fall I met Bill at a party in Connecticut. He was the son of our retail department manager and was in his senior year at Yale. I agreed to go out with him when he invited me to dinner and then later for a football weekend at Yale. I was looking forward to it. Perhaps someone else might interest me enough to shake me out of this insane relationship with Roy.

The week before I left, I made sure that I didn't drink or eat chocolates. I wanted my face to be clear, and I didn't want to look bloated at all. The ride to New Haven was fun, and I liked being away from the executive world and back amongst people my own age. But shortly after I arrived on campus, and met several of Bill's friends, I began to feel uncomfortable and awkward, as though I didn't really fit in there at all. For one thing, I stood out as the only girl who was not attending a college, and when a couple of people asked me if I was Jewish, I became flustered, and ashamed of who I was. When drinks were served before dinner, and never stopped being served throughout the entire weekend, I hung right in there, drinking as many as most of the guys around me. Amazed at my own tolerance and capacity for alcohol now, I watched others gradually get sick and drunk all around me the way I used to. But I held every ounce of what I drank and didn't get the slightest bit sick. In fact, the next Monday mornng, when I had to get up to go to work, I was up, sharp as ever, whatever sharp was for me at that time. I would have liked to hear from Bill again, but I didn't expect to, and I didn't.

Roy now became the total primary focus in my life, and the one area where I had held out, I now began to rationalize to myself. Thoughts came to my mind constantly telling me it was really okay and perfectly acceptable for a girl of twenty-two to have an affair. I found supportive articles in magazines and heard discussions on TV which advocated sex before marriage. Girls my age and older discussed the subject on their lunch-hour or coffee-break at work. Several agreed that a guy wouldn't marry a gal today unless he slept with her at least twice, and that any gal who held back after twenty might have a problem with frigidity. I weighed the facts I gathered, looked at the length of time I'd been seeing Roy on and off — more than two years — and finally concluded that I was strong enough to handle that kind of relationship. Certainly I didn't have much to lose at this point.

It wasn't long, however, before I realized that I could *not* handle the emotional part of a relationship where I was wanted only part of the time and then, only for the physical. Already insecure and rejected many times over, I now had no way of repressing the thoughts, questions and lonely wanderings that went on in my mind, not to mention the constant ache in my heart. I felt more than ever like that little puppy dog that said, won't somebody please give me a home? Now I had two reasons to escape to a bar alone at night on East 86th Street. The first was the intolerable fights with Mother; the second was the insecurity I felt after waiting all evening for a phone call that never came, or the long cab ride home alone, late at night. Instead of home I often went to a lounge or someplace, any place, just to dull the pain inside with a few drinks.

Our Park Avenue apartment was even worse than the Hotel Greystone had been. I felt locked in there and began to loathe going to the bars on East 86th Street, and Madison Avenue was just too stuffy. I had to meet some other people my own age. Even my job wasn't any fun any more. Always counting the hours until five o'clock, I made oodles of mistakes and became more scatterbrained than ever, all to avoid any and all responsibility. Naturally, I blamed everything on Roy and Mother. I just had to do something to change my situation, and so in the summer of 1963, after turning 22, once again Mother and I tried the geographical cure.

This time, we chose our joint fantasy together, and chose to believe in it; anything was better than facing reality.

The search for a new apartment began. It was Mother who found a light, bright, L-shaped two-and-a-half, with a real kitchen, on East 80th Street, between Second and Third. Four large windows made up the entire wall facing the street; I could kneel on one of the sofa beds and watch the people come and go from the building. The place seemed to be teeming with young people; just next door were three girls my age, rooming together.

Bonnie, Jean and Jennifer soon became close friends. Jennifer was an actress, a real one, in a show on Broadway. Bonnie was also an actress, the struggling variety; she never quite landed a part. Jean was an airline stewardess for Pan Am, beautiful and British. On the seventh floor were three boys, all in their twenties. Their apartment became a meeting place where we all gathered. The guys had good jobs — up-and-comers who had come to the city to spread their wings. Nothing more than friendship ever developed, but for me these two apartments became a refuge from home, and made it easier to avoid seeing Roy and to start playing hard-to-get with him. Now, when the scenes at home became unbearable, that's where I headed.

Meanwhile, Iris had married Brian while Mother and I were still living at 1040 Park, and Lynn married Larry shortly after we moved to East 80th Street. I was happy for both of them and proud that Lynn had asked me to be her maid of honor, but my dejection at never marrying and finding a home of my own overrode everything. Dr. Glick, who became our family doctor while we were at Park Avenue, tried to help me sort through some of my problems when he saw me weekly for my extreme case of hives. He would prescribe a weekend in the Catskills, at the Concord or at Grossingers, to find a nice Jewish boy my own age, and settle down. And when my lip or eye would swell up to an enormous size in the middle of the night, and I had to go to the emergency room for adrenalin shots, he prescribed a tranquilizer for me to steady my screaming nerves. But I found that several drinks after work and through the evening hours were a far better tranquilizer than any pill I'd ever taken. Besides, new bars were springing up on upper First, Second, and Third Avenues that were not considered bars per se, but rather, pubs. Resembling the English type of pub with sawdust on the floor, round wooden tables, decorative low lamps and good beer, hamburgers and chili, these new, "in" social meeting places for young singles in New York became a more accepted and respectable escape for me. In a very short period of time, they became a large part of my life. I began to frequent Bogey's, Martel's and Spark's, all of which were within a two-block radius of home. I also began spending more time down in the Village, at places like Downey's and the Union Club.

Between going out with people from work and friends of people I knew in the building, my horizon was broadening, all the way from the fabled "21" to the "Thousand Mile House" in the Bowery. One evening, in the company of a couple of wealthy, blue-blood friends whom I met through Jean next door, we found ourselves taxiing around the Bowery, looking at the bums lying in the street with their hands outstretched for money. The Thousand Mile House was a large room — cracked mirrors, unswept floor, dirty glasses and men leaning against one another. We entered late, having made the rounds. As we moved through the maze of men and maybe two or three women, I felt pity rising from deep within me. "No, no, Al, I don't want to sit at the bar. I can't drink here. I can't take this place!" The faces, the desperate, searching faces, looked gaunt and harrowed from the torments of hell. "It's painful! How can you get a kick out of being here? You must be some kind of sadist!"

I started for the door and saw a man wearing a shabby but once-good-looking tweed sport coat, leaning against a broken window. Breathing on his hands to warm them, he was cold and needed a drink. He suddenly looked straight at me, his eyes penetrating mine. He must have been in his forties, and beneath the dirt and disheveled appearance, he might have even been handsome. I opened my handbag and handed him what money I had. I couldn't bear his suffering; it was as though I somehow knew exactly what he was going through. "I wish I could help you, all of you! Tell me, how did you get here? What did you do — before?"

In a low, soft voice, his eyes never wavering from mine, he said: "I am a professor. I used to teach at New York University." Holding the money I gave him in his hand and waving it in front of me, he added, " It's what I'm going to buy with this that destroyed me, and everyone else here. My life is hopeless now. I don't even have the guts to kill myself."

"No, no, sir! Don't say that!" Pleading for him and me and everyone, I started crying. "There must be a way out for you!" But he just shook his head and turned to the bar.

8

The horrible memory of that night in the Thousand Mile House came back to haunt me, but I became adept at banishing it. Like all the other painful memories, this one, too, was washed away with another drink. Drinking now took the center place in my life, leaving me unable to follow through with any preplanned activities. I gradually lost interest in the theater, cinema and art museums; where once I could happily spend several hours at the Metropolitan, now ten minutes was too long. Books were now too long for me to concentrate on, nor could I focus on politics, though I did enjoy following President Kennedy. When the news came that he had been assassinated, I felt like most everyone my age did: our hero was gone. He represented all we thought we wanted — poise, looks, money and a sense of idealism.

Shattered, I took the Fifth Avenue bus home early that day. All the offices at Rockefeller Center were closed by 3:30 p.m. I did the natural thing for me and went bar-hopping. At the Gay Vienna, on 82nd and Second Avenue, I cried in my beer with all nationalities present: German, Hungarian, Swedish. I don't know if I got home that night, or the next, for that matter. I always remembered where I began my evening, but rarely how it ended. My tolerance for alcohol was still good, but the change in my personality was becoming more extreme. In the meantime, Mother was worried about me, although she didn't seem overly concerned about my drinking; it seemed like the natural thing to do. We really didn't know many people who didn't drink, but then we never really looked for them or took a poll. I suppose when you spend a large percentage of your time in pubs, as I did, you meet mostly people who drink. All my friends and dates were heavy drinkers, and if they weren't, I soon became bored with them.

Mother's main concern was the late hours I was keeping, my growing irritability, and the fact that there were episodes and events that I couldn't recall. And over it all was the fact that I was still single, and it didn't look like my flitting around was going to change my status. I had one other big problem: money. It became harder and harder for me to carry on my new life-style on the salary I was making. Lunch sometimes ran as high as ten dollars, two or three times a week, when I used to be satisfied with a hamburger and coke. I frequented the Champlain, a French restaurant on 49th Street between 6th and 7th Avenues, and would often have three tumblers of wine with my meal. And dinner — well, Mother would have dinner prepared for us, but I often would not show up and not bother even to call her.

My treatment of Mother became shabby, and although it wasn't conscious, I was carrying out what I said I would, back when I was thirteen years old, standing in the kitchenette of our hotel and slugging whiskey out of a bottle for the first time: "I'll show you!" I was making her pay now for any injustice that I felt she had done to me, and I could count many. But then, after some particularly mean acts towards her, I would be besieged with guilt and remorse, trying to make it up to her by inviting her to meet me at Longchamps at 34th and Fifth Avenue, after she and I were through work. I knew she was lonely and wanted my company, so I doled it out piecemeal when my own guilt became overwhelming. But finally this emotional seesaw became intolerable, and I told her that I was leaving.

Jean wanted to share an apartment with me, and one was becoming available on the top floor of our building. She couldn't hack the theatrical crowd or their hours anymore. There were other activities that didn't meet with her English upbringing either, and while she did remark on my drinking, at least it wasn't out of the norm in her society.

Mother was furious when she heard that I was really going to leave. She called me and the girls next door every name she could think of. She even came up to the penthouse floor where our apartment was and banged on the door, trying to shake me into coming home. But Jean and I were roommates. Finally, at the age of twenty-three, I had left home.

A new beginning! Free! Completely free and independent, in my own apartment. So many new things were happening: for one, the entire 34th floor where I worked opened up. The oil company now occupied the whole floor, and they needed a head receptionist. I wanted that job, especially since I was doing worse each day where I was, refusing to concentrate on my work and knowing that the job of receptionist was plush, soft and easy, and wouldn't interfere with my sophisticated lifestyle. I still had the same pull I always had, and I got the job.

My salary was $95 a week before taxes, which was not bad for 1964, but our new rent was $165 a month. Jean wound up paying $100 of it, since her stewardess job at Pan Am afforded her a much higher salary, plus traveling expenses. But now I had to buy my own food, whereas with Mother, I didn't. Also, there were doctor and dentist bills that kept hanging on, plus new clothes.

I took out my first loan at Irving Trust at Rockefeller Center and attempted to clean up some of my bills. But once again, half of that money seemed to slip right through my fingers as soon as it was in my hands. Why, the morning I received the check, I cashed it and spent fifteen dollars on a long, long lunch-hour at the English Grill. I never held on to money and was a compulsive spender, thus my financial affairs were completely chaotic.

But I refused to let myself worry about such unimportant matters. I always said, when a bill collector called me at my office demanding payment, that I'd worry about it tomorrow, or the next day or the next. Those next days never came, though, and my bank loans began to spread. Before long, I had loans at Hanover, Chase, and First National, in addition to Irving. The bill collectors called and threatened me. I must have received over fifty pink slips in that one year, but I swallowed every ounce of panic that rose within me, as if it were a pill, and I drank enough to keep it down.

Our apartment was a spacious, L-shaped room with a kitchen and bath, like Mother's. The windows, though, since we were on the penthouse floor, were on both sides of the L, giving us lots of light. One Friday evening, our small dining-room table, adjacent to the kitchen, was attractively set with wine glasses and a small bouquet of flowers. Warm French bread and salad accompanied *boeuf bourguignon* that was loaded with Burgundy wine. As we shared our experiences over the past ten days, the wine dwindled in the bottle. "Let's open another, Jean."

"No, Barbara!"

"But, Jean, I haven't had a drink the whole time you were gone."

"Barbara, I know you better than that. I'll bet you were out every night at Bogey's or Spark's. Now weren't you?"

Lowering my eyes, I nodded sheepishly. "Yes, but not every night, and I did get home early."

"Well, it's obvious you didn't get home early enough to hoover the apartment, and I left you a note, asking you to please tidy up."

"I'll do it tonight, Jean, I promise. I'll do it, while you're out with Dick." Feeling as though I had been a bad little girl, I waited and then asked her once more, in a barely audible voice: "Jean, please can we have more wine? You're going out tonight, and I'm going to be here all alone."

"Oh, all right, but you can have only one more glass." And she opened up the other bottle which she had brought home with her, pouring a glass and returning it to the open cupboard.

At the end of dinner, Jean hurried to get ready for her date with Dick. I cleared the table, looked at the dishes in the sink, and decided to leave them for later. Tonight I was going to stay home, wash my hair and watch TV. I wanted to get to bed early for a change, but I began to feel edgy the closer it came to Jean's leaving.

Jean was in love with Dick, who was an advancing attorney, and who obviously enjoyed having a stately, beautiful blonde on his arm. Like most of her suitors, Dick was taken with Jean's aloof English mystique and accent. In her company, I felt even more awkward and embarrassed by my Brooklyn accent. It was a pain trying to copy her by saying "hoover" the apartment and "queueing". But annoying as it was, I tried to copy her, because she seemed to draw something I craved very much: respect.

Alone now, I took a shower and washed my hair, which was long and straight, requiring an ordeal to get it looking fashionable. Sitting on the sofa, drying my hair with a towel, I glanced at my watch. 8 p.m. The dishes had to be done, and the apartment vacuumed. Jean's royal-blue carpeting showed every speck of lint and dirt. Well, I had about an hour before I would have to set my hair. I should get started. It was so quiet, except for the purring of Jean's Siamese cat, Mineux, which I had come to love, and which was now curled in my lap. I had to get up and get moving.

Yet the creeping edginess I had felt earlier now began creating anxiety, and depression quickly set in. With the thought of that bottle of wine, minus one glass, sitting in the cupboard, I went over my life. As I recollected bits and pieces of the past few years — the emptiness, the bars, the meaningless dates and collisions, the futility of expecting to eventually marry Roy, the entire pitiful existence — I closed my eyes hard, letting the tears roll down my cheeks and drop onto Mineux's soft grey fur. "Oh Minny, I'm so unhappy!"

As Mineux lifted her little face and looked at me with her deep blue eyes, I wiped my tears and got up. I'll wash the dishes first, I thought. Walking into the kitchen, however, and facing a sink full of dirty pots and pans, I couldn't bear it and turned away. Face to face now with the open cupboard, I peeked around it into the opening, to look at the bottle of wine. It was just sitting there by itself. I was by myself, too, and everything seemed so bleak and unfair.

Some hours later, I curled into bed and turned on the Tonight Show. Minnie was on the bed at my feet. My hair still wasn't set, the floor hadn't been vacuumed, the dishes weren't washed. I fell off to sleep, with the TV on.

I awoke to the sound of Mineux crying for her food. Jean's bed had not been slept in. Groggily, I tried to focus on the alarm clock —no, it couldn't be 11 a.m.? Mineux was after me now, meowing like crazy. Putting on a bathrobe, I groped into the kitchen, searching for her cat food, but I couldn't find it. "Oh you blasted cat, shut up! My head is killing me!" Picking up the empty glass, I looked in the dark green wine bottle on the floor, to see if there was any left. Not a drop. "Oh, Jean is going to kill me!"

Just then, I heard a key in the front door, and voices outside. The door opened, and in came Jean with Dick behind her. "Good morning, Barbara," she said cheerfully, "isn't it a glorious day? Dick and I are going out for brunch, then for a walk in Central Park, and tonight dinner and the theater."

"Oh, that't nice," I murmured, and noticing that the cat was crying and playing up to her, I added, "I looked all over for Mineux's food but I couldn't find it."

"Oh, that's okay; I'm here now. I told you where it was, but you never seem to remember anything any more." Embarrassed in front of Dick, my face became flushed. Dick half smiled, asked me how I was, and sat down to work on the New York Times crossword puzzle.

"Barbara," Jean asked, "did you eat anything after dinner?"

"Well," I thought, "I had a can of tuna fish," I replied, vaguely remembering opening a can and getting out some rye bread and mayonnaise.

In an almost hysterical voice, Jean shrieked, "Like hell you did! There was no tuna in this apartment, and I had one can of Nine Lives cat food left for Mineux. Here it is in the trash can!"

"No, oh no, Jean! I couldn't have eaten the cat's —"

"Oh yes, you did!" she exclaimed, bringing the empty can into the living room and sticking it under my nose. Furious now, Jean demanded to see the opened bottle of wine she had left behind. Giving up, I simply pointed to the broom closet where I had hidden it, until I could throw it away in the incinerator. Jean's anger diminished as she saw my eyes fill with tears. "Barbara, I'm really worried about you."

Dick interrupted her, saying he would meet her down in the lobby in half an hour. When he left, Jean sat down next to me.

"You're on your way to serious trouble. You aren't as tough as you think; you wear your heart on your sleeve. How long can this getting drunk and not remembering go on? Sooner or later it's going to affect your sanity." Jean's stern expression, light blonde hair and blue eyes reminded me of Lynn.

I remembered Lynn begging me over and over again not to drink so much. "Oh Bobbie," she'd say, "I care about you. Look what happened to my mother. You've got to stop before you're destroyed." I never heeded her, but I did feel her loving concern. I valued our friendship and missed her. And now it was happening again.

"Jean, I promise you right now: I swear to God on a stack of Bibles, that I will never drink *a lot* again. From now on, I'll stop like you do, at the second or third. I don't need that stuff. I'm going to change and redirect my whole life. Perhaps I'll go back to school again, or take a part-time job to pay off my debts. Maybe even volunteer work — something, anything, but I will change!"

With this noble purpose in mind, I grabbed two Alka Seltzer, drank a bottle of Coke, and popped two aspirin and a vitamin. In tune with turning over a new leaf, I washed the dishes and vacuumed the apartment in half an hour. It was noon, and a glorious fall day, just as Jean had said. I'll walk down Second Avenue, I thought. With all its interesting foreign restaurants, coffee shops, grocery and specialty stores, thrift shops, and so on, Second Avenue from 80th on down was colorful and full of life. This sunny afternoon, people were out in pairs, alone, or with their dogs. It reminded me of when I used to stroll down 13th Avenue in Borough Park with Meema, looking in all the shops.

As I observed my silhouette in the glass doors and windows, I threw back my shoulders, and stood up straight, proud and intent on leading a new life. Passing the local synagogue on 79th Street, I hesitated and watched the people around the building. It was Rosh Hashanah, the Jewish New Year, a time of serious contemplation for the Jews. Everyone was dressed up, the ladies with their white hats and gloves, the men in suits and ties. This spirit of old-world finery brought warm memories of Shabbes in Brooklyn. I went closer, as far as the second step, hoping to smell the old familiar aroma that I'd known in Temple as a child. But that was as far as I got. With a sigh, I breathed deeply and continued my walk. That wasn't a part of my life anymore. Actually, it never really had been. It was the occasion and ceremony, the pomp and sacredness that I liked about synagogues, but I didn't know what was said. Never understanding Hebrew, I made up my own fantasies about God being the biggest of all men, with white, white hair, way up in the sky. People prayed to this wise old man and he nodded, yes or no. That was all.

I walked faster as I neared the "Zion" Delicatessen. My favorite of all restaurants, I sometimes came here twice in one day on weekends. Ordering anything from matzoh ball soup to strudel, I would sit huddled in a corner, remembering lunches with Peepa in the store. Sitting by the window, we would eat our pastrami sandwiches, knishes, and kosher pickles, and watch the people go by. I came here alone or with Mother, but never with friends. Here I felt secure. I belonged to this atmosphere of yesterday. Letting my mind wander, I would linger over a Dr. Brown's cream soda, and never, never did I spoil the illusion by ordering a beer in the Zion Delicatessen.

True to my promise, I did forgo drinking all afternoon. And by some miracle, I was thereafter able to bring my drinking under control — enough so that I gradually became convinced that I had licked my problem, whatever it was. And so, with the arrival of late fall, and everyone now back in the city and the thrill of being at the hub of the most exciting place in the world, I began to relax. And before long, I was drinking as much as ever.

My way of life was getting increasingly expensive. I had taken out an additional loan at Household Finance that I couldn't keep up, and happily, Aunt Mary took it over for me when she saw the state I was in. My tab at Bogey's and Martel's was so high that they were reluctant to let me charge any more, and I had borrowed from all of my friends. I had even taken money from the petty cash and Toys for Tots at work, which I would never be able to pay back. Yet as the situation grew progressively darker, I became progressively more adept at avoiding looking at it, and convincing myself that everything was fine.

As the Christmas season of 1965 drew close, I became more involved with Toys for Tots, a program in the company to buy toys for underprivileged children. Annette had been chairman before she left the company to get married, and I took it over. This soliciting gave me an opportunity to reach every man on our corporation totem pole. Bypassing all secretaries, I won the approval, smiles and money of most of the executives. These new and older acquaintances took me out to lunch, cocktails and dinner. Their calls home to Darien and Greenwich, to tell their wives that they were delayed on business, didn't seem to bother me. I knew many of the wives; in fact, in more than one case, I had dated their sons. Somehow, I managed to rationalize what I was doing, by fantasizing that I was the lost, forlorn daughter. Feeling more at ease with older men, I noted that it fed their ego, too. I always looked for the sense of warmth and belonging I had felt in Borough Park with Peepa, and it became unavoidably apparent that emotionally I had never left my grandparents' home.

New Year, 1965, took a horrendous toll. The only eating I did was from hors d'oeuvres trays at cocktail parties, the only sleeping, a few hours in strange hotel rooms, with no recollection of how I wound up there. And finally, the following Monday after the beginning of 1965, sitting at my reception desk, all of a sudden my entire body felt as though each of its parts had separated from the rest. Objects began to float, and noises sounded disjointed. I began to scream loudly and grabbed my chest, as my heart pounded wildly, making me feel extremely nauseous and dizzy. Unknown and demonic fears hovered just above my head, threatening to devour me. The more panic-stricken I became, the more I screamed for help. My hands, flailing and trembling out of control, flung the pen and telephone receiver away from me. My entire body was twitching now, and I thought I would fly out of the swivel chair.

As it happened, one of my frequent luncheon companions was waiting for an elevator. Drawing me quickly into the mail department nearby, it was decided that my friend Ruth ought to take me immediately to my doctor. Dr. Glick was waiting for me, as the taxi drove up to his luxurious office on 85th Street and Fifth Avenue.

"What is it this time, Bobbie?"

"I don't know, but my heart is racing so, and the fear — I have these terrible, almost ghoulish fears."

After an electrocardiogram, Dr. Glick gave me an injection and called in a prescription for me. "Your heartbeat is rapid, but apart from that and the heart murmur you've always had, there is nothing critically wrong with you." He looked at me for a moment. "But obviously your nerves are shot. What in the world have you been doing to yourself, Bobbie? Look, you go home and stay in bed, and take this medication only as directed. You've got to get a hold of yourself."

"Oh, Ruth," I sobbed in the taxi, "what's wrong with me? I'm so frightened, and I don't even know what of. My life is so meaningless. I don't care about my job, the men, the constant running. I'm sick of this city. I'll never find a husband here. With a thousand and one airline stewardesses, divorcees, models and actresses, to say nothing of all the secretaries and receptionists and typists, all searching for the same thing in a town where a man has his pick, and is picking them all, I'll never find a husband! Today, you're lucky even to get a married man to have an affair with you!"

"Barbara, that's not true. Look at me. Joe and I have been engaged for six months now. And we are getting married. But Barbara, I've got to say this: I didn't meet Joe in a bar." She paused. "I'm sorry if that hurt your feelings, but this constant drinking and all these bars are only going to get you a man who drinks and is out for one thing only." She took my hand and made me look at her. "Barbara, your health is at stake now, not to mention your job." Ruth's advice was similar to Jean's and Lynn's. I nodded my head and tried to look sincere, but her words floated away, never finding a place inside me.

I did not realize it, but somewhere in those first wintry months of 1965, I had passed the point of being able to stop. True, I did not drink on my job, nor did I on every lunch hour, but when five o'clock rolled around, I was off and running.

Finally, after trying to manipulate my money and bank loans every which way, plus borrowing from mother and anyone I could from time to time, I took a night job. Across the street on Second

Avenue was one of New York's poshest Italian restaurants. One evening after work, I walked in and asked for a second job.

"What is your experience?" the owner asked, all the time eyeing my every move. I drummed up a few make-believe jobs I'd had in restaurants. "What nationality are you?"

"I'm, uh, Jewish."

"Well, I guess you could pass for Italian. You have dark hair. Wear it back off your face, little makeup and don't dress, uh, you know, like Miami Beach!"

He paused and then smiled. "You start tomorrow night as the new hat-check girl. You'll work every night from 5 until one or two, with Sundays free. No fooling around with any customers. I run a fine operation, and remember, the tips all go in the till; you get a percentage. If you steal from me, you get in real trouble! Now, good luck, and I hope you can handle two full-time jobs."

Oh wow! I thought. Whatever I was getting myself into sounded very exciting, and I couldn't wait until the next evening. Dressing myself in black with understated gold jewelry, my hair pulled straight back in a chignon, I tried to look as Italian as I could.

"Very good, very good!" the owner commented, when I arrived. At first, I stuck to the rules. I loved this job. I was making money, but not enough — and so gradually, when no one was looking, I began to pocket some tips. Thrilled about my artistry, I was proud of my "extra" money.

There were other areas that I let down my guard. Right next door was one of my favorite pubs. Before I started working, in order to give me a lift and keep my weary eyes open, I would duck next door for a couple of quick drinks and then slip back intermittently throughout the evening. I would sneak out of the restaurant, always keeping an eye on the owner, making sure that he was tied up. At the pub, I had connections with the bartender, who would have two double vodkas waiting for me, because I was sure vodka didn't smell. Also, in case the owner did look for me, the bartender at my restaurant covered for me by saying I was in the ladies' room, making a phone call or getting cigarettes.

But after a few weeks, the crazy working hours were taking their toll. I was completely exhausted and undernourished, and the owner was getting to me as well. I thought it was stingy of him, not letting me keep my own tips, but I stuck it out for five long months, until one evening just before closing, I just couldn't take another minute and quit.

It was June of 1965 now, and the warm weather was here. After taking one full day at home to recuperate from the double-shift work, I picked up right back where I left off, with my erratic social life, dating, parties and pub-hopping. Mother and I began to frequent the Jersey shore together. She was my main companion again. Since Jean's romance with Dick had long since died, and Ned was her new boyfriend, I had no one to go out with but Mother.

Roy was still occasionally in my life, but I had just about given up hope of anything further developing with him. His sister Ellie and her husband and two children had moved directly across the street from Mother and me. I had always been fond of Ellie, and so I began to visit her and meet her for drinks, usually at Martel's. But she was married and her weekends were tied up.

There was, however, another place I could run to, when I had nothing to do in the city and longed for some family to be with. Aunt Mary and Uncle Leo Sheirr had taken a summer place at Long Beach. Often on Saturday mornings, I took the Long Island Railroad at Penn Station out there. I never left Friday after work, because no one ever missed Friday nights in the city. One particular weekend in late August, Aunt Shirley and Uncle Morty were visiting from Washington. I was eager to see everyone, but I felt lousy. And by the time I arrived at Aunt Mary's apartment, I had a temperature and two enormously swollen cheeks. Everyone insisted I see a doctor immediately, and I weakly agreed. Upon examining me, the doctor there told me I had the mumps, that I was contagious, and that I should go directly back to the city and stay home in bed for two full weeks. "That's it, doctor? No medication, nothing, just stay in bed? Can't I even go out if my temperature comes down?" The thought of not being able to go out to Bogey's, which by this time was like another room in the apartment, panicked me.

"Definitely not, young lady," the doctor replied firmly. "With mumps, we prescribe complete bed rest until the swelling goes down — there are no pills for this."

Two boring, miserable weeks passed. The first three days, I stayed home in bed, but on the fourth and every night from then on, I went out to Bogey's from 5 p.m. when they opened, until 11 p.m. at night. I did not go to work, however, and when I finally did, my face was still swollen but feeling okay. My friend Ruth kept insisting that I go back and see my doctor. "Barbara, something is just not right. Look at you: you're all distorted." Other employees were also giving me strange looks as they passed my reception desk, until one day one supervisor told me that he didn't think it was right for me to sit there, looking the way I did. Finally I agreed to see Dr. Glick, who spent over an hour examining me and taking various blood tests. After having me wait in his office for the results, he decided to send me to see an eye, ear, nose and throat specialist, several blocks away on Park Avenue.

"Have a seat and try to relax, Bobbie, while I call Dr. Greenbaum. He's a great guy. I'm sure you'll like him." Dialing the number and trying to set me at ease by continually smiling at me, I heard him say: "Hello, Dan, how are you? Listen, I've got a pretty young girl in my office, 24 years old. The only problem right now is that, with the swelling, she looks like a chipmunk . . . ." He looked up, "Bobbie, Dr. Greenbaum will see you in one hour."

I called Jean and asked her to please come with me. I couldn't figure out why I had to see a specialist and became a little nervous about it. Dr. Greenbaum was tall, broad-shouldered, greying at the temples and quite dark. His eyes were pale blue and sparkled when he smiled to greet us both. His office was large, with several dark wooden cabinets. Leather chairs and a rather large leather sofa opposite his desk made his office look more like a living room. My eyes traveled around the room, taking in the rich paintings and huge windows overlooking Park Avenue. Impressed with both doctor and office, I found myself envying the blond-haired lady in the picture on his desk and their two small children. What a different life I would have, if only there was the security of a husband like him, and my own family. I wondered if I would ever get married, settle down and get off this damned merry-go-round.

"Well, Miss Scheutz, after looking at your case history, I would like to examine you." Since Jean wasn't about to leave me alone, we all went into a small room. Not a word was said, as the swollen glands underneath my ears were checked over and over again. Dr. Greenbaum looked at my fingernails, my eyes, my nose, my ears, listened to my heart, and at the end, he told me that he would get back in touch with Dr. Glick. His white teeth were whiter than any I'd ever seen before. When he shook my hand goodbye, I felt as though I was in the presence of some very great person — one who knew about all the mysteries of life.

Of all the professions, for me doctors had always ranked the highest. "If I had my choice, Jean," I gushed on the way back to the office, "I would love to marry a doctor. By the way, what did you think of that one? Wasn't he absolutely divine? And did you see his teeth? I've never seen such white teeth before, and his blue eyes. Even the greying at the sides."

"Yes, Barbara, and did you see the picture of his wife and two little children on his desk?"

I thanked Jean for accompanying me, said goodbye, and wished her a good flight. This would be a long one for her; she would be gone for about ten days. No sooner had I swung through the door than Ruth came running up to me. "Barbara, Dr. Glick called. He wants you to call him right back."

Still feeling somewhat elated over the office visit to Dr. Greenbaum, I said: "Hi there, Dr. Glick, what's the news?"

"Bobbie, I'm afraid you're going to have to go right into the hospital."

"What?"

"Now, don't get upset; we simply don't know what is wrong with you. Dr. Greenbaum, however, is concerned and wants to have tests taken. He will be your presiding physician there; this is his field."

"What hospital and when?"

"Mt. Sinai, as soon as I can get you a bed."

Mt. Sinai — the words rang in my ear; that was where Linc had gone and died. Without thinking, I asked, "Dr. Glick, is leukemia one of the diseases I'm going to be tested for?"

"Bobbie, I just don't know, but it may be." He gave me a quick pep talk and told me not to think the worst.

"Oh Ruth!" I cried, "I'm going into the hospital; I may have leukemia!" She and everyone else came running. Surely I was bidding my last farewell to my fellow-workers. I allowed them to treat me to enough martinis befitting the occasion, which naturally called for a total wipe-out!

After I said my tearful goodbye, instead of taking the Fifth Avenue bus home and changing for the crosstown at 79th, I splurged with a taxi — my last. "Take me directly to Bogey's, please, Second Avenue between 81st and 82nd," I told the driver, and settled back in the cab. "I'm going into Mt. Sinai Hospital, as soon as my doctor can get me a bed. I'm an emergency, and probably won't live out the week. They're suspecting leukemia — the fast kind." And fresh tears formed at the thought of my imminent demise.

"Oh, sorry to hear that, ma'am. Life is rough, isn't it?" I nodded, dabbing my eyes, and smiled gratefully at his commiseration. He went on. "I know, I work my fingers to the bone and still can't make ends meet. I've got five kids, and another on the way. What's it all about, anyhow? You're here a short time, it's misery, then you're gone. No one cares or misses you. As long as I leave my missus enough money, she's happy. She couldn't care less about me, driving a hack ten hours a day to keep food on the table, and then she blows her stack if I stop off for a beer on the way home!"

I had opened the conversation, but now I couldn't close it. Getting more annoyed by the minute, I finally interrupted him, saying: "Hey! I'm the one who's sick and dying around here, and I can't get a word in edgewise!" But by that time, we had reached Bogey's.

My last martini had worn off. With tears in my eyes, feeling sleepy and melancholy, I told the bartender to keep pouring the drinks. "George, I've got to get good and bombed tonight, for tomorrow I may die."

The next day was Saturday. Dr. Glick called at 10 a.m., cutting through a horrible hangover, telling me that I would be admitted at 6 p.m. Sunday evening. "I have one question, doctor, just one:

can I drink before I enter, or are they going to do tests right away?"

"No, nothing's scheduled until Monday morning. You might as well have a drink; it'll steady your nerves."

A drink — when was the last time I had had *a* drink? Maybe one pitcherful of gin was *a* drink!

Aunt Mary came rushing over that Sunday to help me pack and to go with Mother and me to the hospital. With tears in their eyes, they looked at the nightgown I had selected and then nervously at each other, as if to say: "What? You can't take a thing like that to the hospital! Are you crazy?"

"No," I said calmly, reading their thoughts, "I want to wear this nightgown, when I die."

"Barbara, please! Don't say such things!" Mother broke down, sobbing. "My baby! My little yettat, my whole life! Mary, what am I going to do?" The ensuing scene was so melodramatic, it would have been hilarious — if I hadn't been the one carrying on the worst of all.

I was pretty loaded by the time we arrived at Mt. Sinai. Slipping into something wholesome-looking, I got into bed and gaped at my three roommates who were all seriously ill. The woman to my right was having a hysterectomy in the morning. Across from me was a woman who had kidney stones, and who cried out in agony every twenty minutes. In the far corner by the window was an elderly lady who had throat cancer. I felt guilty that frankly I felt great and was only twenty-four.

When Mother and Aunt Mary left, I dozed off until I was awakened by a cool hand on my forehead. Looking up, I couldn't believe it; I saw those gleaming white teeth of Dr. Greenbaum. "I couldn't wait until tomorrow morning to see you, Barbara. I was so worried about you here alone, feeling frightened." Actually, I was drunk and sleepy, but I jumped up in agreement about my fear and loneliness. We walked the corridor and sat in the small foyer or TV room talking. He told me about the tests that were going to be done, starting tomorrow.

I interrupted him: "What about the bone marrow test? Are they going to do that?"

"Well, maybe towards the end of the week."

"It'll have to be before Friday, because that's the day I'll probably die." I then proceeded to tell him all about Linc and how, like him, I would probably die on Friday, too.

After he questioned me about my life, Dr. Greenbaum said I could call him Dan. "You've suffered a lot, Barbara, I wish I could take care of you. You need someone to . . . ." He never did finish his sentence as he gently swept the hair off my forehead and kissed my cheek. "I've got to leave now, but I will be here very early. I'm going to take you for the tests myself and will try to be here as much as possible."

"Why are you being so kind to me, doctor? I mean, Dan?"

"I care about people and take my work very seriously," he hesitated. "Sometimes I, too, get deeply involved and get hurt."

Needless to say, I spent that entire night dreaming and thinking about Daniel Greenbaum. I pictured myself gracefully fainting in the elevator and being caught in his arms. I would be so irresistible to him that he would just have to kiss me and postpone all the tests. Falling madly in love with me at the end of the week, he would be the one to have to break the news that I had only a short time to live. I didn't want to die on Friday any longer, but sometime later on, to give Dan and me time together. Because the anguish was so great, he would have to leave his job and family and take me to the Virgin Islands or the Bahamas, where we would spend three or four glorious weeks together, before I finally died in his arms. I pictured myself in a white negligee, my hair (freshly washed) falling down my back, all the way to my waist. Dan's hair would be disheveled, his eyes wet from crying for days on end. Since he played the piano beautifully, he would carry me to a chaise lounge and seat me next to him. I would close my eyes and listen to him play Rachmaninoff, never to awaken again.

At about 3:30 a.m. I was awakened by someone tugging at my arm. Looking up with sleepy eyes, I saw a man in a white smock. Sitting up and looking again, I was now face to face with a young intern, just a couple of years older than I. "Sorry to bother you, but I've got to examine you. I should have been here earlier, but was late getting through my rounds. Don't worry; it won't take long." As this young, dark-haired intern examined my ears and neck, he made casual conversation, asking me if I was married.

"No, and I never will be. I have leukemia and am going to die. What do you think about that?"

"I don't know about the leukemia, but I'd sure like your phone number, just in case you get out of here alive!"

During the next four days of grueling tests, no liquor, and screaming nerves, Dan's constant presence, reassurance and extraordinary bedside manner kept me going, until I finally persuaded Kathy to smuggle me in a pint of whiskey. Kathy was a drinking buddy of mine from Bogey's. But when mother saw her, she became suspicious, and left Aunt Mary in the corridor to follow Kathy into my room. Mother caught her slipping a bottle under my bedding, and confiscated it. It was Thursday, one more day to go. Dan came in and announced that he had conferred with several other specialists, who would be present when they performed a sialagram of my glands and neck.

"Will it hurt?"

"Yes, but I'll be with you every minute."

"I'm so grateful for the kindness you've shown me, Dan; I don't know how I ever would have gotten through this week without you. What will this test show?"

"It'll show everything, Barbara, especially any malignancy, tumor or infection. Tomorrow morning at 8:00 a.m. I'll be here."

"I wish I could go out tonight and have a drink somewhere. Perhaps something could be brought in. It's hard being here and not being very sick, just waiting and waiting."

"I know, I know, darling, and I wish I could, but rules . . . ."

Darling? Had he called me darling? I missed the rest of what he said. I was as high as if I'd just had twenty highballs!

The next morning, I insisted on wearing my black lace nightgown for the tests. The nurses just about had a fit, but they finally let me have my way. "C'mon," I said, "grant a dying girl her last wish."

I felt a mild sense of euphoria from the injection I had been given earlier, but when I saw all the nurses and several doctors too, gather around me as I was strapped into a tilting chair, I gasped. My body stiffened, and I grabbed hard onto Dan's hand. A large viewing screen was directly in front of me and a long needle on my right was being filled with some yellow liquid. "What is that?" I said, pointing to the ominous-looking needle.

"That's the dye we're going to inject into your glands. It will cause any obstruction or tumor to show up on the viewing screen. Now don't worry about a thing. Just sit back and relax while I inject this into your neck...."

Sit back and relax? He must be kidding! I was scared to death. Raising my left hand, I said, "Wait, can't we wait a little longer before we do this? I think I need another tranquilizer or something. Do I have to be awake?"

"Yes, dear, you do," said Dr. Greenbaum. He didn't seem to be the least bit concerned about professional ethics, continuing to call me dear and hold my hand. As a matter of fact, he looked a little frightened himself. "May I please go to the ladies' room?"

"No, not now," came the sharp reply of one of the other physicians. "Let's get on with this now."

I squirmed and wiggled as the needle came closer, but had no choice but to squeeze Dan's hand, take a deep breath, and shut my eyes. There was a sharp, burning pain as the needle went into my right gland first. I let out a shrill scream and yelled, "*Stop!*" But one of the nurses told me to keep quiet, hold on, and that it would all be over soon.

It wasn't over soon, and it was excruciatingly painful. The needle stayed in my gland while dye kept being poured into a tube that ran into the needle. Everyone was watching the screen. One of the nurses told me to watch, too; it was interesting. But I continued to keep my eyes tightly shut, squeezing Dan's hand as hard as I possibly could. My gland felt as though it was on fire, and when I heard a doctor say, "Okay, now let's do the other one," I thought I'd throw myself out of the chair. I didn't want to go through one more minute of this. But as I began to squirm and become just slightly hysterical, hands appeared from everywhere to hold me down.

"Now remember, Barbara, you have got to help us. That's the reason you're awake. Point to the area that hurts the most when you feel the dye."

Finally, it was over. I lay back in my chair crying with one of the nurses holding my head and hand, telling me that it was all done and that I had done fine. The other doctors were in an adjacent room talking medical jargon and studying my glands on the pictures they had taken.

Then I heard Dan's voice: "Great! That's great! Let me go get her." He came rushing in and said, "C'mon, wait till you see: you're all right!" I began to get excited, too, but what did he mean come on? I could hardly get up and walk after that ordeal. And so, Dr. Greenbaum very heroically carried me into the room where the pictures of my glands were being viewed. But I didn't know a good looking gland from a bad one. "Barbara," he said, more calmly now, "this is a miracle. You have two salivary ducts that are so narrow that the saliva is not flowing through them. That is what has been causing the enormous swelling. All we have to do now is dilate them periodically, until they become wide enough to carry the fluid through."

Elated and full of joy, bubbling with anticipation at my newfound life, I flung my arms around Dan. Believing with all my heart that I was in love, this time sensibly, I was certain he felt the same way.

In the weeks and months to follow, I did see Dan — but only on furtive visits to his office. He knew of my loneliness, insecurities and desire to be loved, and have someone of my own. When I questioned him about his wife, who was now expecting their third child, he told me that she didn't understand him, certainly not the way I did. "She's so busy, she doesn't have time for me anymore," he said, with a trace of self-pity. "She takes care of the children, and all my paper work, and is exhausted by the time I get home. She's become matronly and cold."

I continued to feel sorry for Dan and rationalized seeing him. When I first discovered, however, that those rich, wooden cabinets in his office held sheets, blankets, pillows and bottles, I had my first doubts about his sincerity. But by then I wanted so much to believe him, that I accepted anything he cared to tell me.

9

Bogey's was informal — seedy, actually. The atmosphere was similar to a scene from "Casablanca," with a large, low fan spinning slowly over some tables. A juke box and small dance floor were in the rear of the long rectangular room, the lighting was dim, and a beaded curtain separated the restrooms. Oversized poster photos of Humphrey Bogart hung over the cracked grey walls. Since I was allowed to run up a tab there, and knew the bartenders and everyone else, I began spending every night in this place, hoping to drown out every memory of Dan, and what I had thought might have been. His name was now added to the list of rejectors that started with Jack, and then Roy, who still called me now and then.

I never attributed any broken relationship to my drinking, but one evening I was horribly crushed when someone whom I knew and had even dated once or twice, called me a "barfly." But all the girls came here after work, I said to myself. I wasn't the only girl, and besides, where else does one go in New York? But no matter what excuses I came up with, it got to me, just the same: *bar-fly*.

My tolerance for alcohol was still good, and I continued to take pride in the fact that I could drink and drink and drink and not get drunk — sick drunk, that is. However, another change was beginning to take place in my drinking, and that was a personality change. My emotions, when under the influence of alcohol, were becoming intensified. Ordinarily, if something made me feel sad, I'd just get sad for a bit and get over it.

But now, this sadness turned into grief and despair almost instantly. And everything I experienced emotionally became distorted. If I was feeling good, I wanted to feel better, on top of the world. I drank with a frenzied excitement that drove me to run from bar to bar, to dance, to talk to anyone, to go to parties at any hour, invited by people I didn't know, and to trust everyone and anyone.

Naturally, I crashed. I overreacted to any outside instability or bad news. If the world was in an uproar and going downhill, well then, so was I. I talked for hours and hours about events I knew nothing about, telling one lie after another, all the while believing that the people around me didn't know.

I was particularly affected by the intense anger I felt inside when Mother and I had a fight. My anger towards her became increasingly aggressive. Whereas in the past when I sensed an argument developing or suddenly found myself in the middle of a scene, I would change the subject or leave the apartment, now I fought back with venom. I would even goad Mother into a scene that would bring all the neighbors to open their doors.

One evening, after such a set-to, I left the apartment feeling totally frustrated and angry. I went directly to Bogey's, my club, and proceeded to drink as much Tequila as I could hold. Good and drunk, I walked, not staggered, into Sparks'. It was important to me that I never stagger.

At Spark's, a feeling of doom set in, and I had a desire to do something to stop this craziness. I wanted to get out of the situation I was in, but I didn't know what to do. I ran out of Sparks' and back to Mother's apartment. She was asleep. I strode into the bathroom, opened the medicine cabinet, and took out a razor blade. Opening the wrapper and almost wishing I had more guts than I did, I slashed my left arm (well above the wrist).

The blood that came pouring out was enough to scare anyone, and it did me. I wrapped up my arm in a Turkish towel, a white one — and then watched the blood come through. With my right hand, I wiped up the mess I'd made and left the apartment. Walking back in the door at Sparks' again, I felt different, something had changed. Perhaps the people who weren't paying any attention to me before, would now, when they saw my arm. Naturally, everyone wanted to know what had happened to me and some offered to dress my arm. But I stoically said it was fine and proceeded to drink and recount a tale leading up to the events of my attempted suicide. I didn't arrive home that night or the next, but at least I knew where I began my evening.

During that crazy fall of '65, Jean spent all her free time in New Haven, at Yale with Ned. She continued to pay more than her share of the rent, but fear of being alone began to creep over me, until many an evening I slept at Mother's. One particular evening, November 9th, all the lights went out in the entire city. It was mysterious and different, and it brought excitement and a sense of adventure. When I was a little girl, I wanted to be safe inside my home with Meema and Peepa, eating chicken soup, while a storm or a blizzard raged outside. Now I envisioned myself in my present home, Bogey's, with all the other regulars, just having a few martinis at the end of a long day's work.

The super was huddled in the lobby of our building with the doorman and several other residents. "We're having a black-out, Barbara, as far as we know. Looks like a biggy! The entire city is in darkness."

Wow, I thought, fantastic! Running up the flight of stairs that led to Mother's apartment, I found her in her robe, cooking cabbage soup by candlelight. She was sipping a drink and listening to the portable radio by the window.

Not only were the lights out, but elevators weren't running. People were stuck in their offices, the radio announcer had said. I thought of all the men left on the 34th floor at work, who had decided to work late. There were women, too, who were left behind. What a blast they're going to have tonight, I thought. Every other office had a well-stocked bar. Joining Mother at the window, I watched men coming home from work on foot, or taking off their jackets and walking out into the middle of the street, to act as traffic directors.

"Barbara, sit down and have a drink with me."

"No, I can't. I'm going out."

"What? You're going to leave me here alone tonight without any lights on or anything? Why, we don't know what's happened yet. It might even be an enemy attack. How can you be so mean?"

"Leave me alone, Mother. I'm going out."

I never drank alone in the apartment with Mother. I could never bring myself to have even one drink with her. I couldn't bear to drink there by myself either, unless it was absolutely necessary, but those times, too, were becoming more frequent.

What a weird sense of excitement it was, walking from 80th and Second Avenue to 81st and Second. I couldn't see anyone around me, but I could feel them close by. Everyone was laughing; it was fun, a new adventure. And at Bogey's, all the drinks were on the house! We all sat at the bar and listened to the radio.

It must have been about ten o'clock that night, when someone tugged at my sleeve, telling me to look at the door. "Barbara," came a voice from behind me, "that woman at the door says she's your mother."

Lifting my head from my champagne glass, I peered through the fuzzy stream of light coming from the candles on the bar, until my eyes focused on the woman at the door. I looked at her from head to toe. She was still in her robe, and had a small flashlight in her hand. Seeing me, she came towards me, beckoning me to come home with her. Then in a faint voice I heard her say: "Barbara, please come home. I'm very frightened by myself."

I turned my head back to my drink. Lifting it to my mouth, I said in a voice loud enough for the person behind me to hear: "That's not my mother. I don't know that woman at all."

Later on that month I did move home for Christmas and then for good. There was absolutely no way I could pay more than $50 a month, including food and rent. Mother accepted that. In fact, she did all she could to make my homecoming a celebration. She bought all kinds of delicacies and prepared a beautiful steak dinner for us. But it turned sour, because I had gotten a lot deeper into debt, adding another two or three pubs and tabs to my already long list and Mother began to express her concern over the purposelessness of my life.

Christmas, 1966 came and went, and my memories of the Christmas holidays were better off forgotten. Sitting in a bar one Saturday afternoon, after an argument with Mother, I watched the couples outside, walking by arm in arm, often with a little dog tagging along beside them. I stared back at my drink, thinking, "Oh my God, my God, I am so miserable, so lonely — and so frightened." I could cope with the loneliness and the aching despair inside, but not the fear. This was something new that had developed since my attack at work. Impending disasters and doom now hovered around my head with a foreboding expectancy. Only alcohol brought mental relief and physical warmth to my body.

But the alcohol, I began to notice, was wearing off more quickly than it used to; I needed to drink faster now to maintain that sense of well-being. Typically, I never worried about this, instead taking pride in the fact that I was becoming a master at drinking. Whereas once, two or three martinis would set me in orbit, now my tolerance and capacity ranked up there with the best of them. And also, wherever I happened to be, I generally found someone else in the same boat, or they found me. Always they were people in despair over their lives, looking for the answer in a bottle, hoping to find someone else who would erase the pain of yesterday and give some promise of a new tomorrow. It always depended on someone else or something else to fill the insatiable thirst inside, which the alcohol only temporarily anesthetized.

And so, when I met Siegfried, we shared the desire to create a magical world where the answers were found in a person. The more we drank together, the more reality was erased, and the more we were able to construct a fantasy to our mutual liking. My mother at first opposed the relationship: he was older, divorced and pretty much penniless. But nothing mattered to us, as long as we had the bars and booze. Between the two of us, we knew every bartender in town and were always able to drink.

Apart from the make-believe, there was a poignant struggle going on inside this man. His questions, late at night, were as gropingly painful as was the sight of the many deep scars on his back. Fully aware that I was Jewish, and that my family were for the most part skeptical about our budding romance, many times Sig would seem to be looking right through me when he asked, "Why does the hatred still exist? It's not over yet!"

"What's not over, Sig?" Often, he alluded to times in Germany, when he saw Jews being persecuted. But this one particular night, as we sat in a dingy bar on lower Second Avenue, the one where they would keep his double vodkas coming all night long for half the price, he related to me how his father hid Jews and was beaten and persecuted. He, in turn, had also been horribly beaten and whipped for his allegiance to his father, and his disdain for the Nazis. When he was sixteen, his father was killed, and he and his sister had somehow managed to escape to the United States. Living together in an old tenement building on First Avenue, he took odd jobs as a painter, and she worked in the Jewish garment district as a seamstress. Night after night, I would hear stories from her about how cruel the fat, old, bald Jewish men were to her, never letting her forget what her countrymen had done to their kin.

When it came to World War II, I, too, found it hard to forgive and forget the mass murders. In my mind, except for Siegfried, Germans were a different brand of people. He fell in love with me and the day I turned twenty-five, July 1, 1966, he asked me to marry him. His light blue eyes had deep shadows underneath. His face, what little was not hidden under a well-trimmed beard, was lined with sorrow. I wanted so much to make up to him what he had suffered. And I wanted to be needed. But one of the first things Siegfried wanted help with was to stop drinking — not to just cut down, but to stop. He drank around the clock, needing a slug out of the vodka bottle upon rising.

Never admitting that his drinking was a problem per se, I blamed it on the cold, cruel world. "You really don't have to stop drinking altogether, Sig; just take it easy."

"No, I do, Barbara. It's got to be all or nothing. I know that's hard to understand, and I don't want to deprive you of a drinking companion, but this stuff is killing me, and I know it."

"Siegfried, you're being melodramatic. When we're married, and you're happy again, you won't have to drink with such a vengeance."

"Barbara, if you love me, you'll try to understand and help me. I'm not stopping you from your cocktails and wine, I'll even sit with you and have coke when we go out, but *I* have got to stop."

"Okay, okay! If that's what you want!" I was surprised about this sudden, noble attempt to go on the wagon, and also disturbed. "It's not going to be much fun drinking by myself, Sig."

"Well, then, unless you have a problem yourself, it shouldn't be too difficult for you to stop, even if it's just for my sake." Inside, my heart skipped a beat at the thought of stopping. That would leave me . . . . I couldn't even identify what that would leave me, but I knew it would be completely empty, abandoned, insecure, and above all, frightened.

As the days passed, and Sig came closer to making the commitment, increasingly my own drinking felt threatened. "If Sig is sober," I confided to Kathy, one of my friends from Bogey's, "he will notice how much I drink." So the very next night, before meeting him at our most frequented bar, the one we had met at, on 76th and First Avenue, I had the taxi stop several blocks before my destination. Inside a nearby pub, I downed three quick martinis, believing that would sustain me through the evening. But time somehow slipped away from me, and I was half an hour late when I arrived.

Siegfried was furious: "Why are you so late? Where have you been? Don't you know how hard this is for me? Today is the first day I've stopped, and I'm ready to climb the walls!"

"I'm sorry, but I had to work overtime a little bit," I lied. "But my God, it's only been half an hour! Are you so weak that you can't control yourself?" That last comment hurt him terribly. I could see his cheeks flush with embarrassment. His eyes filled with tears. He probably would have cried, if he had not then pulled me to him, and caught a whiff of my breath. "You damned liar!

You're reeking with gin! What's the matter, Barbara, are you weak, too?"

Feeling that the source of my existence was being threatened, I retaliated, "You're just jealous, because I can drink, and you can't." I ordered a martini, finished it quickly, and motioned to the bartender for a second.

Sig got up. "I'm leaving. I can't stay here with you."

"Where are you going?"

"Upstairs." He lived directly over this bar.

"Okay, I'll be up in ten minutes."

Five hours later, I knocked on his door — or rather, banged on it. When he didn't open it, I hammered on it and hollered at him. But he never answered me.

A whole week went by in which we didn't see each other. It was the first time in many months. Then he called me, his voice filled with sadness. "I'm drinking again, Barbara. We can have fun and go out. I couldn't do it without you, and I missed you terribly. I love you and don't want to lose you."

We began seeing each other again, but it was different now; he got sloppier and sloppier, losing more and more control of himself. In my eyes, he had become weak and unmanly, and gradually I lost interest. "Kathy, he's too poor. He can't offer me anything, and besides, I could never marry a German!"

When I told Siegfried that it looked like it was over for us, he pleaded and cried for me not to leave him. That Saturday night we had plans to go dancing in Germantown on East 86th Street, with my friend Ruth from work and her new husband. It was obvious that both Ruth and her husband didn't approve of Sig for me at all. He was very drunk. The next morning he was lonely, frightened and shaking, but I had no mercy. As the weeks followed, I was besieged with flowers from him, phone calls at work and to Mother at home, telling her how much he loved me and would try to make a good husband. Finally, at a nearby bar he insisted I meet him after work, he presented me with an engagement ring.

But all I could think of was how much I wanted to get away from him, and from then on I refused all calls from him, instructing Mother to screen my calls. At work I said hello and then goodbye when I heard his voice. Once again, I returned to my nightly pub-hopping alone or with Kathy. Almost a month had passed when I saw Siegfried. I had walked home from work, up First Avenue, trying to avoid the hot, sticky buses and subways. I passed by the pub we used to frequent on 76th Street, and inside, I saw him at the bar. He looked awful.

The proprietor came out when he saw me pass. "Barbara, you've hurt him terribly. He's drunk all the time now. Several times he's mentioned something about being sick, very sick. Says he has cancer of the lung."

Putting my hand to my face, not wanting to hear any more, I said I had to leave, and that I would get in touch with Sig. But I never did.

Some were strong, and some were weak, and poor Sig was one of the weak ones. I shuddered and thanked my lucky stars that I was strong enough that drinking would never destroy my life the way it had his.

One afternoon a couple of days later, I got home before Mother, and curled up on my sofa bed next to our big window facing 80th Street. The sun had not yet set, and people were coming home from work, getting out of taxis, or hailing them for an evening out on the town, or perhaps a movie or the theater. Everyone I saw from my window looked as though they were whole, had a purpose to their lives and were living normal, healthy and happy existences with others they loved. Recalling some of the recent events in my own life, I sighed: "God, what in the hell is happening to me?" And in one of those excruciating flashes of reality which I drank and partied so hard to avoid, I saw my life as it really was: an empty, endless, meaningless hell.

Badly shaken by the glimpse, I frantically reasoned: "I had better get married and settle down. I go to bars, because I can't just stay home with Mother. We argue too much. Besides, I feel confined, trapped when I'm cooped up in the apartment for too long. I get depressed. Other people go out, too; I'm not the only one. But marriage is definitely the answer — a home of my own, emotional security, and my very own family. That's all I need, all I've ever wanted."

Quickly going over the beaux in my life, I stopped at Courtney as the only possible candidate for marriage. I had met Courtney when I had lived with Mother, before moving upstairs with Jean. It was at a party that the boys on the seventh floor gave.

"Courtney has everything you could possibly want, Barbara. He's nice-looking, a Yale graduate, wealthy, has a fantastic job and background, and is definitely going places. He's crazy about you and you're crazy to throw him away." Jean's words had been similar to Mother's. They were both quite fond of him.

I liked Courtney; in the beginning I liked him very much. But through the years, though I continued to date him, I just couldn't get to the place of ever thinking about spending a life with him. At first, when I wasn't sure about his feelings, he had been a challenge. But as soon as it became obvious that he was falling for me, calling all the time, bringing me flowers, taking me home to his parents and so on, I gradually lost interest. Yet I hadn't completely broken all ties — because of times like now. I got up and went to the telephone and called him, hoping that this time, my feelings about him might change and that he might look like less of a marshmallow.

It had been a good five or six months since I had last seen him, I thought, as I dialed; he could be engaged for all I knew. But when he answered the phone, cheerfully and on the first ring, as he always did, I knew he was still free. We made a date for the following evening for dinner at Saito's and anything else I might want to do. When Mother came home, and I told her that I was going to try again with Courtney, she was thrilled. "Oh Barbara, please give him time. It's such a shame that you haven't been able to appreciate him. He's such a good boy, from such a good home and with such a good future, and he treats you like a lady. That boy has respect. Oh how I wish it would work out!"

"Mother, please! I'm just having a date with him! Remember, I can't even kiss him."

"Barbara, that's not the most important thing in the world. It's a person's character and upbringing. You can learn to love him. In fact, those marriages are probably the best. Look at the mistakes I've made by wearing my heart on my sleeve and being such a romantic. Your father and I were in love from the moment we met, and he was romantic, but so what! I built castles in my mind about our life abroad together, and they came to be for a while, but then he left me. There were many things about him I ignored in the beginning of our courtship, because I was a starry-eyed girl of twenty. Be wise, be sensible, and don't throw yourself away on some bum."

I didn't know if Mother was referring to Sig, or if that was just a general statement about where it looked like I was heading, but whatever it was I became angry. "Okay, I'll close my eyes when he kisses me, and pretend he's Omar Shariff, or I'll be so drunk, it won't matter."

By the time we got through cocktails at the Yale Club and then dinner at Saito's, I was doing so well at feigning interest in Courtney, that I actually began to believe that I *could* learn to love him. Certainly I could love the promise of security and a life of everything I never had. But no matter how much I drank, and there were many drinks at various pubs along the East Side, Courtney still remained a marshmallow to me.

A whirlwind of dates with Courtney followed. He took me everywhere, bought me flowers and had me to his home. On one such occasion, his parents threw an elegant formal party. Along with everyone else, I proceeded to get good and loaded, and jumped up onto one side of a piano with a bottle of Brut champagne, flirting with the piano player for the rest of the evening. How Courtney ever forgave me and resumed our relationship was beyond me, but he did.

And I couldn't stand it; the more he seemed to care, the more I turned on him, just as I had with Siegfried. But I didn't have the same excuse for hurting Court; he wasn't poor, German and divorced, and I had actually been attracted to him when we had first met.

In my mind, I went through the dates and times that showed how much he really cared for me. He had seen me sick, drunk, and without my make-believe facade. And he had come to my aid during times when I needed help, including financial help. I had called him, and he was there. He never questioned or interrogated me, just stood by. Yet he fell lower in my estimation, because he loved me, because there had to be something wrong with anyone who really loved someone like me.

I saw a pattern developing in my life then, a very sick one. For some reason, I refused to accept love, the very thing I craved. I couldn't think about it, or wouldn't think about it. Why, why, would I turn in anger on someone who loved me? It was too perverse to be believed!

My own emotions and behavior began to frighten me now, even when sober. I was destroying what I wanted and whatever good I found. Doing what I didn't want to do was becoming a pattern, an insane, inexplicable pattern. Well, I would break that pattern, come hell or high water!

The next day, I called Courtney from work and cancelled our date for that night. I wanted to have the evening free and so I met Kathy at Martel's for drinks and dinner. In the summer, I loved to sit at the tables outside Martel's and watch the people go by — the couples, the oddballs, the singles and the drunks. It seemed as though they all passed 83rd and Third Avenue. After cocktails outside, and a hamburger at a table inside, Kathy and I joined the hard-drinking crew at the bar. It was there that I heard that Ralph Martel had opened a summer place in Amagansett, Long Island. He needed waitresses and as Kathy and I both had vacations coming, we took the jobs, from 5 p.m. until 2 or 3 a.m. I was entitled now to a month's vacation at work and took the entire month of August for my new endeavor at Amagansett. There I would get away from home, from the haunting memory of Sig, and from Courtney. I had to have a break from Courtney, and who knows, maybe this would be the place where I would really meet someone special and fall in love, to live happily every after.

Amagansett, however, did not turn out to be quite the place. I worked hard at waitressing, in a rushed but sophisticated atmosphere that catered to the New York East Side crowd with the money to come out there and spend it. From 10 a.m. until 3 p.m. I slept on the beach, getting more and more tanned, then I returned to the little room I shared with Kathy and changed into my uniform. It was a long walk from my rooming house to Martel's, so I stopped half-way at a little Italian restaurant and bar for a couple of martinis to warm me up.

After several nights had gone by, I began also stopping at a local liquor store to buy a pint of vodka. I did it, just because I felt I needed to know that a bottle was there, in case I needed to liven up at midnight or became anxious. This was the first time I ever bought a bottle and hid it in my handbag. Throughout the evening, say every half-hour, I would get my bag and head for the ladies' room, where I would swig at the vodka until it was gone, sometimes by midnight.

I didn't tell Kathy what I was doing, for fear she might not understand. For that matter, I didn't understand it myself, but I didn't try to figure it out. I merely rationalized it by telling myself that I was on vacation, and therefore drinking all the time was acceptable. After closing, I went to an after-hours place with several other waiters and waitresses and drank until five in the morning. I slept from six to nine for those entire three weeks — three weeks, not four, because Ralph's assistant fired me one evening. "Barbara," he said firmly, after calling me into the kitchen in front of all the others, "I am going to have to fire you. Something is wrong with your behavior. I know you're drinking on the job, and that we cannot tolerate."

"What? How can you say such a thing?"

"Don't bother to defend yourself; the owner of the Italian restaurant told me how you drink one martini after another before coming to work here."

"So? Everyone else on the staff drinks too. I know they do —"

"They may drink and party, but they don't stop at the local liquor store after several martinis and pick up a pint of vodka to bring to work with them and stash away somewhere to nip on, like an alky. Also, you barely eat dinner with the rest of the crew, and then by 10:30 you're ravenous, sneaking leftovers from people's plates into the ladies' room and gobbling them up like an animal. You —"

My eyes burning with tears, I ran from the restaurant down the street, one block after another, the whole fifteen or twenty blocks back to my rooming house, where I flung open the door to my room and fell on my bed, sobbing.

There wasn't any way I could get back to the city until morning, and I couldn't stay in that room by myself, listening to the echoes of those horrible words. It was torture being compared to some common, ordinary alcoholic in front of all my co-workers in the kitchen, even Kathy. I couldn't bear the thought of facing Kathy again. What must they all think of me?

"Oh God, oh God, oh God!" Suddenly, Mother's face appeared in my mind. She wore a pleading, desperate look; she was worried about me, her little girl. I was being destroyed.

"No more, no more!" I screamed, jumping to my feet. I washed my face in the sink in the hallway and then walked outside. Not knowing which way to turn or where to go, my eyes caught the bright neon sign of the town bar across the street. It was advertising some kind of special for that night, and trucks were lined up next to each other in front. I knew the kind of place it was, but I had no other choice.

All that fall of '66, I tried again with Courtney as hard as I could, but was unable to work up enough love for him to consider marriage. So I finally did what I thought was noble and made it clear that we couldn't be more than friends.

Apart from Mother, my job was the only constant factor in my life, for while the bars were the same, the men changed. Living in a world of total make-believe and "if only," I went from one to another to another to another, until I became desperate, unable to pay my debts and tabs. I had to get another part-time job, anything.

Down in Greenwich Village, the Village Gate was known for its good entertainment, food, drinks and attractive waitresses, some of whom later went on to work as bunnies at the Playboy Club. Kathy was still a friend, and we took jobs as waitresses there. I worked from 5:30 sharp until 4 a.m., without a break. After one week, I was exhausted. My head hung low every day at my reception desk at work. The managers and other executives that passed commented: "Hey, where's your cheerful smile, Barbara? You aren't free for cocktails any more; got a steady beau?"

I didn't dare tell anyone at work that I had another full-time job, nor did I tell them at the Gate that I had a daytime job. I knew no one could long exist with such crazy hours, mixed-up meals and quickly-downed cocktails, whenever I could buy or steal one. I learned how to hustle — to pad checks and not return the right amount of change to customers, and all the while becoming more and more adept at smiling, walking, appearing and disappearing at just the right time.

I made money all right, but I spent it, too. Some of my bills got paid, the bar tabs first, and some didn't. Frail yet bloated, my stomach was in a constant knot that was only alleviated by the heat that came from a quick martini or fast slug from a vodka bottle in the ladies' room. I drank now just to give me enough strength or fuel to keep going. This crazy existence continued on through October, November and December. Mother was afraid to talk to anyone about where I was at. She couldn't come to grips with it herself emotionally, and blocked out all reality. The only reality that crept into my life was the gut feeling I had on those long cab rides home from the East Village at 4:30 or 5 in the morning. "Driver," I would plead, "must we go through the Bowery?"

"Well, I'm just trying to save your money, lady."

The men with their arms outstretched, lying on the curb, saliva drooling out of their mouths, were a pitiful sight. There was no way they could possibly take care of their bodily functions, as they lay there, dirty and sick, with vomit all over them. And yet if one of them had an eye open, and we were still waiting for a light to change, he would crawl on hands and knees to the taxi, not knowing whether he'd be run over or not, and all for the remote chance that somehow it might mean another drink.

"Sorry, lady, I know it gets to ya," said the cab driver, "but these bums aren't worth thinking about. They're worse than animals!" I could not dispel the slow knot that formed in my stomach each night, as we drove past these Bowery bums. How could anyone sink so low?

And then I would remember the alcoholic I had met at the Thousand Mile House, who had once been on the faculty at NYU.

Mercifully, one evening in December, the nightly ordeal came to an end. Shortly after I arrived in my short black skirt and skimpy white blouse, I was told that I was fired. No explanations or reasons were given, except that I was to leave at once. Was it the drinking or the stealing? It didn't matter; I could barely function and needed sleep desperately.

Mother was glad to see me come home early and relieved to learn that I wouldn't be working at the Village Gate any longer, but the worried look in her eyes had become set — so set, in fact, that she was afraid to leave me alone. She made me soup and bought my favorite foods and begged me to talk to her, to tell her what was wrong with me. But I couldn't. I didn't know myself. All I knew was that I wanted out badly, very badly.

10

"Mother, I can't stand my life any longer. Nothing ever works out for me. I feel as though I'm going round and round." I was in one of my desperate moments when Mother was my only confidant. I poured out my heart to her, only I didn't want to hear her reaction.

"Barbara, I'm so worried about you! I want you to settle down with a nice boy, just the way Iris and Lynn and Jean and Ruth have. You've got to change your luck. You really should concentrate on building a relationship with Courtney. You're a fool to let him go. He's such a fine boy, and he's so crazy about you. Oh well, there's no sense in my telling you all over again the same old thing. You don't listen to your mother."

I didn't listen to my mother, but this time, after she fell asleep, I decided that I was going to learn to care for Courtney, no matter what. And so I called him, once more. The operator surprised me, when she said that the number was no longer in service. Where could he have gone to? I know: I'll call his parents' home on Park Avenue. When a young woman answered the phone, I felt a little uncomfortable and asked her who she was. When it turned out that she was Courtney's fiancee, I hung up.

Sitting on the edge of the sofa, I went over and over our last date.

It hadn't been that long ago; how could Courtney have met someone else so fast and gotten engaged, too? Why, that's crazy! I continued to sit by the phone, numb and rejected. Perhaps I was wrong all along; I should have gotten involved with him. No, that's not true; I'm well rid of him. Perhaps . . . oh phooey, perhaps nothing, it's over! I'm going out for a drink.

It was raw and cold that December night. I planned to have about two or three quick drinks and get to bed by 11:45. When I reached the corner of 80th and Second Avenue, I decided not to go to Bogey's. I didn't want to see anyone I knew or listen to that loud jukebox, so I walked across the street and headed towards Spark's. It was dark inside as usual, and it took a few minutes for my eyes to focus on where the bar and tables were. Soft, romantic music issued from the rear. I could smell the charcoal hamburgers and raw Bermuda onions that were being served at the bar to a couple who seemed enthralled with one another. Taking a seat on a stool away from everyone, I gradually became aware of a familiar hacking cough. I'd heard that cough on Saturday afternoons before Spark's became crowded. I had also heard that cough late at night, like tonight, when most people had gone home because they had to go to work the next day. Only the few regulars that always came early and stayed late remained. I looked to see who was coughing, and my eyes looked into those of a man down the bar from me. He couldn't seem to stop coughing. Finished with his drink, a tall Scotch and water, he pushed his glass forward for the bartender to refill it.

I couldn't take my eyes off him now. The bartender filled his glass with Scotch and added just a dash of water, saying, "That's your ninth, Frank. How are ya doing?"

"I'm okay; keep them coming." His voice was deep; in fact, I'd never heard such a deep voice. I watched this man Frank drink his Scotch as if it were water, cough and lower his head and occasionally look up, but never at any particular person or object. He seemed to look through everything. His blond hair fell slightly over his right eye, as he noticed that I was looking at him. Actually I was studying him: his shoulders were broad and his face looked weatherbeaten and strong. He was handsome, with straight features, and had a pensive-looking forehead that gave him a mysterious, intelligent look.

I wonder what he's thinking about, and why he has such a hacking cough? Why does he smoke like that, one unfiltered cigarette after another? He's definitely a loner. He looks as though he's burdened with great problems. Maybe he's a writer . . . he looks like a writer . . . . Noting that the bartender didn't attempt to make conversation with him, I began to draw an imaginary picture of his life. He was lonely, searching, brilliant, political, romantic and very sick; as a matter of fact, he probably didn't have long to live.

The more tragic and dramatic my imaginings became, the more I felt the need to introduce a helpmate — someone who would come to his aid and love him, nurse him, and bring out his great hidden talents. And naturally, as the tale grew, this someone became me. Then, as I became aware that I was staring hard at him and not even drinking my drink, I quickly looked down, only to hear another repeat of that hacking coughing. This time it was so bad, I didn't think he'd catch his breath. I just couldn't help saying: "Are you all right, sir?"

"Thanks, I'm fine. I'm used to this cough. Sorry to disturb you, though." Oh, his voice was even deeper than I thought! And this time I noticed his eyes were the most beautiful shade of green. I couldn't see the exact shade in the dark, but they looked like the ocean, when it was more green than blue, the color so rich, you just wanted to dive right into it. I wouldn't have exactly dived into his eyes, but I now found this man fascinating, full of intrigue. I wanted to know all about him and believed that he must have had a life as interesting as a pirate's. As I continued to create my own illusion, he raised his head and barely looked at me, saying: "Can I buy you a drink?" I felt excited about the offer but also panicky.

"Gee, thanks, but I told my mother I had to get right home." I gasped after saying such a stupid thing. Why did I ever mention my mother? I always say the wrong thing at the wrong time, I thought, as I quickly paid my bill and left. Oh well, at least I'll be getting to bed as planned. It was 11:40 p.m.

All the next day at work, I found myself thinking about this man Frank and his cough. Remembering that I'd heard that cough before, around 5 o'clock, I made sure to leave work in time to get to Spark's early. And guess what? He was there at 4:45, even before they officially opened. He was on the same bar stool he had been sitting on the previous night. We were the only two people in the entire place.

The bartender dropped about five quarters in the jukebox and told me to pick anything I wanted. Feeling a little nervous and full of expectancy, I sensed that Frank was aware of me. All I could select were two: "Second Hand Rose" and "Georgie Girl," and I asked the bartender to finish the selections for me.

The silence was awful. Was he going to offer to buy me a drink again? Or did he lose interest last night, when I said I had to go home to my mother, like some twelve-year-old? Hmm, how old *is* he? At least ten years older than I. Is he married? Divorced? Children? On and on I went, until the coughing again broke the silence between us. Now I felt embarrassed for him; perhaps he was dying of TB or lung cancer. Then, when he ordered his second drink, I heard him say to the bartender, "Give her whatever she wants." He didn't even ask me. He just took over. Now I knew for sure that I liked him, his whole manner, even his cough.

In that entire evening at Spark's and then around the corner at Bill Mac's, I learned that Frank Maloney was Irish, an ex-marine who was bitter about the service, fifteen years older than myself, divorced, and of all things, he lived with his mother who was alone too. He was serious and brilliantly witty, a writer and one-time owner of several restaurants and bars in New York. He was now waiting for a contract to be signed for a new place, to be called Maloney's on 81st and Second Avenue.

It was obvious that Frank drank with the same relentlessness as Siegfried, but Frank had control over himself. Not once did I see his personality change or his mood waver back and forth. He seemed strong, silent and steady, and I became more and more taken with him. When the evening drew to a close, and he walked me home, he didn't ask me out for the next night; he just told me where he would meet me. During the next few nights and then the weekend, and some more long evenings the following week, I decided that I was in love. Frank had one lung left, which made me feel needed. I listened like a little girl to one fascinating episode after another. It had been three years since his left lung had collapsed. I didn't really know what brought it up, but it was obvious that he could lose the other as well, if he continued to keep such late hours, smoking one cigarette after another. "Frank, aren't you afraid that the same thing will happen to your other lung?"

"No, not really, or I would do something about it." He shrugged. "Look, let's not talk about my lungs. You're the nicest thing that has come into my life in a long time. I've had a broken marriage, my mother paces the apartment day in and day out, talking to my dead father, living in yesterday. The women I've known the past few years have meant nothing to me. I've had no one to talk to, really."

I was flattered, and I, too, was lonely, with a list of unfairnesses. I wanted someone older, solid yet warm, that I could lean on and turn to, like the father I never had, and the boyfriend, too. He would be both in one. By Christmas of 1966, I knew I was in love, and this was one relationship I really wanted to work out.

To Frank, I seemed together. I gave an okay appearance, and my job and my living with my mother were enough respectability to divert him and other friends and questioning relatives. Aunt Mary, for instance, continually asked me how things were. I told her okay, fine, but she only half-believed me and made it clear that she was there if I ever needed her. This new relationship that made me particularly star-crazed had her worried.

"Who is he? Where's he from? You don't know anything about him; give it time." But I knew all I cared to know, and I was sure that Frank was absolutely perfect for me, and did not want to hear any more about it. When Aunt Shirley and Uncle Duddy invited me down to Washington for the holidays, I refused. And then when Aunt Shirley came up to Brooklyn instead, and got together at Uncle Leo Karl's with the family, and wanted Mother and me to come out there on Christmas day, I again refused, letting Mother take that long subway ride from New York to Brooklyn alone. I spent that entire day barhopping with Frank, collapsing somewhere that night at Bill Mac's apartment, the owner of the bar we closed down. Barely able to walk, I made my way back to East 80th, where I showered, changed my clothes, left a note for Mother, and met Frank at another bar. This continued on in the same fashion for the next month, day in and day out, with hardly any sleep, getting to work late and bleary-eyed — and finding that when I lifted my first cocktail to my mouth at five p.m., my hand shook uncontrollably. I had to ask Frank to get me a straw.

Whatever remaining interests I had, prior to meeting Frank, were now gone. Never had I missed so many days of work, not even caring if I was fired. For now the most important consideration in my life, interrupting all plans, days and events, was Frank — and the next drink. Distorted dreams and visions tormented me, telling me that if I lost Frank, I might as well not live any more. Somehow, this relationship drew on all the previous ones, bringing to it all my unhealed hurts and emotional scars. It all erupted now, in this one person whom I simply had to have, and that meant marriage.

On New Year's Day, 1967, Frank said, "Okay, let's get married. I'll give it another shot." Thrilled with this news, I called everyone in town I could think of: Kathy, Aunt Mary and Mother. We celebrated with eight Bloody Mary's the following day, and then went down to City Hall after I called my employer, saying that I didn't know when I'd be back to work; I was getting married. But when I heard from the clerk that we couldn't get married until we had blood tests, made an appointment with the Justice of the Peace and so on, I panicked. Since I was born to lose anyhow, I feared that Frank would change his mind if he had to think about this whole marriage thing too long.

During the next few days, we had our blood tests taken. Dr. Glick was obviously upset when he saw the two of us arrive, looking run-down and disheveled. "Bobbie, are you sure you know what you're doing? This man is so much older than you, and well, he just doesn't seem right. Why can't you wait and settle down with a nice —"

"A nice Jewish boy!" I finished it for him. "Doctor, look: I don't *want* a nice Jewish boy!"

As we left Dr. Glick's office after the blood tests, I sensed a change in Frank's attitude. He was quiet, unusually so. As my own insecurity mounted, I talked a blue streak, and then I, too, became quiet. I couldn't wait until we got somewhere where we could drink ourselves into oblivion again, and just stay that way until the following day when all the arrangements would be taken care of, and we would be married. Then I knew that everything would be fine. Frank would have someone to care for and love him, and I would have what I wanted. With each drink I drank that day, I couldn't squelch the tormenting doubts from overriding any joy or eagerness in me.

Coinciding with our wedding day was also the opening of "Maloney's." Frank had been spending his free time at his restaurant and bar, drinking and painting, and telling friends who had volunteered to help, where to put what. I drank champagne like crazy, dipping a big brush into a large can of paint and splashing it on the walls. By the wee morning hours, the restaurant was ready for opening. I was absolutely wiped out, and went home after Mother had left for her job at Lord and Taylor's. I showered and changed my clothes, and realizing that I hadn't anything new to wear on my wedding day, I put on an old but smart grey-striped wool suit. I wore a black turtleneck wool sweater underneath and a wine-colored, wide-brimmed hat. Black leather gloves, bag and shoes completed my ensemble. With my hair pulled tightly back into a bun under my hat, I felt okay about my appearance, though I looked a bit like a French spy, instead of the portrait of purity and properness I'd seen in all my girlfriends on their wedding day. That didn't bother me; I was different, and my life was going to be different, and I was marrying someone different, not some silly little boy just out of college, who wasn't really a man yet.

It was a clear, cold day in January. I was freezing without an overcoat, but an overcoat would have spoiled the entire look I'd created. Trying to run, but finding it difficult in my high-heeled shoes, I hobbled up Second Avenue to 81st Street, to a bar directly opposite Frank's new place. Neither of us had ever frequented "Joe's," and I wasn't even sure why Frank had selected this place for us to meet at noon that day, but he did.

I arrived early, 11:45, just in time to have a couple of dry martinis to ease my nerves. Excitement began to rise within me, as I realized that in just a short time, I would be married! At twelve noon, I got up from the bar and, glass in hand, I stood at the window. A cab pulled up, and my heart leaped, as I expected Frank to get out. But it wasn't him; it was another man whom I knew. He came in and ordered a beer. Seeing me staring out the window, he asked: "Hey, Barbara, who are you waiting for?"

"I'm waiting for Frank Maloney. You know him? We're getting married today."

"What? You're crazy!" His face took on a look of unbelief. Walking over to where I was standing, he said: "Don't count on him showing up."

"How dare you say that!"

"Barbara, I don't want to burst your bubble, but that man isn't for you. First of all, he hasn't got a dime. That place of his across the street will fold in two weeks. He's borrowed so much money, it's unbelievable, but that's not the worst of it. Not only is he a sick man, but, Barbara, he's an alcoholic. In fact, he's probably passed out somewhere right now."

Those hard words tore into me. I couldn't even answer them. Returning to the bar, I looked at my watch — 12:15. I ordered another martini. Drinking it feverishly and hoping to speed up the dragging moments, I ordered another and another, until finally, at 1:00 p.m., I put my head down on the bar and sobbed. The man who had told me those horrible things about Frank had long since left. I was all alone with the bartender, who didn't know me and didn't seem to care to, just so long as I paid my bill.

"This can't be happening; it just can't be!" I moaned, as I left Joe's and staggered across the street, weaving among cars that came to a screeching halt as I went right in front of them, almost hoping that one would hit me. Across the street, I peeked into Frank's restaurant, but saw no one. It was dark and obviously closed. I continued to walk down Second Avenue, past Spark's. As I looked into the drugstore next to it, I saw Frank. He was all dressed up in a suit. He even had a tie on and overcoat. Why, he looked as prominent as the highest-ranking executive at work.

"Oh, Frank!" I burst in. "What happened?"

His words were sober — very sober. His voice was dry, without a trace of emotion. "Barbara, we are not getting married. Not today or any day. It's a mistake, no use."

Frank lectured me briefly about how bad marriage would be for us. "I would destroy whatever good there is in you, Barbara. You're really a nice kid. I've had a tough life, and a lot of shady involvements that you would never understand. Besides, my lifestyle is fixed, and you could never adapt to it. It would kill you. It's killing me. Give yourself a break, and find a nice guy your own age and —"

"No! *No!*" I screamed.

Waving goodbye, Frank quickly walked away, turning the corner on 79th Street. I ran after him, begging him to wait, to listen to — But he refused to listen to me, to turn back, to look in my direction again.

For some reason, I could not and would not accept this final rejection. He *must* love me! He can't just abandon me. I followed him on the street for a long time. I called him, and wrote him notes. But it was the night that I saw him with his arms around another girl at Bill Mac's that I became completely distraught. Having had quite a lot to drink, I left that bar, intending to take a cab to Frank's mother's apartment.

But one of his friends, Fred, followed me outside. Fred, who had been in the Marines with Frank, was a mean and bitter man. Knowing how I felt about Frank and totally disgusted with my behavior, he stopped me before I could get into a taxi. Signaling for the driver to continue on, Fred began slapping me in the face, and calling me the ugliest names imaginable. He threatened to kill me, if I ever tried to contact Frank again.

Drunk and sobbing, half-crazed with dizziness, I fell off the sidewalk and into the gutter, after Fred flung me away. I don't know how long I lay there, quietly crying, hoping a car would come and run me over, when a pair of strong arms lifted me to my feet, and a man asked me if I needed help. "I need a cab," I barely mumbled. My face was cut, and blood was trickling down my cheek. Giving the driver Frank's address, I made my way into his mother's apartment. It must have been very late; she told me that Frank was asleep in his room. I watched her walk around the living room, not noticing me, as she reminisced about the past. I went to Frank's room and woke him up. He let me cry and tell him what had happened and how I felt, and then before dawn he put me into a taxi and sent me home. It was over between us, and at last I had to accept that.

All the next week I didn't go to work, but wandered in and out of bars all day and all night, losing track of time and life. But I do remember the rain, falling on my long dark hair. Stepping into puddles, I would often lose my equilibrium and fall face down, waiting for someone to help me. "If only I had the guts to kill myself.... If it weren't for Mother, I'd...."

I spent most of 1967 brooding over Frank, trying to put my life back together again, and at least going to work. Dulling the heartbreak inside with gin, vodka, or anything available, I became bloated, living in constant depression. Often I would walk up and down Second Avenue at night, hoping to catch a glimpse of Frank behind the bar of his restaurant. When I repeatedly saw the same girl whom he'd had his arm around at the time of our break-up, I decided to go inside. It had been months since we had sat opposite each other. I smiled, as Frank nodded. His blond hair was still over his eye and his cough was as loud as ever. "Barbara," someone said behind me, "congratulate Frank; that's his new wife, Kim." Stiffening every muscle in my body, I turned my head to see Fred, the guy who had slapped me around the night I had gone to Frank's mother. Fred was gloating; his thin mouth looked almost sinister. Sitting down beside me, he told the bartender to keep filling my glass. "This little lady here likes to drink. Watch her drink, watch her go wild."

I should have gotten up and left, but I didn't. I stayed and accepted the free drinks, feeling so sick, so degraded, so cheap and shabby. Outside, it was dark. I couldn't hear anything but the noise that the jukebox was making in the background and the hushed whispers of those around me. I knew the familiar faces of the regulars who, like me, made the nightly round of upper East Side bars. I couldn't bear the thought of what they must be thinking. Everyone knew how much in love with Frank I'd been. And now they were seeing me degraded to the core of my being in front of him and his new wife, who sat next to him giggling. Frank wasn't smiling, though; he looked straight at me, as I swallowed every bit of liquor in my glass. I couldn't return his look, which I had waited for for so long. As I finally got up from the barstool and tried to leave, Fred began to chuckle, putting a hand on my arm. "C'mon, Barbie, the party's just starting. Don't go now."

"Leave me alone, Fred! Leave me alone! You're mean, and I hate you!" Pulling away from his grip, I stepped back, then turned and headed for the door. But he followed me, continuing to laugh and taunt me, and as I turned to scream for him to go away, I noticed Frank calling out to him to leave me alone. I covered my face with my hands and ran to the door. Everyone knew, everyone was watching!

"My God, my God, I'm so ashamed!" I sobbed, when I got outside. "Please, I want to die, please, please . . . ." Over and over, I kept repeating those words, until I drank enough to wind up somewhere and not care.

11

For the first time in eight years, I lost all interest in my job, or remaining at the company, the one thread of security that I had going for me. It was only a matter of time before I was fired, anyway; how long could upper echelon connections keep me on, especially when I didn't show up? Refusing to take any responsibility for the emotional mess I was in, I accused everything and everyone around me. It was all Mother's fault — how she had raised me, what she did and didn't do, and so on. And New York — the city was becoming an unsafe jungle, everyone out to win, either the best job, marriage, money or bed partner.

Competition became tougher when prettier and brighter girls than ever moved into town, as airline stewardesses, secretaries, and models. These were young women who had left their out-of-town homes to find themselves and establish careers. Encouraged everywhere by magazines, movies, books, TV and society to have affairs, it became the "in" thing to do. And at twenty-five, I no longer had the innocent, dewy-eyed enthusiasm and interest that had once fed into whatever fantasy the men were temporarily engaged in. Watching those with whom I worked become ever more reckless in seeking outside sexual relationships, I no longer felt drawn to them, but began despising their long-distance calls to their wives in the suburbs which consisted of nothing but lies about spending a night in town on business. I wondered how many of the wives knew where their husbands really were and if so, what was going on inside them? What did they do, if anything? I promised myself that when and if I got married, my husband and I would live close to where he worked, so that he wouldn't have any excuse to stay in town at a hotel. I wanted to make sure that I was there and not stuck in the suburbs in Connecticut, New Jersey or Long Island.

Our company had a new president, and the new broom was certainly sweeping clean. Long-term employees were suddenly let go without warning, replaced by someone younger, or just different. These men did not know how to cope with the sudden loss and life-change. A few dropped dead of heart attacks and some turned to booze early in the morning. For most of them, all they had was their job, and when that was gone, there was nothing. I was particularly concerned about one man who had become like a father to me, the advertising manager who had taken me with him from my first job as mail-girl to a position in the advertising department. One Friday morning, he swung through the doors without the vigor he usually had and his big smile was gone as he walked past my desk.

"Cy, what's wrong? Don't you feel well today?"

"Barbara, I was just fired!"

As he continued to walk back to his office, I sat at my desk stunned, until tears filled my eyes, and I ran to the ladies' room where I cried and cried. Cy had thirty years with the company — I couldn't believe that such a thing could happen without any warning! Why, he had made that department, acquired the new agency himself, and often worked well into the wee hours of the morning — it wasn't fair! And now, as I continued to cry, I shuddered at the thought of Cy having to tell the entire department.

His last day was torture for me, as he and his wife carried piece by piece, different mementos which he had acquired over the years. He didn't cry or fall apart. He walked with his shoulders back and his head high, but inside his life was crushed. "Barbara," he confided to me one afternoon, "I can't figure this out. I have gone over and over the facts, and I still can't come up with any reason, nor have I been given any. But it's not only that; I see now that what I have dedicated my whole life to is heartless and worthless. My dream is shattered. Where do I go from here, at fifty-five years old?"

Of all the men I knew at the company, Cy was the first and dearest man in my heart, and I had to watch him leave that way. More followed — some took it well, on the surface, while others, who looked stoic, cried like babies. It was pathetic and cruel, one of the most emotionally heartbreaking and disillusioning experiences I'd ever had, watching these men who had given totally of themselves, come to this kind of end after twenty-five, thirty, or forty years at a proud, profitable and prestigious firm.

July in New York City is always brutal. The sidewalks shimmer from the heat, and the humidity is so heavy that you can be freshly showered, with a cool dress on when you leave your apartment for work in the morning, and be soaking wet before your bus or subway has gone ten blocks. That July of '67 was unbelievable! People were barely existing until the weekend arrived, and they could escape the heat wave. I had three weeks' vacation coming to me, and took a part-time job at the Warren Hotel in Spring Lake, New Jersey. An extra week without pay gave me a full month of sun and surf.

Since I had never learned how to swim, I slept on the beach all day, until it was time to relieve the girl at the magazine stand in the lobby at 5:30 p.m. Finished at ten, I joined my friend Ellie, since she and her family spent weekends and part of their summers at the shore, too. We toured the swinging hotel circuit, and all the while, in the back of my mind, was Princeton, where Ellie and her family lived. It was becoming a more and more tangible possibility . . . . One day, I accompanied her to her dentist in Princeton. Strolling up and down Nassau Street, I agreed to meet her for lunch at one o'clock.

In the meantime, I felt drawn to this charming, tree-shaded, quaint town that just reeked of old wealth and culture. The university campus stretched along the main street, making the town look colonial and pictorial. "Okay, town," I said under my breath, "I love you, and I'm going to an employment agency right away." And I did.

"Ellie, you won't believe what just happened to me! My luck is finally changing. I went to the employment agency down the street and to an interview at Princeton University Press. And do you know what? I got the job! Isn't that the most fantastic thing?"

"Wow, when you make up your mind to do something, you get right to it! How much will they pay you?"

"Not a whole lot — about $90 a week, but now can you help me find a place to live?"

"Okay, but that's going to be a little rough. Let me talk to Brad Erickson; he knows everything." Brad was a tall, lean, very attractive man in his middle thirties, who owned the biggest real estate agency in Princeton. If anyone could find me an inexpensive place to live in town, Ellie said, he could, and after meeting briefly once at a party, he agreed to rent me an empty office right in his real estate building.

The location couldn't have been better, directly across the street from Bellows and the Brown Jug, and a block and a half from the University Press. I wouldn't need a car, which I didn't have, anyway. Brad's father, old John Erickson, had the only other apartment, directly above my office-room. And there was a Chinese psychiatrist, Dr. Lee, who had his office down the hall. "Tell Brad I'll take it, Ellie, but make sure he gets the typewriters and office equipment out of my room." Having absolutely no furniture of my own, I needed a small ice box, a hot plate, some pots and a teakettle. Confident that I could find a mattress somewhere to sleep on, I gladly accepted Ellie's offer of an old, broken-down sofa.

"I have a new lease on life, Ruth! Everything's going to be different now — no more late hours, no running around, and *no drinking!* At least, not as much."

Saying goodbye to my friend and co-worker Ruth was hard. But she, too, had gotten married, and I had been a maid of honor for the last time, I hoped. Mother cried and cried, and finally accepted my decision. "Princeton isn't that far away, Mamashena, and if it doesn't work out for you there, just come home. I'll come and see you on weekends or Tuesdays, my day off." Mother's full-time job at Lord and Taylor's kept her busy and largely out of trouble, and that was a load off my mind. But since I had never been further than an elevator-ride away from her at age 26, it wasn't easy to say goodbye. As for the oil company, well, the men were sad to see me leave; the women weren't. Over the years, I had accrued some $800 in their provident fund, and left after a farewell luncheon at Rockefeller Center.

During the taxi ride to Penn Station, I fought the tears welling up inside me. I looked around at tons of luggage, and considering leaving the only city I really knew, Mother left alone, all my bills, and a broken relationship with a man called Frank, I sighed, "Oh God, let it be different! Make it all different from here on."

Once in Princeton, I took another cab and asked the driver to go slowly. I took in every quaint shop on Nassau, the tree-lined main street. The A & S newsstand and soda fountain looked lively. Youngsters and students were gathered inside and out eating ice cream cones, carrying books and laughing. Looking through the window, I wished my life had been like that. It all looked so clean, so good and right. P. J.'s Pancake House was a folksy, family-type of place. There was a florist, an art store, an optometrist, a five and ten, Thorn's Pharmacy and the "Brown Jug" package store and local pub. What was it Ellie had said about that place?

"Don't go there alone, Barbara. It's full of town people who talk. Students go there, too, but just to pass away the time and watch the games on TV."

"Here we are, ma'am, Erickson Realty. That'll be one dollar with the luggage. Hope you make out here. It's a nice town, all right, if you know people."

It *was* a nice town, and life in my small, square-shaped room was fun, the first month. I saw a great deal of Ellie and her whole family, whenever I felt lonely or troubled. They seemed to genuinely like me, and I certainly enjoyed being around them and gradually began to develop a real love for them. There were dates, parties and some social life connected with the University Press, and I liked the people there, too. They were businesslike, keeping their distance and not getting too personal. Gradually I became friendly with two girls who roomed together, Lalor and Claire, who were two very attractive editors. They, too, had moved to Princeton to try their luck at business and husband-hunting. How could you miss in this town, with an all-male campus?

My job was different than anything I'd ever done in the past. It was spelled w-o-r-k, and that was something I was not used to. Believing that I was incapable of working under pressure, I nonetheless found myself required to do just that. With tons of manuscripts on my desk that had to be checked in and given to the appropriate editor, galleys of proofreading to check, and book jackets also to be logged in at my desk, and then distributed to the art department, I panicked. Breaking out in a cold sweat by midafternoon, I would feel uneasy and anxious and would watch the clock until it was 5:30, and I could head for the Annex, for a drink with the girls. In the meantime, I made frequent escapes — to the ladies' room, the water fountain, or to run an errand. Sometimes I would even pretend to have left something at home, so that I could run the block and a half to my room just to sit down and try to relax.

"What's wrong with me?" I asked Ellie. "My nerves seem to be shot."

"Barbara, you've just had a big change in your life. Working at the Press requires a lot of concentration. But don't worry; it'll all work out. Just give it time."

Ellie's words comforted me, and the martinis seemed to make my worries a figment of my imagination, and so I went on. But late hours of tossing and turning found me exhausted in the morning, barely able to wash and get dressed. Taking tons of Alka Seltzer, Bufferin and Pepto Bismol, I gradually became convinced that I had ulcers. And when one morning, during working hours, I had to excuse myself and go home, where I vomited and vomited, until my stomach was so sore I could hardly move. I spent the rest of the day on my couch all curled up, frightened and lonely.

Early one evening in September of 1967, after another long weekend of running around, I was feeling unusually despondent. My stomach was now burning with pain, despite the fact that I was now consuming Maalox tablets as if they were peanuts. In desperation I had resorted to drinking a concoction of beer and tomato juice. My hair was pulled back and clasped with a barrette in the back and hanging down, almost to my waist. Since I wasn't eating much and was living on my own, I looked thin. Wearing a tight-fitting skirt and blouse of my favorite shade of grey-blue, and a cardigan sweater draped loosely over my shoulders, I decided to take a walk. I didn't know where to go, since it was a Monday night, and everyone whom I knew was home. There were many nights like this, when I found it impossible to stay home alone. Fear began to creep into my room. The small windows facing the courtyard had no shades or curtains, and shadows cast eerie figures that looked as though they were going to get me. It was stupid, of course, but I still couldn't let go of the fear.

It was a warm, balmy evening with just a hint of a breeze. Crossing over the other side of Nassau Street, I saw a glow of light coming from the Brown Jug. Several cars were parked in the area, including one green Austin Healey directly in front of the door. The door was wide open, and looking in, I was recognized by the bartender who waved. He was young, probably a graduate student, and he was intensely involved in a conversation with three young men at the bar. They turned to watch me enter and take a seat on the stool nearest the door. There was complete silence, as the bartender, ignoring the comeback of one rather caustic fellow, asked me what I wanted to have.

"I'll have a stein of light draught with just a trace of tomato juice, please." Three heads turned in my direction, as I repeated my order to the startled bartender, adding, "Really, it's not that bad."

Listening to the conversations, it soon became obvious to me that the others at the bar lived in Princeton but were not University students. Probably older, working types, I thought. Periodically they would glance in my direction. Two fair-haired boys called Eddie and Bill, were sitting nearest to me, and seemed rather shy. But the one farthest from me, the dark Italian-looking one with the strong, brooding features and rather long face, like a Modigliani painting, made a couple of cutting remarks about my drink. He was also the most discursive of the group, seemingly knowledgeable on everything from sports to politics to the arts. Instantly I knew he was the one I liked the least. But I wished he would stop talking enough to give Bill, the one nearest me, a chance to say something.

Seeing that he was not about to let up, I shoved my drink down the bar towards him, saying: "Go on, try it yourself. You think you know everything and how awful this drink is; well, I dare you: drink it!"

Taken aback by my sudden gesture, he picked up the stein of beer and tilted his head back. He looked all neck, as he drank half of it. "Mmm, not bad, not bad at all — oh, what did you say your name was?" Getting up from his stool, he moved around to the empty one between Bill and me.

Annoyed, I replied, "I never mentioned my name, but it's Barbara — Barbara Scheutz."

Aware that everyone was quiet now, listening to our conversation, I hoped he wouldn't ask me what kind of a name that was, or what nationality I was, so I went on, hastily, "I moved here about a month ago, from New York City."

Every eye focused on me now, as if I had come from outer space. "You moved here — alone?" the tall one asked, leaning towards me.

"Yes, what's so strange about that?"

"Nothing. It's just that we don't get many attractive single girls like you here from the city. You are single, aren't you?"

"Yes, I am."

"That's great! My name's Ray Tamasi; where do you live?"

Suddenly aware that these three might be thinking that I might be an easy mark, I tried to change the subject. But he kept on until, with my face flushed, I hurried out the door.

More frustrated than before I'd left my room, I kept on walking until I reached P.J.'s Pancake House. I decided to go in, figuring I'd eat until I could no longer breathe. After finishing a hamburger, a tuna on rye and a hot dog, plus an ice cream sundae for dessert, I ordered another to go. Paying my check, I waited in line at the take-out counter for my sundae. Instead of feeling satisfied, I felt disgustingly bloated and could hardly walk.

Suddenly, a hand tugged at my sweater, and looking down, I saw, seated in a booth, Billie, Eddie and Ray.

"Fancy meeting you here," one of them said. I quickly explained that I had had dinner, when Ray asked me what was in my bag.

"Um, an ice cream sundae."

"Well, how come it's in your bag, if you live alone, and you just ate?"

Why didn't he mind his own business! But instead of ignoring him or telling him off, I lied. "My cousin is staying with me for the night, and I'm taking her a sundae."

"Great, go home and get her; we'll all go to the Annex for a drink."

"I can't do that. She's sick — not feeling well, and won't come out."

"If she's sick," Ray persevered, "what makes you think she'll want an ice cream sundae?"

Completely hassled, I replied: "Look, I'm taking this home to her, and if she wants it, fine; if not, I'll put it in the refrigerator and eat it myself tomorrow."

And then, all of a sudden, I noticed his grin — he was kidding! I gave up and began to giggle a little. "C'mon Barbara, let me buy you a drink at the Annex. You'll be safe with three clean-cut Princetonians — how about it?"

Ray's smile made his whole face take on a different look. I noticed his teeth now — straight and white-looking. I liked his high cheekbones and the sparkle in this greyish-green eyes. Taking in all I could about him in that instant, I noted his grey flannel slacks, brown loafers and grey Shetland crew-neck sweater. As he continued to smile at me, one side of his mouth curled up slightly. He's not that bad, I thought — young, must be in his early twenties, just a boy, really, but . . . I think I'll say yes. "Okay, I'll meet you all at the Annex in half an hour."

My first date with Raymond was on a Sunday afternoon. Aware of my interest in art, he took me on an afternoon tour of Princeton University's small museum. I was impressed with Ray's knowledge of art, his Ivy League clothes, and his green Austin Healey, and discounted the fact that he was eight months younger and not what I considered "my type." Yet his slow smile, elusive air and dry sense of humor began to grow on me throughout that day. After a scenic drive to New Hope, a small rural artists' colony, we had dinner and two liters of wine back in Princeton, at a quaint, informal restaurant on Witherspoon Street called the Grotto. It served hearty, home-cooked Italian food, heavy on the spices the way I liked it, and it was to become one of my favorite restaurants.

The next day at the Press, I thought about Ray and hoped that he would call me again. There was a hometown stability about him. My friend Ellie, who knew everything that went on in town, told me as much about him as she could. "He lives at home with his parents who are as Italian as can be," and then she added thoughtfully, "Barbara, he's a nice guy, but remember that he's Catholic and you're Jewish."

"So what? I'm not going to *marry* him! Besides, I never was very Jewish."

"Well, okay, but be careful about drinking and smoking. I wouldn't do either around his parents, if I were you."

That afternoon, the telephone rang, a little before three. When I heard Ray's voice on the other end, my face became a little flushed, and I lowered my voice to a whisper. I eagerly accepted a date for Wednesday night, at a French restaurant I'd heard a lot about — "La Haires." Wednesday finally came, and that night over candlelight and escargots, we found out as much about the other as each wanted the other to know, leaving enough unsaid to allow for that mystical curiosity that draws people to each other. Ray was a graduate of Rutgers, had a younger sister named Linda, and a grandmother who owned "Toto's" grocery store and meat market. "She's a tough woman. Started that store with nothing, and now it's a goldmine."

Ray had a large family, many of whom came over here years ago from Italy. "The elderly, widowed women still wear black; you must have seen them on Nassau Street. They're all proper, never drink or smoke. My parents are like that, too. They don't know much about what I do, or where I go when I'm out of the house. My father runs the home with an iron fist. My mother is definitely under his dominion." Ray grinned. "That's the way every woman should be." He went on with his recollections. "I can remember times when my buddies would leave me off in front of the house, and I'd be scared to death to face my dad at four in the morning when I was so drunk. I'd fall asleep in my own car. Once, I came home all bloody. My date and I had been out in a rowboat, stoned, and we went overboard. I was cut and bruised — and dead drunk. When my mother opened the door and saw me, she screamed. And sure enough, a little later, my old man came up the stairs with his belt in his hand . . . ."

Ray was chuckling now about those early incidents in his life. And I loved hearing about them; they sounded so stable, somehow. I shuddered to recall my own memories which seemed like a murky, surrealistic nightmare, in comparison; in fact, they were so unreal that I began to regard them as just that: bad dreams, best forgotten.

"Yeah, they're simple, *Daily News,* home-type folks," Ray went on. "Maybe you'll meet them someday." I wanted to meet them, I suddenly realized. I was aware now that I really liked this character, even though it was only our second date. Here was a clean-cut, wholesome American boy — no wife or ex-wife, no children or psychological hang-ups. And not only did Ray have a job, he had a good one. Working for Market Dynamics, a division of Opinion Research, he was recently made research executive of that firm.

I sensed that Ray was attracted to me, but he left enough unsaid and concealed his thoughts and feelings so that I never felt as though I was sure of him, as I had felt before, so destructively.

I was somehow hoping it would stay that way, that he would play the game for awhile. For past experience was finally beginning to show me some ugly things about myself, things I didn't want to face at all. I recognized that there was something crazy inside me that, while I wanted what was "good," the moment I had it, I threw it away. It was as though I felt I was beneath anything good or fine.

The only men I felt secure with were those from broken homes, or those who had emotional problems as deep as mine. And for the most part, the men I liked treated me shabbily. I didn't consciously want that, yet I seemed to draw it to myself repeatedly, suspecting deep inside that I deserved only to be ill-treated. Why did that keep happening? Wretchedly unhappy, I nonetheless plunged into relationships that were almost guaranteed to produce even more unhappiness. *Why?* What was it in me that shunned light and craved dark?

Whatever it was, I hoped that this time things would be different. Sitting across from Raymond Tamasi now and looking at his face, watching him smile, laugh or frown, I knew I wanted him. But I also wanted *this* relationship to be different. There were not going to be any overnight stays anywhere! Determined to stick with that and not allow this to turn into just another affair, I recalled again, as I did frequently now, my mother's counsel and that of my friends' mothers, about remaining chaste until marriage. How I had scoffed at that when I was in my late teens, thinking it pathetically old-fashioned and meaningless in today's society!

And yet through the years, I had gradually, painfully, discovered that physical relationships — whether one was in love or not — invariably brought emotional consequences that wounded deeply. Giving myself to someone I was in love with only tied me more deeply to that person. Yearning to belong to that person, to become "one," made it impossible for me to let go emotionally and continue in my daily life with any degree of normalcy. And I was jealous to the point of paranoia. I feared what he was thinking, or losing him, or his changing his mind about marriage, and so on, always ending with: "I just couldn't go on without him." And I couldn't. It was no exaggeration. Twice I had been torn apart inside, desperately wanting to have the other person completely, trying to find fulfillment in my already empty world.

And with Frank Maloney, this last and most painful rejection threw me into a state of acute anxiety. Physically, I felt worse than ever before; it was as though my body no longer belonged to me, or anyone else. All personal values were gone. I didn't see it as such, but I was in a form of torture — giving, hoping, waiting — only to be left with less than what I'd had, before I ever entered into a physical relationship. And what about all the men in between? The ones I didn't give a damn about — single and married, drunk and sober, rich and poor? They had all left me alone, with my guilt.

Turning my head on some strange pillow, barely able to see who was next to me, I often wanted to just close my eyes, never to open them again. The litany that would go through my mind then, became all too familiar: "Oh, Barbara, how could you have! Don't you remember where you met him? Or how you got here? Barbara, Barbara, what's *happening* to you?" Reliving such memories was more than excruciating; it was impossible. There was no earthly way I could get rid of the shame, the guilt, the utter self-loathing and disgust.

And partly because there was no way to end it, to wipe it away and start all over, it repeated itself — the same episodes and tragic one-night-stands that left me cold, shaking, and trying to cope with something so personal. I would tell myself it didn't matter; everyone was sleeping around these days, yet it didn't work. I was just that much more guilty, when I finally did manage to pull myself together.

So, I simply did not let myself think back on those days, once I was in Princeton. I stuck to my guns: this time things were going to be different! And it was going to start here and now, with Raymond Tamasi. Raymond lived at home, and if his parents were really as strict as I'd heard, well, then, it shouldn't be too difficult!

Our dating began to develop a regular pattern: we went out on Wednesday nights, usually to dinner, and on the weekends. The

Brown Jug became our regular hangout all day Saturday and sometimes Saturday night as well. I eagerly looked forward to the times when I would see Ray. By now, my job at the Press had lost a lot of appeal. I became fidgety, nervously expecting to be fired. The cold nights in my room with only a small electric heater were bleak, dreary and depressing. Now, more than ever, I hated to be alone. The nights I went out with Ray, I usually drank enough to enable me to sleep through. But the rest of the evenings were tormented by creeping fears that engulfed me, as I lay on the old torn mattress on the floor. Staring up at the ceiling, I watched the shadows on the walls, as they hovered over me threateningly. Since I was seeing only Ray, I usually went directly home after work, if I wasn't going with some of the girls from the Press for a drink. Even then, I was home by 6:30. I had no desire to date anyone else and was not about to ruin my reputation by running around to different drinking spots.

But in order to quiet my frayed nerves, which I was now convinced were due to the fact that I was living alone in a small, quaint and gossipy town that had its spies out watching me, I went to a local doctor for a cure. "Dr. Tan, I used to take whiskey for monthly stomach cramps, and it helped, but I can't do that on the job I have now. Are there any pills that can help me with this awful pain I get?"

"Of course. And I'd much rather see you take pills than liquor, anyhow. Here's a prescription for some pain pills. They should give you a sense of well-being and help you relax at your difficult time of the month. If you like them, let me know, and I'll give you a prescription for six months." And so, it wasn't long before I began carrying these round yellow pills with me, wherever I went. I felt a small sense of security, listening to them jiggle in my pocket book, as I walked down Nassau Street. Discovering that they not only took away pain, but the "blues" as well, and even late night eerie fears, I popped one when I felt low, or in the evening alone.

A month went by, and it was October, the brilliant fall foliage making the university campus as picturesque as possible. Ray would drive me around the campus in his Healey, telling me stories of how he and the other guys — always Eddie, Bill, John, Georgie and Tommy — would crash various fraternity parties. As many episodes as Ray could gather from his youthful past, he proudly related. And yet, this was but a small part of the Raymond I sat next to. Serious and thoughtful, he seemed to have many values and beliefs about life. And although they sometimes seemed confusing and radical to me, I nonetheless envied him. For I had no values of my own. I didn't care about the world around me, let it all go to pot.

12

For the first time in my life I was in love with someone and it all seemed right, good and clean. Knowing only failures, never tasting joy in anything after leaving Meema and Peepa, I hoped against hope, wished upon every star and turkey bone at Thanksgiving, for this relationship to become lasting. "Oh God, oh someone, if there is anything out there beyond me, please, please, let me marry Ray. I love him. I know I do. He's the most honest person that ever came into my life." Sipping a glass of sherry next to my bed eased the screaming fears and doubts that kept me awake, tossing and turning night after night. Even the little yellow pill that I took an hour or so before the sherry wasn't helping much. So afraid that everything was going to crumble all around me again, I even wished I had never met Raymond, so that I wouldn't have to be hurt any more.

But when we were together, I felt at ease. Ray seemed to not just like me but really care for me, and I yearned to be needed by him, not just wanted. As a young girl, lost in fantasy of who Prince Charming would be in my life, I had once seen sex as something very personal and intimate, the culmination of two persons' love for one another, sanctioned by marriage. Emotionally, I had always felt that way, but somewhere along the line, I had changed my mind and attitudes, and abused the notion terribly. One result was that my fear of rejection had become so great that in desperation, I hung on every word Ray said, going over and over it in my mind later. And I read things into everything; my mind was like the bottom of a woven tapestry, with loose ends scrambling to hook on somewhere.

So when Raymond told me that he was very much in love with me and that marriage was in the future for us, every fiber in my being leaped for joy. Yet almost immediately that joy was taken away by negative thoughts that shot through like darts. Does he mean it, or is he just leading me on? Why doesn't he set a date? Why haven't I met his parents? Why can't I tell everyone I know that we're getting married? Why. . . ? When I periodically erupted with one of these "why" questions, Raymond just calmly told me, "*Relax,* we have plenty of time. It's only been two months that we've known each other."

But I wasn't able to relax. I didn't have plenty of time. My life was now on a threshold, hinging on one thing only, marriage to Raymond Tamasi as soon as possible. It had to be that way, because I did not believe for one minute that, in time, it would all come about. How could it? It never had before. I was sure that time brought only destruction. Good promises for me never became realities. In order to make something happen, I had to grab hold and take, fast. I hated myself, my insecurities, my stupidity, and above all my inability to ever be what I always envied in a person, cool, aloof and mysterious. I always let everything hang out, even if I didn't want to. Lynn, I remembered, could go for months without letting a guy know that she cared for him. With me, it was obvious on the first date, and it usually frightened the boy away. Somehow, I had to hide my emotions with Ray, and the only way I knew to do that was to drink, and play-act. Almost always that was a part of Ray's and my being together. And it was giving me, in a way I'd never seen before, the power to be as cool or as warm as I wanted to be.

When we were with Ray's friends, we drank. If occasionally a discussion arose about the latest books, I sat in my seat dreading that I might be asked a question, especially one that I would be expected to know the answer to. Inevitably, one Saturday night it happened. The occasion was a birthday party for one of Ray's friends, and when one of the girls mentioned a well-known book, I gave the wrong author. Everyone just stared at me. Blushing, I left the room and headed for the bar. Ray followed me outside. "Barbara, what's wrong? You must know who wrote that book. Where have you been the past five years?"

Where had I been? As the tears flowed down my cheeks, scenes flashed through my mind — Bogey's, Martel's, Spark's . . . a blur of parties, homes, offices, hotel rooms. . . faces of men I knew and barely knew. "Oh Ray!" I sobbed, "I'm not what you think I am, I —"

Ray's soft voice interrupted, "Forget it, I don't care whether you know the author or don't. I love you anyway, Princess." This was the second time I had heard him say that. Those words were so comforting, but inside of me, the fear remained. The fact that I didn't know the author wasn't what was upsetting me; it was *why* I didn't know who the author was. It was what took the place of acquiring knowledge that threatened me. Ray actually believed that I was a young woman who had somehow remained chaste up until this point. I had conned him into believing that, I had lied to him, and now I was reaping the anxiety of that lie.

After much persuasion, Raymond finally conceded: he would introduce me to his parents on Sunday. I had been asking to meet them for several weeks. He talked of marriage, told me he loved me, and everyone in town knew that we saw only each other. But each time I brought it up, he would shrug his shoulders and say, "It's not important that you meet my folks." That was strange. I meant, here he was, living at home at age twenty-six. One would think it would be very important to him. I was curious, anxious, and very nervous. Insisting on meeting Ray at the A & S News stand on Nassau Street at one o'clock, I had a mental picture of the Grotto. Sundays are out for cocktails anywhere, except if you are eating, but I could never meet the Tamasis cold sober. So, at 11:30 a.m. I stood outside the Grotto on Witherspoon Street, waiting for the owner to open the restaurant. Finally he came. I couldn't bear the thought of heavy Italian food; to me, it was still Sunday morning. Besides, I would soon have another lunch, for which I had better have an appetite. The waiter obligingly said an antipasto would be sufficient with my two extra dry martinis. I still had fifteen minutes before I was going to meet Ray, but as much as I wanted a third drink, I dared not order it. Taking my check, the wife of the owner, a dark, round, short Italian woman with a shrill voice said, "Hey, don't you go with the Tamasi boy?"

"Uh, yes?"

Looking at my check she read every item aloud: "Antipasto, two martinis. A little early, isn't it?"

"Yes, yes, it is. I uh, have stomach cramps."

My heart was still pounding by the time I reached Nassau Street. Ray, who was usually late, was there waiting for me. The martinis had done nothing to calm my nerves. I lied and told Ray I had had something to eat and a glass of wine. Conservatively dressed, with little makeup on, I waited with Ray at the front door of the Tamasis' white Cape Cod house. Complete with neatly trimmed shrubbery all around, it had a screened porch to the right of the entrance, something I had always dreamed about having with a house of my own someday. I loved houses, especially cozy and compact ones. In my mind, they spelled home, something I did not believe I'd ever had. The folksy, small-town picture became complete when Mrs. Tamasi opened the door. Surprised, she shouted for Ray's Dad: "Oh Don, guess what? Ray's brought a friend home to meet us. Come in! Come right in, it's nice to meet you." Jabbing Ray lightly with her elbow, she jokingly scolded him for not giving them any advance notice. Surprised myself, I turned to Ray, a little annoyed

"Gee," I whispered "you might have told them I was coming; we've known about it for three days!" But that was the way Raymond was. Either he was supercasual about everything or just plain forgetful.

Looking around the living room at the simple, early American furniture, I was impressed with the order I saw. Completely opposite from any place I had ever lived in, everything was in its proper place. Ray's mom kept smiling and chatting away. About 5'4", she had salt-and-pepper hair that was short and curly, and not a hair was out of place; in fact, her entire appearance and dress was tidy and wholesome. She kept calling for Don to come out into the living room and meet me. She was so obviously cheerful, I now wondered what Mr. Tamasi would be like.

He walked into the room with about as straight an expression as possible for the occasion. It wasn't until after we were introduced that I caught just a hint of a smile. But when he did smile, his dark Italian eyes twinkled, giving his already attractive appearance a rather roguish look. Of average height and well built, Mr. Tamasi had a deep, deep voice, and it soon became obvious that he was a man of few words, unless he felt like talking.

"Sit down, sit down," Ray's mother kept urging. "I'll bring out some Coke and cookies, or would you like some tea or coffee? I know Ray just loves his Coke."

What was this about Ray loving Coke? Why, Ray downed martinis at the same rate I did. "Coffee will be fine, thank you, Mrs. Tamasi." Ray's Dad joined us while Mrs. Tamasi was in the kitchen, and Ray proceeded to pick up the New York Times crossword puzzle. He sat in silence, talking only when I tried to ask some simple questions, hoping to start a conversation. Silently, nervously, I could feel my back tense up, as we listened to Mrs. Tamasi singing away in the kitchen. How I wished Raymond would say something! Wait until I get him outside later!

Suddenly, Ray's sister Linda came running down the stairs with a knit hat on and a scarf thrown over her shoulder. Like Raymond, she was tall and lean, with thick dark hair, and she smiled as we were introduced. I was glad she was there. I hated long silences, absolutely hated them, and always felt as though I had to do something to break them, almost as if it was my fault that no one was talking.

Afterwards, driving towards the Marroe Inn, a favorite restaurant of ours outside of Princeton, I bombarded Ray with questions. "Why didn't you make conversation? I felt so peculiar just sitting there. Doesn't your Dad talk much? Or do you think he didn't like me?"

"Oh Barbara, it's not you, that's just the way he is, a man of few words."

"He sure seems stern and strict. Now I know what you mean about being afraid to be bad as a kid. I wouldn't want him angry at me."

"Italian men are like that," he said, smiling at me, "but they can also be quite warm and sincere."

"I hope you are sincere about us, Ray."

"Why is it so hard for you to trust me?"

"I don't know; I guess I'm afraid of losing you."

"Don't worry, you won't lose me, Princess, unless I die."

"Don't say that!" But there was something in the way he'd said it that made me go on. "By the way, what is it you said you'd tell me sometime, if we got serious enough, remember? When I told you about my cousin Nancy being really sick, you said you knew what it was like to be that sick. Can you tell me now? Not knowing what you meant has made me wonder all sorts of things." I hesitated. "Were you ill — very ill — too?"

Ray's smile vanished. "I don't want to talk about it now. Later — I'll tell you later, at dinner." Now I was worried. What could it have been, or be? Old thoughts of Linc flashed through my mind. God, I hope it isn't anything like that, like leukemia! But what if it is? What if my fears are true and I lose Ray? We drove in silence to the restaurant.

Half-way through our second drink, I insisted that Raymond tell me what had happened to him. "It can't be that bad! Ray, what's wrong?"

"TB. I had tuberculosis when I was twenty-three. I was away in a sanitorium for eight months. It was awful."

I didn't know what to say. I was relieved that it was not some terminal illness still latent. On the other hand, I didn't know anyone who had ever had TB, or anything about the disease, except for the dramatic way in which "Camille" died. "Is that all?" I laughed. "I didn't know what you were going to say." But Raymond still seemed distressed about it, as though having TB would ruin his reputation.

"Well, would you tell me about it?" I went on. "It must have been a rough experience for you."

"It was. My mother's had it twice, so it's in the family."

"Well, so what? Is it contagious? I mean, can you pass it on to a child?"

"No, you can't!" Ray said, signaling to the waiter that we wanted to order. "But the tubercular germ is a precarious one. It lies dormant, perhaps for years. You think you're fine and then, wham! You're sick and sent away. That's why I still live at home at twenty-six. I was twenty-four when I got out of the sanatorium, and needed lots of rest, plus my parents worried a lot."

"So that's why you like to get home early during the week. I've noticed that you seem concerned about getting enough rest and nutrition. But you *are* okay, aren't you?"

"Yes, but I'm still on medication. I take 30 pills a day. Look at my mother: she was apparently healed — yet had a relapse. There is no cure for tuberculosis. It is only arrested."

"Ray, you make it sound so bleak; what about —"

He cut me off. "I don't want to talk about it any more. It was a nightmare — suddenly pulled away from a good job, my home, friends, and. . . ." He stopped.

"And what, Ray? You look so sad."

"And sports. I always loved basketball. It's been my game. I still don't play." Ray looked at me, and there were tears in his eyes.

"Oh, Ray," I said, taking his hands, "it's all over now. You won't get sick again, and you mustn't live in fear of it returning. Your parents probably worry. Now I know why your father was so upset when you went to Philly in the snow. I'm sure it's gone for good," I said fervently. But in my heart I wondered.

The months went by slowly and still Ray avoided setting a definite date for our marriage. Finally, one night at the Marroe Inn during after-dinner drinks at the bar, I looked at Ray and demanded an answer. "Raymond Tamasi, you have told me that you love me and are going to marry me. Well then, let's make it definite. Either you set a date, or I'm going back to New York."

Confident and sure of myself, the enabling power of alcohol sustained me. I smiled rather coyly and waited for a reply. After the longest silence of our relationship, Ray pulled out a calendar from his wallet.

"Okay, Princess, let's set a date."

"Oh, Ray! You mean it?" Flinging my arms around him, I said, "Anytime. I don't care, but not later than October. We've waited long enough."

"Well, I like September, Barb. How's about September 21st?"

"Perfect! Now tomorrow is Sunday. Pick me up at one o'clock and we'll go right over to your house and tell your folks."

"My folks?" he said, shocked at the thought. "What have they got to do with this?"

"Oh no, you don't, Raymond. I know your tricks. Let's tell your folks tomorrow." He looked at me with a frown that gradually turned into a smile.

"Okay, tomorrow. Let's have another drink."

The following afternoon was not exactly the cheery scene a bride-to-be might fantasize. Raymond, with his black sunglasses and trench coat on, was slumped down in a corner armchair in the living room. His mom was in the kitchen, and his dad was watching TV in another chair. After ten minutes of back-breaking silence, with Ray just nodding out, I got up and went into the kitchen. "Mrs. Tamasi, we have something we want to tell you. Ray and I are going to get married."

"Oh my God!" she shrieked. "*Don!* Don, listen to this: they are going to get married!"

Everyone seated in the living room was suddenly alert, straining for words. Mr. Tamasi spoke first. "Well, I hope you're not pregnant?"

Flushed with embarrassment, I was speechless and shook my head.

Ray finally spoke. "Well, it's no big deal, Dad. We're going to get married in the fall, and it's only May now."

"Do you love her?"

"Yes, we love each other."

"I love Ray very much, Mr. Tamasi," I added, fighting back tears.

"Well, I hope you two know what you're doing. Remember, if things don't work out, you can't come back here," he said to Ray, not even looking at me. "You want to get married, get married." Trying to muster up a smile, when I felt like sobbing, I put out my hand. He shook hands with me, and slapped Ray on the back. His mother and I attempted to hug each other.

The long silence that followed was finally broken by Ray, saying, "Well, I guess we'll go now. See you later."

"Don't stay out too late," we could hear his father's disapproving voice as we closed the door behind us. "You both stay out too late. Don't drink too much."

13

It was sealed. We, or rather I, had finally told Ray's parents that we were going to get married. But my flood of relief soon turned once again to worry. Did Ray's folks like me? Would they talk him out of marrying me? And the place where I was staying had finally gotten to me. It was time for another "geographical cure" — especially since I was now taking wine and pills both, to get a decent night's sleep. So, one afternoon, at my place, I said, "Ray, since we're going to get married anyway, why don't I look for an apartment for us? We'll need something larger, and I can get it ready, in the meantime. Please, please, Raymond, I can't stay here any more. I know I'll feel a lot different someplace else. You know I even have to take some sherry at night in order to get to sleep. So you see this place is affecting me."

"Okay, okay, Barbara, look around and see what you can find."

"Really, Ray, it'll be just that much less that we have to do later. You'll be able to move right in with just your clothes, when we're married."

"I said, okay, you don't have to go on convincing me. But I hope the next place does what you want it to."

Intent on finding a new place to live for myself and also as security for our forthcoming marriage, I looked all over Princeton for an apartment. Somehow I got word that there was a five-room apartment available on Witherspoon Street above the Princeton Clothing Store, next door to La Haires, and across the street from Harry's Luncheonette and the Grotto, and I called Ray at work to tell him the good news.

Down an alley and up one flight of stairs, I was somewhat reminded of our old apartment in Brooklyn when I was growing up. There was even a Mazuzah above the door, that let me know that someone who lived there had been Jewish. That added to the warm memories and I fell in love with the apartment.

"With furniture and utilities — $150." It was twice as much as I could afford, but I didn't care. "Yippee! I'll take it! I can't wait to tell Ray!" And then, afraid that they might misconstrue that, I added, "Um, Raymond Tamasi, my future husband."

"Ray Tamasi? Why, he's a friend of ours. Is he going to live here with you after you're married?"

"Yes, yes. You mean, Ray has more friends than I know of? They're coming out of the woodwork all over Princeton."

"Raymond," I said, later that evening at the Brown Jug, "you won't believe this apartment! It's spacious and even some dishes and silverware are included in the rent. Oh Ray, I'm so happy and excited about this! You know, I've never had a real kitchen since Brooklyn. I'll just love cooking and entertaining your friends. Finally, I'll have a home. And when you move in, you won't have to do a thing. Raymond, I love you, and I know we'll be happy here."

On the following Saturday, Ray and his friends moved me. I promised myself that from here on everything was going to be perfect, just right. And I was not going to drink anymore — in the daytime that was, and then only on dates with Ray. Never alone, again. My insecure days were over and everything was going to be different from now on.

I loved looking out of the living room window onto busy Witherspoon Street. Ever since the Hotel Greystone facing Broadway I had enjoyed looking out and watching people go by. But here, unlike Broadway, the opposite sidewalk was much closer. I could even look into someone else's apartment on top of the luncheonette or laundromat.

Everything was old and lacked any style or taste, but despite the creaky, tilted floors and torn furniture, it was clean. In one corner of the living room stood Raymond's favorite piece of furniture, an antique-looking grandfather clock. In another corner, Ray set up a bar out of an interesting wooden bureau with a glass door that locked. Bottles of Scotch were put inside, along with some good red and white wine and a bottle of vodka for our martinis.

The living room led directly into the kitchen which literally leaned to one side. With a couple of drinks under our belt, we almost had to hold on to the sink or stove so that we didn't slide from one end of the floor to the other. But it was fun — everything was fun and held many warm moments. The table in the middle of the square kitchen was encircled by a refrigerator, window, sink, doorway to the bedroom, stove and another doorway leading to the dining room. There were no halls in between rooms; one step from the kitchen and we stood in an enormous bedroom with cross-ventilation. The bright, airy room with a dresser and bureaus around the walls made me jump for joy. I just couldn't believe that I was going to have a big bedroom like that, even though it was a little dilapidated. And the formal dining room off the kitchen had everything from a large table to a mahogany glass closet for dishes.

At the end of a hectic moving day, I insisted that I cook dinner for Ray the first night in my home. After serving some caviar (which I had taken from a local grocery store without paying), I drenched huge shrimp in white wine and garlic. We had shrimp scampi and three bottles of wine that night after I don't know how many martinis.

"Ray," I said, asking him for the tenth time, "tell me, do you really like this apartment?"

"Well, if you really want to know, it's okay for a rickety old couple who like having a lot of junk around."

"You're kidding! How can you say that? You're just spoiled, because you've always lived in a nice house. This place is a haven for me. I love it and am so happy here. I'm not going to want to move from here for a long, long time, you'll see."

It wasn't long before we began making plans for our wedding. I had to push, push, push, to get Raymond to discuss anything to do with that subject — where we were to get married, by whom, and how many people should be invited.

"I don't care," he said finally, his tone betraying his frustration, "let's just get married at a justice of the peace."

"Ray, I don't care either," I lied. "I'm Jewish and you're Catholic, but your folks will have a fit if you're not married in a proper church. They were upset enough about the fact that I didn't have an engagement ring. I told them I had a choice, a ring or a trip to Spain and that I picked the honeymoon in Spain. It's obvious they don't like that."

"Oh, all right, Barbara! We'll get together with them and discuss the plans."

My family, my Aunt Mary, Uncle Leo Sheirr, Aunt Shirley, Uncle Morty, Aunt Edith, Uncle Duddy, Uncle Leo and Aunt Gerie, along with my cousins, were thrilled about my forthcoming marriage. Some even came to Princeton for my birthday on July 1st to celebrate with us. We had dinner at the Marroe Inn and champagne kept flowing. I cried as I looked from Mother, who was beaming, to Aunt Mary who had worried about her little Pussy Cat for years. "Finally, you'll have your own family, Barbara," she said, "and someone who'll love you and take care of you. I'm so happy."

But my joy was soon interrupted by the doubt and concern of Ray's parents about our life — where we were going and how much we drank. Ray's Dad would pull me in a corner after dinner at their home, to lecture me about Raymond's illness and that late nights and drinking could bring it back. I began to feel guilty in advance, as though I would be to blame if Ray ever did get sick again. My mother, who didn't have much money, offered to give me a small wedding, with a wedding cake, hors d'oeuvres and champagne, but Ray's parents wouldn't hear of that. They offered to pay for all the wine and liquor, if we had a sit-down dinner. It made Mother and me feel guilty again that we couldn't afford to do the whole thing ourselves. But on the matter of the Catholic Church, we both stood firm. Since I had worked at Princeton University Press, I knew the secretary to Dean Gordon, the Dean of the

University Chapel, and was able to arrange for us to be married by him at the Chapel.

Every other day, I walked up and down that aisle on my lunch hour when no one was around. I was awed by the regal beauty of that distinguished place. It changed the picture I had of myself as an awkward girl, hunched over, grasping for security and a place to belong; hurt, and rejected, unlucky in love, counting the days until my wedding date. The long aisle seemed never-ending, and the warm summer sunlight filtered through the stained glass windows, casting beautiful shadows of light on the carpeting. Holding my head as high as I could, with my long hair twisted neatly on top, the way I planned to wear it on the day of our wedding, I pretended that Raymond was standing in front of the altar waiting for me. He was tall and handsome, and I was experiencing the day I had waited for. From the time I left Meema and Peepa, I had begun to search for love, first inside, then outside. I was light as a feather, radiating joy as I walked slowly down the long aisle, preparing myself for the day when I would actually become the Princess that Ray called me.

Actually I had left the Press some time before, and had managed a tiny mod dress boutique for a while, until I decided to get into something eminently respectable. The day that I went for an interview at the Clark, Dodge brokerage firm, a high-ranking, prestige outfit, was the day Bobby Kennedy was killed. It was 6:30 in the morning, June 5, 1968. Ray had called to tell me the horrible news. Since he had always been a Kennedy fan, he was taking it especially hard. His voice choked up, as he asked what countless millions of Americans were asking over and over: "Why, why?"

During my interview, I spent most of the time talking about Bobby Kennedy's assassination; nothing else seemed to matter. But having had quite an interesting employment record, I somehow charmed the man interviewing me into giving me a job. How I ever convinced him and myself that I was interested in the stock market beats me. But I knew Ray and his friend John were avid investors, playing the market all the time. This would impress Raymond, his friends and his parents. After all, one couldn't get any higher than being employed by Clark, Dodge.

Raymond *was* impressed. He braggingly told John and everyone else where I had started working. With me, though, he expressed some concern: "Barbara, I hope you know what you're doing. It's not going to be easy working there, but I do feel proud that you got the job."

I set my mind on learning whatever it was I had to learn, but stocks, brokerage terms and tickertape machines, the whole darn thing was a complete snarl of confusion to me. At the end of the day though, I felt good, better than I had in a long time. I was doing something respectable. I had an apartment two blocks from work, and in three months I was going to be married. I forgot the past completely until one day when I was called into my employer's office. "Barbara, I want to know if you have ever been bonded? If you haven't, you will have to get bonded sometime in the near future for this job, and where it could take you."

The word *bonded* shocked me out of the dream I was having about Snow White marrying Prince Charming and living happily ever after. I nodded no, as if in a daze saying, Sure, I'll get bonded, but inside I knew I would never get bonded. I had a record. I had forgotten that completely. My fingerprints were on file, from the one time I had been caught shoplifting. Raymond and this town must never, never know about that. There would be no getting bonded, and hence no future at Clark, Dodge.

Gradually I began to lose interest in my work. My drinking picked up, as Ray and I began to see each other now almost every night. Dinner always included wine, cocktails and after-dinner drinks. But this never struck Ray or me as unusual. All our friends drank. In fact, anyone who didn't had to be a little strange or kooky. The only people I knew who didn't drink were Raymond's parents, and they *were* strange — strangely strict.

Much of my morning was spent lingering over the water fountain or the coffee machine. I lied and told my immediate supervisor, a woman who looked as if she could see right through me, that I had mononucleosis and had to stay home for several weeks. During that time, I went out, met Ray for lunch and shopped. I didn't do it secretly, and obviously I was seen. When I "recovered from mono" and returned to work, dreading going back, I was called in to the office of the man who had interviewed me, and fired.

Never knowing whether he had discovered my record or not, I cried and cried all the way home that day and into the night. Ray, seeing how unnaturally torn apart I was, tried to console me by saying, "The stock market is a hard field to work in." What he really meant, I thought, was that it was a heady business and I didn't have the head for it. I felt so low, so very low, I walked around in despair and fear again. Unable to bear thinking what Ray's parents thought about me, I began to imagine what they must have thought, such as: "What kind of a girl is she, anyway? Doesn't she have a family? I'm sure she's divorced, maybe even with kids." And such was my paranoia, I soon believed my imaginings to be the truth. Walking the streets looking for another job to get me through the eight weeks until our wedding, I found myself often suddenly turning to see if any of Ray's relatives were watching me.

I landed a job as a sales girl at a local department store, where I worked for the month of August selling clothes. I also pocketed lingerie and underwear when no one was watching me. And in Cox's grocery store, a Princeton landmark, I often took cans of expensive salmon or whatever — until the day I was caught. Following me out of the store, the son of the owner angrily asked me what I had in my handbag. Pulling out a small package of cream cheese, that couldn't have cost more than half a dollar, I handed it to him. As I cried and pleaded for forgiveness again, he let me go but told me never to come in the store again.

How can I describe how I felt? My arms were full of groceries that I purchased, more than $5.00 worth. Why had I done it? Certainly not because I needed it. It must have been because I was hooked, addicted to shoplifting, or was it that perverse thing in me that made me do something that would ruin what was left of my reputation, just as surely as the past I was so desperately trying to hide? Seeing young Mr. Cox on the street, I would purposely cross over, deathly afraid of him telling my future in-laws about me, or Ray, or anyone. Would I have to leave Princeton less than a month before our wedding?

Breathing a sigh of relief when no serious consequences followed, I swore up and down that I would never, never steal another thing again and during the *days* preceding my wedding I didn't touch a drop of liquor. I watched my diet too, so that I wasn't bloated or my face didn't have any blemishes on it. Mother and I went over the wedding plans with the Nassau Inn, where the reception was to be held. Since Ray's Dad had been an employee of the entire Palmer Square area, and had acquired a good solid reputation in the community, the name Tamasi was well respected, and it made me feel proud that I was marrying Ray. However, Mr. and Mrs. Tamasi weren't as enthused about our wedding as much as they were concerned that everything go well. I was constantly asked to convince Raymond to do this or that, and in my desire for their approval, I always did.

But the times spent at their home for dinner or dessert became increasingly tense. Backbreaking silences and looks left me wondering and worrying about whether they accepted me or not. Ellie, who was my only close friend and confidante at that time, knew of my anxieties, and told me simply not to think about it; I wasn't marrying them. But nevertheless I felt like a dirty piece of newspaper everyone had read, and was then thrown on the street to blow away.

The day of my wedding, I walked down the aisle at 11:00 in the morning, reeking of vodka and orange juice because I didn't think I could make it sober. I saw my mother and all of my relatives sitting up at the altar. Their faces were wet with tears, and they were beaming. However, Raymond's mother kept her head lowered and didn't look at me at all. Ray's Dad looked directly at both of us, and I saw the faint hint of a smile on his face. I wanted to really know him, to love him, to call him Dad.

Suddenly, my eyes focused on a tall, grey-haired, blue-eyed man, who was definitely smiling. Dean Gordon's eyes were telling me to smile, be joyful, this was the happiest day of my life. I fixed my mind, my entire being on him, hoping to capture something he had. He stood tall and straight, and somehow his assurance wasn't at all pompous. I remembered how he was behind his desk at the chapel, when Ray and I went there to arrange the wedding. Nervous, wondering what he would be like, I relaxed the moment I sat down. He had greeted us with a genuine warmth that radiated from him. We told him we wanted to be married there at the chapel, because it was so beautiful and meaningful, but neither of us believed in God. Studying us for a while, his face took on a more pensive look. "That's too bad," he said, and then startled me by asking, "Well, why do you two want to get married? You can live together, you know." We hunted for an answer, but were still left feeling strange, even questioning ourselves. "Look," he went on, "I will be glad to marry you both, but I want you to know that God wants it that way. He wants the two of you to be married. I believe that." And then he added: "God does love you."

I didn't think any more about the God stuff, as Ray and I happily strolled down the walk from the dean's office across the campus to Nassau Street. It was a hot, sunny day; some students who were in Princeton for the summer sat with their legs crossed, secretly smoking pot and watching the people go by. But only a few dared to be that open; the rest of the people that crowded the green lawn were on their lunch hour, having a picnic, or lying flat out on a blanket to get some of the noon rays.

"Gee, Raymond, I really liked Dean Gordon, didn't you?"

"Yes, surprisingly. I didn't think I would. As a matter of fact, I was dreading this meeting. I hate churches. You know, I used to be an altar boy at St. Paul's. I even went to parochial school — oh, forget it, I don't want to talk about it." We walked on in silence for a few moments. "One thing I did like about that man was that he wasn't pushy. I figured he'd sit there and lecture us or something. You know, I could have stayed longer."

"Yeah, me too. I'm really glad he's marrying us..."

"And who will give this woman to this man...?"

"I will." Uncle Leo Karl's voice was loud, deep and proud, as he stepped to one side, letting me continue on down the aisle to join

Raymond, who was standing at the altar, smiling. His hair was neatly parted and combed, but just a few hairs had fallen on his forehead, giving him a boyish look. I couldn't believe this was happening. It was 1968, I hadn't lost Raymond; we were getting married! Feelings welled up inside me, and I wanted to explode with gratitude. I wanted to thank someone. Looking to Mother and Aunt Mary, who were crying and jubilant, I answered all Dean Gordon's questions with "I do," as if in a trance. Somehow, for one quick moment, I wanted to ask this minister if I could see him again. There was something behind those blue eyes that held me — something quiet and peaceful.

All at once it was over. Outside the chapel, we stood in line hugging and kissing everyone as they congratulated us. My family encircled me, while Raymond's relatives, some of them unable to speak English, showered us with warmth.

My own mood swayed from moments of extreme nostalgia to hysterical glee. Our friends, "the Princeton Town group," were anxious to hit the bar at the Nassau Inn, and so were we. Billy drove the wedding car. Turning around, he handed me an open bottle of beer. Grabbing it, I tilted my head back, saying "skoal," and with no relatives around, I chug-a-lugged the bottle. We stopped briefly at a light, and out of the corner of my eye, I noticed the look of an astonished pedestrian.

"Who cares? Who cares about anything now? We're married. I'm finally blissfully happy, safe and secure, forever and ever." I was so excited, I couldn't sit still. Ray was thinking about the envelopes with money — some we had received, and some we were to receive. What we collected that day was going to pay for half of our trip. "I need a drink, a real one, Raymond. Leave those envelopes or put them in my suitcase. You can count the money later. We don't want to miss the party."

"Barbara, the party for us is just beginning. It'll go on and on and on."

And that night, it did. At the reception, at Ray's parents' to pick up a traveling iron, out on the town afterwards, and finally at my mother's apartment, which she vacated for the night, I drank for the first time in months all that I wanted — with the inevitable result.

Somehow Raymond managed to drag me on to a bed. He yelled and yelled at me. "Why the hell did you get so damned drunk at my folks' house? Today, of all days!" I heard him as I lay unmoving, unable even to kick my shoes off. Apparently he soon fell asleep somewhere, because it was quiet.

We both awoke the next morning sick. "Oh, Barbara, I don't ever want to look at another drink again."

"What? I feel bad, too, but look what Mother's left for us for a wedding breakfast: champagne and smoked salmon and bagels... We've got to have champagne for our wedding breakfast."

"Well, you have two glasses, one for me and one for you."

"Raymond, that's awful. I don't know one husband who wouldn't drink champagne for breakfast with his wife on their wedding day."

"Well, Barbara, I am the one, the only one, and that's it." He held his head: "I honestly don't know how you can stand to drink it. I'm a boozer, but, boy, you sure have a hollow leg or something. Besides, we've got another big night ahead up in North Salem. That's going to be some party Annette's throwing."

Somewhere in the course of the day, Ray softened, and we had a bottle of champagne together, aside from the one I drank myself at breakfast to celebrate my own wedding. That night we were greeted with rice, given a huge master bedroom with a canopy bed, met tons of local and state politicians — who spoke with affected speech, which became more affected as the evening wore on. Money and wealth were talked about and flaunted. Ray and I had a ball, got absolutely smashed, and decided to fool everyone. Ray put on a stuffy phony British accent; I pretended to be a socialite who had recently had the biggest coming out party ever. We mingled with everyone and convinced them all. Every once in a while we huddled in a corner and laughed till our sides ached.

But the next morning, when I looked up at the canopy above and heard Annette scurrying around in the kitchen, I turned over with a groan. "Oooh, my head! Ray, I'm sick, very sick."

"No sympathy from me; I feel the same."

"How will I ever get on that plane for Spain at 5 p.m.?"

"Well, if you take some Alka Seltzer and eat, and don't have any liquor all day, except maybe one with dinner, you'll be okay by tomorrow." No liquor all day? He can't be serious! What's with him? I don't want to go all day without a drink! Projecting about the day ahead without any liquor at all, spelled complete boredom. Yet I knew my heart murmur was back, as I listened to the skipping beats and palpitations. Yesterday the champagne cured all that. I would have to figure out a way to get a drink for lunch.

Mother met us back at her apartment. When I suggested that we all go out for a martini before Ray and I took a taxi to the airport, I received a flat no from both Mother and Raymond. "Ray," I chided, "you're a real dud on our honeymoon." I couldn't figure Mother out. Insistent on getting my way, I demanded that we eat at the "Fish and Claw" restaurant across the street on Second Avenue, rather than Burger-Q. I knew I could order a drink there. And indeed, when the waitress came, I ordered a dry martini before Ray could bat an eyelash. But now, he looked almost frightened.

"Why did you order that drink when I told you no? Do you have to have it?"

"Of course not, Raymond. It's just that I've got to have a few drinks before I board a plane. I'm petrified of flying and have never flown anywhere sober."

Later, at the airport, we called Mother again to say goodbye. Then I cheerfully dialed Ray's parents' number. His father's somber, deep voice on the other end let me know he was not happy to hear from me. "Is something wrong, Dad?"

"Is something wrong! You were a cheap disgrace on your wedding night, here in my home. You were drunk! Don't you ever get that way here again, because my wife and I will have nothing to do with you if you do."

I held the phone stiffly to my ear. Unable to move or speak, I yielded the receiver to Ray, who talked to his Dad outside the booth. I just stayed where I was, frozen. Later, as we went to the plane, I couldn't cry. I was hot with shame and humiliation, desiring only to forget, to run away.

While Ray slept, I sat for eight hours, staring out the window, my nose pressed to the pane. The vacuum I had felt inside of me in the car when I left Meema and Peepa to go to New York was back.

I ached and didn't belong. Alone and lonely, trying desperately somehow, through the darkness of my mind, to understand my hurt, my pain, I looked at Raymond, I watched him sleeping so peacefully, while I churned inside. The security of our marriage was lost already. I became anxious and worried. Harassing thoughts of Ray leaving me sometime in our life plagued my tired, sleepless mind.

14

But the culture shock didn't fully hit me — until we were smack in the middle of a noon-day traffic jam. In lieu of honking their horns, which was forbidden in Lisbon, people were banging on the sides of their cars with all their might. Indeed, the doors of the drivers' sides of taxi cabs (old black Citroens, for the most part) were permanently dented, and the sound of all that thumping and banging was a little like being in the middle of a metal foundry. People were loud. Traffic lights and directional signals might as well not have been there; policemen waved their hands and held back cars so that we might cross the narrow, architecturally quaint, busy main street of this old, clean city.

I loved it! Every bit of the excitement and the noise, and the strange language, and swirling colors. Raymond and I held hands and watched with wonder as the short, attractive Portuguese people followed their daily routine.

Even the fragrances were exciting — exotic aromas from different restaurants followed us all the way to an elegant hotel, where we had several glasses of port while waiting for the flight that would take us to Monte Gordo, a small, quiet, idyllic spot on the southern coast of Portugal.

My brown-and-beige checked wool suit was a bit too warm for a sunny September twenty-second, I decided, as I looked at the thin, dark-skinned women enter the cocktail lounge. I couldn't take my eyes off them; they were chic, petite, with trim features, and their jet black hair was worn off their faces and foreheads. Trying to brush back my hair as I finished my third glass of wine, I decided I didn't like the way I looked. The new going-away suit that my Aunt Mary had gotten me seemed ordinary now, making me look chunky and shapeless. Raymond didn't seem to notice — he was talking about everything, unusually alive and filled with excitement. But until I looked more like these other women, I would be miserable. "Excuse me, Raymond, I'm going to the ladies' room to change my appearance."

"What's the matter with how you look?"

"Everything! I'll see you in a bit." A "bit" turned out to be three-quarters of an hour, spent taking all the curl out of my hair, sleeking it back and upwards into a chignon and redoing my entire face. I emerged strikingly different, and looking not too dissimilar from the almond-eyed beauties who were gracing the hotel's cocktail lounge.

"Yipes!" exclaimed Ray. "What did you do to yourself?"

"Raymond," I assured him, "I'm much finer-looking this way. Maybe I could even pass for Portuguese or Spanish?" Raymond laughed at me, with me, and together we took a cab to the airport. Although we were both exhausted from the flight — especially me, who hadn't slept at all — we couldn't wait to take in every bit of this adventure we were on. "Raymond, I couldn't be happier! Never, never have I had so much to be grateful for. I love you, and being here, it's — I'm so excited, I can't stand it! It's true, Ray! I've been alone and unhappy for so long, I don't know how to stand it."

Recalling some of the loneliness in the past, I bowed my head. Raymond lifted my chin and kissed me, reassuring me that our lives together were going uphill. "It's always going to be like this, Princess. None of the 'establishment life' for us. We're going to taste everything — one big party, with no one telling us what to do ever again."

Being the only Americans on the small airplane added to the

sense of adventure we were feeling. Somewhere during the plane ride I developed stomach cramps, and because they were familiar, I knew they would increase. I asked Raymond to get out the bottle of brandy that I had insisted he bring along for this purpose, but he told me I'd have to wait until we landed. Waiting for anything was never one of my virtues, and before long I began to be as nasty as I could be. But even this incipient temper tantrum was abandoned when the plane came to a halt, and I looked out the window and saw endless flat land. There were Portuguese people dressed in blue work clothes with large hats to shield them from the hot sun. It was so different from anything I'd ever seen before, that even my stomach cramps couldn't keep that sense of anticipation from welling up inside me. We picked up the little Volkswagen we had rented for our trip, and I curled up inside the front seat and waited as patiently as I could for Ray to produce the pint of brandy that I now wished that I had kept in my handbag. When all of our luggage had been stowed in the back seat and we had finished all unnecessary business, Ray finally pulled out the bottle I had been waiting for. "Whew! Ray, if you only knew how much I hurt, you wouldn't have made me wait so long."

"Boy, when it comes to a drink, I've never, never heard you say no!"

"That's ridiculous! And for heaven's sake, don't start getting picky on our honeymoon."

Ray was about to reply, when his attention was distracted by something happening in the street. "Hey! Look out there! Look at all those people marching in line. They're all in black and carrying a box — it must be a funeral!" He shook his head. "It must be about 110 degrees outside! I wonder how far they have to walk? These people look much poorer than the Portuguese we saw in the center of Lisbon, especially at that hotel we had a drink at."

My head was tilted way back, as I listened to Ray, my mouth tightly hooked onto the brandy bottle. His voice startled me, and brandy began to run down the corners of my mouth, as I moved my head forward to see what he was talking about. "What a sight!" I exclaimed. "All those people, young and old. . . . Look at the lines on the faces of those old men. It must be from the hot sun. Let's stop the car and watch the procession."

After feeling the warm brandy ease the tension in my stomach, I knew I wanted more from that bottle. There was only one way to get it: my cramps would apparently have to persist. Periodically moaning from pretended pain and doubling over so that I was practically on the floor of the car, I drew enough sympathy from Raymond that he let me finish the bottle of brandy. I felt so warm, so filled with romantic illusions of grandeur that they were no longer a daydream. They were real! The brandy did more than take away stomach cramps; it picked me up and put me on top of a mountain, where I could remain high, looking down over the entire world, yet not touched by anything.

Once on top of that mountain, I was not about to get down, and I didn't, not for one hour in one day of the glorious three-week honeymoon we had together. The hotel we were staying at was magnificent. Directly on the beach, it couldn't have been more romantic or picturesque. The lobby, with its handsome bellboys, desk clerks and guests that all looked as though they had recently been at a garden party at Buckingham Palace, made me feel like a debutante. I was beautiful, rich, and in love, and the more I looked around and the more brandy I drank, the more I became that debutante. Later that evening, I floated around the dance floor in a dark green chiffon dress. The only thing missing was a diamond tiara.

I wanted to impress Raymond, and he wanted to impress me. And that was what we did: impress each other into believing that even though I had grown up in Brooklyn, and he had come from plain Italian folks, we had somehow managed to overcome these inadequacies (we saw them as curses) and attain higher places for ourselves. At night, we would stand on our terrace and dream of all the things we wanted for our future. Our plans did not include a house of our own, or furniture, or children, or "American things". We talked of traveling, dining out, omitting Coke, milk and cocoa from our diet, along with hamburgers and hot dogs. Instead we would have bouillabaisse, scampi, paella, wine, brandy and champagne. We even agreed to do away with the American martini. "After being here," I mused, "I really believe Americans don't know how to eat or drink or even live, for that matter. Even the siesta is great! Maybe you can arrange to come home from work every day for a two-hour nap instead of a martini lunch."

Ray laughed. "I doubt if Market Dynamics would go along with that, but I'm only a block from our pad, and I'll be there when I can."

Tears of gratitude again came to my eyes. "Raymond, our lives couldn't be more perfect. We have such a fantastic start! My job at Mathematica is only one block from home, too, and with Marilyn as my immediate boss and friend, I've got it made." A tiny cloud drifted across my horizon. "What would your parents think if I ever lost that job, too? I hate clerical work. But Marilyn did say that I would be moving out front to the reception desk soon. It's quite a firm. They do a lot of work with the Institute of Advanced Study at the University. The people I'll be working with are all brains; actually, they're kind of square."

"Well, I'm sure that won't affect you. You'll brighten up the place, Princess, when you're there."

"C'mon Ray, really, I'm scared. You know, I'm even afraid to return to Princeton. I'm afraid of your folks. Never mind, I just won't think about anything that bothers me. Now, tor tomorrow: where are we headed?"

"Seville!"

The drive to Seville was beautiful. We had stopped for a picnic of bread, cheese, sausage and wine under an old oak tree, and so did not arrive in Seville until the shadows were lengthening towards sunset. The light of the day was softest then, and the whole city seemed bathed in a golden glow. Raymond and I agreed as we walked down the narrow streets and studied the beautifully wrought bronze doors of the old houses, and occasionally getting a stunning peek into floral courtyards, that this city would always be our favorite. It had everything — flamenco, bullfights, the best restaurants, shops and fleamarkets. I couldn't believe the price of leather goods, so much cheaper were they than in the States. Up well before Ray each morning, I embarked on jaunts where I smiled at everyone and had coffee with the local Spaniards at eight o'clock. Who could sleep! I was so excited, I didn't want to miss one minute of anything.

In my enthusiasm, I started trying on leather shoes. Before I knew it, I had bought six pairs. Carrying them in two bags, suddenly I wasn't so sure how Ray would react. I'd never done anything like that before with his money. Or was it our money now? The time had slipped away from me. It was eleven o'clock, and I'd been gone since eight. Growing increasingly anxious, I happened to glance into an old cafe, where men were lined up drinking brandy and coffee. Impulsively I decided to walk in and, standing alone, as far away from the looks of all these men with their black berets and cigarettes down to the butt, I quickly ordered and drank two Tio Pepes. That made all the difference. Back on the mountain top again, I even stopped to buy another pair of shoes on my way back. Quietly opening the door to our hotel room with my key, so as not to wake Ray, I was greeted with a loud "The door's open."

Raymond was angry. I'd never seen him so angry at me. "Where the hell have you been! This is my honeymoon, too, you know. Great, just great! Take my money and go out on a spree alone, leaving me here in a hotel room."

"Ray, I'm sorry, I thought you were sleeping. Wait till you see these shoes I bought, and so cheap."

"Shoes? How many boxes do you have there?"

"Seven."

"*What!* You mean you bought seven pairs of shoes and have the nerve to come back here with them, why. . . ." I didn't hear the rest, for I was dissolved in tears.

Later that evening at dinner, Ray apologized and wiped my eyes, but I continued to stay in my self-pity, feelings of unfairness and most of all, a broken heart. "You should have been glad that I bought those shoes," I rebuked him. "Don't you want to make me happy? You should. . ." On and on it went, until we finally made up around two in the morning, as we watched some exciting and fiery Flamenco dancers and drank ourselves drunk.

The following day was blistering hot. Our feet burned as we toured the city, looking for the right restaurant to have lunch in.

My mouth was getting dryer each day. "I don't know what's happening to me, Ray. I feel as though I'm becoming dehydrated or something. I can't wait until we get some wine."

"Well, you're just going to have to. I'd like to see a few things first. You know, we're not here just to eat, drink and barhop."

"Don't be so damned ugly, Raymond. What do you think, I'm uneducated? It's hot and I'm tired. . . ." The hassle continued until we sat across from each other, sipping wine.

Raymond spoke now, and in his voice was genuine concern. "Barbara, you seem to be getting more and more irritable lately, unless you're in a restaurant or cafe."

"Don't be ridiculous! That's your imagination."

"Well, maybe; I hope so." Unnerved by his solicitude, I wanted to devour the entire bottle of wine as fast as I could. I felt as though I was suffocating, and only the liquid in that bottle would revive me, but I didn't dare refill my glass myself. My opportunity came when Ray went to the men's room. I quickly poured another glass and drank it down before he returned.

When we finally left the restaurant, two hours and many brandies later (for Ray, too, loved the stuff), we headed back to our hotel for a siesta, then a bullfight. I was reluctant to attend, but Raymond persuaded me to go. "It's El Cordobes, and he's supposed to be the best." We went, and at first I loved the wild excitement, the festive occasion, the band, the handsome matadors and even the bulls. But it got so that I loved the bulls so much, I sobbed uncontrollably when they were brutally, and at the same time, artistically, killed and then dragged off. That was a side of the Spanish character that I didn't think I could ever accept.

Torremolinos, our next stop, was on the southern coast of Spain, and like Monte Gordo, it was a time to just bask in the sun, stroll, nap and live it up at night in the various cantinas along the side streets — dancing and singing and standing on tables and talking to strangers, and we did it all. Torremolinos was not as quiet as Monte Gordo; there were more tourists from all over, but especially the Scandinavian and German countries. I liked it there. Even cheaper than Portugal, it had more to offer, as far as shops, restaurants, night life and hotels.

I was glad we wouldn't be doing any more sightseeing until Madrid. September was a hot month to be walking city streets, unless the soles of your shoes were really thick. Our hotel was simple, but there was still a terrace, and the chamber maids always draped my nightgown over the bed. It was here that we drew closer than ever. The adjustment period after the wedding was over. Arguments about what place to visit first and when to go where, ended as soon as we departed from Seville. Now we could truly devote time to each other without any interruptions, including sleep. Raymond and I believed that we had more in common than most couples and knew how to make a marriage work. We began to feel quite superior to our friends back in Princeton, who had never traveled abroad. We were European travelers now, and intended to keep home, children, and parents' demands in the far, far future, as we lived each day to the fullest and laid plans for our next trip back to Spain.

Madrid was super — very chic, very old, and very magnificent. New buildings balanced the old ones, wealthy people who were dark and beautiful balanced the poor people in their shabby clothes. It was like Fifth Avenue or Broadway, but the people were different; they weren't American. We found ourselves sitting at a cafe, watching men and women go by, and lifting them above the Americans in just about every way. The way they carried themselves, looked, dressed, ate, drank, laughed, lived. On our last day in Madrid, Raymond bought me a really gorgeous gift — a rose beige suede coat that was handmade and all one skin with rich fur on the inside. That night we dined at Casa Botin, Hemingway's favorite restaurant, which was now ours, too.

The next morning, we would fly back to the States, and I wanted this night to never end. We talked about what our life would be like when we got home, and I was thrilled that Raymond agreed that we would have wine with meals. I couldn't wait to set up house and really become Raymond Tamasi's wife. I vowed that I would be eternally grateful and in love, and remembering the lonely times in the past, I threw my arms around Ray for protection. He was going to be my protector, and I would always be safe with him, just like Peepa.

That night, I could not sleep. I dreaded going back, and tossed and turned and wandered around our room, moving quietly so as not to wake Raymond. Could this really be the end of our honeymoon? I tried to tell myself that our love would grow steadily stronger, as we commenced our daily lives together, but as I looked out over the window at the sleeping city, tears came to my eyes. Overwhelmed with remorse, I found a bottle of wine we were going to take back with us. Assuring myself that it was perfectly okay to drink some of it because I was thirsty and dared not drink the water, especially with an eight-hour plane trip coming up, I opened the cork and took a long swallow. Careful not to wake Ray, I slid back into bed. However, I still tossed and turned. Feeling just the slightest warmth in my stomach, I craved more. About five or six times during the rest of the night, I stole out of bed and unscrewed the bottle cork in a corner of the bathroom with the door shut.

It must have been dawn when I finally fell off to sleep and late morning when I felt a rough shove on my arm. "Barbara, what the hell is this? Did you finish this bottle of wine last night? How could you? You knew I was planning to take it home. What's the matter with you?"

Trying to focus on Ray, who was standing by the bed in his pajamas holding out the empty wine bottle, I frantically thought for a moment, and then turned on him. "Raymond, how dare you accuse me of drinking that bottle of wine! Last night, I was dying of thirst while you were sound asleep. I didn't dare drink the water. You've had diarrhea for three days because of it. So, naturally I went to the wine. I had to have something. What did you want me to do? Anyhow, when I opened it in the dark — I left the lights off, so as not to wake you — I spilled most of the bottle. I happened to be standing over the sink, because that's where the water glass was, and well, the wine just went down the drain."

He looked at me with his head tilted, and one eyebrow raised. "Are you sure?"

"So help me, God; it's the honest truth. Why would I lie? I love you so much. Don't be that way. We can buy another bottle before we go to the airport. As a matter of fact, let's buy as many as we can carry; they're so cheap here."

Raymond apologized and put his arms around my waist. Relieved and somewhat shaky, I clung to him, holding him tightly around the neck. Looking over his shoulder, I seemed to see an old scene. I was sitting on Peepa's lap with my arms around his neck, and we were in the center of a circle. I clung to him, afraid. All around me was a raging storm. I was safe with him in the eye of that storm, but the storm moved, I was torn apart and left with nothing to hold on to. Clinging tighter around Raymond's neck, I shuddered. Was I in the eye of another storm?

15

It was October now, and Princeton, with the fall foliage in the university campus and along the suburban side streets, had to be one of the most picturesque places on earth. It was fun to see Witherspoon Street again, as we unloaded the taxi with all our baggage. All the evenings I walked down this street alone, not knowing where I was going but going just so I didn't have to stay in my room with the walls closing in on me, were now a memory that would never be a reality again. I had Ray. The first thing I wanted to do after putting our suitcases aside in our apartment, was to walk up and down the length of Nassau Street together. I imagined meeting people we knew and didn't know, smiling as we walked, prouder than anything that we were now one. I was jubilant and yet couldn't get used to this new-found happiness. Happiness that lasted more than a day was something new to me.

"Wow! Wait till you see what my folks have done for us, Princess," Ray called down the stairs. Hurrying up to see what he was talking about, I left my suitcase and ran. Standing inside the doorway, I looked all around the living room, then the kitchen and then the bedroom. Raymond's Dad had painted our entire apartment while we were away, and his mother had cleaned it, leaving little lace doilies and touches of warmth in different nooks and crannies. I jumped up and down and couldn't wait to thank them. "They must like me, Ray, to do this."

"Sure they do, Barbara."

I punched him. "Hey, you noodnik, you forgot to carry me over the threshhold."

What was left of October and the month of November was a continuation of our non-stop, merry-go-round honeymoon. Raymond was working in a new position with Market Dynamics in Princeton, bringing in a much larger salary than he had ever made before. I told myself that I liked my job at Mathematica, but the truth was, I was finding it difficult to cope with a marriage, apartment and job, especially since we didn't get to bed until the wee hours of the morning.

I did exactly as planned, and entertained — with one lavish dinner after another. My confidence in my cooking soared, with dishes like filet of sole covered with champagne, shrimp scampi in vermouth and garlic, boeuf bourguignon soaked in red wine. Raymond would arrive home weary from a day at work, to find the living room lights low, pillows all over the floor, shrimp and pieces of steak roasting and a full-course Japanese dinner, preceded by six or seven sake martinis. We even had little sake cups that whistled when we drank hot sake from them. And most evenings we took off, after we had come alive again at ten, to go to the Peacock Inn, La Haires or Black Bart's.

As November turned to December, the weather grew nasty now, and we blamed our colds and state of exhaustion on the New Jersey climate and too much work. It took me a long time and several cups of black coffee, aspirin and Alka Seltzer, sometimes Maalox too, to get going in the morning. The first month of bacon, eggs and toast for breakfast was soon just a fond remembrance.

"Ray, Ray, something's wrong with me. I must have some kind of illness. I don't feel at all well until evening. My hands shake and my stomach is queasy. My nose and mouth feel dry for most of the day, and sometimes my heart races terribly. You know, the other day, when I was typing at my desk and I felt sick?"

"Yeah?"

"Well, suddenly my heart jumped and then began to beat fast

and loud. It was so frightening, I started to scream. I thought I was having a heart attack and insisted Marilyn get me to a doctor. The doctor listened to my heart, and ordered an electrocardiogram right away."

"I know all that, Barbara; why are you bringing it up again? You were all right."

"Yes, but the fear is still with me and it's so awful, Raymond. I find it hard to function like this. What the hell is wrong with me?"

"I don't know, but I have noticed how moody you are. You go up and down like a yo-yo."

"Well, Scott, maybe I really am Zelda, after all?"

"C'mon, don't say things like that. You're not nuts. But I do know one thing that will help, and that is getting to bed early. I can't keep up with these hours and wild weekends myself. Tomorrow's Saturday. Let's not do a thing all weekend, okay? I did promise some of the guys at Market Dynamics that I'd help them move some boxes tomorrow morning, but after that we're free to just relax and catch up on our sleep."

"Raymond, can I please come with you tomorrow morning? I'll help, too. I'm afraid, lately, to be alone."

I usually tried to make a fairly decent breakfast for Ray on Saturday, but it was all I could do to get out of bed and put water in a pot to boil. Saying that I must have a virus or something, maybe even severe anemia, I stayed in bed as long as I could.

"Barb, why don't you stay home, while I go to Market Dynamics for those boxes? You don't seem to be feeling well, so rest at home. I'll only be gone for an hour or two."

"No, please let me go with you, Ray," I cried. "I don't want to stay home alone. I'm depressed for some reason."

"Okay, do whatever you want."

Barely able to get dressed, I tried to hide my sudden state of anxiety from Raymond. I'd felt queasy before and been hungover. In New York, prior to our marriage, I'd had intense periods of dry heaves, cold sweats and shakiness, but this, whatever the hell it was, seemed different. It was as if there was a vibrator operating inside my body. The racing and skipping heartbeats began to make me sweat and feel nauseous. I felt just awful and had no idea what was wrong, or what I could do to get straightened out. Rubbing my hands together, running hot water over them, even biting my wrist in the bathroom — I did everything I could think of to distract myself from this roller coaster I was on. Perhaps some fresh air would help, or even just going with Ray. I've got to get some fresh air. Listen, I'll meet you downstairs. I want to walk up and down the block myself."

My legs felt wobbly, as I hurried down the stairs from our apartment. Once outside, I gulped deep breaths of air, but they didn't seem to help. Standing in front of our landlord's clothing store, I began to feel as though the salesmen inside were watching me. Feeling uncomfortable and frightened, and not sure of what I might do, I went back upstairs.

"I thought you were waiting for me downstairs. What's the matter, Barbara? You look awful."

"Ray, oh Ray, I don't know, but I'm scared. Hold me, just hold me."

"C'mon, this is ridiculous! Call a doctor and get a check-up on Monday."

Monday? How could I ever survive until Monday? I was getting worse each minute. "I just won't think about how I feel; it's probably all in my mind anyway. Let's go, Ray."

Since it was such a nice day, I thought for sure I'd be better after the walk. I held Raymond's hand tightly, saying very little and trying not to listen to my heart, as it beat irregularly and loud. Market Dynamics was empty, except for one of the secretaries who had once dated Ray, and who now slunk out of an office in her bare feet, completely ignoring me and beginning to flirt with Ray, right in front of me. I had intended to stay and help Ray, but with each passing moment, I felt worse and worse. Suddenly gripped by a heavy feeling of impending doom, I asked Ray to take me home quickly. "Please don't ask me to walk home myself, I can't. I'm scared, and I don't know what of. Something is terribly wrong. Oh God, Ray, something is happening to me! Please help me!" I wished that I could cry then or break down, anything to relieve this tense, rigid state of anxiety.

Raymond didn't know what to make of it. "C'mon, snap out of

it. You only have two blocks to go, nothing's going to happen to you. It's broad daylight." But seeing how earnest I was in my pleading, he took my arm and helped me down the stairs. I now found it extremely difficult to put one leg in front of the other and my hands were shaking and flailing around uncontrollably. "Get into bed, Barbara. I'll be home as soon as I finish up with those boxes."

"Hurry, Ray, please, I'm petrified of being alone."

The door closed behind me. The sunlight glared through the room, blinding me. Looking out the window, I saw Jamie French across the street, the boy who cleaned our apartment every month. He was staring at me. Then I looked into another apartment, where I saw someone in there, too, staring at me. I ran to the side window and hastily pulled the shade, not daring to look in any more windows. Pulling down the living room shades, and then those in the kitchen and finally, the bedroom, I paced from one room to the other, wringing my hands. What the hell was wrong with me? With one hand I could feel my pulse, and it was racing. We had a clock with a second hand. Watching it, I sat down on the living room sofa and timed my pulse for twelve seconds and multiplied by five — 125. That's impossible! Yet I felt as though my body was about to throw itself all around the room.

Slowly raising my head, I found myself staring at the bar in the corner of the room. Ray had bought a bottle of sherry for the weekend — should I take a glass? Maybe that would calm me down. Looking at my watch, I noted it was 11:10. Ray was at MDI, and so was that secretary. My mind went skittering off in a thousand directions.

What were they doing there alone? I shouldn't have left him with her. I hate her, hate her, that bitch. Would Ray cheat on me? We've only been married a couple of months. No, of course he wouldn't do anything like that. I'm just having crazy thoughts. I needed help but didn't know whom to call or what to do. I felt trapped, locked in.

Rushing towards the bar and not knowing if the sherry would help or not, I thought I'd at least try it. With fumbling fingers, I struggled to get the new cork top off. I took a glass from the bar shelf, and attempted to pour myself a drink, but my hands were shaking so badly that I missed the glass and spilled sherry on the floor. "Damn it!" Grabbing a kitchen towel, I bent down and rubbed the liquid into the rug. It felt as though blood was rushing to my head, and the whole room began to move.

In the distance I heard an eerie whistle, and it became louder. But I heard it only in my right ear. "Where was that coming from?" I screamed. Frantic now, I picked up the bottle of sherry and put it to my mouth, drinking as much of it as I could. After coming up for air, I did it again, until I could feel that faint warm glow in my stomach. I put the bottle down and sat back down on the sofa. In a few moments my hands stopped shaking and my entire body calmed down. My pulse was down to 80. "That's it. *That's it!* Thank God, I thought of taking that drink! That's the answer, all right. That's all I need."

In fact, I felt so much better that I found it hard to believe I had been distraught an hour before. It was twelve thirty now, and Ray hadn't come home. Angry, I picked up the phone and called him at MDI. The secretary answered and made me feel all the more insecure, with her hard, almost taunting voice.

"Why haven't you come home?" I shouted, when Ray came to the phone. "You knew I wasn't feeling well. You said you'd be right home, and it's been two hours. You're there alone with that tramp — how can you do this to me?" and I slammed down the telephone and began to sob.

Another half-hour passed and there was still no sign of Raymond. I began to feel edgy again; those creepy, sick feelings were coming back. This time I didn't question why or what, but went instantly back to the place of relief, the bar. Since most of the sherry was gone now, I panicked, thinking Ray might get angry. Remembering how furious he was when I had finished all the wine in Spain, I took the bottle to the sink and mixed the remaining sherry with water. I believed that I had to do this, because Raymond just wouldn't understand and would make a scene that my nerves simply couldn't tolerate now, and I was proud of myself for thinking to add water to the bottle, as if I was the only person who ever thought of such an ingenious scheme.

When Raymond finally did come home, and attempted to explain why he was late, I slammed the bedroom door in his face and told him to go to hell. We didn't speak for several hours, while I remained in the bedroom and he in the living room. But then the effects of the alcohol began to wear off, and I felt the anxiety returning. That I could not handle alone, nor could I handle it without a drink. I still did not make the connection that what was happening to me had anything to do with the alcohol — only that alcohol brought relief. I emerged from the bedroom apologetic and awkward, clasping my hands together so that he wouldn't see them tremble, and asked him sweetly if we couldn't take a ride and go out to dinner.

"Gee, Barbara, do we always have to go somewhere? Couldn't we just stay home one night and relax? You always want to go somewhere."

"I know, and I'm sorry, but please, Ray, I feel as bad as I did this morning. The rooms are closing in on me. Bear with me and take me out. Please? I'll see a doctor on Monday, I promise."

"Oh okay, damn it all. I guess I have to give in to you, or you'll be miserable."

Within a matter of minutes, I again began to sweat and shake, my heart jumping. Wishing that Ray would disappear so that I could get a drink — just one to tide me over until we got to a restaurant — I asked him to go to the bathroom first to wash up. He did, but kept reappearing for one thing and then another. I was too frightened and not skilled enough at sneaking drinks to get myself one, so I paced the bedroom until we were ready to leave.

One of my favorite things to do was to ride in Ray's Austin Healey. I didn't drive, never having had an opportunity to learn, living in New York, but I loved sitting next to him with the top down, as the wind tossed our hair around the faster he drove. And the faster he drove, the more I liked it. However, this time, it was different, and not just because it was winter. As Ray stepped down on the accelerator, I panicked. "Don't go too fast. Slow down."

"What's the matter, Barb?"

"I don't know; I don't feel well." But even a normal speed began to bother me. Instead of feeling better as I thought I would,

I was worse. A pounding heart and cold, clammy hands, followed by nausea, made me grit my teeth and sit as straight as possible. I grabbed my stomach and doubled over, feeling suddenly as though my stomach was again being massaged inside by a vibrating machine. But this time the machine had apparently lost control and was running away wildly. I didn't know how long my body could continue to function with my heart pounding and skipping beats the way it was.

Fear gripped my mind. Ungodly, damnable horrors began to sweep in front of me. And I felt a presence, a power resting on my shoulders, that was now in control of me. I even heard this power echo orders to me: *Throw yourself out of the car. Put your right hand on the door release, open the door, and throw yourself out onto the highway.*

"No, no!" I screamed aloud.

Do it. Do it now. Now!

"Help! Help! Ray!"

"What's going on? Get ahold of yourself!"

"I can't!" My voice was frenzied. "Stop! Stop the car. I'm going to throw myself out."

"What? Are you crazy? What the hell is the matter? You're not going to do any such thing."

"Yes, yes, I am. Hurry! Hurry, I'm going to jump."

Ray brought the car to a screeching halt along the side of the road that went to Kingston. It was raw and damp outside. I flung open the car door and got out, breathing deeply. "Oh, Raymond, hold me, hold me. Something horrible is happening to me. I've lost control of my body and my mind. Oh God, oh someone, help me." Falling to my knees, I began to sob.

Raymond bent down and gently tried to tell me that this wasn't such an unusual experience. "Lots of people sometimes have fears of falling out of cars, jumping off bridges. You'll be all right."

"No, no, I won't. Listen, let's stop somewhere for a drink, please. Can't we just sit somewhere and have a drink?"

"Barbara, I thought we were going for dinner in the country. Can't you wait for a drink until then?"

"No, I want one now! Something is really bothering me. Can't you see I need to relax?"

"Okay, okay, the Embers is just up the road; we'll stop there."

But when I turned to get back into the car, I again felt the presence on the back of my neck. It was laughing at me. I actually heard its eerie laughter. It, he, was waiting for me to jump. He was still waiting and laughing. "No, no," I froze. "I can't get back in the car."

"C'mon, this is crazy! You can't stay here on the highway. Now get in." Seeing that I couldn't move, Raymond began to push me into the car. I cried and screamed, but got in. And once he started driving, I heard those damnable orders again. I locked the door, put both of my hands around Raymond's arm and made him promise to hold me and not let me jump. Somehow I knew that if I could just get to the Embers and have a drink, I would be okay. As soon as we pulled up in front of the door, I leaped out and ran inside, leaving Ray in the car. It was dark and dingy. A man sitting at the bar with a red, pocked face and bulbous nose turned to smile at me. Ignoring him, I sat on a stool at the other end of the bar. The bartender had his back to me and was wiping some glasses.

"Bartender? Bartender, please, I'm in a hurry."

He turned to face me, rather surprised. "What is it, ma'am?"

"Give me a double dry Rob Roy, and hurry." I wasn't sure at that point if Ray was even going to come inside, but in any event, I didn't want him to see my hands and arms so shaky.

The drink sat on the bar, in a cocktail glass, full to the rim. The amber-colored liquid glowed, and I watched a twist of lemon peel float to the top. I reached out for the glass, but as soon as I touched it, the drink spilled. Without thinking, I lowered my head and sipped as much as I could. I could feel the eyes of the bartender and the pocked man watching me. Then I tilted the glass and drank some more. Now I could lift the glass and finish the drink. As soon as I put the empty glass back on the bar, I looked up at the bartender who never once stopped watching me.

"Quick, give me another." I saw his eyes move from mine. He was now looking over my shoulder. Turning to see what he was looking at, I saw Ray behind me. He had been there watching, too.

16

It was a crisp, wintry Thursday evening. Ray had gone to play basketball with some of his friends, and I had gone to the liquor store. "Tony, may I please have a pint of vodka? Uh, Ray went to a game, and I think he might bring the guys back for a drink; I don't want to use the good stuff, understand?"

Tony smiled, but I felt uneasy. This was the third time this week I'd been in his store alone, and always for a pint of cheap vodka. My hands were trembling now, as I searched my bag for the right amount of money. But once that bottle was in my extra large handbag, I felt secure again. Upstairs in our apartment, I quickly poured some in a glass, added a dash of orange juice, and drank it down. That was better! I took off my coat and then had another. When I had finished half the pint, and had made several long-distance phone calls to relatives and friends, I suddenly thought of Raymond playing ball all this time. It was mean of him to just leave me. He must be sweating. He'll get sick and his parents'll hold it over me. Putting on my coat, I poured what was left of the cheap, lemon-smelling vodka into a plastic bottle and then stuck it in my handbag under scarves and makeup.

Steady and no longer frightened, I thought of Raymond proudly now, as I hailed a taxi on Nassau Street. I couldn't wait to see him. I thought he was the best player in Princeton, apart from Bill

Bradley. Remembering how, before he got sick, he had loved to play basketball, my eyes filled with tears. I paid the driver and ran off. His voice called me back: "Hey, lady! You dropped something."

Walking back to see what I had left, I followed his finger downwards to the plastic bottle filled with vodka lying in the street. "Oh, thank you, that's just some cheap perfume." I hope that wasn't one of Ray's relatives, I thought. Did he suspect or smell my breath? I banished those thoughts by finding a lonely stairway and finishing off the pint. Looking for Ray, I stumbled down the corridors leading to the university gymnasium. I heard noises and saw lights in the distance. Running now, I tripped over myself and landed face down on the floor. My bag opened, and everything fell out, including the plastic bottle.

Afraid to look up, I felt an arm, and heard the voice of one of Ray's friends, Augie: "Hey, Tamasi! Your wife's here. Hey, somebody get Tamasi; she seems out of it."

Trying to get to my feet and at the same time pull away from Augie's grip, I ran down the hall right into the gym. Ray was up at the near basket. I ran towards him, yelling, "Oh, Ray, here I am. It's me, Barbara. I've come to. . ."

I fell again and blacked out, not remembering the rest. . . vomiting at the gym, the looks from Ray's friends, and more than anything his own shock, disbelief and humiliation. I woke up the next morning with black and blue marks all over me, unable to get up, let alone go to work. I tried to remember, and tried not to remember. "Ray, I'm so ashamed! I promise it will never happen again!"

"What do you mean, never happen again? This is the fourth time this has happened in two weeks! I carried you home from your boss's party last week, and at Lalor and Claire's party you threw up all over their house and then passed out, after combing the place for booze. What's happening to you, Barbara? It's happening so quickly. Last night, you were hysterical, and I hit you so hard, I could have knocked a tooth out or worse. God, this is one hell of a nightmare!"

"Raymond, please don't turn away from me. I'm so sorry. I

love you. I do promise that it'll never happen again. I swear, I swear to God. I don't know what's wrong with me. I've never had trouble drinking before. I must be emotionally upset about something. Please, oh please, bear with me."

"Okay, okay, this is the last time I'm going to believe you. Now get dressed and try to get to work. And remember, we're having dinner at my folks' tonight, and we're *not* going to meet at La Haires first for 'a couple'. No booze at all, today, okay?"

"Okay, Ray. I really don't care if I have any or not."

Somehow I got to the office and made it through the day — at least until 4:30. I slipped out a half-hour early. My intentions were good in the beginning, but there was no possible way I could get through that day without a drink, rather ten drinks or whatever it now took just to feel normal, let alone high. I told Marilyn some story about a sore throat. Ray was going to be home about 5:10 tonight; that didn't leave much time. I couldn't go to Tony's again for still another pint of vodka. . . where could I go? Everyone, everyone in Princeton knew Ray's dad. There was another liquor store just past Toto's market, where Ray's grandmother and aunt and uncle worked. I hurried as fast as I could past the store, got the vodka, crossed the street and then ran quickly past his Uncle Willie's dry-cleaning store. But Betty, Willie's wife, was outside. She stopped me to chat. I always liked Betty, but if I didn't get into that bottle fast, something awful was going to happen. I ran past her, down our alley and opened the door leading up to the stairway. Already my hands were flailing, my head throbbing, and eerie sounds were drifting in and out of my mind. *You are going to die,* said the voice I had come to dread.

"No!" I screamed, as I stopped on the stairs and fumbled to open the bottle and guzzle down as much as I could. I hoped no one, especially Ray, would come through that door or down the stairs, but I couldn't take the time to get into our apartment. I sat on the stairs, repeatedly tilting the vodka bottle, dribbling it all over me and the floor, like a baby. But the wonderful, colorless liquid did its warming, calming, reassuring thing.

My body functioning again, I ran up the rest of the stairs and let myself in. I raced against time, first pouring the remaining vodka into two small plastic bottles, which I closed tightly and dried, then sprayed with perfume. I quickly finished the last of the pint, but just as I was about to hide it somewhere, I heard the downstairs door open, and recognized Ray's footsteps on the stairs. I grabbed my handbag, threw the plastic bottles inside along with the pint, and ran down the hall to the bathroom, where I frantically slammed the door. There was no lock, but there had never been any concern about anyone opening the door, if it was closed. I heard the upstairs door open and close, and then Ray' voice: "Barbara, are you home?"

"Yes, yes, I'm in the bathroom. I'll be out soon, I have an upset stomach."

I couldn't leave the bottles in the handbag. Ray had seen one of them in my stuff at the gym, and would be checking my bag, especially before going to his parents'. Taking them out of my bag, I tucked each one inside my bra, then buttoned my blouse, which fortunately was loose-fitting. I brushed my teeth, washed my face and gargled with perfume, drinking some of it. Trying to decide where to hide the vodka bottle, until I could throw it out tomorrow, I heard Ray's footsteps coming down the hall.

"Oh, *no!*" I opened the window facing the alley and flung the bottle an instant before Ray threw open the bathroom door. We both heard the loud crash of glass on pavement.

"What the hell's going on in here? Are you nuts? This morning you said this wouldn't happen again. And that you wouldn't drink today. We were going to my parents' tonight. I don't know what to do any more."

I stood there, numb, as Raymond turned and walked down the hall. His head hung low, he seemed beside himself with despair. I begged and promised and pleaded, and he finally agreed to take me along with him. The plastic bottles tucked inside my bra were empty when we returned home.

Christmas 1968, our first Christmas, had passed. Raymond bought me a present that meant a lot to me. Knowing of my love for art and that I had stopped painting years ago, he was thrilled when I opened a beautiful set of oils, an easel, brushes, palette, every possible piece of equipment. I just hugged him and cried. I loved Raymond and wanted to show him that I did. Yet I was afraid, too, afraid of losing him. At least once a week I was plagued with nightmares of Raymond standing at our door ready to leave. I would be at his feet, pulling on his trousers, begging him to stay. In my dreams, there was another woman he was going to.

I hurt, ached and dreaded these dreams of Ray leaving me, and the even worse realities of noises and faces on the wall when I closed my eyes. That awful clown, his mouth drooped open, kept getting bigger and bigger. Once I jumped out of bed and ran around the room, landing on Ray's chest. He awoke panic-stricken, believing that I had completely lost my mind. By now, he was also on to my bottle-hiding. So I had to spend every lucid moment figuring out new hiding places. I had bottles folded in towels in the linen closet, in empty cereal boxes, in my tall high-fashion boots, even in the oven (and it was lit once). And I always tried to slip one under the mattress, in case I needed a fast slug in the middle of the night. What we had stocked in our bar I was constantly drinking and watering down. Each night, Ray searched the house in a grim game of hide-and-seek. He'd pull my pints, flasks and half-pints from everywhere, and always I discovered new hiding places. I made a slit in the sofa, stuck a flask inside and then sewed it up. I put vodka in my paint jars, filled turpentine bottles with it. But I had to have it! I had to drink to live! And each time I was discovered, I begged and pleaded to Ray, on my hands and knees, to have mercy, to help me, to stay with me and even to kill me.

He did everything he could think of, even slapping me and flinging me across the room. One night, he came home early and found me with a bottle of whiskey in my hand. "That's it, I've had it! It's me or the bottle," and he wrenched it out of my hand.

"Don't, don't say that, please! I want you, but give me back that bottle."

Raymond shook the contents in my face. "You're nothing but a drunken slut. I'm getting out of here now. You can have your bottle."

He threw it on the floor, and slammed the door. I got down on the floor in the kitchen and tried to lick up whatever whiskey was left. Then I stared at my left arm. There was an old scar there, where I had drunkenly slit my arm with a razor once. Sobbing loudly, unable to catch my breath, I pounded the kitchen floor. "What's happened to me? Someone help me. Oh, I want Raymond or I want to die."

Ray did come back, and somehow our marriage limped along. Spring 1969 came, and it was unusually hot for May, so with our friends Joe and Kate, we headed for the Jersey shore early Sunday morning. Any time we had an opportunity to be with them, I was more than agreeable. Joe was never without a drink and always had an extra batch of something made up for the car ride. When he pulled out a beer at 10 a.m., and offered me one, I grabbed it. Raymond winced, as if to say, here we go again. He pulled the can out of my hand. Leaning over to me in the back seat of the cream-colored convertible, with the top down, I could barely hear him tell me to "cool it for the day". The wind felt good against my face, blowing my hair off my shoulders. I tried to concentrate on the crisp air, but my mouth was dry, my hands were taut and my heart began its usual palpitations. I had nothing in my handbag, or anywhere. Somehow, if he wouldn't let me drink Joe's booze on the beach, I would have to find a way to get something. But Ray watched me all day. It wasn't until 3 o'clock that I was able to steal away for a pretend hotdog. I drank as much beer as I possibly could in fifteen minutes, but it didn't even scratch the surface.

My chance came later that evening, when Joe ordered two bottles of red wine with dinner. I drank mine as fast as they were poured, counting on the fact that Raymond would not make a scene in a restaurant. I even invited them back to our apartment after dinner for a goodnight drink. "Why did you do that, Barbara?" Ray whispered to me, as we were leaving. "I have to be in New York early tomorrow."

"Oh Ray, just one. Anyhow they've been so hospitable to us, bringing all this food and liquor and beer to the beach, even offering to pay for dinner." I got my way. I could always find a reason, an excuse to arrange for another drinking situation. I had to! But I didn't know I had to, then; I just thought Ray was becoming a drag.

Now my mind began to work overtime at planning and figuring out ways to drink. I knew that, back at our apartment, I wouldn't be as conspicuous with two other people there, and I wasn't. When it came to pouring my own drink, I made it tall and very weak. Ray was impressed. To and from the bathroom, however, out of sight of the living room, I opened the broom closet and managed to drink a fifth of Ray's bottle of Campari that he had been saving. Somehow, sometime that night I got to bed.

The next morning, I felt the same as I had been feeling for the past seven months: lousy. For that matter, I couldn't even remember when I had last woken up bright-eyed, hungry, and eager to start the day. I looked in the mirror and was grateful for the redness of the windburn that would distract attention from my bloated skin and puffy eyes.

My face felt unusually hot as I walked to work, greeting people, mostly Ray's relatives. The vibrations that I usually felt throughout my body after a weekend's bout with booze were more intense than at any other time. At my desk, I squirmed and made excuses to go downstairs for coffee or cigarettes. Up to now, I had not done any drinking on my job, or on my lunch-hour for that matter, except for a rare special occasion. The hiding of bottles and sneaking of drinks were confined to after five and throughout the weekend. And because I did not drink anywhere around my job, I didn't agree with Ray who was now saying that I drank too much, no matter what the reason.

"Raymond," I would reply, insulted, "a person who drinks too much or has a problem with drinking has to drink when they wake up and all day long. How dare you accuse me of overdrinking, you stuffed shirt."

But even the three tuna-fish sandwiches and two milk-shakes at 9:30 a.m. didn't help. No amount of coke, ice cream or Alka Seltzer lightened the effects of this unusually bad hangover. And when I had positively stuffed my gullet, I suddenly threw up in the ladies room; however, instead of feeling relief, I felt worse than before. At about 11:30 that morning, Marilyn, my immediate boss and friend, asked me to have lunch with her at the Chinese restaurant on Witherspoon Street.

"Yes, sure. I feel lousy today. Maybe some Chinese food will help. Besides, I'd like to hear all about your vacation." I usually had lunch at the Princeton Tea Garden alone or with someone three times a week, that was how much I loved Chinese food. Often I ordered a double bowl of Won-ton Soup and Shrimp Chow Mein as I did this day.

My stomach was empty now. We were chatting about her vacation, the job, nothing really important. I was aware of feeling very hot, especially on the top of my head and in my face. Very hungry by the time the soup came, I finished it quickly. Marilyn was talking, and I had taken about three bites of Shrimp Chow Mein when suddenly my face felt as though it was on fire. The fork I was eating with flew out of my hand. I began to shake violently.

"Barbara, what's the matter?" Marilyn put down her fork and began to get out of her seat to call for help. Sounds and voices were distorted and echoed in my ears. My heart was running away with itself.

I began to scream. "Help, *help!* Something terrible is happening to me! Help, quickly, I've lost control, I'm. . ." Within a few minutes, people were turning around in their seats, waiters were circling around our booth. Marilyn was quiet and stunned. Every part of me was trembling uncontrollably. It was the most horrifying experience thus far, physically and emotionally.

I felt a hand on my wrist and looked up into the face of a tall grey-haired man. "It's all right, ma'am. I'm a doctor, a psychiatrist. I was sitting at the next table. Now try to relax, your pulse is very rapid. Calm down!"

Calm down! What a joke! That would be like telling a laughing hyena to stop laughing. As far as I knew, I was in the middle of dying, and he was telling me to calm down! "Doctor, I have to throw up, I'm very nauseated."

"No, no, you can't. You can't throw up now. Try to hold it. A police car is coming to take you to Princeton Hospital."

"Oh God, what's happening to me? I can't breathe, I've got to throw up! Why am I going to the hospital? Am I having a heart attack, a nervous breakdown, a seizure? *What is it?*"

"I don't know what's wrong; that's why you're going to the hospital. Your whole body is shaking, and your heartbeat is very rapid. Relax." Relax, relax, relax — I had come to hate that word. What do you mean, relax? What do you do when you can't relax?

I heard a loud siren and saw people gathering in the doorway of the restaurant. The Chinese waiters were running around frantically, telling everyone to make a way for me to get through, and also adding that I was having some kind of an attack that had nothing to do with the food. I was scared to death when I saw two policemen come towards me. Yet I was glad to be getting away from this psychiatrist who kept telling me to relax. He handed me to one of the policemen, who tried to lift me to my feet. I had lost all control of my legs and fell down on the floor of the booth. The policeman bent over and tried again to pick me up and lift me out. He motioned to his friend, and they took an arm on each side of me and carried me out into a waiting police car.

"Marilyn? Where's Marilyn? Please tell her to come with me. I don't want to go alone. And oh, my husband. He works at Market Dynamics, but he's in New York today!"

Across the street I could see Willy and Betty's cleaning store. They were standing outside, probably wondering what all the commotion was about. I hoped they didn't recognize me. I lowered my head in the sunlight and bit my lips as tears rolled down my cheeks.

The two policemen carried me into the emergency room. One of them I didn't want to leave; he looked concerned, as if he cared. This policeman said, "You'll be okay, ma'am. Good luck." He held up his fist to me as if to say, "Hang in there; you'll make it."

Two nurses were around me, asking questions. I could barely tell them my name. "Please, please what's happening to me?" They were cold as ice and didn't say a word. They didn't touch me; they just kept staring at me.

"I feel worse, I'm so scared. I want my husband." Tiny pins and needles that began in my feet, worked their way through my entire body. Each muscle became taut. I could feel my mouth twist to the left. My hands were curled and unable to move. I had become catatonic. I couldn't talk, but I could think. The doctor who had glanced my way ten minutes earlier and walked away after I begged him to help me, now came over with a needle. The nurses were standing over me.

"Give her oxygen." A mask was put on my face. I felt as if I was suffocating. A stroke! That was it! Either I had had a stroke, or a heart attack, or a severe nervous breakdown. The movie "Freud" quickly flashed through my mind. The female patient had become paralyzed. Had I gone mad? Then I thought of Ray, and how much I loved him. How I wished he were there with me, to hold me, to look at me. I might never see him again. Oh God, God, where are you? I called out to God, to some power that might be out there, that might be good and that could help me. I began mentally to ask for help. Oh help me, *help me!*

I don't remember how long I was like this, but all of a sudden, as quickly as the attack had come, it passed. My hands and fingers moved. The nurses sat me up. I could move my legs, although I was still wobbly and unable to stand. I began to throw up as soon as I was upright. Someone took me to a bathroom, where I sat on my hands and knees, hovering over the toilet bowl for about an hour with the dry heaves.

Back on the cot, I saw Dr. Ullman. He had been to see Ray for pneumonia, and I had used him once or twice for a virus. Since I gave his name as our family doctor, he was paged. "What happened to you, Barbara? No one here seems to know what the problem is yet."

"Oh doctor, I'm so glad to see you." Sobbing, I told him what had happened and how frightened I was.

"Well, let's go over your entire day and see what we come up with."

I recounted the day, the restaurant and then added: "Oh Dr. Ullman, we were at the beach most of yesterday and well, I drank a lot all weekend. Doctor, I wonder if this could have anything to do with alcohol?"

"Why, that's ridiculous, a nice Jewish girl like you. I've seen drinkers, and you don't seem to be one of them. Don't worry, we'll get to the bottom of this. In the meantime, I'm giving you another shot and sending you somewhere to rest and sleep. Now, is anyone home?"

"No, my husband is working. I have no one in town except my in-laws... Yipes, I can't go there like this."

"Well, you'll have to. Give me your mother-in-law's telephone number; I'll call her."

He came back a few moments later. "It's all set, Barbara. Your mother-in-law is home waiting for you. Now I'm also sending along a prescription for Librium. It's a tranquilizer. I want you to take two right away, and then one four times a day. I'll see you Wednesday morning in my office."

"Doctor, will these pills help me, I'm so sick?"

"Just take them as prescribed and I'm sure they'll help."

"Uh, one other question. What about liquor? I always have a drink to relax in the evening. Is it okay to mix cocktails with these pills?"

"No, definitely not! Remember what happened to Dorothy Kilgallen?"

"Yes, I remember."

Waiting to take me was the same nice policeman who had brought me to the hospital. He had waited, never leaving the emergency room. Marilyn, too, was there. As he took my arm, he smiled: "You're Mrs. Tamasi. I know your husband, a fine boy."

"Yes, thank you, he is. I wish he was here."

"Well, I'm to take you to your in-laws; they'll take good care of you till he gets home."

Marilyn and I were in the back, the policeman driving the car. I soon got panicky again. "I don't want to go up Nassau Street. I don't want people to see me."

"Okay, Mrs. Tamasi, we'll go the back way."

We drove just a few blocks and my hands started to shake again, and my legs, too, were trembling. I looked down and saw my stomach moving in and out. "Marilyn!" I screamed, "look, look what's happening!"

"Oh, no! You must be convulsing or something."

"Sir, take me back to the hospital."

"Mrs. Tamasi, let me try to get you to your in-laws' house; the doctor said you'd be okay."

We drove one more block. I was shaking violently now. The power that had told me to throw myself out of our Austin Healey was back, resting on my shoulders. He was big and loomed over me. I felt him. *You are not being taken to your husband's parents' home,* he told me. *You are going to an asylum for the insane. Your husband was called at work and gave his verbal agreement.*

With a shriek, I looked out the window. Seeing a store that I didn't recognize, I began screaming. "I know where you're taking me, all of you. I'm going to a hospital for the mentally insane. No, no I won't go. Help, *help.*" I began to roll down the window and scream. Everything became distorted in sight and mind. I hallucinated, rocked and shook.

I was back at the hospital in minutes. After throwing up some more and having another injection, I was again carried out by this policeman, who had to be a saint. I tried to apologize to him, but it didn't matter. His concern had become so genuine. Marilyn was still beside me, stiff and unable to speak.

My father-in-law was waiting outside as the police car drove up Southern Way. As the policeman lifted me out and handed me to him, I could hear Ray's mom say: "Hurry up, Don, bring her in. I don't want the neighbors to see this." Ray's dad carried me, still weak and shaking all over, to the sofa. He left for work, and Ray's mom and I were alone until Ray came to get me many hours later.

I took the pills the doctor had given me all that day and night, but discontinued them the next day. "Remember what happened to Dorothy Kilgallen," he had said, and if I had to choose between alcohol and medication, there was no choice; I had to drink.

"I'm much better, Raymond. I don't need those pills; a couple of drinks will relax me just fine. By the way, I mentioned my drinking to Dr. Ullman in the hospital, and he said that I definitely don't have a drinking problem, so that's not it at all. I have a feeling it's this town and place and. . . it's driving me nuts. Everybody knows what you're doing all the time. I can't take it!" But then my mood suddenly changed from anger to fear. "Ray, I'm scared. Please come with me tomorrow to the doctor's. I don't want to go alone. I'm afraid to go to work, to go to lunch, to go anywhere alone. What if this awful thing happens to me again, anywhere, even on the street? Oh Ray, what is *wrong* with me?"

Ray shook his head. "I wish I knew. Look, I have to go to work. You'll just have to go alone. Maybe Marilyn can drive you or take a cab."

The next morning in the doctor's waiting room, I paced the floor with anxiety until I was called into his office. "Barbara, it's so good to see you." Putting out his hand to greet me, he sat down behind his desk. Dr. Ullman was a middle-aged man, dark and rugged-looking with an unusually deep voice. "Well, I've got some very interesting news about what I think is wrong with you. I went back to the Princeton Tea Garden that day to do some investigating. Won Ton soup and all their food is loaded with monosodium glutamate. And a recent article from Columbia Medical School relates some of your symptoms to the effects of MSG. As a matter of fact, I'd like to have you appear before a group of doctors at Princeton Hospital to answer questions — will you? And aren't you relieved?"

Relieved — I was stunned. "Yes, yes, I will answer and go anywhere, but are you sure? I eat Chinese food all the time and have never gotten sick."

"I know, that's what the waiter said too. He said you were always in there, eating double portions of everything. Well, maybe it's cumulative."

"But doctor, I still feel anxious." Crying now, I looked up at him. "I hope this is all it is, because frankly I don't know what it is to feel good or normal. I've thought it was my mind."

"You're fine, fine. Go along now, and I'll get in touch with you."

"Okay. Er, it's still okay to drink liquor, isn't it?"

"Sure, sure, just don't mix it with those pills I gave you."

I walked outside, took a deep breath and tried to feel happy about what I'd heard, even excited about the fact that I had something unique and might appear before a board of doctors at Princeton. But it was no use; I was completely driven by anxiety. I had that presence with me now all day and all night long. That power, that awful, horrible power, told me what to do, what not to do, what people were thinking about me, and what would happen to me; it sat resting on my shoulders, laughing, gloating and mocking me.

You can't go to lunch like other people. You'll have another attack. Stay at your desk or go home alone. Draw the shades at home; the neighbors are watching you. Raymond doesn't like the way you're acting. He's going to leave you one day, the way your father left your mother. You are going to end up alone, lonely and crazy.

"No, no!" I often screamed back in terror to myself. Sitting at my desk, unable to type, aware of everyone's curious glances, I wrung my hands together, bit my nails, ran to the ladies' room, walked the halls, rode the elevator, anything to kill time till five o'clock. Over and over again, I would envision what it would be like at five o'clock, drinking that first drink, then the second and third. Each day I promised myself I'd stop at three, just until I got enough of life's blood into me, to enable me to function. And that is what alcohol had become to me — life's blood. I could not live without it.

And every evening, beginning at five o'clock, the pattern for the night until the wee hours of the morning had been established. I always awoke the following day saying: "Ray, I'm sorry! Please, oh please, forgive me. I promise I won't do it again." But I'd said the words so often they sounded hollow, even to me.

"What the hell is going on here? You refused to come home, and so I left you at Black Bart's at 10 o'clock. You didn't get home until 5 a.m. Where the hell were you? You crawled up the stairs. I actually found you on the stairs. I don't know who brought you home, or how. Barbara, I don't know what to do any more. We've got to do something. The whole town knows. You are not to set foot in Tony's liquor store again. I'm cutting off all charge accounts."

"Okay, okay, I'll do anything you say." He put his coat on. "Ray, where are you going?"

"To visit Linda at the hospital. Remember, it's Saturday." Saturdays had become difficult days for both of us since Ray's sister had come down with tuberculosis. For Raymond, it was a reminder of the dreaded disease running through his family, and the suffering they all went through. I dreaded going to the hospital, but dreaded staying home alone even more.

"Oh God, take me with you, Ray."

"Who are you kidding? You can't even walk. Stay in bed all day. I've got a Rutgers reunion tonight. You've got to shape up." Ray turned to leave. As he opened the door, I got out of bed, and practically crawled after him into the living room.

"Raymond, don't go, please. I'm scared. Something horrible is going to happen to me."

"Don't be ridiculous. Now, look: I've got to go."

"Nooo, I'm scared to death." The door closed. I turned to go back to the bedroom. Looking down, I saw a huge black bug running fast across the kitchen. I screamed and made my way back to bed. This power loomed over me. I pulled the covers up over my head. My heart was racing. I was sweating. I uncovered myself. Across the wall was a shape. I stared more intently at it. I saw a big ugly mouth. 'Oh God, someone help me, help me." I finally decided to call Dr. Ullman. "Please, please, doctor. Something terrible is wrong with me. My pulse is 125; Ray took it this morning. I'm seeing and hearing strange ghoulish things. Please help me. Is this normal?"

"No, Barbara, it is not normal, but I don't know what is wrong with you."

During the next few weeks, he tried to find out, but since we had ruled out my drinking as a possible cause for my "anxiety seizures," we were both mystified. Finally, the only thing he could suggest was extensive testing.

17

"No, no, I don't want to go away! I'll do anything but that. Ray, I'll stop. I promise I'll stop. I swear to you that I won't take another drink. Please, please believe me this time."

Ray looked grim sitting beside me. His pale face, unusually drawn, was showing the strain. At Ray's prodding I had begun to see Dr. Ullman weekly. He offered his counsel and guidance, along with medical advice, in the hopes of getting to the bottom of my sudden and extreme anxiety. We had just come back from my third Monday noon visit. Up to this point, I had been building a case for myself, causing both me and the doctor to see my environment as the cause for my "breakdown".

Raymond had decided to accompany me on this visit, which raised some concern in my mind. Things were going very well between me and the doctor, and I didn't want Ray saying anything that might disrupt our relationship. My fears came upon me, though, as soon as Ray burst into the doctor's office and took a seat alongside of me. Looking from me to Dr. Ullman, his eyes filled with rage. "Booze!" he exploded. "That's what's ruining our marriage, doctor. I came here to tell you exactly what's been going on! Has she," pointing his finger at me, "told you that she hides bottles all over the house?" Dr. Ullman leaned forward, stunned. "Has she told you that she's drunk every afternoon by

5:30, when I get home from work, with dinner usually burned or not even made? Has she told you that she's up in the middle of the night, bouncing off walls and trying to find the bottles she's hidden? Has she told you that we have a pile of empties in the back yard, that she's thrown out of the bathroom window?"

Dr. Ullman was speechless. His face reddened with embarrassment at having been so taken in, and when he finally spoke, it was with the utmost gravity. He outlined medically exactly what I could expect, if I continued drinking this way. He ended by telling me that if in the next three days I didn't stop, I would have to go away alone for several months, where I would not be allowed to have one drop of liquor. "And even after that, if you are a true alcoholic, you may never be able to stay stopped."

Reality hit hard. My God, I thought, what he must think about me. All this time, all these hours alone in his office and I never once was honest with him. But for him to suggest that I might be an alcoholic — that if I had one drink, it controlled me and my actions from that moment on — that was too much. I would show him who was an alcoholic!

For the next two and a half days, I used every ounce of self-control I had in me, to stay away from alcohol. I felt lousy, and deprived, and I determined to make Raymond pay for divulging my secret. Every minute, every hour, was extenuated. When would these three days be up? I looked to and longed for that third day. For in my mind I believed and convinced Ray that if I could abstain for three days, then I was certainly not an alcoholic. "A true alcoholic could never go without a drink like this, Ray. And I don't even miss it. As a matter of fact, I don't care if I ever have another drink again. I just wonder if you could stop and feel the same way."

My three days were up early; at the end of work on the second day, I rewarded myself with just a half-bottle of wine for two at dinner. And if Ray had not conceded that, I would have found some way to do it anyhow. For beneath the detached facade, I was chafing, like a mad dog, to feel the warm glow inside that had become an inner lining, protecting me from the cold outside. But I was careful to sip my wine and even leave a little in the glass, demonstrating to Ray that, now that "my system had been cleaned," I could, in fact, drink like a lady.

It was a little harder convincing Dr. Ullman the following Monday, that I really didn't have that big a problem with booze. Despite all my persuasion, he insisted that I stop drinking altogether for several months. "See how you feel and what it's like for, say, three months."

"No, I don't think I need to do that. Certainly, I could stop for three months, even six, but there's no reason for it. I know exactly what happened to me. I simply began to rely on alcohol for a while, because I had just gotten married and — never mind, I know why. I will not allow myself to ever drink that way again. And since I know the reasons now for my anxiety and excessive drinking, I don't think I need to come here any longer."

"Suit yourself, Barbara. I wish you lots of luck and really hope you can stop; otherwise you're in for a long, lonely trip that often ends in suicide." The words rang with authenticity, as did his tone, manner and handshake. It frightened me, as I turned to leave his office for the last time.

Throughout that summer of '69, I continued to exhaust every excuse I could think of for my drinking. I also found new hiding places, new liquor stores, and ways of procuring liquor. One time, I arrived with a pint of vodka tucked in the seat of my jeans. I tried to hurry down the hall to the bathroom, but Ray insisted I sit down on the sofa. When I refused to sit, he became suspicious, stood up, and pushed me down. The bottle didn't break, because I fell to one side on my thigh. Another great secret hiding place had been discovered!

It was a long, depressing summer. With Linda ill at Deborah Sanitorium, both Ray and his parents were depressed. Their deep sense of unfairness was aggravated now that this insidious illness had reared its head again. The long car ride each Saturday, and the visit at the hospital became almost intolerable for me. It pointed to the fact that my craving to drink was becoming increasingly worse.

One afternoon at the hospital, I thought I was going to have another "Chinese restaurant" attack. I shook and came unglued, throwing up uncontrollably in the bathroom in Linda's room. I paced the hospital floor with a cold rag on my head, waiting for the moment when my body would become catatonic again. Things did not progress that far, however, and several Libriums later and several drinks later that evening, I found myself functioning again. After that, I made sure that I never went anywhere, unless I was supplied with my own liquor and was near a bar or liquor store.

Afraid to ever be alone, especially at night, I also made sure I had someone stay with me every evening I was alone, which meant four or five nights when Ray finally consented to have a hernia operation, and it turned out to be a double hernia. I sat across from Mrs. Tamasi in the hospital waiting room, drunk. I was drunk when I kissed Raymond goodbye as he was being wheeled up to the operating room and I was drunk when I slumped over him when he awoke hours later. And in the middle of the night, after sneaking up the hospital stairs with Giuseppe, a co-worker of mine at Mathematica who had become a good friend of ours, I was so drunk that I drooled all over Raymond, telling him I loved him and was worried about him. Even through sedation and pain, Ray glared at me. "Get her the hell out of here, Giuseppe, before I kill her!"

In a constant stupor, I continued going to work while Ray recuperated for six weeks at home. The last time I was carried home from work at 11 in the morning in a blackout, I hailed a cab and went somewhere, where I continued to drink until I wound up home again somehow. This time was different. The next day I collapsed at the reception desk at 9:30 in the morning and had to be dragged home by two co-workers who took pity on me. They thought perhaps that the fresh air might revive me, but it didn't. In a blackout I could function, even though I didn't know what I was doing or where I was going, but this time Ray found me cool to the touch and had to strain to find my pulse. It was weak and irregular, and when he finally revived me, his face was agonizing. I was so cold. No amount of blankets and hot tea could warm me. "Oh my God, Raymond. I'm so sorry. I'm killing myself, us, our lives.

Oh my God! Raymond, I'm going to die." This time Ray was unable to do anything but fold his arms, bend over and cry.

One hour later, after swearing up and down that I would never, never again take another drink, I retrieved an unopened pint in the guest room under the mattress. Half the bottles I hid, I never found anyhow. But oh, how I needed a drink! I was so cold. On my hands and knees, I lifted up the bedspread and stared at the neck of the bottle. "I've got to stop this. Oh my God, help me." I saw Ray in my mind before me, now asleep in our bedroom. How I wanted to keep my promise to him! I ached to keep it, if that's possible. Yet my body craved that drink. My clammy hands were shaking as they both grabbed the bottle, my mouth twitched, and I dribbled like a baby as I drank.

The next morning, I was unable to get out of bed. When Ray left the apartment for something, I crawled to the guest room to see if there was any more liquor in the bottle. One bottle was empty, but there was another, half full of rye. I didn't remember going out last night; how did I get another bottle so late? I drank as much as I could of the rye and crawled to the telephone. Hoisting myself up against the wall with the help of a kitchen chair, I called Marilyn at work to tell her I wouldn't be in that day. No matter how much I drank, I couldn't get high. I wasn't even able to completely steady the shakes, so when Raymond returned and found me resting in bed, he thought I was sober.

"Are you going to try to go a day without —" The knock on the door interrupted his sentence.

From the bedroom, I could hear Marilyn's voice. "Hi, Ray, may I come in for a few minutes? I'm on my lunch hour. I'd like to see you and Barbara."

"Sure, come on in, Barbara's in bed, but I'll get her."

Ray didn't have to get me, I had already gotten to my feet. I stood behind him, facing Marilyn.

I motioned to her to have a seat on the sofa. I sat down huddled next to Ray. Marilyn turned to face us both. It was obvious that whatever she had come for, it was not to bring good news. A wrinkled brown paper bag was in her lap. Marilyn handed it to me and told me to open it. I took it, my hand trembling as I opened it and looked inside. Every muscle of my face tightened.

"Take it out, Barbara," Marilyn said. I shook my head, and handed the bag back to her. She opened it and pulled out a pint of Four Roses, three-quarters full. A long silence followed. Finally Marilyn said what she had to. "I'm sorry to be the one to have to tell you this, but Barbara, we're going to have to let you go. You will receive. . ."

Whatever followed made no impression, nor did I hear it. I couldn't speak, nor could Ray. After polite formalities and a goodbye, Ray and I were left alone on the couch staring at each other. Ray sobbed, "What are we going to do, Princess?"

"I don't know, I don't know. Oh, it hurts so much! I'm sorry, I don't know anymore, I. . ." A thought flashed through my mind. A picture of Meema and Peepa, and old feelings of warmth came back. They were protection. My home in Borough Park was *a place of protection.* There must be another place!

"I know, Ray. Let's go away for a while. Let's go to Washington to my relatives. I'd never drink there. I'll dry out. You'll see. I'll change, everything will change in Washington. C'mon, let's go today, now! I'll call Aunt Edith and Uncle Duddy. Okay? Please, please?"

"I suppose. It doesn't make any difference where we go or what we do. I don't care any more, Barbara. I just don't care."

Aunt Edith said, "Sure, come on down." Always naturally warm and hospitable, she asked no questions. I told her we simply had to get away for a while. But as much as I tried to think of the forthcoming trip that afternoon, and the love that would be waiting from Edith and Duddy, Shirley and Morty, I still felt sick and hot at thoughts that were too fresh to be memories.

"I wonder if they found the other bottles hidden in my desk? What about the ladies' room? There were bottles there every day, that I threw in the trash. The cleaning lady must have found them. Ray's dad works at Palmer Square. They're sure to tell him. No, no, I won't think about it, not today. I'll think of my only hope, the only thing worth living for: Ray. I'll stop drinking for Ray. I have to." I concentrated on Ray and focused on Washington as my hope, as though somehow I'd find something there to enable me to stop. It would be almost what I found in Peepa, and that would be enough!

The train ride down seemed long. I felt so sick. I knew Ray was beyond the point of following me to the bar or wherever I went to drink, but it didn't matter. No matter what, this time I was not going to drink, even if it killed me. I thought about being a little girl in Brooklyn. Still a little girl, years later I had never given up the agonizing search to once again feel the love and security that I had known then. Holding hands with Peepa in the movies, or having breakfast with Meema and Peepa, or rushing home from school to see them, or waiting eagerly for the weekends when we would all be together — in each glass, in each man, I looked for the warmth of yesterday.

It never occurred to me that perhaps leaving Brooklyn *wasn't* the root of all my misery, that perhaps the root was simply — me.

18

"Ray," I whispered in the back seat, "it's been six hours since I had a drink today. Six whole hours!" Uncle Duddy was driving us from the station to his house, and it was so good to see him again. I must have been six when he came home from the service, or younger. How I clung to my childhood! When I was with my family, I even became again that little girl in Borough Park, doing comical things I did for attention, as I had before. Why did I have this insatiable desire for attention? Why did I exaggerate, why did I lie, why did I steal? I always came back to the stealing — it was the bottom line. I felt guilty, unclean. No one in my family had done anything like that. I craved love, craved attention, craved a drink. Always craving something, I clung to Ray as he kissed me and tucked me into bed later that night.

It was 11 P.M. It had been twelve hours since my last drink. I couldn't remember when I had gone so long without one. The physical suffering I had felt earlier had changed now to mental anguish and fear. But I was determined, no matter what, not to drink. Tossing and turning, I thought about the evening, the wonderful Jewish dinner, the laughter, the TV. I tried to think about anything cheerful, even flowers or colors, but in the corners of my mind, the darkness was building, advancing. Like some sentient, amorphous being, it began to make inroads upon the light. Like a frightened little girl in a big hall, I ran around lighting candles in wall sconces, bright thoughts: wasn't Uncle Duddy funny with Raymond at dinner, both of them with their dry sense of humor. Wasn't it fun, recalling what the family meals were like, when we were all together?

But it was no use; a wind seemed to blow out the candles almost as quickly as I could light them. The big hall grew darker, and I grew more afraid. I lay in bed, wide awake, my eyes staring into the darkness, while Ray slept. The Venetian blinds were slightly opened. A street light was casting eerie shadows on the wall, as it cut through a tree. The shadows were getting larger; they were spreading, like amoebas.

I knew what it mean. The power was back. He was back. He was back, hovering over me like a vulture. And then I heard his old familiar laugh. I covered my ears and closed my eyes. But even with my eyes shut, I could see this black amoeba getting larger and larger, engulfing me, devouring me. *"Noooo!"* I jumped up. Shaking my head violently, as if to shake out these ghoulish horrors, I whispered, so as not to wake the house, "Ray, Ray, wake up! I'm having trouble. Ray, I'm in trouble. I need help. Please wake up!"

Damn it, why doesn't he wake up? Never mind, I'll make it by myself. I've got to." Pulling the covers up over my head, as if that would shut out the power, I huddled under the blankets waiting for time to pass. But each moment became worse than the previous one. My heart raced faster than ever; even in the dark abyss, I could still make out ugly shapes and colors. Mouths floating in the air were horrible to look at. Inside, they were rotten, with decaying teeth or no teeth at all. It was impossible to go on this way! Knowing that I was further from sleep than when I had gotten into bed, I pushed back the covers and sat up. What was I going to do? Putting both my feet on the floor, I began to feel it shrink away from me. "I'm losing my mind," I whispered. "I've got to get a drink! There must be something in this house, but where? They don't drink. Still, Edith must have a bottle of something here for company. The kitchen? Where else could it be? Either the kitchen or the living room."

Tears filled my eyes. "I don't want to do this! It's been almost a whole day. Why must I have one when I don't want to? Why, damn it, why?" My tears stopped as I became filled with anger about the unfairness of my situation and my helplessness. I knew I was about to lose my mind if I didn't get a drink. I'd gone too long this time, too long. "There's no hope. My only hope is in a bottle."

Stooped and shaking, I cowered past Raymond, who was sleeping peacefully. "I love you, Ray, and I really tried. I'm sorry; I don't know what's wrong with me. I'm ruining your life." I muttered my shame, as I hobbled down the long hall of this one-floor ranch, into the kitchen. It was after two in the morning. Everyone was asleep, and Edith and Duddy's room was at the other end of the house. Confident that I wouldn't be heard, I took a desk chair and climbed up on it. Opening the tall cabinets, I peered inside. With trembling hands, I moved boxes and jars and bottles. But my grip was unsteady and I dropped a jar. It fell loudly to the floor, and I froze in silence. Time passed, no footsteps. I had not been heard. "Luck is on my side this time."

After climbing down for the third time and then getting back up on the chair again to look in more cabinets, I finally struck paydirt. There were several bottles together in one area. My mind was efficiently calculating, in spite of the continuing onrush of fresh monsters and horrors. I knew I had to drink something strong quickly. My eye caught a brown and yellow label. In the moon's soft light I could read it: "Myer's Rum". I recalled that dark rum was strong and heavy; that should do it all right. "Afterwards, I'll fill it with coffee mixed with water. It'll look just as dark, and they'll never know it was me. Months will pass before Edith ever serves it again."

I didn't dare try to get down from the chair with the bottle in my quivering hands. Being careful not to drop it, I unscrewed the top, grateful that it was an easy bottle to open. Drinking as much as I could in one gulp, I came up for air and repeated three large swallows — until there were the first sensations of warmth once again in my stomach. I smiled as that warmth began flowing through my veins, and put the bottle back and got down. I whispered to myself, climbing back up on the chair and setting the bottle again.

"That was stupid, it's only three in the morning. I've got lots of time. If anyone wakes up, I'll say I'm drinking coffee." The alcohol was giving me courage now, as well as easing my frayed, screaming nerves. I boiled some water as quietly as I could, and added three heaping teaspoons of coffee to it, then cold water. Quickly drinking more rum, as much as I could, from the bottle again, I then poured a large mug full, leaving a little room at the top to add some strong coffee. The rest of the coffee went into the bottle of rum, and the bottle back where it was on the shelf.

"Yippee, I made it! And I did it with hardly a sound." Then I sat down at the kitchen table with my cup of "coffee", sipping it as I watched the dark night slip away with all of its secret distortions and ugly lies, leaving me feeling safe again, warm, sunny and at one with my body.

Light peered through the kitchen curtain, as I heard a boy's voice call out to me: "Oh hi, Barbara. What are you doing up so early?" It was Uncle Duddy and Aunt Edith's son.

"Oh, Eddie, hi. I uh, couldn't sleep, so rather than fight it, I came out for some coffee. Where are you going? You're all dressed up, and it's only 5:30 in the morning?"

"It's Shabbes (Sabbath). I'm going to Temple with my grandfather. It's a long walk, we have to leave early."

"Yipes, it sure is a long walk. Are you going to walk that distance by yourselves, now?"

"Yes, we do it every Saturday morning, and we stay there until early afternoon and then walk back."

"What are you going to do all that time?"

"Pray."

"Oh, well, are you going to have some breakfast?" Somewhat stunned by Eddie's answer to my questions, I hastened the conversation along, since I didn't know a thing about praying, nor did I even remember much about Synagogue. "Can I get you something to eat, I'd like to?"

"No, thanks, I'm fasting."

His reply left me a little speechless and I said goodbye and hoped he had a nice morning. Actually, I didn't know what to say to my cousin Eddie. I liked him and always had, but his life and belief in God was something very alien to me. There had to be something wrong with a boy sixteen being that devout. It couldn't be for real, I thought. Disappointed that he was leaving, nonetheless I now felt quiet, amiable and happy, thanks to the rum. Careful to wash my cup well, I dried it and put it away, then strolled through the house, ending up in Aunt Edith's room. Sitting on the edge of her bed, I chatted aimlessly away, smiling, beaming — swaying. Unaware of her concern, I now decided to go back to bed, so that I would wake with Raymond. "Maybe now I can get some sleep. See you later, Edith; I'm a little tired now."

I was not aware that I was already drunk. The rum had done more than its job. The last thing I remembered was climbing into bed. Then, hours later, I got up and hit something sharp. There was blood. Raymond was kneeling over me. I was put back into bed. An eternity later, I awoke, looking up into Aunt Shirley's deep blue eyes. "Ohhh no, Shirley," covering my face, I cried, "not again! Not here! How did you get here?"

"They called me. Barbara, what's wrong? What's happening to you?"

"I don't know, I don't know."

"Get some more sleep, honey. I'll see you later."

"Can we, I, still go out with you and Uncle Morty tomorrow night? Will you still take me?"

I completely lost that entire day, Saturday. When I did get up and walk into the kitchen that evening at six, I found Raymond at the table with my family having dinner. This was the first time my family ever saw me like this. My secret was out. An insecure, emotionally high-strung young girl had now grown up into an insecure, neurotically sick beyond help, young woman. Sick with shame at who I was and what I'd done, I humbly took a seat at the table. Quiet, lost in the confusion of my mind and body, I began again to crave a drink — drink that would keep me from going mad. I bit my lip and waited as long as I could, even after Ray, Edith, Nancy, Tina and Eddie left the kitchen, leaving my uncle Duddy and me alone. I looked at him, remembering how he used to call me "Bobby Shafto" when I was a kid, how he had picked me up and hugged me when he returned from the war, and how he took me for long walks and ice cream sodas.

"Duddy, I'm very sick. I'm so sorry." Trying to hold back the tears, I watched him get up and go to the refrigerator. He turned to ask me the most loving, uncondemning and truly understanding question: "Would you like a beer?"

Tears rolled down my cheeks. I felt the comfort of his love. He knew where I was, he knew, he knew. And he didn't just say, "Stop." Wouldn't I have stopped all these years if I could? I craved to be able to stop, almost as much as my body craved that drink. Who the hell wants to be chained like an animal, without a choice like this, who?

"Do you think that beer will help, or do you need a shot, too?" Nodding yes to both, it was obvious that he didn't know I needed enough alcohol in me hourly now, just to keep from going stark, raving mad. But then, I didn't know that either; it was just something that was happening. One of these things you learn as you go along, and boy, was I learning.

But that shot and beer, and then another, two hours later, and another beer before bedtime, were enough to keep me together. And I drank it all in front of my husband and family, and they watched me, silently, and I wanted to die.

"Barbara, Barbara, I'm so upset!" It was Aunt Mary, calling from Brooklyn. "Please, please, promise me you'll see a psychiatrist as soon as you get back to Princeton. Oh Pussycat, I love you so much. What's wrong, is it your marriage?"

"No, no, I don't know what it is, but my nerves are shot."

"Why didn't you come to me, tell me? I knew that night at your apartment, when I saw you with a bottle to your mouth in the bedroom, something was wrong." For a minute I didn't know what Mary was referring to, and then I remembered that she stayed over one night because I was so afraid of being alone when Ray was in the hospital. "You told me that you were drinking more because of Ray's operation and you were worried. I suppose I wanted to believe you. I didn't want to believe that you were —" and her voice broke into a sob.

"Aunt Mary, don't cry. Don't worry. I'll do whatever is necessary now to get help. I don't know what's wrong with me, but I'll go to a doctor for a checkup as soon as I get back. We're leaving here on Monday."

"No, not a checkup. You need a psychiatrist. Something is terribly wrong. Don't waste any time."

"Okay, Mary, okay. Don't tell Mother, please. She'd never be able to handle it."

"Barbara, I already called your mother. I had to tell her the truth. Yes, she is upset; we all are. But she doesn't believe what is happening to you, she doesn't want to."

"Oh God, Mary. I wish she didn't know. I've got to go. I'll call you, I promise."

Even without seeing it, I could feel the small bandage on my head. It was a reminder of that ghastly day at Edith and Duddy's. It reminded me of what was happening to me — worst of all, what was happening to me every time I picked up a drink. But I was not ready to face that. I couldn't even bring myself to see a psychiatrist, or even go out of the house except for booze, in the days that followed our short stay in Washington. My fears and blackouts grew worse than ever. Now the monthly phone bill had become a thing I dreaded. Long distance calls were made everywhere, and I never knew whom I called. A frantic search for my father and an attempt to call Stockholm, Sweden, were interrupted one night by a slap in the face from Ray. Boozy calls to him at work during the day, sometimes ten times in a single day, made it impossible for him to concentrate. Ray terminated his job at Market Dynamics and started a new one with Chesebrough-Ponds in October. It paid a higher salary and was quite a promotion. But Raymond's lack of sleep and worry about me added to the pressures that were already on his shoulders. Not sure whether marketing research was really his field, Ray began to gradually detest the lies to the public and downright fraud. The commuter ride from Penn Station to Princeton had long since lost its charm. "As a matter of fact, this whole middle-class American way of life stinks. I don't see much hope here, not for America, after Kennedy's assassination." Ray often became moody and philosophical, his thoughts, dreams and ideas taking him round and round, leading him nowhere.

But one thing Ray *was* emphatic about: "You have *got* to get help! I insist you see a psychiatrist or..."

Dr. Evans' office was at the other end of Nassau Street, on the corner of Harrison. It was a long walk for my first appointment that afternoon, but several martinis before leaving, an additional stop at the Pink Elephant across the street, and a flask filled with vodka in my bag, gave me all the courage I needed to lie down on a long sofa, followed by a rather emotional and dramatic recollection of my childhood. I thought Dr. Evans, a balding, middle-aged man with glasses, would provoke me, but instead he said practically nothing. I sat on a straight chair opposite him.

When he said, "Well, why are you here?" I gave him a thousand and one excuses. "Dr. Evans, my husband tells me I drink too much and —"

He interrupted with, "Do you?"

"Well, yes, but just listen to what I've got to put up with here and my life, it's been awful, anyone would drink."

When my hour was up, and I finished talking, I said, "Well, what do you think my problem is, Doctor?"

"I don't know, Mrs. Tamasi. But I suggest you continue coming, and I do think you ought to stop drinking. It certainly isn't helping your life, now is it?"

Now, that was true, but just ask a dog to stop barking, or lovingly tell a newborn baby not to cry or wet his diapers.... I smiled and said, "Yes, doctor, I will stop. It's easy. I just never really wanted to until now. And when I stop, everyone will see that I am not an alcoholic and never have been."

"That's fine, Mrs. Tamasi. See you next Friday at 11:00."

"Sure — uh, Doctor, are you married?"

"I don't discuss my private life with my patients."

"Oh, sorry, sorry." Gee, I thought, walking down the stairs, I was just curious. What's so private about that? He's not even friendly.

After an evening a few weeks later, where I was exceptionally drunk and disorderly, and I insisted that Dr. Evans do something immediately to help me, he came out to his office to see both Ray and me. Only Ray was summoned inside his office, not I. I stood outside crying and banging on the door. When the door did open, Ray was beside himself, that was obvious. Dr. Evans looked straight at me. Through the veil of drunkenness I heard his words, much like Dr. Ullman's had been. "Barbara, you have got to stop drinking *now!*" Again I nodded, yes, I would and, oh, how I wished I could. But I continued to drink, fearing all sorts of horrible things, even death, if I were to stop. A few days later, a friend, a casual friend who was running for political office, asked me to address some envelopes for him. I said, "Yes, Marty, I'd love to." I wanted to feel useful again and was so excited, when I told Ray that I was going to address envelopes for Marty the next day and maybe even get involved in his campaign later on. "Maybe this will help, Ray. Give me an interest, something like that. You know what I mean?"

"Yeah, Princess, maybe."

But who was kidding whom? The next morning came, and there I was, as usual, on the bathroom floor hanging over the toilet bowl, until I felt I could make it down to the corner liquor store to get a bottle when it opened. I'd long since given up caring what Tony, the proprietor, thought. Everyone knew what I was and what was even worse, who my husband was.

Marty's letters were on the kitchen table, still waiting to be addressed. Another false hope and promise. "There isn't a damn thing I can do now, except drink and throw up, damn it all." Disgusted, I walked up Witherspoon Street to the liquor store. Across the street, I noticed Charlie. Charlie, I knew — we all knew, had a ferocious drinking problem. Yes, Charlie wore the title alcoholic with everything that meant — and now Charlie was crossing the street in my direction. La Haires had just opened. He must be going in there for a drink, I thought. Charlie always started out in the nicer places, like me. "Hey, Charlie," I called, waving my hand as though I'd seen a long-lost friend, "Charlie!"

He slowed to a halt, quietly listening. "I'm in trouble, please help me, Charlie; I have a drinking problem." This was the first time I had admitted such a thing to anyone, even myself.

"No, you couldn't have, Barbara. *I've* got the problem, dear, not you."

"No, it's true! Don't leave me here. I'm desperate."

His curiosity turned to worried concern. "C'mon, then, I'm headed toward LaHaires."

We sat across from each other and after several martinis, Charlie sort of smiled: "Okay, you do have a problem. Have you been anywhere for help?"

"I'm seeing a psychiatrist; he's okay, I suppose — a thousand dollars okay. But it's not helping. I feel as though I just have more reasons to drink. Oh yes, he told me I had to stop."

At that we both laughed. That was the first time, too, that I could laugh with someone about this horrible dark hidden nightmare of mine that erupted when I did. "Look, Barbara, I know what it's like. There is a group of people who can help you. You can trust them. They will help you. They know what it's all about. They helped me, but — well, forget about me. It's too late for me. Go home now, and call them. You can get the number from Information. Good luck, honey. I'll say a prayer for you."

19

Our first anniversary had come and gone. It was October 1969, and the leaves had turned once again from green to gold to red. Princeton in the fall was beautiful. A year ago this season Ray and I had returned from our honeymoon — a glorious honeymoon that marked for me the beginning of a life that was supposed to be devoid of loneliness and anxiety. I loved Raymond more than anyone or anything in the whole world. He was my answer to all the emotional insecurity I had battled all my life, after the sheltering years with Meema and Peepa.

Now, just one year later, I sat at the kitchen table, looking at the envelopes I had promised to address for Marty, and the telephone book in front of me. The envelopes were shoved to one side. They would never be done. But the telephone book held a number that might mean help. Charlie had told me who to call. "Do it right away, Barbara!" he exclaimed, and his words had rung with urgency.

But now, sitting there, I was angry. I demanded to know why, *why,* had this happened to me, so fast? It's unfair, damn it all. Haven't I suffered enough? I pounded the phone book, until it became another pillow, wet with tears. Drawing back from calling, I decided that only I could help myself, and obviously I wasn't.

But then I saw a picture in the front of my mind. Lynn and I were fifteen. She was smiling, beaming as she told me about her mother. "Barbara, my mother is well now, thank God. A group of people helped her to get sober. These people are marvelous, I've met them. Do you know, it's been almost two years since my mother has had anything to drink?"

The picture of Lynn and me slowly faded from my mind. In its place stood one of Lynn's mother. Her blond hair, neatly combed back off her face, shone, like Lynn's. Possessing delicate features and a slim figure, Lynn's mom was the farthest from looking like an alcoholic that I could ever imagine a person to be. And as her face faded too, I heard again Lynn's words: "A group of people helped her to get sober."

Wiping the tears from my eyes and pouring myself a tall glass of vodka with a squirt of orange juice, I knew that I was to make that phone call right now. But as with everything else, I needed the courage to even dial the number, let alone speak to a perfect stranger. And this stranger was to be someone I confided in, someone to whom I told what I myself couldn't bear to look at, let alone believe, that I was, in fact, an alcoholic.

No, no! I wouldn't use that word! I didn't know if I was one. I'd just say the truth, which was that I was newly married, had lived in this small town for one year, had had a miserable life, was adjusting to marriage, and therefore was having some trouble with alcohol. No, I wouldn't even mention the word alcohol. I'd say I was having some trouble drinking, and that lately I'd been overdoing it and would like to learn how to handle liquor the way I used to.

So I called. And a man spoke to me and was as understanding as Charlie had led me to expect. He told me that a group would be getting together that night, if I cared to come. I said I would, but as the day grew longer, I began to get cold feet. Finally, it was getting near the time.

"Ray, will you come with me, when I meet these people? Do you think I should go? Maybe I never should have called them. I don't know what I'm getting into, and I'm scared, so scared."

"I'll go with you, if you like. And I do think you should follow through with the call and go. What've you got to lose?"

"Okay, okay, but I've got to have a drink before I go."

"No, damn it, you've had enough today! What is this, a game? You're going so that you won't have to drink."

That scared me even more. I couldn't bear to think of not drinking. And I had to have a drink, a bottle to take with me. There was enough time before we left, for me to slip out when Ray was in the bathroom. It would take only two minutes to leave and get back with another pint of vodka. I'd leave the music on and the door slightly opened; he'd never know I was gone. Just one more, one more pint tonight. My last forever, maybe...

That night seemed longer than forever, and while our new-found friends couldn't have been more accepting, they were, like Lynn's mom, clean-looking and radiant, not at all like my idea of alcoholics. They smiled and laughed more than any bunch of people I knew, and they weren't even drinking! I couldn't figure it out. "How can you have had the trouble that you say you've had, been where you've been, loved booze with a passion, and now be so free to laugh like this? I don't believe it."

"Honey, when you're sick and tired of being sick and tired and are ready to live again, without one drop of booze, one day at a time, calling for help instead of reaching for the bottle, relying not on yourself, but on God and all of us, whom He has given to help you, then you, too, can be free."

One of them, Emily, gave me her phone number, and so did several other women, while their husbands drank coffee and ate donuts, laughingly reliving one horror after another. But underneath the laughter, I sensed an earnestness — a fight for life. An air of lightheartedness did prevail, but so did the unwritten law: "You do not take one drink for one day, one hour, one moment. You live your life one day at a time. Because an alcoholic is always one drink away from a drunk. There is one power alone that can help you," they said quietly, "and that power is God. May you find Him now."

For days my mind was filled with questions and all sorts of pondering, like that word, power, that was used. Power being from God? I'd often felt ruled by a power. The power I knew told me to jump out of moving cars. It sat on my shoulders weighing down on me and putting eerie phantoms before me that threatened to devour me.

"Raymond, these people talk about God as if He were real. That's crazy! There can't be a God. If there was one, why did He let this happen to me? I like Emily, though, and Ed and Jim and Clarence, and I feel as though they really understand. But, Ray, I am not an alcoholic. I have not been through all the horrible things they have."

"So what? Remember what Jim said: keep drinking, and you'll get there. Please see them and call them. I'll tell you, it's been a help to me. Now I know that you're not completely nuts. You're an alcoholic, and that's curable."

"Don't call me that! You miserable — don't you or anyone else call me an alcoholic!"

In the weeks and months ahead, I saw a lot of these people who had been defeated by liquor and who had come through into a life of sobriety. They let me be myself. Drunk or sober, I was accepted. But most of the time I was drunk. I could manage to stay dry for a couple of days at the most, biting my fingernails and counting every hour, always living for the moment when I would "break out" and drink again. Even as I sat in their homes, with a bottle hidden under a scarf in my handbag, somehow, for the first time in my life, I felt a small glimmer of hope.

Yet still I could not bring myself to think of myself as one of them. "Clarence, even though I'm not an alcoholic, I like you. You've been such a help to Ray and me. You know, if I ever really become one, I know that I will be able to stop, too." Clarence, a black man who was short and slim and reminded Ray and me a little of Sammy Davis, Jr. had been in more than thirty institutions, tried suicide, been in jails, and had been declared hopeless. He had been sober now two years and lived just a block down the street from us on Witherspoon. He became our closest friend during this time.

And a time it was! My drinking, more frenzied than ever, took me out and away on benders that became progressively wilder and more degrading. After each one, Clarence was there to help me start over again. "It's a new day, girl. Let's start it sober. Whoever gets up the earliest will be sober the longest. How's about it?"

"C'mon, Clarence. What a time to call — 7 o'clock in the morning! I promised you I wouldn't drink today. Did you have to call this early to remind me?"

"Yeah, I did, sugar. Someone took the time to call and remind me."

To Ray, Clarence was the best friend he ever had. There was no one that Ray could confide in the way he could with Clarence, and at all hours of the night and day, while he waited for me, not knowing whether I would show up dead or alive. Clarence felt the pain with him, helped him to get out his feelings of disgust, hate and even murder. For at this point, Ray often wished me dead. He even imagined and hoped it would happen, so that the noose around his neck might be released.

And Clarence let him cry. Sometimes they cried together, like that awful night in March of 1970. I had been dry an unbelievable two weeks, and both of them dared to hope that I had finally turned the corner. How could I tell them that I was once again chafing at the bit to be free — free from the control and tyranny of these people (and I now included among "them" my husband) who were treating me as if I were an alcoholic and had even railroaded me into admitting it. They had practically forbidden me to drink again, although they would never out and out tell anyone what to do, just suggest. Anyway, I was angry and looking for any opportunity to "break out".

Since no opportunity did come my way, I created one. I continued to see my psychiatrist, Dr. Evans, for a while longer. He was pleased when each visit I gave him more information about alcoholism as an illness. "I'm glad to see you've talked to some people who've been and come through a similar experience. It *can* be done."

"Doctor, do you think going back and reading some of the diaries I kept as a child might help me?"

"I don't know. Read them if you want to."

That night, grabbing onto that "Read them if you want to," I gave Raymond a twenty-minute dissertation on why I needed to go into New York the next day and get my diaries from my mother's apartment.

"No, I think that's crazy, Barbara. You've only been two weeks without a drink. Don't chance it. It's too soon to go back."

"Don't order me around! I'm not a sick cripple. If I want to go, then I'll go. And besides, Dr. Evans said it would be helpful for me to go back and read them," I said, bending the truth a little, to get my way.

But Ray knew me pretty well, by now. "Are you *sure* he would agree to your getting on a bus and spending the whole day in New York on your own?"

"Definitely; I wouldn't lie, Ray."

"Well, I still don't like the feel of it. Let's call Clarence and see what he thinks."

"Call Clarence? What the hell do I have to do that for? He's not my guardian."

"No, but he is our friend and he does know what's best for you now."

"Well then, go ahead and call him, damn it, since you're going to, anyway!"

Clarence did more than talk over the phone; he came rushing over and spent the next two hours desperately trying to convince me that it would be a terrible mistake for me to go into New York the following morning. "What on earth is suddenly so important about getting those diaries tomorrow? Can't you wait and go in with Ray on the weekend?"

"No, I can't, and don't tell me what to do, Clarence." Shrugging his shoulders to Ray, as if to say, I've done all I can, he left. Ray was so hurt and angry that he refused to speak to me that night, except to tell me to call him at work, when I had gotten the diaries.

That night, as I took a shower and washed my hair, I planned what I would wear the next day. Eagerly looking forward to this adventure alone in New York — the sort of thing I'd sorely missed — I decided to wear my favorite coat, the rose beige suede that Ray had bought me in Spain on our honeymoon. I had worn it only three or four times, never wanting to soil it in any way, thinking that I'd cherish it for years, my one big memento from that trip of a lifetime.

Waiting for the bus at the corner of Witherspoon and Nassau, the cold, clean air biting my nose, I tossed my hair back and let it fall over my shoulders, flipping up at the ends. Taking off my long black leather gloves, I brushed my hand along the skirt of my coat, admiring the soft suede. Knowing that I looked better than I had in a year, after losing some bloat, I felt like a bird whose cage door had suddenly swung open. "I'm getting out of prison," I hummed to myself, as I stepped into the bus.

Watching the skyscrapers and onrush of traffic and busy people as we pulled into Port Authority, I wished we could move back to New York and start all over again. "Now that I've learned something about alcoholism, I can protect myself. I can control my drinking. It's been two weeks. I'm no damn alcoholic. Clarence and Emily and Jim, they just want everyone to be like them. Well, I'm not going to be. I'll show them." As I finished murmuring "I'll show them," a cab pulled up in front of me, and I climbed inside.

"222 East 80th Street, please, between Second and Third Avenue. And would you please drive up Third?" I wanted to see all my old stomping grounds, though I felt a little like a grown woman returning to favorite childhood icecream parlors and candy stores.

But that "I'll show them" had rung a bell. When had I said that before? Straining to remember, I saw before me Mother's and my apartment at the Hotel Greystone, on the West Side. And then I remembered when I had said it before: when I saw the kitchenette with the door swung wide open, a bottle of whiskey half-full on a counter. Mother was asleep, and my first date, Tommy, was shortly coming to pick me up. Filled with hate and a sense of unfairness, wanting to get even with Mother for all I accused her of doing to me, I had impulsively grabbed the bottle. Saying, "I'll show you," I had gulped as much as I could, holding my nose. It's odd, I thought, how I can actually recall saying the same thing, and then remember the incident in such detail. Why, that happened nearly fourteen years ago! Slightly shaken at the similarity of the replay, I refused to think about what happened to me afterwards. I sensed the same thing could happen, only this time I was older. The result would be even worse. As much as I tried to think about other things, look into passing shops, even chat with the cab driver, I had an eerie feeling, almost as though I had been warned.

Finally the cab turned the corner of 80th and Third Avenue. I couldn't wait to get out. The bright, airy feeling I had had earlier when I left Princeton was gone. Instead, there was a kind of foreboding and stuffiness, in spite of the crisp air and bright sunshine. As soon as I paid the driver and got out of the cab, saying hello to the doorman, I asked for Bill, the superintendent. "He's not here today, Barbara. Took the day off."

"What do you mean, he's not here? I have to get into my mother's apartment."

"I'm sorry, but he and the missus have gone away for the whole day, and I don't even have a key to let you in." Furious, I stood there, glaring at the doorman, as though he was just one more person who didn't believe in me and was out to make things tough. In spite of what he said, I proceeded to take the elevator up to the second floor, where I knocked on the door loudly, and then turned the knob back and forth, in the faint hope that Mother was either home sick or had left the door unlocked. When the reality of my first disappointment for the day sank in, I ran down the stairs and out of the building, down the block to Second Avenue. There I stood on the corner, watching warm air come out of my mouth like smoke.

"What am I going to do now? It's only 11:00 in the morning?" I could have gone to Lord and Taylor's, borrowed the key from her, used it, and left it with the doorman. But that would have interfered with my subconscious agenda for the day, and so it never occurred to me.

"I know! I'll call Mother and ask her to meet me at her apartment, right after work. But that won't be until six, and even Ray will be through before then. He won't want to hang around, I'm sure. I'll just have to call him later and tell him to go ahead back to Princeton by himself, if he doesn't want to come up here. It would be stupid not to get my diaries, after coming all this way for them."

I eyed the phone booth across the street; it looked stark and cold, stuck on the corner by itself. Turning towards Second Avenue and

81st Street, I walked up the block. There was a bar and grill on my left, and I turned to look at myself in the glass window. But my eye fixed on a glass of amber liquid that the bartender was passing over the bar to a man. I watched him tilt his head back and swallow. Boy, I'll bet that feels good, I thought, especially today. I was so cold, too cold to call from an outside booth. I walked in, and asked the bartender if there was a phone there.

"Yes, ma'am, there's one behind you on the wall." Looking in my handbag for a dime, I had only a fifty-cent piece, a nickel and two pennies. The bartender looked busy, although there was no one else around except for his one customer and me. Hating to ask him for change of a dollar just for the phone, I decided to order a coke. "Excuse me," I said, looking at the warm, inviting drink that the man at the bar had, and feeling more sorry for myself each moment, champing at the bit for a mouth-watering martini, detesting the thought of a cold, fizzy coke, thinking of Ray, seeing Clarence's face before me and unable to wish it away. I stood by the phone with my mouth open, not knowing what to do.

"Yes, ma'am, did you want to order a drink? What'll it be?"

"A martini. It'll be an extra dry martini, straight up with an olive, please."

20

"Get your own ride back tonight and go straight to hell. I'll be damned if I'll meet you at 5:00 anywhere."

"Why, Raymond, wus da matter wit you?" Slurring my words and leaning on the phone, I almost sobered up hearing the loud *click*. "Hello? Hello, Raymond, you there?" I replaced the receiver. "He hung up, the rotten. . . I'll show him and everyone else that I can drink. Trying to make me out an alcoholic. They're all against me. I feel as though I'm being kept in prison, locked up in that small, hypocritical, bigoted, stinking, no-good town. Who cares whether he meets me or not. I'll get my own ride home tonight. Gee, I'd better order another drink. I'll meet Mother back at the apartment at 6, or was she coming here? Don't remember, better call: Hello? Lord and Taylor? What the hell's wrong with your operators? I've been waiting here ten minutes, and this is an emergency call."

"Sorry, madam, I'll put you right through."

"Hey, Mom, where ya gonna meet me?"

"Barbara, is that you? You sound awful."

"Oh c'mon. I can't go home. I'll meet you at Dresners at six for dinner, and let's not have any scenes tonight, ya hear?"

All in all, I'd had around ten martinis by the time the night bartender came on. He looked familiar, very familiar, and when he turned his head I whispered, "Frank!" And then, louder, "Frank, Frank Maloney, hi, it's Barbara."

"Oh, hello, Barbara, how are you?" Frank was unusually composed. We talked briefly about what had happened to each of us during the past few years, or rather I talked about me.

"Frank, I'm married. Married to a wonderful guy and guess what, I'm an alcoholic, but before I tell you about that, can I have another martini?"

Expressionless, Frank mixed me another and set it in front of me, saying, "Go easy."

"I am, I am. You know I can't drink. Never could. I'm a real alcoholic; that's what they tell me. I've stopped drinking though, except for today. I know people who've hit rock bottom." Taking a large swallow, and looking at my watch that read 5:45, I proceeded to tell Frank and everyone else around me why they shouldn't drink. "It'll kill you. Drive you nuts. Boy, the things I've seen on my bedroom wall —"

"Barbara," Frank cut in, "you've had enough to drink. I'm not serving you anything else. Frankly, I understand the problem. I've been on the wagon myself for eight months."

"What? You? Eight months without a drop?" I was speechless, stunned, feeling as though I was all alone. The heaviest drinker I knew had stopped, and I couldn't. "Eight *months* — wow!" I paid my check and left. Wishing the fling I was on would pick up some momentum, I began to drink with a hurried, frenzied passion. I met Mother at Dresner's, arriving late, and insisted that we go back to the bar where Frank worked. Mother, in order to avoid a public scene, conceded. I couldn't believe it. Frank worked with the stuff, touched it, and was sober. I watched him as I ordered each drink I drank from another bartender who was more than willing to serve me. The more I watched him, and the drunker I became, I remembered our romance, how I felt, how we drank, how he treated me, and now, how I blamed him and all the others, for making me what I was.

"Who wants to hear my favorite song, 'Second Hand Rose'?" I called out. Then, "Hey, what about 'Georgie Girl'?" and I slumped over in my chair, sobbing, as I listened to the words and melody of "As Long as He Needs Me." Since no one needed me, I sniffled, whimpered, cried and wailed. "Sheer schmaltz!"

When Mother had finished her martini, we sauntered out and made our way back to her apartment. Functioning without awareness or memory afterwards, even moments afterwards, was, I had learned, a blackout. I was in and out of them every other moment, saying and doing things that were bizarre and out of whack. For instance, after searching the apartment for my diaries and not coming up with them, I believed I was under attack! A conspiracy had been planned by my mother, and I didn't know who else, to destroy everything I'd ever written as a youngster. "Mother, you . . . I know that you don't believe in putting anything, anything, down on paper. Now get those diaries out of hiding, or I don't know what I'll do."

Mother began to cry and scream in loud shrieks. "You're trying to give me a heart attack. You're going to kill me! You've always had a mean streak."

"I'm getting the hell out of here! You're starting one of your scenes!"

"Oh no, you're not! You're not going anywhere; it's 11:30 at night!" Even I was taken aback at that bit of news; the last time I looked at my watch it was 7:30. As if I had suddenly come to again, my mind began to clear.

"Mother, you're not going to keep me here against my will. I'll open all the windows and scream. I'm calling Ray." Mother grabbed my arm, as I attempted to take the telephone from the living room into the bathroom. I tried to push her away, but her grip was too strong. We struggled together. I tried to break loose, but she was holding my wrists too tightly. Then I kicked her and pushed her down to the floor, leaving her absolutely hysterical. Quickly I snatched up the phone and locked myself in the bathroom. Barely able to hear Ray's voice on the other end, I cried and begged him to come and get me.

"Look, I can't get you now. It was your choice. Get a cab down to Port of Authority and come home, or stay overnight. It would be better if you stayed there. You're in no shape to travel."

"Raymond, I'm cold sober," I lied. "I've hardly had a thing to drink. It's just that I'm so upset, half out of my mind here with Mother. You know what she's like when she's been drinking."

Just then, Mother broke through the door. She yanked the phone from me, and there was another struggle. We fought, scratched, kicked and bit each other. Raymond and the telephone got lost somewhere. Another blackout followed, until the phone rang again. When it did ring, I struggled to my feet from somewhere and picked it up, crying, "Ray, Ray! Help me, help!"

"Barbara, this isn't Raymond. It's Clarence. Do you hear me? It's Clarence. Barbara, I want you to listen to me very carefully. You have been drinking and the situation is terrible. You have got to calm down and stay the night there. Don't, whatever you do, go out like this. Ray has been beside himself all night long."

I listened to Clarence's deep voice, and his instructions which were almost orders, and yet I knew he loved me. He really cared about me, and us. I couldn't understand it, but it brought a flood of hot tears to my eyes. "I'm not drunk. I want to come home. I've got to come home!" Continuing to beg and plead on the phone, I lost control and dropped the telephone, becoming hysterical. Mother appeared from somewhere. Obviously she rallied and, taking the phone from me, she started to rant and rave about me to Clarence. I couldn't get the receiver away from her. We fought and pulled each other's hair and swore, each one calling the other every ugly name we could think of. With the receiver still lying on the bathroom floor, and Mother slumped over the tub, I made my getaway, after taking all the money in her pocketbook.

Shaking badly and needing a drink more than I ever had since I could remember, I went straight to my old hangout, Bogey's. "I'll have just one or two to calm down, before getting a late bus back to Princeton," I told myself. But as usual, the one became ten, and then I insisted on finding an after-hours place, one that would be "safe."

"C'mon," I wheedled the bartender, "there must be another place that stays open around here, and by the way, where's George, the other bartender?"

"He's working at Edward's in the east sixties. It's open after hours, if you know what I mean."

"I know where Edward's is; I used to go there. But I don't know what you mean."

"Card game. All men — an all-night-long card game."

Somehow I found my way over there, and was directed outside and down a few steps. I tripped on the last, and through a window saw George and a group of guys seated around a table. Cards and bottles were on the table. Every eye turned in my direction, and George smiled and told me, "Pull up a chair, honey." My gloves were in my bag, my hands outstretched, sliding along the smooth, soft suede of my coat. This was the only time I had looked at it or even thought about it since waiting for the bus to leave Princeton.

"Take off your coat, honey, and have a drink."

"Thanks, George. But I'm cold; I'll keep my coat on. But I will have that drink."

Someone pushed a bottle of brandy in my direction. Someone else passed a glass. The same ominous, eerie feeling that I'd had in the cab on the way up to my mother's house, returned. No longer did I want to scream or tear my hair out. I wanted to run, but I was here and it was three o'clock in the morning, a bottle was in front of me, and Raymond was so far away.

"Okay, everybody out, I mean it. I'm turning off the lights."

"Wait a minute!" I cried in the darkness. "I can't see! Where's George? I'm scared."

Mocking laughter and cynical voices were whispering in the dark, and I didn't know where any of them were. Clutching my coat, I fell, unable to get myself up. "Somebody help me, I've fallen. I can't see where I'm going. *Please* — don't leave me here."

The laughter continued, but the lights flickered back on. George came over and helped me to my feet. "What're you so scared of, honey?"

"Nothing — I don't know. I'll be okay. I want to go now. I've got to get home to my husband. I shouldn't have come here, but I didn't know where to go. I — I love my husband." And I started to cry.

"Okay, okay, nobody said you didn't, baby. We're all going now. The party's over, but you ought to watch it." I fell again on my way up the few stairs I had come down. With nothing to hold on to, I wound up going up the stairs on my hands and knees. Holding my breath until I got outside the door, I waved goodbye after I turned sharply to my right, intending to walk down to Second Avenue, where I could get a cab. Morning was waiting for me just around the corner. My heart began to pound. Would I make it? Falling several times, once in a puddle, I got to my feet finally, after many tries. "My coat, my beau'ful coat. Don' wanna dirty my coat."

Talking to myself, staggering in a drunken stupor, I turned to my left, hoping a taxi would be coming down the street. A car drove up and pulled alongside the curb; someone, or two or three, waved to me, saying, "Hi, how ya doing?" as if I knew them. Or was it one person, just the cab driver?

"I don't know. Must be a taxi," I mumbled. "Thanks, thanks for stopping. I didn't know if I'd get a cab this hour of the —" Before I could finish, an arm grabbed me and pulled me along the street, off the curb and into the cab. "Wait a minute? Who is this? What's going on?"

I couldn't see anyone or anything. It was black as coal in the back seat of that car. Young men were huddled together in the back, and there were others in the front. I could hear voices, their mocking laughter, sneering, filthy comments, their hands all over me. *"No!"* I screamed. *"Noooo!* Let me out of here! Oh my God, oh my God, oh my God, help me, help me! Please let me out of here." I wrapped both my arms around myself in self-protection. But those hands, hands of an octopus, kept crawling all over me. I screamed at the top of my lungs, choking with tears, "Don't! Don't do this to me! My husband. Raymond." I shrieked his name, *"Raymond!* Oh God, please. God help me, *please!* Let me go, let me go!" And as abruptly as I had been dragged into the car, I was thrown out while it was still moving, landing face down in the gutter, in the middle of a huge puddle filled with debris. I didn't care. I sobbingly cried: "Oh thank God, thank God, I'm free."

Time meant nothing. It was dawn, and I, oblivious to everything, lay there in the gutter, until another car slowed to a halt in front of me. Barely able to lift my head and petrified that it was the same car that had dropped me, I looked up. Above the black tire I saw a yellow fender. A taxi? A man's legs dressed in dark grey trousers got out of the car and walked towards me. His black shoes were well shined. He stooped down to lift my head. "Are you all right? I saw you lying there and I couldn't just leave you. I'm on my way to work. Can I take you somewhere? Is your home nearby?"

As if an angel disguised as an executive on his way to work had been sent by God, I responded immediately. "Yes, yes! My mother lives on East 80th. Please take me there. My husband, my Raymond..." Tears streamed down my cheecks — tears of relief, tears of shame, tears of tragedy.

From the cab, I was helped into the lobby and handed to the doorman, who rang my mother. He took me up the elevator and handed me over to her, as she waited, fearful and expectant, in the doorway. "Oh no, oh God, no! I can't take it. Barbara, what horrible thing happened to you?"

Unable to walk, to move, I felt swollen everywhere. Bruised and sick, oh so very sick, I collapsed on one of the studio couches by the window. Touching my coat, my favorite rose beige suede coat, I could feel the tar and grime and debris. "My coat is ruined, isn't it, Mommy?"

"Yes, my baby — oh my poor baby." Mother sat next to my feet at the end of the couch, crying softly, pitifully. "Let me take your coat off, let me —"

"No, don't touch me. I don't want anyone to touch me." I wept.

"Mamashena, what shall I do?"

"Call Raymond. He should be at work soon."

"Can you tell me what happened?"

"No."

"You must tell me what happened." And getting upset again, she added, "You look as though you've been beaten up."

"Please, nothing until Ray gets here, if he'll ever, ever come for me again."

Mother, fearful for my marriage, and now my life, began crying uncontrollably. She was desperate, despondent and beaten. I couldn't get up or even move my head. After throwing up all over myself, I fell on the floor and crawled with my coat on to the bathroom; I had to at least get to the bathroom. Like an animal left for days in the cold, starving, yet unable to eat, I groveled and whimpered and pleaded and cried, and inside, I died.

A soft, familiar voice kept asking me if I was all right. A gentle hand was on my forehead. Opening my eyes, I looked up into Raymond's face; tears were streaming down. His mouth was held together as tightly as possible, until it quivered, then broke. Raymond, with his head on my shoulder, kneeling on the floor beside me, wearing his overcoat, the one I always recognized him in, was in anguish.

"Barbara," Mother broke in, half-hysterical, "this poor boy has been up all night, frantic; he's falling apart!"

"Oh, Raymond, I never meant to do this to you! I'd rather die than go on hurting you like this. I won't blame you if you leave me —"

"Stop it! Stop it now." Then he pulled himself together, and lifted me up and took off my suede coat. Looking at it, we both cried again when we saw what had happened to it.

"The one thing I owned, Ray, that I wanted to protect, is ruined."

"Barbara, you'll have to snap out of it and tell me what happened. Do you think you need a doctor?"

"No, I'm okay."

"*What* happened?"

Almost in a hush, shamefully embarrassed, I told Raymond exactly what I could remember of the night and morning, and it was sketchy at best.

"Well," he said, when I had finished, "somehow you were saved from being raped, but honestly I don't know how."

Two days later, after being spoon-fed and washed and having much sleep, and rarely getting up to even walk, I held on to Ray's arm as we took the train at Penn Station for Princeton. "Your job, Ray — I'm so worried about your job! I've ruined everything for you, calling you ten times a day, drunk, and now this..."

"Don't worry about my job any more, Barbara. I was fired."

21

By the summer of 1970, I was about to take the geographical cure — again. I had convinced Raymond that it was Princeton's fault that I was an alcoholic. We had never had a chance in that little town — the only town he had ever known — and I was certain that if we could just get away, we would have a chance, a real chance. Perhaps our last.

Ray was willing. He had been out of a job for four months, with no motivation left to ever get back into advertising or market research, despite the good money. Fortunately, he had been able to set aside enough, so that we were not hurting during this time, and ironically, my tolerance for alcohol seemed to stabilize during this period — so much so that I began to believe that I could control my drinking after all.

And now, for the first time in months, we had a joint project that we could share: the planning of our escape from Princeton! Night after night, we would sit at a table of Good Time Charlie's, plotting each detail with all the conspiratorial thoroughness of a prison breakout. "We should start with a clean break," I said, sipping my vodka gimlet, and I mean sipping; I did not want to risk destroying the illusion of my new-found ability to control myself. Reflecting on the time we spent in Spain on our honeymoon, before all our problems took hold of our lives, I said out loud: "And Ray, wouldn't it be wonderful if we could go back to Spain, to the place where we were happier than we have ever been in our lives? Of course, I realize it's out of the question — way too expensive..."

"I don't know, Princess," he said, excited as I was at the prospect of our again having a dream to share. "If we were to buy a VW camper, and live in it, instead of hotels or pensions, we might just be able to swing it, at least for a few months. Of course, we'll be flat broke when we get home...."

"Don't even think about that! You'll find yourself over there, and you'll find new work — the work you really want to do — as soon as we get back, and maybe in a new location."

Ray shook his head. "I don't know. There are so many things we need to take care of first. We'll have to find someone to pick up the remainder of our lease and store our stuff somewhere...."

So many dreams turn into ashes, it was almost too much to dare hope for, when the pieces of ours began falling into place. We found someone to take the apartment, and Ray's parents agreed to store the few things we had. And despite the long wait for VW campers abroad, Ray was able to arrange to take delivery on one in late August, almost as soon as we landed there. The most important possession Ray had was his Austin Healey, but he didn't think he'd have a problem selling it. However, when our last buyer kept putting us off, we became a little desperate. We knew that our entire trip hinged on the sale of this car and the money that it would give us. Finally, the details were worked out, and just weeks before our departure, the car was sold for $2,000. That night we celebrated by having dinner out at La Haire's.

"We'll be leaving this stinking town in a few weeks. We're going to start all over again, without all these people around who've known me all my life and can't mind their own business."

"I know, Ray. I know it'll be different. Just getting out of here and being alone with you will change our whole marriage. It's this place that's caused my alcoholism. I know it. You know, we've never really been on our own, and you've lived in this town all your life. It's about time you moved."

And so, on August 24, 1970, we were once again airborne, heading back across the Atlantic. I sat by the window, looking out on the soft, billowing cloud cover below, while Ray dozed beside me. Could nearly two years have passed since that time? Considering all we had been through, it was a miracle we were still together. For that matter, it was a miracle that I was still alive. I shuddered at all the grief and agony those two years had held, and made myself think ahead.

And now, we were being given a chance to start over, a second honeymoon, as it were. And I determined that that was what it would be: a new beginning.

Wiedenbruck, where we picked up our VW camper, was charming, even though it was Germany. I had tons of preconceived feelings about Northern Germany, most of which were verified when I saw the efficiency with which the Germans worked and organized things. I imagined vehicles coming off a VW assembly line by computer. Our camper was ready on time, and everything was in its proper working order — except us. I was cold, it was cold, and we had no luck finding sleeping bags on our first day. Hence, our first night in the VW was an introduction to camping that I will never forget. "Brrrr," I groaned the following morning, "my head, my throat! Ray, do something; I'm sick and freezing."

"Look, it was just one night. I'm sure we'll find sleeping bags today. You've got to stop demanding American luxuries. We're European campers now."

"European campers, my foot. I've got to have a warm place to sleep tonight, or I'll get pneumonia and die."

We walked and walked, and still had no luck in finding any sleeping bags. And now it was raining. It had also been more than a day since I had had any wine. The hell with this abstinence. Everyone knows a person has got to have brandy when he's cold and freezing. "Ray, while you're in that store over there, I'm going into that coffee shop for some hot bouillon for my throat. I can hardly talk."

"Ah, peace and quiet at last. You can no longer talk! Okay, go ahead, but don't be long and for heaven's sake, don't go off on one of your jaunts."

"What a terrible thing to accuse me of! Haven't I been good for three months now with my drinking? You haven't seen me drunk once, and the other day I was just sick."

"Well, we'll see, we'll see. I'm not holding my breath. I remember what Clarence said: 'Once an alcoholic, always an alcoholic.' There's no going back."

"That infuriates me!" I retorted. Walking away from Ray, I groped for an explanation for our constant disputes. It was easy to find one: lack of trust on Raymond's part in his wife, who loves him more than anything in the whole wide world.

It was amazing how the dampness turned to sweet-smelling dew in my mind and all seemed euphorically beautiful, after several schnapps and beer and wine. Strolling in and out of grocery stores, losing all track of time *again*, I decided to forget about my cold and buy some herrings, wurst and whatever else I could find for Ray. I would eagerly cook him our first dinner in our camper, by candlelight and with good, dry German wine, of course. Proceeding to carry out this romantic ideal, I spent all my spending money we had budgeted for five days in Wiedenbruck and bought two bottles of wine. I was smiling from ear to ear when I met Ray, who had been waiting for me for an hour. Gleefully, I told him of my plans for us for that evening. He was furious. "Barbara, I have two words for you: drop dead."

"Brrrr, it's cold!" I complained later that afternoon, as we tried to nap. "Ray, do something!" But he made no move to get up. "Do something, or I'll scream my head off."

"What do you want me to do, damn it, get a blanket from thin air?"

"Well, you could go walking around the campsite, looking for someone who might have an extra blanket for your sick wife. You're so mean and selfish and —"

"Oh, shut up! I'm going, I'm going. Boy, this is some great beginning!"

"Ow!" Ray exclaimed, as he hit his head on the ceiling, trying to get out of the camper.

I had barely screwed the cap of the wine bottle back on after several slugs, just to warm up, when Ray returned, a different person. Bubbling over, he was transformed.

"What's happened?" I asked. "You're actually smiling?"

"Our luck has changed! I knew it would! I met a family, a Jewish family, in fact. They're from Chicago, and they're doing the same thing we are, only they know already what they want out of life and where they belong. And wait till you hear this: the father was a high school teacher. Both he and his wife and daughter, who's about 18, were fed up with the 'rat race'. He just quit his job. They've sold their belongings and are going to Israel, to work and live on a kibbutz."

"Lots of people are starting to do that," I said. "It's the 'in' thing now amongst Jews, to return to Israel."

"Well, I don't feel so discouraged, somehow. This man is much older than I, and he finally found his dream. There's hope for me. Besides, I like them. They said they'd give us two warm blankets for tonight, and they invited us for dinner tomorrow."

"Oh, okay," I replied, a little reluctant, knowing that Jewish people weren't drinkers, especially Jews going to Israel. I had really been looking forward to having the two bottles of wine I bought for dinner. But I had to be careful and not show Ray how much I suddenly wanted to drink. So far, so good. After we were ready to leave our camper, as an after-thought I suggested we bring some wine. "We shouldn't go over to their camper empty-handed, Ray."

"Barbara, this is Nate, Roz and Naomi."

"Hi," I said brightly, "it's nice to meet you and thanks for inviting us. It's been pretty cold, and we don't have a heater yet." Looking around their VW camper, I was struck by the radiant, beaming smiles they each wore. Nate had a yarmulkah on and was wearing one of those tasseled black shawls I remembered seeing on the men in Borough Park when they went to Temple.

"I'm glad to meet you, Barbara. Shalom, shalom. Your husband told me you were Jewish. You must be familiar with the Friday night dinners, then. We're going to have prayers and read from the Torah."

Nodding yes, I knew I was lost. I was familiar with the delicious Friday night dinners, the candles that were lit, and the bowing of heads over the Jewish candles, but I knew nothing of prayer. Embarrassed, I smiled my best smile and said, "Oh, sure. I come from

Brooklyn, Borough Park. You know where that is, near Flatbush?"

"Sure, I do. I have relatives there. Isn't this wonderful, meeting one's own here in Germany?" He then looked up to the sky, or rather the ceiling of his camper, cupped his hands and said something in Hebrew, as if to thank someone for this.

Nate told us about his job in Chicago — the street gangs, the racial problems and the continuing decay of society. "I said to myself and Roz one day: there has got to be more to life than this. I don't want to die this way, with nothing meaning anything to me, aside from you and Naomi." As he talked, he held our attention between the wine and the flickering candles and the Israeli music on the portable record player in the background.

"That's partly why we're here, too, " I put in. "My husband and I are searching for something, something more...."

"You know, Barbara, it is a blessed thing to be born of a Jewish mother, to be a descendant of Abraham, Isaac and Jacob. I hope you find that out some day, the way we have." And they all looked at each other as though there were something holding them together that transcended normal human experience. Feeling a little uncomfortable now, a little sticky, I glanced at Ray, hoping he'd motion to leave. He didn't. But when Nate said he would like to pray for us and our trip, a sense of acute embarrassment swept over me. Watching everyone lower their heads, including Ray, I assumed that was what I was supposed to do as well. But I was still able to see him again raise his hands to the sky. He spoke in Hebrew and then in English, and all I could hear was Moses, Abraham, Isaac and Jacob.

"Abraham!" I jumped. "That was Peepa, my grandfather's real name. I loved him more than anyone in the whole wide world." Tears filled my eyes. It was like being in Synagogue, but it was more personal, much more. "Jacob was my other grandfather's name and, come to think of it, my great-grandfather's name was Moses — how's about that!"

I slept well that night, dreaming on and off of Peepa and life in Borough Park. In the morning, my throat was still sore and the weather was still cold and damp, but I awoke feeling happy again.

Ray, too, seemed eager to get on with our trip — it was as if anger had been banished from our camper. Once again we tried our luck shopping, and this time we found sleeping bags and the rest of our camping gear. We took the camper out for a run and it did beautifully.

"The traffic is crazy here," Ray said, chuckling. "The people are nuts; look how fast they drive. And I hear Italy and France are even worse." We laughed and joked about the road signs, and that evening we went to a little bar in Wiedenbruck. I regarded it as my reward for not getting drunk the past several months. I had read somewhere that if you could control your drinking for three months, you're not an alcoholic. Well, my ninety days were up, and best of all, I had what I wanted, yearned and waited for, my drinking partner to return. That night he did, and we had a ball — laughing, imitating people, romantically looking into each other's eyes the way we used to. One stein followed another, and my tolerance was truly back; with not even one hiccup or slur in my speech, I shouted for joy: "Prosit, un autre vin, please!" It didn't matter that I mixed German and French, both made-up versions.

Before very long, it became obvious that Raymond was not going to stand for a trip that consisted mainly of going out at night. He seemed to enjoy camper life and just hanging around, doing nothing.

"Ray, we're missing the life style of the people! Conversations in a congenial atmosphere — like a cafe — are the other half of a camping trip." But I had to be careful, not too insistent, or Ray would suspect that once again I was becoming obsessed with a craving to drink. The truth was that while Ray was content to sit for an hour or two and read, or fool around with a piece of equipment, I had to be on the go. I simply could not sit still for more than five minutes. But after two years of having given in to my impulsiveness and the subsequent hell that it had brought both of us, Ray was determined not to passively allow me to have my own way. And I was equally determined that I *was* going to have it, come hell or high water. Our close quarters allowed for no escape from each other. Arguments became more frequent and louder.

Traveling on, we headed towards Denmark. Raymond's insistence on picking up hippies began to irritate me, especially since the last two Italians, who were sitting behind me, looked as though they were going to stick the point of a large, cold stiletto in my back. At least I could legitimately say my nerves were shot when they finally got out of the camper, and I needed to stop and have a drink!

Copenhagen was modern and expensive. Tivoli at night was impressive with all its beautifully lit gardens, music, concerts, stage shows, amusements, cafes, and eye-popping scenery — which was torture, because we could afford nothing! The mosquitoes at night were the size of nickels and during the day the bees were like armies encircling us. We did not stay long in Denmark; the cold, damp weather just aggravated my cold which continued to hang on. I was eager to leave and head further north. There I was finally going to meet what I'd always fantasized about — the other half of my lineage, the Swedish half. What was it going to be like meeting relatives I'd never known but seen pictures of and heard glamorous stories about? I'd see the way my mother used to live, a world so foreign to Borough Park in Brooklyn. But most of all, was I going to meet my father? Was he still there in Stockholm? Would we finally meet? What was it going to be like?

Hesitant, anxious, and excited about what I felt was going to be the greatest adventure of my entire life, my dream come true, I made certain I was in "good shape," cutting down on my alcohol intake, until it would almost pass as "normal." And after we checked into a hotel, I called Bjorn, a cousin, whom I had met years ago in New York. He was thrilled we had arrived and was going to meet with us that very night, to take us to the home of Eva, my father's sister, and her husband Karl. Eva, warm-hearted, had endeared herself to Mother. She remained close, writing always, as had all of the relatives who knew we were coming, and were awaiting the arrival of "Harriet's daughter."

Taking in as much as we could, we walked up and down the great, long, wide streets, looking at all the impressive buildings, and as Ray said, "the fantastic chicks."

"How do I look, how's my hair, my makeup? Are you sure I

look refined? Ray, for Pete's sake, will you look at me? This is important!" The time had arrived for us to drive to Bjorn's house. It was huge, high on a hillside, the view indescribable, and Bjorn looked the same, except for being chunkier with age. His wife Minnie and their children welcomed us right away.

But it was when we approached Eva and Karl's old Swedish house with rich red paint shining in the darkening twilight, and white trim on the windows, similar to almost every house in Sweden, that my heart began to pound with anticipation. And when she opened the door, and we stood, all of us, facing each other, I began to cry, as did she, when we embraced. "Little Barbara, Harriet's little Barbara. I already know so much about you from your mother."

Behind Eva stood a wooden mantel with pictures of the whole family. My eye ran through all of them, landing on the one of my father. But I said nothing, at least not in the beginning of our visit. Our visit brought love, warm memories and a place for Ray and me to camp, just outside their home in a large, lovely yard. Eva and I took to each other, and Karl, who was a famous artist in Sweden, gave me a beautiful watercolor.

There were maudlin times, too, during our stay. Those times alone in the camper brought down self-pity, and jealousy, for the starry-eyed girl who loved to dream elaborate dreams of what could have been hers. For she was just now taking a peek at the life she had missed, longed for, and was convinced could have brought her emotional stability and happiness.

And all the time I was waiting for either the right opportunity to find out where my father lived, or the courage myself to go into a phone booth and call the man who would answer to his name in the phone book. But my father was never mentioned, and so I got fairly high one evening out alone with Ray, leaving him whenever I could and hitting a bar to and from visits to the ladies' room. Holding a piece of paper in my hand, I dialed a telephone number. Waiting almost breathlessly, Ray outside and angry about my repeated disappearances and semi-intoxicated state, I heard a man answer. It must be him, I thought, and I identified myself as my mother's daughter, giving my maiden name, his name. There was a long silence. "No, I'm sorry," he replied in heavily accented English. "I am not the person you are looking for."

My heart dropped. "But you're the only one in the telephone book by this name. Are you a relative?"

"Why don't you call your father's brother's widow? She's in the phone book, and she can point you to the right man. It's not that unusual over here that names are similar. Goodbye now."

"Goodbye, sir, and thanks." I stood in the telephone booth, holding the receiver, suddenly cold sober, stunned. "Who was that man, who was he?"

Frustration set in; I was building towards a real drunk. It had been too long now, this pussy-footing around, a couple of drinks here, a couple there; I needed it and wanted it badly, lots and lots to drink. At that moment, I determined to create a situation where I could have as much as I wanted. And it was going to be soon.

22

We were almost due to leave Sweden, and I still hadn't found out what I wanted to know about my father. So I finally came right out and asked Bjorn where my father was.

"He's in Florida, Barbara."

"Florida, the U.S.? I came all this way, and he's back there!"

But in many ways, it was a relief to at last find out for certain. Fear of rejection had been traveling with me since we had left the States. I could relax now, and I did. The following night, Ray left to go into town alone, while I stayed behind to nurse my cold which had worsened. Eva and Karl had left that afternoon for England to visit her daughter. Now I finally had the chance I had been longing for. I had already noted a bottle of Aquavit, a strong Scandinavian liqueur, in the pantry. Thinking I would have just one, but already smiling at the unthinkable possibility that one might not be enough, I convinced myself that it would be such a long period of time before they ever touched that bottle that, if they did notice it, they would automatically think it was the cleaning lady. After all, a nice girl like me wouldn't do a sneaky thing like that!

The next morning, of course, I had to face Raymond. But I was ready for him: "It's because you're always watching me, that I've turned into a sneak! It's not my fault that you don't let me be any more! I have to hide everything! It's your fault it happened, not mine! And yet, in spite of you, this will not happen again."

But it did happen again. It happened again at the Carlsburg Brewery, in Copenhagen, just two days later. We took the tour and in the biergarten at the end, I sampled the free beer they offered and two hours later walked out with several bottles tucked under my coat and in my handbag. And it happened yet again, the very next night. Once again came the forgetfulness, and mornings became dreaded times, when I felt queasy and shaky, as I tried to remember.

During our drive to Heidelberg, I found myself dreaming of Clarence, of all people. His words of caution echoed in my ears: "Alcoholism is a progressive illness, Barbara. It *never, never* gets better, just steadily worse. Even when the alcoholic stops drinking and doesn't touch a drop for a long time, the illness continues to progress, so that when and if he resumes drinking, he doesn't start again where he left off, but where he would have been, had he kept on drinking. That's one of the things that makes alcoholism such a cunning, baffling disease." I sat bolt upright in my seat at this replay in my mind.

I knew something drastic was happening again. These past few months of control seemed sharply over. "No, no," I whispered to myself. "I'm *not* an alcoholic! And why *should* I stop? Germany is ahead of me. And Italy — how could I ever go to Italy and not drink wine? How could I go anywhere and not drink? I must remember to drop Clarence a card and tell him I'm doing just great."

I wasn't, of course, and it wasn't long before the reality of that overcame Ray's patience, and his own desperate desire to believe that I really was all right after all.

"Barbara, cut this damn stuff out! You're starting again!"

"I'm sorry, Ray, but I know why I lost some control," I said brightly. "It was because I was so upset about not finding my father, and on top of that, I've had this terrible cold, plus the weather is nasty and damp. You'll see, once we get to Heidelberg, and further south, things will be different."

From his look, I knew he didn't believe me; he had heard it too many times before. And yet, the alternative to believing me was so much worse, that in the end he chose to accept what I had told him, and said nothing.

Heidelberg was charming. We had a picturesque campsite, right alongside the Neckar river. I cooked delicious fresh herrings, wursts, and red cabbage and we had the most marvelous Rhine wines and cheese. It was a beautiful, travelogue day, which deserved to be capped by a night on the town. And so we went pub-hopping, and this time, Ray stayed right with me from tequila to beer to schnapps. We got drunk together, and the next morning we were hung over together. But we handled it in different ways.

"Ooooh, my head, my stomach," Ray moaned. "I'll never get so bombed again. I couldn't look at a drink today!" He looked over at me and shook his head. "How can you sit there and drink beer at 11 AM? Don't you *ever* have enough?"

For once, his concern really bugged me, and so instead of bothering to reply, I simply raised the half-empty beer bottle in a mock salute and smiled a taunting smile.

That did it. Realizing how far I was gone from that moment on, Ray watched me like a hawk. And my skill at deception developed far beyond anything it had ever been before. I would have made a great field spy for some espionage agency, except that I was utterly unreliable. I escaped to drink, and drank to escape. Round and round on the carousel I went, somehow managing to stay in the saddle, even though my mind was in a state of confusion and fear.

We spent our second anniversary, September 21st, at a quaint pension in Baden Baden, Germany. After a week to ten days of camping, often with cold showers (when there were showers), a night or two in a room with a real bed and bath was sheer luxury. We both loved the out-of-the-way inns and restaurants that we found, and Ray was amazed at my stamina. "I never thought you'd get the hang of camp life, Princess!" What he didn't realize was that it was the alcohol which was now constantly in my system in varying amounts that was keeping me warm and content. It was only when it began to wear off that I would become irritable, uncomfortable and shy.

The Black Forest, on the way to Zurich, was the most beautiful country either of us had ever seen. Up thirty-eight hundred feet, we stopped at an extremely luxurious mountain resort. But all we did was stop and look, as in our daily expenditures we dared not exceed $10 a day at the most. So our lunch was spent dreaming of the future, as we gazed around us at the silent green beauty of the forest. Only the constant buzz of bees all around us and our food kept us moving on.

Zurich, Switzerland, was a place I never had any particular desire to see, but it surprised me with its clean order and beauty. The shops were smart; the people had style and were well dressed. And now I knew why my old roommate, Jean, and the Swiss banker she had finally married, loved it here. I had written her that we were coming and couldn't wait to call her and tell her that Ray and I had arrived. And as we drove to her home, where she had invited us to stay for a while, I reminisced about our life together on East 80th in Manhattan. Jean had had to work hard for her apartment and upkeep then, but she had known what she wanted, and she had gotten it. I turned greener than the greenest tree I'd seen in the Black Forest, when her maid answered the door. She had her own home, her own car, and most of all, what I couldn't bear to look at, two beautiful children. Her husband had a top job with a Swiss bank, and her whole life seemed perfect.

As Jean told me about the parties, theatres, exercise salons twice a week, and how much Ned loved and worshipped her (which she didn't have to report; it was obvious), I looked down, went down, and drooped my shoulders, feeling sorrier than ever for myself. Certainly Ray had long since lost respect and perhaps love for me. When we were out with them, Ned was constantly looking at Jean, holding her chair for her and showing obvious signs of still being romantically drawn to her. It made me acutely aware of who I was, and what was happening to me, and it brought home a stark picture of where we were headed.

Feeling that I couldn't possibly stay in that frame of mind, or the depression would drive me insane, I leapt at the first chance for a change of scene. When a Swiss fellow named Peter, whom we met at a restaurant one night, invited us to come and stay with him for a while, Ray urged me to accept. Peter's life seemed to be focused on heated discussions about politics. Ray loved the political discussions, I, the booze that Peter drank and had a good supply of. So, my fears of staying at this man's apartment, a man whom neither of us knew, were soon alleviated. Ray and I told Jean and Ned about Peter and that we were going to spend a few days with him before we left Zurich. I couldn't bear to face any longer the kind of life I so wanted, yet was walking further and further away from. How I wanted a home of my own, something I had never had. And children? I had begun to believe that I would never have children and inside, I was afraid — afraid that as a mother, I would destroy the very children that I would come to love. So I sat with them that night in the restaurant, sipping vodka and dreaming dreams of owning my own home, and watching a little boy and girl running in the sand, calling out to me, "Mommy, Mommy, I love you." I could see glasses of cold milk on the kitchen counter when they came home from school, baked brownies waiting for them, a little dog jumping up and down, and the whole family sitting down to dinner together. There would be bubble baths, the smell of clean sheets that had been sun-dried in the fresh air, and bed-time stories before goodnight kisses. Later, Ray and I would have coffee and dessert together. He would enjoy just being with me, sharing everything, including the latest news and books.

"Hey, Barbara? Barbara, wake up, where are you? I've been talking to you for the past five minutes."

"Huh? Oh, I'm sorry, Peter, what is it?"

"Just wanted to know if you wanted another drink?"

"Yeah, sure, thanks."

Peter and Ray were involved in another discussion now, about what might be the true meaning of life, and what is truth? Peter's wife was away, he said, as he pointed the way to his house. He certainly was hospitable, inviting us to stay with him. Why did he do it? The following night, I found out why. In the middle of the night, wide awake and ridden with anxiety, I repeated the pattern which had become my *modus operandi*, wherever we were house guests. I slipped silently out of bed and tiptoed down to the kitchen, to see if I could find a dusty, half-forgotten bottle of liquor somewhere. It was better if it had been around for a long time, because they wouldn't be so likely to notice that it had been tampered with, or if they finally did, they would be less likely to put two and two together. It was dark, and I stumbled over something, and then I froze: I heard something that didn't make any sense — whimpering. Turning on the kitchen light, I found Peter sitting on the kitchen floor, drinking vodka out of a bottle and crying like a baby. Looking up at me with bloodshot, bleary eyes, he sobbed, "So now you know! I'm an alcoholic!"

It was a pitiful sight, and should have sent icy tremors down my spine, and perhaps sparked some compassion, yet all I could feel was revulsion and a desire to get our of that place as fast as I could. It was like a horrible nightmare. He maintenance-drank all day, he told me, keeping his job, but at night, all night long, he would sit on the kitchen floor or in the bathtub with the water running on him and drink out of a bottle. "Sometimes I call for my wife, sometimes my mother. I've lost my wife and my little children. Oh, my little ones!" and he broke down again.

"I'm sorry, Peter, but what can I say? Can't you stop drinking? You must be able to stop."

"No, I can't. There was a time when I could. Everyone warned me then that this would happen, but I kept on, and now I'm ruined. I plan to take my life, you know. And I'm not just saying that; I mean it. This — existence — isn't worth a damn!"

The next morning, Ray was totally mystified at my abrupt reversal, and insistence that we leave immediately.

"But, Barbara, *why?* Peter's let us come and go, and he's pleasant enough company."

"I just want to move on. Besides, it's not decent staying here with a man whose wife is away."

"But he's not like that; he doesn't notice you, other than as my wife."

"I know that, but I want to leave, do you hear, now! I've got to get out of here, or I'll go nuts! It's too depressing."

Facing Peter's bondage was more than I could handle; it forced me to look at my own.

Our trip from Zurich to Locarno was rough. No longer could I sleep through the night — Peter's face, pitiful, longing, full of despair, haunted me. After seeing him with a bottle that night, I decided never to drink vodka again. Convinced now that all alcoholics drank vodka to hide behind it, I was going to stick with good wines. "Wine is safe, Ray. You never hear of anyone getting into trouble with wine, right?"

Ray let me have my way. He had no choice, knowing that if I couldn't drink with him, I would invariably find another way. And I did, like our second night in Locarno. "Ray," I said in the camper, "I'm restless. Let's go someplace. You never want to go out at night any more. We can't just stay in this camper and stare at each other, day in and day out."

"You know, Barbara," he said sadly, "we really have very little in common. I was fooled. Now that I don't care about drinking, there's really nothing, nothing at all. It's a shame you don't like to read. Come to think of it, I don't think I've ever seen you with a book in your hand. For that matter, you don't like to sit still, period. The only thing you seem to enjoy doing is hopping around from bar to bar. You're a barfly, a common, ordinary barfly."

These words pierced my heart, as I listened to the sound of the pounding rain against the metal roof of our camper. Ray, with a book in front of him, never looked up at me as he spoke. I felt so low, so cheap — locked in, and there was no defense. He was right about me and reading, and even my daily diary was something to be ashamed of, so poorly written was it next to Raymond's. Ray could converse with anyone about anything. He explained himself well with a few words and was able to write what he saw and felt clearly, unlike my rambling descriptions of scenes and sights I was now barely able to see clearly.

The sting of truth hurt. I wanted to cry so badly, but instead I took the book out of Ray's hands and hurled it to the floor. He sat silently, never once looking up at me, while I yelled and screamed, cursing him and ultimately threatening suicide. Finally, utterly defeated, he spoke. "Barbara, I don't care *what* you do any more. Go and kill yourself, if you want to."

"I will, I will, you bastard!"

The rain whipped against my face, as I ran along the road in the dark, looking for a place to drink. It was late at night, after eleven, and it occurred to me that women didn't do this sort of thing in Italy, unless they were loose. Cars stopped, men whistled and called out to me, offering me rides and much more — all. I looked straight ahead and ran all the faster, suddenly remembering that horrible drunken night in March when a car stopped and men pulled me inside. I became frightened at that recollection, and fearful that it would happen again. Memories now came back of the times when I had left our apartment in Princeton in the dark, in the rain or snow. I had always come back, but inside I had sensed that there would come a time, and perhaps it was tonight, that I would not come back. Someone would attack me, maybe kill me, or I'd run out in the street drunk and be hit by a car, or be dragged off to the woods and be beaten and stabbed to death. My body would be ripped apart and thrown away.

Cringing, I ran and ran, until I couldn't catch my breath any more. How long could I keep on like this? How much more time was left? Breathless, my eyes caught a dim light in the distance on the other side of the road. Falling and crawling on my hands and knees, bruised and wet, I made my way to the light in the distance on the other side of the road. When I was close enough to see what it was, I strained to read the neon sign. Tears streamed down my cheeks. It was as if I had been on a desert for days and finally saw ahead a well, filled with cool, clean water. *Cafe* — the blessed word cafe, my oasis, beckoned. I could drink as much as I wanted all night long. Only a few more feet to go. Ignoring the cars splashing me, some on purpose just to taunt me, I crawled up the three front steps to the cafe. Then, hoisting myself up against the door, I walked in.

Couples were sitting at small round tables together, some holding hands. Soft music played in the background, waiters were busily taking orders. They stopped, turned, and stared at me for what seemed like the longest, most embarrassing moment. Lowering my head to where I couldn't see anyone, I found a chair at an empty table by a window. A soft male voice whispered in my ear, "Madam, are you all right? Have you been hurt?"

"I'm fine, fine, thank you," I said to the waiter. "Just give me a litre of red wine, please." I was curt in my reply and had my money out on the table before the wine came. Hardly ever looking up, blocking out as much of everything in me that hurt and was in anguish, I drank the litre.

"It's time to close, now, madame. Would you like a ride home?"

"No, I don't want a ride home!" For an instant, I was back in front of Edward's again, being pulled into that car and seeing hands, thousands of hands. Scarcely able to walk, I managed somehow to get outside. It was a mile back to the campsite, and in the dark, I stumbled and fell, sometimes out into the middle of the road. One oncoming car stopped, just in time, before I was hit. I cried and pleaded, out there in the night. I cried just like Peter did on his kitchen floor with his bottle of vodka. I called for help — for Mother, for Raymond and for Peepa. "Oh Peepa, my Peepa. If you only knew what's happened to me, your little baby, your little Mamashena. Peepa, I'm coming to you soon. I don't want to be here any more. I can't take it, Peepa. Please, please take me away."

23

Crossing the Alps was not really as difficult as we were led to believe. Passing through beautiful villages and mountain scenery, I made Ray stop the car every half-hour in front of a cafe. I told him I had to use the ladies' room. But on the way to or from each ladies' room there was usually a bar of some sort where I could down a fast drink.

With each drink I took came another threat from Ray. Fear upon fear, I lived in torment over the day that would finally come when our marriage would be over. And I knew that once our marriage was over, so, too, would be my life.

It was a long ride from Locarno, Switzerland to Rapallo, Italy. An Italian traffic jam, we decided had to be the worst in the world —everyone yelling at everyone else, and yelling at us, too, till Ray finally rolled down his window and yelled back, in choice Italian, which I'd hardly ever heard him speak. But finally we found a campsite, and bedded down for the night. The next morning was a beautiful drive along the coast, with a short stop at Portofino, a picturesque village with lots of cafes. Later on, the road became incredibly curvy and mountainous, and we were slowed to a crawl. But once we got on the Autostrada, our speed picked up and we rolled into a so-so camp at Pisa, about three blocks from the

Tower. After dinner and some stop-offs on the way back home, we went to bed. The next morning we went to see the Cathedral, and then visited one of the architectural wonders of the world.

"Yipes, that tower really does lean. Are you sure it's safe to go up there, Ray?"

"Of course, people go up and down every day." Since everything frightened me, I knew I must be over-reacting. Up the stairs Ray and I went, with the rest of the tourists. Once on top, I took a big step after Ray, outside onto the leaning tower. And did that tower ever lean! My whole body felt as though it was going forward. There wasn't even a railing to stop me from falling over. Certain that I was about to fall off the tower in the direction it leaned, I felt myself begin to lose my balance. Nauseated and dizzy, I screamed: "Help, I'm going over, help — help!"

Suddenly things came into focus, and I became aware of a burning sensation on my right cheek. Raymond had slapped me hard. "You nitwit," he hissed, "hold on to me and stop making a scene. You're not going over, though that might not be a bad idea!"

"Whew, that thing was unbelievable!" I said, when we had gotten back down. "You've got to be nuts to go up there," I told everyone waiting in line for their turn. Heading straight for a cafe, I sat alone at a table and drank as much as I could until I knew Ray would leave. And leave he did. He picked me up in the camper, I picked a fight, and he let me out of the camper somewhere along a deserted beach. He drove off, and I turned into the nearest bar.

An hour later I came out. Standing in the middle of the road, I yelled, "Oh Raymond, where are you? Aren't you coming back for me?" And just then the camper turned the corner. Ray got out and walked towards me. His head was low. But instead of the anger I expected, I saw tears.

Trying to hold all the pent-up feelings, hates, fears and loneliness that he had felt since we started this trip, he broke. Bursting into tears, Raymond sank to the ground, pounding it with his fists, crying, "Why, why why?" The pain of watching him suffer was even worse than my own. I couldn't bear it. I was causing it. I was ruining his life.

"Oh Raymond, please, *please,* don't!" Kneeling down on the ground beside him, I begged him to stop. "Oh God, my God, please forgive me, help me, I'm sorry." Not even aware of what my words were, I cried out like I never had before. "Raymond, I'll do anything, this time, anything it takes to stop! I'll do anything you say. We'll find a place, some people who can help me, something. There's got to be a way. There's got to! Give me another chance, please, I beg you. I love you so much. You're the only decent thing that ever was or is in my life."

He quieted, but still shook his head. At least he had stopped crying. "Maybe, Ray, when we get to Rome, when we're in one place for a period of time, things will be different. We'll be a whole month in Rome. I'll get help there. I'll go to the American Embassy. I'll do something, anything."

Getting to his feet, Ray lifted me alongside him and put his arm around my shoulder. "C'mon, let's take a walk on the beach, Princess."

The next morning we drove down the beautiful coast to Cicino del Mare. We found a perfect three-star camp with all facilities right on the beach. Arriving at about 6 P.M., I clung to Ray as we checked in. This was the first day since my drinking had gotten out of control again, that I hadn't touched a drop. With every fiber in me, I wanted to keep my promise to Ray. How I wanted to be sober, to be normal! We turned a corner in the camping area, looking for our site. I saw other families together, enjoying one another. I yearned to be like that woman, and that one over there and that one, and then, my eye caught a sign — "Camp Store." Every camp store, I knew, had wine. No, no, don't even think about it!

But Barbara, you must drink! As soon as you get to your site, steal some money from Ray's wallet and leave him and go to the store. Make sure to take everything for a shower with you. Then get a bottle and drink it in the shower. It's the only way. You have to, you know, you have to. After all, it's your life's blood, isn't it? The power, that awful power, was back, dictating to me, making me do what I didn't want to do, and I was putty. I couldn't fight it. I was so weak, I did exactly what it said.

I came back fairly quickly. I was bright but not too cheerful, and I didn't get too close — but somehow he knew. The look on his face, which had been so hopeful for the first time, now took on the most bewildered picture of disappointment I'd ever seen. It was so awful, so childlike and sad. "I'm sorry, but I only stopped for one drink. I just had one to get me going." He turned and walked away from me, far away. I climbed into the camper and pulled out the bottle from the towel I had wrapped it in. Sitting on the floor in between the seats, so that I wouldn't be seen, I finished what was left in it.

Siena was an enchanting old walled city that caught my heart. I loved it. For once, I made myself walk and walk and walk through the narrow cobblestoned streets and out into the large piazza, which was scalloped in shape and surrounded by umbrella-ed, outdoor cafes. "This place is just like the color siena, Ray — rich, warm and glowing." We found a villa for $4 a night for both of us, where we could get a bath for $1.25, and a quart of wine for only 40¢. The lobby of this villa was filled with old oil paintings and all sorts of tasteful art. Our room looked out on the whole city and was above the most beautiful gardens imaginable. It was everything and anything that I'd ever imagined beautiful to be. Romance was everywhere, and I decided that this would be a very special few days. But in the end, I spoiled that too. . . .

"But Raymond, all these salty black olives make me thirsty. And you know we were warned about drinking water."

"Look: you'll come up with anything to have your own way, Barbara. If you want to stop, you can buy bottled water. I've had my heart set on coming to Italy, and now I'm here. You are *not* going to spoil it for me. So from now on, you're on your own. I won't say no to you or chase you. It's obvious to me now that nothing short of a miracle, if there is such a thing, will be your final refuge."

Our campsite, outside of Rome, was in the country. It was the largest camp we had been at so far and was full of young people. There were some "straight" families, but for the most part, there were long-haired, sandaled hippies from everywhere. Every tent, camper and puptent had bottles of wine stacked outside. In the evening, soft guitar music could be heard, and to our surprise, we noted the sweet smell of marijuana. The paths leading to each campsite were curved and bumpy. Restrooms were located next to the large camp store and restaurant, so I was in luck. With the camp store so close, I didn't have to hunt around for other excuses to get to the bar at all hours; I was just going to the ladies' room. I got up as usual in the middle of the night and stole lire from Ray's wallet. The store was open at 6:30 in the morning and closed at midnight, which left only six and a half hours when I would be without a drink. Even so, that was an ordeal. I sat on my hands, bit my nails, twisted and turned all night long, rarely catching more than an hour's sleep at a time. At 6 a.m. I headed for the restrooms and then straight for the bar. Two large water glasses filled to the brim with white wine began my day, but it wasn't until I had consumed several more hourly doses that I became functional by 9:00 a.m.

But no matter how hard it was physically for me to abstain from alcohol, it was harder emotionally. I found myself going through nostalgic moments when I missed my mother terribly. I missed Clarence, Emily and everyone who had tried to help me. How could I have been so wrong, so blind, so sick?

Rome bustled with hectic traffic; the Italian men on our bus were ready to fight at the slightest provocation, or flirt at any opportunity, always making a woman aware of her sex. The women were chic — at least, those strolling the fashionable Via Veneto. Their olive skins and shiny dark hair pulled off their faces gave them a magnificent appearance. Rarely did we see a woman wearing slacks, and so whenever I went into town, I too wore a skirt, except for the cold, damp, rainy weather. I went to the Catacombs, to the Forum and the Colosseum, but caught only glimpses of these places, traveling now in a continuous alcoholic fog. Blackouts were frequent now — sometimes several occurring in one day — talking, moving and being without any recollection afterwards of where I was or even with whom, although I never left Raymond for long. At the Colosseum, I made a fast exit after hearing a guide tell a story about lions and gladiators hiding in caves. I could have sworn I saw a gladiator coming at me, but then the weather had turned quite warm, and it wasn't unusual in those days for me to envision all sorts of things.

Most days consisted of a litre of wine before 11 a.m. Then we would take a bus into town and tour the city, stopping at some small groceria for lunch in the back of the store with all the local Italians. By four o'clock, I had consumed another couple of litres of wine and was getting ready for the evening and some serious drinking, either back at the camp or anywhere and everywhere feasible. And if Ray ever got disgusted with my drunken histrionics and let me slam out of the camper without a dime or a bottle, I would wake up sleeping strangers, complaining of pains in the stomach from the food or water. "May I please have some brandy?" And eventually they would help me back to our campsite.

Ironically, through this bizarre behavior of mine, Ray made friends with various people, including one fellow from the Midwest, Gil. He began to tag along, so that Ray could have some company. Gil loved to play cards, and Ray didn't mind staying back at the camp in the evenings and playing cards or visiting friends in other tents, discussing everything from the war in Vietnam to God is Dead. Conversation bored me; my thing was to sit by the Trevi Fountain and throw lire in, wishing that either I would die or everything would change. I cried and cried and wished and wished, as people passed and watched me make a fool of myself.

But somehow, everything was different the day I went to St. Peter's Basilica. I felt as though I was almost whole, instead of broken, shattered and drunk. Taking in all I could, I stared in wonder up at the Sistine Chapel ceiling and Michelangelo's great masterpiece. I felt as if I was in the center of some divine presence. Even the hands touching on the ceiling above seemed to reach down towards me. I wanted to stay there. And when we came to the last work of art for that day, the Pieta, I stood in front of it for one hour, and an hour for me, on my feet, standing still, I would have thought was impossible. Tears filled my eyes at the wondrous, poignant beauty — that seemed to beckon me. Later that night I sneaked a glimpse of Raymond's diary, to see what horrors he'd written about me for that day. But this time I was surprised. "Great spirituality filled us all, especially B — she could so use a tower of strength such as this whole area around St. Peter's exudes." What did he mean? Ray never talked like that. What strength was he referring to?

Our money was running low. We had to make it stretch. And so I reverted back to an old skill which I had sworn I would never use again. In the supermarket I passed the cheese counter and impulsively grabbed a large hunk of blue cheese. Then I went to the fish counter and took several tins of canned fish. Then olives, nuts and so on.

Outside, Raymond went bananas when I brought out, one by one, my stolen goods. "Oh, c'mon Ray, everybody does this sort of thing. Let's go in again and take some other things. Don't be such a square. Haven't you ever stolen anything?"

"Yes, when I was eight years old, I attempted to take a pack of cigarettes from my grandmother's meat and grocery store on Witherspoon Street. She caught me and spanked the daylights out of me."

But to my surprise, Ray did agree to try his luck at taking a jar of instant coffee. Walking behind him, I watched him clumsily put a jar into his boot. He took two steps and it fell out. He turned to me and yelled out: "You damned nut, you're insane! Why did I listen to you? Why did I marry you?"

Why *did* I do it? I wondered, suddenly jolted back to reality. Haven't I been through enough, having almost been arrested? God, I don't want to end up in an Italian jail! Ray doesn't even know about the stealing. I mustn't do it again.

For days I pondered my actions. Why did I go into that supermarket and so blatantly take those items? Did I *want* to be caught? Maybe that would be better than this, I thought, one afternoon, holding my head and kneeling over a filthy toilet bowl. But the dry heaves wouldn't stop, and I couldn't keep even liquor down. Looking at the blood I had just thrown up, I ran back to the bar. "There must be something I can keep down, bartender. I've got to have a drink that will stay down." The bartender came up with something cloudy-looking.

Putting it in front of me, he said: "Try this, it's Pernod." It did the trick, and after two and a half drinks, the vomiting ceased. Several more drinks and once again I breathed, moved, smiled and lied.

"Raymond, do we have to take Gil with us to Capri? And I hear Positano is about the most romantic spot on the Italian coast. We can get a room alone overlooking the blue water. If we stay there for a few days, I promise to dry out. It'll be easier there. This camp is dirty and inconvenient, and I'm cold."

"Do you think I'd be so crazy as to go off for a weekend alone with you? There's no telling what you're capable of when you're drunk, and you're drunk almost all the time now. I don't know what to do with you."

I didn't want to hear that, and I didn't. In Positano we had a magnificent view from a room in a pension that was built on a hill, just as I had predicted. The lights at night, glistening on the black water, made this spot the most romantic thus far. "Ray, will you take me dancing downstairs, if I promise to be good?"

"Fat chance of that. I'm playing gin rummy with Gil tonight; you'll just have to find someone else to dance with."

My legs gave way the following morning when I tried to get out of bed. My body shook and heaved. Ray said nothing, but I could feel his cold stare as he watched me crawl to the bathroom. After dressing, my long hair still tangled, I quickly left the room. It was 8 a.m. and I hobbled down a steep cobble-stoned street in search of a cafe that was open. But it was so early on Sunday that everything was closed. I had to find something! We were due to go to Capri.

As I swayed and staggered down one alley after another, I finally came upon a bar that was open. "Whew, saved again!" I couldn't allow myself to think of what might happen to my body if it was deprived of alcohol at this stage. Several hours later, I arrived back at our room, ready and raring to move on. The boat trip to Capri was rocky. Ray refused to look or talk to me at all; Gil barely nodded. So I wandered around the boat, and down some stairs, where I tripped and slid right smack into a pigsty. There among some fat, filthy pigs, I sat in the mud, "oinking" back at them; at least they allowed me to sit in their company.

From that scene on, I blacked out totally, until one night a week later, I came to in the camper. Ray was asleep next to me. I saw his diary beside him. Quietly I turned the flashlight on and opened to the day's entry. "Sunday, October 18, 1970 — This was almost tragic. I experienced desires to kill, maim, leave, suicide. The whole bit — let's chalk it off."

24

Waiting for the end of our Italian month to arrive, so that we could go to either Spain or Greece, I continued my scheming and devising ways to drink. Deception had become such a part of my daily life that I began to deceive myself and others even when I didn't have to. Physically and emotionally, I was in a constant down. There was no hope for the future, except for the possibility that things might somehow be different in another country. "Raymond, I'm sure if we go back to Spain and wait out the winter, I'll be able to recapture what and how I was on our honeymoon. The warm weather will be good for me, and I just know I can stop drinking there." Ray nodded his head, but it was automatic for him to do that now. It was even automatic for me.

The truth was, I was empty, devoid of any hope for the future. It wasn't long before I even gave up saying to myself, "I'll stop tomorrow." I began to believe that Raymond was punishing me; intense paranoia about everything set in. At night, I was sure snakes were wrapped around our tires, or there was a big bear outside waiting for me. Darkness and especially silence frightened me — the long, black, silent, cold nights were steps of torture that only made me loathe waking up to a new day. There was no place in our camper to stand up, let alone pace the floor.

Truth no longer existed. I lied about everything. I had to; there was no self-respect left, nothing. I was a total shambles, unable even to stand in a shower alone, because of my horrendous fear of running water. Believing lies that I made up about myself and other people kept me in perpetual fantasy. And fantasy, any way I looked at it, was infinitely preferable to truth and reality. I would have gone stark, raving mad if all my "props" had been taken away from me, and I was left alone — with myself. Fear that Raymond was soon going to commit me somewhere, to an asylum, haunted me. Only drinking to oblivion blocked out these fears, but even then not completely. I clung desperately to the fact that he couldn't possibly put me away in Europe. That at least gave me some time to . . . to . . . I never knew. Instead of ending that sentence with, "to get dry and shape up," I now began to end it with "to get up enough courage to kill myself."

The fleeting thought of taking my own life brought horror and shame. Emotionally I fell apart just thinking about it, so I didn't think about it. I didn't think about anything. Every thought had to be deadened with alcohol. There was nothing, nothing good left for me. Sometimes at night, after waking up in a cold sweat, screaming and crying, I would plead with a sleeping Raymond not to let anyone lock me up. "Oh, I'd rather die than be locked up in an asylum!" But inside, I was torn to pieces because there was still a part of me that wanted to live. "I want to live . . . if only . . . ." And then it would become if only this, if only that, and if only he, she, they, this place, yesterday, tomorrow . . . .

Gil and we parted ways in Rome on October 11th, and Giuseppe, our Italian friend whom we had met in Princeton, now turned up. So I put up as good a front as possible when we all went out together, but he was clearly aware of how I looked and behaved, though he had seen me in pretty bad shape back in Princeton. Giuseppe didn't ask any personal questions, but let Ray know he cared about him. He offered us his "villa," as he called it, outside of Rome. "Look, you two, go there for a week. You'll have sunshine and a rest. The people don't speak English, but the fresh air and quiet will be good for you. I'll come up and visit you on the weekend."

Oh, how I suddenly felt a surge of hope! Ray agreed to go, and I was thrilled. "This is it, Ray! That is where I am going to sober up."

If it was going to happen, it had to happen soon, for the situation was getting worse, if that was possible. One morning, I returned from the ladies' room after a series of dry heaves, then wine and more vomiting. Looking up at Ray as I tried to climb into the camper, I burst into tears: "Oh my God, my God. Isn't there any help for me? Ray, please, I beg you, come with me to get some help. I've *got* to try to get some help now, before it's too late." My pleading and crying became obsessive, as I sensed impending doom all around me.

At first, Ray shook his head. "You've had help before, and you threw it away. Besides there simply isn't any way to get any help here in Italy."

"I'll find a way; there *must* be a way. We can go to the police or the American Embassy —"

"All right, come on, or you'll be harping on it all day. We'll find the police station in Rome. Maybe you'll get lucky, and they'll lock you up," Ray said, chuckling and hoping I'd see the humor. But I didn't. I feared they really might lock me up. At that moment, though, anything would be better than where I was.

And so, after a frantic driving trip around one traffic circle after another, and loud jeers for going every which way but the right way, we found the police station. Ray stayed a good distance behind me, as I proceeded to charge through the station. I stopped the first policeman I saw. "Sir, I don't know how to tell you this, but I am very sick. I need help. I, uh, have a drinking problem."

"You have a drinking problem, eh? Well, do you drink wine?"

"Yes, yes."

"How much wine do you drink?"

"A lot. I don't know, two bottles a day?"

The policeman burst out laughing in my face. In between laughs, he asked me if we were vacationing. When I told him we were on an extended camping trip, he consolingly tapped me on the shoulder, saying: "Young lady, we don't have such a problem in this country. It is good wine, good for the blood. Drink, eat, have yourself a good time in Italy."

"But you don't understand. Can't you tell me where to go to —"

"Go out and have a good time; that's all I can tell you. There is no place, young lady, for you to go, do you understand?"

Walking out of the police station into the bright, sunny streets of Rome, I wasn't aware whether Ray was still with me or not. More despondent than ever, I hung on the officer's words: "There is no place for you to go." I crossed the busy street, hoping to be hit. Not looking up, hearing brakes screaming and drivers yelling to me to watch where I was going — "Do you want to get killed" — and tons of Italian phrases and gestures from open windows, I looked for a bar or cafe or restaurant or candy store. Finding one, I sat there until I drank myself into a stupor. When I could no longer walk or talk, I just sat slumped over on the table, drooling.

Giuseppe had said his villa was in a tiny hill town called Monticchio, about a three-hour drive from Rome. From there we planned to go to the small town that Ray's father had come from, and where Raymond intended to meet his Italian relatives.

We reached Monticchio on October 27th at 4 o'clock in the afternoon. "We must have gone the wrong way, Raymond. It doesn't look to me as if there could possibly be a villa around here." Chickens were running loose in the street. Oxen and donkeys were everywhere. Men and women, mostly old, were all shabbily dressed. The women wore black with black kerchiefs around their heads. After much insistence on my part, Ray got out at the local grocery store in the village and tried to find out if Giuseppe's "villa" was, in fact, here.

I saw Ray laugh for the first time in a long time when he emerged with some old men, chuckling and pointing his finger up the street to me in the camper. When he took the wheel again, his face was alight with a boyish grin and he told me the good news: "Right up that street is Giuseppe's villa."

"What? You've got to be kidding! Why, that place looks as though nothing but an animal could live in it." And then I got suspicious, "Is this a joke?"

"Nope, no joke. That's Giuseppe's house. Look at it this way: we're *really* away from tourists now. And when would we ever have an opportunity to live in a foreign country like this?"

"Well, okay. But I have a feeling that camping is luxury compared to what's in store for us."

It turned out that apart from my being ill, very ill, this was the best week of the whole trip so far. The village had approximately a hundred people in it. Our neighbors peeked and stared but gradually got used to us, smiling as we came and went. We went down to the store for wine and food and up the hill to the country for picnics. There was no heat, and worse of all, the bathroom facilities didn't work well, which was critical because, considering the fact that my whole body was now reacting to alcohol abuse, I needed to spend a lot of time in the bathroom. Chills and freezing temperatures at night and my complaining drove Raymond in search of help one evening. But when the man who returned with Ray saw the kerosene stove in Giuseppe's room, he raised his hands and screamed in fear, saying "No, no," and left.

A loud knock on the door after we piled sleeping bags and hot water bottles on ourselves, got us to our feet and outside, to face a fiasco that we had caused. All we could see were livestock and donkeys screeching, piled up along our street. It took forever in pantomime for Ray to finally figure out that the way our camper was parked made it impossible for these animals to use the street. Ray got the camper out of the way, but then ended up pinned against a big wall. He couldn't go forward, because he was spinning wheels in reverse. Four men from the town came to the rescue and lifted the entire car up off the wheels. Ray got out unscathed.

We ran out of hot water, and then had no water at all. In a way I was grateful, for I felt like I was going to die. It had been a day and a half that I had gone without a drop of alcohol, and was I sick. My legs wouldn't support me, and I had to stay in bed, but that was the least of what I was suffering. So when Ray brought home a freshly made liter of white wine for twenty cents, and it was powerful stuff, I resumed drinking and functioning once again. But even with the wine, I stayed in bed for two days, ceaselessly shivering and shaking, unable to keep anything down.

It was obvious to me that if I stopped drinking by myself, I might die, or worse, go out of my mind completely. It was at this time, when Ray caught a glimpse of my dependence and helplessness, and was aware that I really had tried to stop, if only for one day, that he looked at me and stroked my forehead one evening. "It's too bad, Princess," he said with compassion, "it's just too bad."

The rooster on top of our "villa" woke us faithfully at five o'clock in the morning. So we were ready and waiting for Giuseppe when he arrived to take us to Abruzzi. Petoranello was the little town in Abruzzi where Ray's dad was born and raised, until he came to America at twelve years of age. Just as my meeting my relatives in Sweden was an experience I would cherish, so was this meeting with Ray's relatives in Petoranello. As Giuseppe's Porsche drove up to this immaculate old village, we were suddenly bombarded by Italians from every direction.

They *all* turned out to be Ray's relatives, and none of them spoke a word of English! But Ray and I had our cheeks pinched over and over again, and they all cried and cried on our shoulders. "Li'l Raymond" was one term of endearment that I made out and heard over and over. After a while I joined in and cried, too. And since I had a lot to cry about, it was easy.

We took pictures, Giuseppe translated, and began waving his hands with the same gusto as these people. When we came to the home of the oldest lady in town, Ray's dad's aunt, she wept to see us, knowing that she would never see us again. She did say repeatedly, as did some of the other older people, "I'll see you in California." We asked Giuseppe afterwards what that meant, and he said it was a common expression that they used for the after-life.

The Italian meal that was prepared for us would have put any restaurant in Rome to shame, and the brandy and wine — well, they kept pushing it our way. Giuseppe knew how to say no, and so did Ray after a while, but I kept on, and by some quirk of fate, I did not get drunk that day and spoil things for Ray. And I hugged the little old lady in black, with the wrinkled tan face and tear-filled blue eyes, and I cried and almost wished that she would take me with her to "California."

We returned to Monticchio for one more day, then said goodbye to the milkman and the cow and the owner of the grocery store and all our Italian neighbors for that week. We left Monday morning at 7 a.m. for Assisi. Of all the sights we had seen, for some reason I yearned to see St. Francis' Basilica. I remembered reading something written by St. Francis once and having been drawn to it: "Lord, make me an instrument . . . ." Forcing myself to remember where or how I'd seen that, I somehow thought it related back to Clarence and Emily in Princeton. I kept seeing Clarence's face before me, remembering how freely he had given of himself as he tried to help us, and yes, how he had even cried for us. There was one man who certainly was an instrument . . . .

Off in my own little world, my head pressed against the window, I said: "Ray, when will we get to St. Francis's?" It was almost as if St. Francis himself was going to be there, waiting for me. I wanted to hurry and get there, before it was too late. But it *was* too late, as it turned out. I was drunk when we arrived, barely able to walk and very sick. How horrible I felt when I later learned where I had been and what I had done — again. To find out that I had staggered and fallen up to the Basilica and back, disgracing myself in front of everyone else again — what could I do, but bow my head in shame.

Moving along quickly now, we headed for Florence, where I wandered in and out of flea markets. I bought a brown leather shoulder bag and cherished it, remembering the suede coat Ray bought me in Madrid on our honeymoon. I'd always loved to bargain someone down in price, though it embarrassed Ray terribly. "But it's such fun to bargain, Ray, and they expect you to here, and I do get such great deals!" Strolling through the flea markets reminded me of Borough Park. I was a little girl again, walking with Meema on Saturday, to the big open air market on Thirteenth Avenue.

There were galleries and palaces, and I was at the Uffizi, the Pitti Palace, and other places, so I was informed. But like the Pieta, there was one visit to which I came alive, and that was seeing Michelangelo's "David." We spent half an hour in front of it, looking at the strong sculptural lines, the incredible power and detail of one hand. The magnificence of this work of art drew me, and I didn't want to leave. But still there was nothing that could take me for long away from the next drink, and that was always there waiting, at every turn.

On our way to the French Riviera, Ray insisted on picking up a hitchhiker. Philip was his name, about twenty, a camper with no money, though apparently from wealthy parents in England. "Oh I come from terribly good stock, you know, but what's money? I'd rather fast, and that's exactly what I'm doing."

"You mean you haven't been eating anything, Philip?"

"No, ma'am, not for three days. It's good for the system, cleans one out." Philip had called me ma'am, and I liked that, so I invited him to come have dinner with us when we found a campsite. He was quite ready to break his fast.

I had bought some hamburger and milk and put it under the camper where it would be cooler, after saying goodnight to Philip who was going down to the beach, not too far from us. Hours later, we awoke to munching and footsteps.

"Good grief! What's that noise, Barbara?"

"Shhh, I don't know. It's the middle of the night."

"I'm going out there with my knife."

"What! Are you crazy? How do you know whoever it is won't kill you?"

"Yeah, you're right, I'd better not go."

This went on for quite some time until I was sure that the culprit was Philip who was supposed to be sleeping down on the beach. "You know, Ray, the English eat steak tartare, and Philip was famished — what if he eats us next?"

"Barbara, your imagination is unbelievable."

The next day, when all was calm, we saw Philip again. He came and ate and ate and ate and ate, until we dropped him off at the next port, Monte Carlo. Even though he addressed me as *Mademoiselle*, I would not let him come to dinner again.

As for Monte Carlo, my uncle Leo Sheirr used to say that Miami Beach was God's waiting room for the retired. If so, then Monte Carlo was the waiting room for Italian and French gigolos. But Nice was exciting, fun and daring, and I suddenly felt like being devilish. So after drinking what I could, we went shopping. In a small department store, I stole a pair of gold earrings and a deck of cards. When I emptied them out and other things back in the camper, Ray went bananas. "What's the matter with you? You swore you'd never steal again. Is that too going to be like the drinking? Boy, you're going to wind up in a French prison, if you keep this up."

"I won't do it again, Raymond, I promise. I'm sorry." It seemed that my vocabulary was growing very limited; all I seemed to be saying was, "I'm sorry, I won't do it again. Please, please don't be angry with me. Can't you ever forgive me? I don't mean to do these things, I don't know why...."

25

Something pretty drastic had to happen, or we were finished, and both of us knew it, though we didn't talk about it. In the two-year nightmare of our marriage, I had destroyed any trust and almost any love Raymond might have had for me. My refusal to stop drinking, no matter how awful the consequences, had driven a wedge between us that nothing could heal. And yet, incredibly, Ray was still willing to try. Now he had a radical solution, one that we both thought just might work — if I cooperated.

He would not let me out of his sight for one single minute, except when I had to go to the ladies' room, and even then he would escort me and wait outside the door. Drastic, yes, but it was our last chance.

And so, the morning we left for Barcelona, we began. It was going to be in the country that was my last hope, Spain. From 5 a.m. to 1:30 p.m., I went without one drink of anything. Trying desperately to put forth my best performance, I kept insisting on how well I was doing. But the suffering was unbearable. My nerves were screaming, and I knew I could not go any longer without a drink, but still I couldn't ruin Spain, not yet. There was always tomorrow to get serious about stopping, after I have just a few, I thought.

The only way I could possibly get out of the camper and off on my own was for us to have an argument. So I proceeded to precipitate one, about not wanting to go to the Gaudi Cathedral. "What do you mean, you don't want to go? How can you come to Barcelona and not see the magnificent works of Gaudi?"

"Well, Raymond, I can. Now leave me alone, just leave me alone!" He left the camper, and I got what I wanted, to be alone. As quickly as I could, peeking around corners to make sure I wasn't being watched, I headed for first one bar, then two, then three and so on, until I arrived back at the bus, I don't recall how, at around six in the evening.

A fight ensued. Then I weaved after Ray, as he searched for a restaurant, where I continued to drink, until I was shut off. But at this point in my alcoholism, there was no shutting me off; there was always a way. Someone once said that if alcoholics put all their effort into something constructive, apart from constantly figuring out how to get the next drink, one would surely become President of the U.S.

Out of the corner of my eye, I noticed that the kitchen was near the ladies' room. Standing in line to go to the ladies' room, and not really sure what my next maneuver might be, I quickly ducked around the corner into the kitchen, right smack into a bottle of dark red wine on a counter. Not even looking up to see where the kitchen help was, I lifted the bottle to my lips and drank and drank and drank. Somehow I was not seen and proceeded back to my table. "Raymond, I have a great idea: remember you mentioned seeing an opera sometime, if we got to Barcelona? Well, let's go."

"What, are you kidding? With you?"

"Yeah, me, I'm a lover of the arts, too, you know. Besides, neither of us has ever been to the opera before."

Lo and behold, I got my way again. As it happened, there was a pair of cheap seats available in the balcony. Ray was now watching me like a hawk, afraid that I would make one hell of a scene if I had any more to drink. But as we joined the crowd in the foyer, I managed to sneak away from him, run to a nearby hotel bar, and proceed to drink myself rapidly into oblivion. After falling off the bar stool, mumbling about the opera, I was reminded that curtain time had been half an hour ago. With the help of strangers, I was escorted or pointed to the very top balcony, where I climbed and fell and teetered, until I found Raymond by yelling "Raymond! Where are you? I'm here!" For some strange reason, Raymond did not respond, so I called him again and again, until I finally spotted the back of his head, hunkered down, several rows below. I was angry now, because I knew he must have heard me; everyone else did. Making my way through masses of people, stepping on toes and falling into strange laps, I landed on the lap of someone I thought was Ray for sure. It wasn't. The man's wife pushed me, and I fell down in the row. But finally I got to Ray, and he sat me down.

"See, Ray, I'm sober, and I'm here!" I exclaimed, proud of myself for this accomplishment.

"Shhhh, *shhhh!*" came from all around us.

"Barbara," Ray hissed, "will you keep your mouth shut? You're ruining the performance for everyone!"

"Oh, I don't want to do that! I'll keep quiet," I said meekly, and I did so — until the beginning of the second act. Then I noticed that the performers were singing in Italian. Whatever made me think I could translate the Italian into German, I will never know, but that is what I proceeded to do, standing up in my seat and declaring in a loud voice that I spoke German, and would now translate the opera. I got off to a good start and was doing fine, I thought, until Ray took me firmly by the arm, and led me out of there and out into the rainy streets, until the camper was in sight. Outraged that he would treat me in such a rude manner, I shrieked at him like a banshee and tore my wrist from his grip, losing my watch in the process. Then I laughed at him, as I got down on hands and knees, looking for it, and lost my balance, pitching forward on my face.

The next morning, I awoke alone in the camper, which was parked alongside a busy thoroughfare in Barcelona. As my eyes focused, I saw in front of me Ray's diary. Dared I look at yesterday? I dared: "Decided to go to the Opera for 110 pesetas and supped first at a cheap place (42 pts). Later, on to an opera by Donizetti. The opening was excellent; the end was just heartbreaking — we had to leave in Act II, more scenes in pouring rain, etc, etc, etc. I can't even write it down. Am completely and totally and thoroughly finished!''

The next day and a half were a blur. I remember that we tried the geographical cure again, going back to Casa Botin when we got to Madrid. And once again I discovered, as so many others had before me: there was no going back to better times. I managed to ruin that evening in typical fashion, getting drunk and dancing on a table by myself.

We tried once more, the next day, visiting some of my favorite artists once again, at the Prado, the museum that we had both fallen in love with two years before. But Goya and El Greco could no longer move me. Gripped by something much more serious than just another hangover, I had to beg Ray to get me to the camper. As soon as we got there, I reached for the one sure antidote: more wine, and made another discovery: it didn't work. My legs were puffy, my ears still heard sirens and the pain in my right eye was excruciating. There wasn't even going to be any more numbing left. No longer did alcohol do the trick — the thing which I lived for and in which I had put all my trust had betrayed me.

"What am I going to do? Oh God, now what am I going to do?" Over and over again, I moaned, "I've deteriorated into a drunken bum!" From Madrid, 1968, my honeymoon, to Madrid, 1970 — in just two years, I had hit rock bottom. All the hopes that marriage was going to be the answer, and was going to provide the emotional stability I had craved all my life, were shattered. "What happened? What went wrong?"

"Lady, I don't know, but I suggest you finish this drink and get back to where you came from. It's seven in the morning. You must have a place, someone to take care of you. I'm sorry, but I've got to ask you to leave."

"Place, did you say place? I'm in hell. I'm living there now. My husband is too, but I'm lower down. There are different levels in hell, you know. It won't be long before I get to the bottom one. In fact, I think I'm going there now, bye, bye, bye."

Turning around, I waved goodbye to all my fellow Spaniards standing at each end of the bar, watching me and whispering. "Oh dear, someone must have spilled my drink; my jeans are all wet.

Oh, someone get me to the bathroom, I'm sick." The next thing I remembered was coming to in a bathroom stall. The door was cold, and as soon as I lifted up my head and remembered where I was, I became uncontrollably nauseated and threw up again and again, until, after several tries back to the bar and a sympathetic bartender, I was able to keep some brandy down and begin my new day. Catching another glimpse of myself in a mirror, I looked more closely — straggly hair, streaked face, bloated and pale, vomit-soiled jeans . . . . I began to sob again. "Should I do it now, or wait a little longer?" My mind was made up; it was just a matter of when.

"Scum of the earth, scum of the earth . . . ."

"What? Who said that to me, who?" Looking up from the barstool after another blackout, I saw men around me, different men. They were younger than the earlier group, and their smiles were cynical and leering, haunting, depraved. "Gotta get out of here, out of here . . . ."

Falling off the stool and collapsing, I somehow, by some divine or crazy intervention, woke up or came to, once again mysteriously, in the camper. "Ray, did you bring me back here?"

"No. Don't worry, I wouldn't bring you back from anywhere."

"How did I get here then, and when?"

"I don't know. I wasn't here. I went out for breakfast and when I got back, you were slumped on the floor. You'd thrown up on yourself again — nothing different, just the usual daily routine."

As I lay in the back of the camper with the bed down, on a blistering hot day, on our way to Toledo, I could see people walking and smiling and talking to each other and children playing and wives and mothers shopping. What was it like to be normal? To walk a straight line, to eat breakfast without throwing up, to brush your teeth and not have to give up because you can't hold the toothbrush with a steady hand? What was it like to have control over bodily functions, to be really human? "Oh why, why can't I be normal, or at least dead?"

"Barbara, shut up back there. You're giving me the creeps with all your crazy mutterings. You're hallucinating!"

"He's going to lock me up. And I have no strength to fight him.

I've got to get my strength back. Ray, stop quickly and help me across the street to that hotel! Hurry, I've got to go to the ladies' room now!"

Afraid of what might happen if I didn't get to the ladies' room, Ray pulled the camper alongside a big building, across from a hotel. We had just gotten into Toledo, and he had the map out for directions. I looked at him for a moment, half-smiling, half-crying, totally insane, and then went into the hotel. There seemed to be in front of me a long corridor with thick, wine-colored carpeting, as if it was especially rolled out for me. I weaved back and forth, making my way up the corridor. My heartbeat was loud and irregular. I could barely catch my breath, and there was excruciating pain in my right eye.

"I won't have to kill myself," I muttered. "I'm going to die anyway. And Raymond, poor Raymond. If he only knew that I never wanted it to be like this, I love him so. I'm chained, like an animal."

"Yes, madame, what are you trying to say?" I had wound up in the bar, not the bathroom.

"Huh? Oh yes, a drink; give me a double whiskey, the cheapest you have." And now at this point, I needed to drink around the clock, at twenty-minute intervals. My body told me the time and made the demands. I followed obediently, whether I wanted to or not. It didn't matter. I drank several doubles, and went to the ladies' room as I had intended. On the way out, I walked back down the long carpeted corridor again, not wanting to stop at the bar, almost pleading to have the power to exercise some last bit of control over myself, even if I just walked out of this place and into another, but I wanted to remain human enough to walk away from that lousy, stinking bottle with all of its power.

"Yes, ma'am, do you want the same?"

"Yes, I do, the same as before, and hurry, but I must tell you something. Are you listening to me? *Will you please listen to me?*"

"Yes, ma'am, I'm listening."

"I've got to stop. Do you hear me, I've got to, got to, got to . . ." The next thing I knew, I was outside the hotel. Raymond was still at the wheel of the camper, going over his map and waiting for me. He rolled down the window and told me to hurry. I looked from the hotel to the camper and down to the ground. Pulled to the left, to the right, and to the bottom which I knew so well, I suddenly felt a pull upwards. I found myself on my knees, and looking straight up, as high and far as I could, I saw a cross. Squinting, I looked again. There was a white cross on top of this building, so I assumed it was a church. Looking at it, without any previous thought, I cried out very loud and clear: "Help, help, help me, please." And when I was finished, it was as if I wasn't, so with the same impulsive, unpremeditated action, I made the sign of a cross as best as I knew how, touching my finger to my forehead, then to my heart directly underneath, then one shoulder, and then the other. I got to my feet and walked slowly to the camper, remembering nothing else of that day, or the next, until I awoke in my sleeping bag one evening, alone. Once again I opened Raymond's diary with shaking hand and throbbing head: "It was a disaster! She continued her binge and was totally wiped out early. So that blew the day, the most horrible thus far. My back feels the tension of this horror and has tightened up. Sat in the car all day, while she was half passed out in the back. It deteriorated to slapping around — I'm afraid I'll soon break her jaw. Pulled into a hotel lot and slept after more horror. Am writing this on Monday — didn't have the heart yesterday — it surely will end soon, for I see no hope, and I'm exhausted." And then a line by itself: "I am so lonely!"

Closing the diary, I stuffed my fist into my mouth, wishing I could somehow shove it down my throat. His pain and agonizing grief was beyond what I could endure. Suddenly one recollection of that lost weekend leaped out in my mind. I remembered the red corridor, and then, *then,* being on my hands and knees in front of a church. "No, not me, not me," I groaned. Then I remembered a cross, and I saw myself make the sign of a cross. "No!" I shouted, determined to wipe out that thought or picture or whatever.

When Ray returned, I accosted him. "Ray, tell me one thing — no, please don't turn away; I want to know something: was there a church or a cathedral yesterday, anywhere around me? Was I in front of a church?"

"You certainly could have been! Not only were you in front of an ordinary building, but you got down on your knees and looked up and begged for help. And on top of that, you made the sign of the cross."

"*What?*" I was shocked, as if I had committed the most blasphemous act possible. "Raymond, I am *Jewish!* I would never do anything like that! Are you sure?"

"Yes, and you said you saw a bright white cross on top of this building. It proves that you are losing your mind completely, Barbara. When we get stationed in Torremolinos, we are going to have to do something about you — us."

"But I'm Jewish! I'm Jewish, and I'm an atheist. I couldn't have done that!"

"Look: I saw you do it from the window in this camper, so what? So you're a drunken Jewish atheist. You've done many more senseless things than that, let me tell you!" He started the engine. He intended to drive around a little longer, in search of a respectable-looking and safe street to bed down for the night.

Throughout the night I tried to put the pieces together of what was left of my mind, still unable to figure out how and why I would do something so stupid, and every once in a while, I moaned with agony, drifting in and out of sleep, and asking out loud, "why?"

Cordoba followed Toledo, and blackout followed blackout, until I was more out of reality than in it. Days, weekends, and then a whole, solid week was lost — until Ray finally said something that shocked me into full consciousness. It happened on the beach at Torremolinos, where we seemed to be camping in the midst of a bunch of other young American wanderers. Torremolinos — the most idyllic memory of our honeymoon was about to become the place where our marriage would end.

"Barbara, you're messed up again," Ray was saying calmly, "and these days too will be lost. I have to take definite action this time, for your sake and mine. I'm being pressed by my conscience. We've both been kidding ourselves for a long time that somehow, by some miracle, things were going to get better. We've tried everything, and nothing has worked. Now we have got to face reality. It's futile for us to go through the best years of our lives — in

Europe no less, and be burdened by this loneliness and emptiness."

I burst into hysterics, and he stopped speaking of it, but I could see that an idea had taken root. I sensed the root going deeper with passing days, and it drove me in search of alcohol more desperately than ever. Ray didn't try to stop me; his capacity to care had finally been burned out.

One afternoon, I found myself coming to from another blackout. I was in a ladies' room. Not remembering how long I'd been there, I opened the door and peeked out. Seated around a table outside this cafe were Ray, and some other young people. Then I remembered. We had come here for lunch about an hour or so ago. Whatever else had happened didn't matter. I was unable to move, literally move, one inch from where I was in that ladies' room. All I could do, frozen, shaking — freezing in 90° weather — almost catatonic, was to call out loud, "Waiter? Hurry, waiter — help!"

A waiter came from somewhere and opened the door. "Ma'am, are you all right? What's the matter?"

"I'm not all right. Go quickly and get me a drink. Don't let anyone see you, but put it down on the floor and shove it into the ladies' room."

"I cannot do such a thing!" he said, shocked.

"Yes, you can. And you will. And hurry, do you understand? If I don't get a drink fast, something horrible will happen; in fact, it's already happening to me. I'll pay well."

Within moments, a water tumbler filled with something was slid into the opening of the bathroom door. How would I ever manage to stoop down and lift up that glass? I couldn't, without spilling it. So I got down on my hands and knees on that filthy, verminous bathroom floor in that old Spanish cafe and put my mouth to the rim, carefully trying to tilt it with my fist because my fingers alone were too shaky. Somehow I managed to get enough alcohol in my veins that way so that I was able to get up off the floor and order another drink brought into the bathroom. I was not yet able to go to the bar, and I did not dare have Ray see me like this. I was so ashamed that I rocked with silent grief, covering my mouth to keep myself from screaming out in horror at what I had become. But the pain I was experiencing throughout and in different parts of my body was enough to get me to concentrate on figuring out the next drink, and the next and the next, and there were no more lucid moments to torture me. I drank almost non-stop now, unable ever to get enough at one time.

My next jolt into reality came several days later, when we made our usual stop at American Express to check if there was any mail for us, and I found a letter waiting for me from Mother. The return address was St. Claire's Hospital. With a shriek, I ripped open the envelope and grabbed hold of my stomach, as I read that Mother had suffered a heart attack. She had been alone and was admitted alone to St. Claire's in New York, where she had been in intensive care for quite a while. Apparently the attack and the several-week stay in the hospital had passed, and Mother was now home from work for a period of three or four months. "She never told me; no one ever told me!"

"What could you have done? It would only have made her worse, if she had known you were like this, Barbara."

Incoherent groanings were all I could get out as Raymond pulled me along out of the American Express. Every other street, I pulled backwards and began screaming. Raymond continued to drag me, until we finally reached the place where we were to have our Thanksgiving Day dinner with some Americans. It was on our way home that he informed me that after our upcoming trip to Morocco, he was planning to send me home on a plane — alone.

It was a Friday morning, the second week in December, just before we were due to go to Morocco. It was early when I crept out of the camper and across the street to a local hotel and bar which I frequented when I knew Ray was asleep, not that he cared anymore. I sat there drinking, until I had enough in me to allow me to walk fairly well, and to talk and do the other things that normal people did without having to drink a quart of wine on an empty stomach at 6 a.m. The sun was just coming up over the blue, hazy sky, bringing with it bright orange and red hues. There was a soft smell in the air, and it was warm outside — the beginning of a gorgeous day.

I was the only one up, as far as my eye could stretch across the sandy beaches of Torremolinos. Crossing the street over to the beach side, I hastened my steps when I noticed that our camper's curtains were drawn apart. Ray up, so early? As I climbed into the bus, I noted that the bed was still down, but the sleeping bags had been put away. Raymond sat on the edge of the bed, his head in his hands.

"Ray, what is it? Why are you . . . ?" But my heart began to leap as I sensed a more total finality about Ray, about us, about everything, than ever before. Barely lifting his head, Ray looked up at me. "Barbara, it's just no use. I cannot go on like this. I'm losing my own mind. We have got to separate. Without me, perhaps you'll have a chance. I'm obviously no help."

Choking, hot sobs caught in my throat, as I motioned Ray to stop: "Oh my God, my God, no! Dear God, please, I beg You, don't let this happen!" Feeling as though my heart was in the process of being torn into small pieces, I begged and cried and said: "Oh Raymond, I know. I know some of what you've been through. And I won't stop you. I'll let you go." Now different sobs from deep inside wanted so much to come out of my body. As if *these* sobs had been there for a long, long time, heavy and full of guilt and fear. These were the same sobs that tried to surface when I was pulled out of Meema and Peepa's house in Borough Park. In one way, this couldn't be happening, and yet it was, it was. I was about to lose the thing I treasured the most — again. And although I had said I would let him go, I knew without a doubt that I couldn't. For me, it had to be "until death do us part." With a loud cry, pounding both my fists on the bed with the same abandoned desperation I had felt in Toledo, kneeling before the church, I called out, "please, please help us." Raymond took a deep breath and exhaled, with tears and wracking, broken crying. His hand was resting on my shoulder, and the more he cried, the more I pleaded with God, the God that wasn't. And if He did exist, then He most assuredly had cursed me and let this happen. I yelled at Him, hated Him, and begged Him to please, please help us.

We fell asleep, slumped over exhausted, just the way we were. But when we awoke, Ray was drained of all emotion. Coldly he looked at me and said: "We are going to part very soon. Either you'll fly home, or I will. I'm not sure just how, but it will be soon."

Weary and sick, letting what he had just said somehow glide over me, yet hearing every word, I got down from the bed, took my purse and without speaking, left the camper. Crossing over to the other side of the street, away from the beach and the camper and Ray, I walked up the one long street I had remembered and loved, the one we had stayed on and strolled on eons ago on our honeymoon. I had a particular hotel in mind to go to, a particular bar. And the agony of Raymond's face appearing before me, like Peepa's, tore deeper and deeper into my heart. "Oh God," I cried again. "I give up now. No more pain. I want Ray so much, our marriage. But if it can't be, then I want to die." I couldn't verbalize death or dying even in my mind, but there was a sureness now, and not a pondering or wondering about it. I knew what I was going to do. The day that Ray and I were going to part finally and for ever, that was the day I planned to end my life.

26

Standing in the center of the busy drugstore, with people clamoring for the attention of the only druggist behind the counter, I steeled myself and walked slowly towards him. To my surprise, he turned to me and asked if he could help me.

"Yes, sir. Please may I have a bottle of twenty-five-milligram Librium, as large a bottle as you can give me. You see, I'm going to be traveling, and I don't know if I will be able to get these over the counter in other countries."

"You won't be able to in other countries, but I don't have twenty-five milligrams. We carry only ten milligrams of Librium. I can give you a bottle of fifty of those."

"That'll be fine, and also some Darvon. I take Darvon for stomach cramps, the red and grey capsules. There they are, over there," I said, pointing to them like a kid pointing to penny candy behind a glass counter.

"I can give you fifty of those, too. Do you want that many?"

"Yes, yes, thank you. I'll take both."

I remembered Dr. Ullman in Princeton warning about taking pills and drinking. Coupled with the quantities of wine I was now consuming, they should certainly do the trick.

With the two bottles in my handbag, I felt prepared for the inevitable, trying to push back the oncoming tears about what had happened, what was happening and what now would soon be in store for me. The only way I could do that was to drink some more. There in the closest bar I could find, I drank wine, trembling uncontrollably, desperately hoping to erase all thoughts from my mind, and yet also arrive at that place of functioning without getting totally blotto. That was me — always trying to achieve that certain high that enabled me to walk a straight line and go unharmed from life's darts, without going overboard. "To drink enough and yet stop just in time, the elusive, tantalizing goal of every alcoholic," I said aloud, shaking my head. "You would think one poor schnook would make it!"

But after paying my bill and walking back towards the camper, seeing Raymond's face, unconcerned and sullen, I knew I'd missed the mark again. "Ray, oh Ray, please take me back. Keep me with you. I don't want to do this. If only there was a way to live, to live with you." All my crying and pleading were futile, I knew that; yet I hoped against hope to once again see that softening in Ray's eyes, that smile that let me know everything was going to be okay and that I was safe in him. It had been so very long since I'd seen it. I yearned, ached and begged to belong. Any sense of belonging that I had ever had in my whole life was always fleeting, giving me only a taste of what security was. But having tasted it, and then been abandoned, I lived in morbid dread of being abandoned again.

It had never, ever been any different. Life was cruel, a hellish torture. What else was there?

Raymond's eyes met mine. Coldly he looked at me and said: "Barbara, you're drunk again. Get out of my sight."

Turning, I staggered across the street, to the hotel bar I frequented the most. The only place I knew to go, I sat there and drank. Maudlin memories of my life and childhood filled my mind with an aching yearning to join Meema and Peepa wherever they were; I cried out to them to take me soon. All the drinking didn't squelch the fear of death and my fear of life. It was as if I had been outside in the cold rain for so long, looking for a place of hiding, a place of protection. I had had that place with Meema and Peepa, and it was taken from me. Now, after years of searching, running wild, I had found it again with Raymond. And I destroyed the good I found. Why, why, why? Why did I ruin the very thing I craved? Why couldn't I have accepted and abided in the love and security I had?

Somewhere on the way back from the bar, with the death pills jiggling in my handbag, I blacked out, coming to sometime later on the beach in front of our camper. Raymond was sitting quietly next to me, digging a stick into the sand, drawing small curving shapes. We said nothing; there was nothing left for us to say. A long silence was abruptly broken when an unusually tall, grey-haired man, walking his dog, approached us saying: "Hello, I'm John Taylor, a resident here. I noticed your international license plates; are you Americans?"

"Yes, we are," replied Ray, volunteering no more, in the hope that this inquisitive man would take the hint and leave. He didn't, and the inquisition continued.

"So your name is Tamasi and you're from New Jersey — why, that's really amazing!"

Puzzled, I spoke for the first time. "Why is that so amazing?"

"Well, you see, just two blocks from here is the Evangelical Community Church. The minister is also Italian *and* from New Jersey. He came here seven years ago to build this church."

"So?" Ray glanced up at this man with sudden disgust at his mention of church.

"Oh, nothing, really. I just think it's a funny coincidence. My wife died shortly after we retired here three years ago. I've been a very lonely man. I'm an ex-colonel, and now I attend that church on Sundays. Listen, I know this minister would just love to meet you, especially since you're Italian. Why don't you stroll over there sometime?"

"No, thanks."

"Well, remember, in case you change your mind, it's the Evangelical Community Church, and the pastor's name is Daniel Del Vecchio — a great guy, even though he does get a bit carried away about God and all that stuff."

"Look: the last thing we're interested in is anything to do with God or church." Raymond's voice was now quite cutting, and it caused Colonel Taylor's good-natured smile to vanish, as he said goodbye.

For the remainder of that Friday and all of Saturday, Ray and I acted as though we were in mourning — which we were, for our marriage. The veil of drunkenness couldn't mask the hopeless despair and self-loathing I felt. Every drink took me away from Raymond. I now hated the very thing that had destroyed me and which was, at the same time, keeping me alive. But this particular Sunday morning at the beach found us in the middle of a blinding rainstorm. It was about 6:30 a.m. when I returned from my morning jaunt and eye-opener at whatever bar was open. Soon it would be seven and I would have to go again for more....

Rather than bring a bottle back and drink it in the camper in front of Ray, for fear that he'd go into a rage and break it, I kept continually going out and hiding, or trying to hide, my habit. Knowing that I had to get into town for a period of time, in order to get enough liquor in me to take me into oblivion, and also knowing that I could never walk, I began to yell at Raymond: "Wake up, wake up! I've got to go now."

Wearily, Ray turned over. "You crazy nut, it's pouring out there! Where do you have to go?"

Completely unprepared for what would come tumbling out of my mouth, but also aware that I was adept at finding any new excuse to get a drink, in my mind I saw a picture of Colonel Taylor on the beach. "I want to go to church. Will you take me there?"

"*What?* You want to go to *church?* You're completely out of it!"

"Ray, please, please just take me there and drop me at the door. I've got to go — now. Do me this one last favor, please I beg you."

"All right, damn it all," he said, getting up and slipping behind the wheel. "Frankly, I can't wait to get away from you. I never know what insane thing you're going to pull next. So I'll take you, mainly to get you out of my sight!"

There wasn't any time for hurt feelings, they would come later, as usual. Now I just breathed a sigh of relief, knowing that there was a way to get some booze into me for the afternoon. Assuming that Ray took off as soon as he dropped me in front of this church, I would then head for the nearest bar. All I could remember from Colonel Taylor was that this church was near the center of town.

But as we drove up the main street of Torremolinos, the rain became heavier and heavier, making it difficult for Ray to see out of the windshield. When he finally pulled in front of the church, we saw people getting out of cars, and running to the church door which was held open by a short, grey-haired man, who was slightly bald. Ray said sharply, "Okay, get out of here, quickly! It can't be more than an hour in there. I'll wait for you here."

"What? You're going to wait for me? You don't have to do that. I'll walk back." My whole body rebelled at the thought of having to go into that church. That was never my intention, not for one minute.

"I can't let you walk back in this torrential downpour, and besides, I can't drive in this myself. I'll have a cup of coffee and read the paper."

"Um, look I'm not so sure I want to go now, Ray. Look at those people, they're all dressed up in suits and dresses. I've got these old jeans on."

"Oh no, you don't, you little liar. I suspected all along what you had in mind! Now you get the hell out of this camper now and get into that church! You said you wanted to go, now go! And no running up the block, because I'll come out and drag you in there." Opening the sliding side door before I could say anything, I felt a shove, and suddenly I was on the street, standing in a puddle.

I took two steps towards the door hesitantly, and it swung wide open. That little gray-haired man stood there, his arms outstretched to me. "Come on in! The service is just about to start." He surprised me with his distinct Scottish accent. Like a mule being pulled and pulled, I tugged and tugged backwards, but this man left the door and came out in the rain to lead me inside.

"Ooh, what have I done now? I know: there must be a side door a fire exit. I'll leave once I get in. Then I can get to a bar, drink as much as possible and come back in through that same door, or even another way, letting Ray think I really did go to church." Pleased with my brilliant answer to this dilemma, I sort of smiled at this man, who never stopped beaming. We were the only two people in the foyer, with wet coats hung everywhere. All that I had on was sopping wet. In an attempt to do something with my long straggly hair that was knotted and matted-looking, I flipped it as far back over my shoulders as possible.

Before I knew what was happening or could even excuse myself to go to the ladies' room, a door opened wide and another man in a dark suit emerged, taking my arm. Lifting my head to see what was happening inside, I looked down a long carpeted aisle. On either side were rows and rows of people, all of whom seemed well-dressed and "normal" looking. At the far end of this aisle stood a man of medium height with dark hair, balding and of medium build. A magnetic smile and intensely penetrating eyes held my attention, as I was blindly ushered to a seat in the back.

Once seated, I gathered my wits about me, and looked from one side wall to another. "Where the hell is the exit?" I muttered. "Damn it, I don't see an exit."

"Good morning, did you say something?" Turning to my right, I found an elderly lady smiling and talking to me.

Embarrassed now, my face flushed with confusion and annoyance, I answered her: "No, I didn't, sorry." How in the world was I going to last a whole hour without a drink, when I was already coming unglued?

People opened books, and the man way up front, standing on what looked like a stage, lifted up his arms. "Come, let us praise the Lord." I didn't know what he was talking about, but it didn't matter. Caught between needing a drink and trying to hold myself together by sitting on my hands and keeping the twitching to a minimum, I didn't get up at all, for fear I'd start flailing about.

My body sat rigid, taut and shivering. I stared down at my jeans, embarrassed by the thick, sticky stains of vomit. Hovering in shame, feeling completely degraded, apart from the entire human race around me, I heard in the distance a tune being played on the piano. The tune began to loosen the taut grip I had on myself, and I raised my head to see where it was coming from. Way up front on the stage, this man or minister, the one that I assumed was this Del Vecchio guy, was introducing his wife Rhoda. "And she will now sing 'How Great Thou Art.'"

Almost as soon as she began to sing, a flood of tears rushed to my eyes, soon making it impossible for me to see. I lowered my head again, in worse embarrassment than before, and dared not look up. Trying not to create more of a disturbance than I was sure I had already done, I sat there and sobbed, as I listened to the most beautiful song and voice I had ever heard. It seemed to beckon me, pulling me up and forward. That feeling reminded me of something that had happened before, a similar experience — what was it?

Trying to remember, I recalled Toledo and dropping to my hands and knees, feeling a pull upward and forward. Then I remembered, as though a rain-blurred windshield was suddenly wiped clean, that I had begged someone, God to help me, and I remembered, too, making a cross on my body. Ray had told me the next day that I had done this, and I hadn't wanted to believe him. And then I remembered something else: he had insisted that there never was a church between the hotel and the camper, let alone a bright white cross on top in the sky, all lit up. "It must have been an hallucination," he claimed, though I was equally certain that I could never have imagined it. The memory of that experience now made me quiver. What's going on with me? Am I stark, raving mad and don't know it?

There didn't seem to be time to figure anything out. The next thing that happened was the sound of a man's voice — deep, strong and captivating. Practically forgetting that my body was with me, I stared in amazement at this "preacher," who began to speak out boldly about God and Jesus Christ.

"Yipes," I murmured. Hating to hear the very name Jesus Christ, as though it was worse than the worst swear word I knew, I shuddered and felt still more embarrassed. But every time he used the word God again, I felt myself relax a little more. Now where did I hear about God in the same way this guy was speaking? A picture of Clarence and some of his friends back in Princeton who had tried to help me, flashed before me. They talked about God and believed in all that stuff. Seeing them in my mind, I remembered how I felt with them, so comforted and accepted.

But there is no such thing as God; there couldn't be.

As time moved swiftly on, my shaking became more obvious and my lack of control more evident. My shoulders began to shake, and I sobbed and sobbed, holding my head as low as I could, with my hands covering my face. "Do you want to come out of Egypt?" the voice asked. "Do you want to come out of the hell you are now in? There is a way, and only one way: Jesus Christ. I would now like everyone present here this morning to bow their heads in prayer, and those of you out there — and maybe there is just one — raise your hands if you need help, if you want to come out of bondage, out of Egypt. I will pray for you, do you hear me? You don't *have* to stay there; there *is* a way out. Come, Jesus says 'Come to me . . .' " I could not hear the rest. It was as though lightning and thunder struck, separating my mind, body and spirit. I responded to something, to the word help, the faintest possibility of a way out, and I hoped against hope, raising my hand barely above my shoulders and crying both inwardly and out for help.

I heard myself say aloud, "Oh God, oh God, if You are really out there, if You are God, please, oh please, help me."

Barely able to get the word "help" out of my mouth and engulfed in tears, I heard this man say, "I see you. I am going to pray for you now. God sees you. He is here, and He is going to help you. Do you hear me? I tell you as sure as I'm standing here that God will help you."

Suddenly it was as if all the people were gone from their seats, and I was all alone in this church. I heard the words of the prayer that was said for me — for me to become freed from bondage to hell, to alcohol and to drugs. Unable to comprehend the personalness of this experience, I could only cry and continue to ask for help, hoping more with each new plea that someone, perhaps God, was there and going to help me. And now, a sense of excitement rushed through my body. It was mixed with anticipation that something good *was* there . . . something . . . I didn't know just what.

"I have to hang on to this," I murmured. 'It's my last hope, the only thing left. I've got to hang on to whatever this is."

When the music stopped, and the prayers ceased, the preacher began going through a list of activities in that church this week. "And on Tuesday evenings, we have some people meeting here who try to help one another with their alcohol problem."

My heart leaped as I heard that announcement. That was meant for me! It must be. But he didn't know. I never thought of looking for that kind of help in a church, not after being turned down in Rome.

Somehow, in some way, my heart and mind made a connection, telling my body that help was at hand, practical, oh so practical a help: someone was putting that help in my path. God? Could it be *God* who is doing this for me? A whirl of excitement caused me to jump up before anyone else. This sudden hope and excitement made me want to inquire, to find out what was happening here in this place, inside me. I couldn't remember the last time I had gotten excited about the possibility of hope or help, except long ago with Ray, and the ache of that disappointment had driven me down so deep that I had given up completely.

Could there be another hope, other than Ray? A hope more than Peepa *and* Ray? "I've got to get out of here, to tell Raymond what has just happened. He'll be as amazed as I am."

Crowds were gathering and forming a line at the back door, or front door, or whatever door it was at which I had come in. Hating to wait to get out, I tried to push my way forward, but people from everywhere turned and smiled — they were smiling at *me*. Why? I was a mess, compared to them, a bum. Could they be crazy, too? Where am I? What is this place?

There was no other choice, but to wait. And as it came my turn to face this man, expecting him to give me the same ear-to-ear smile that the little man with grey hair had given me, I looked with surprise at his face — a face that, when it rested on mine, changed expressions. He stopped smiling and looked more pensive, concerned. "It's good to have you here, Miss . . . Miss?"

"Oh, Barbara," I said, startled. "My name is Barbara. I've never been to church, I mean, this place before. I, uh, have to go now, thank you, 'bye." Suddenly feeling squeamish, as though God Himself had come down, if there was such a person, I was tongue-tied, aware of our differences, yet still drawn to something.

Walking out slowly, I turned to watch this man resume his big smile and continue shaking hands with people, even hugging some. The woman who sang, his wife, joined him. They looked so happy, so one. I felt different, almost envious now that I hadn't gotten a big smile, and a hug. Oh, how long had it been since I'd had a hug like that! The thought of Peepa, smiling and warm, hugging me, made me remember how long it had been.

The moments of nostalgia left, as soon as I turned again to see our camper. Inside with the light on, at our small eating table by the window, I saw Raymond. How I loved him, I thought, and how I couldn't wait to get across the street to tell him about all of this, and especially that there might be hope after all, and help too. "Oh God, if You *are* real, let this be true, please, oh please, don't disappoint me. Let this be real."

27

"Boy, you've *really* gone over the edge!" Ray exclaimed, when I tried to explain my experience in church to him. And within moments I agreed, becoming angry at myself for even daring to believe that there might be a God, and that somehow I could get help at this time. I wondered how much was actually in that church, and how much was in my mind, sheer hallucination.

By now it had been about two hours since I'd had a drink, longer than I'd gone for quite some time. Every nerve in my body tingled, and inside I was screaming for alcohol of any kind. Somehow I got out of the camper, perhaps when we were at a halt to let people across the street. Vomiting somewhere, in some dingy, dirty bathroom, followed by half a dozen drinks, the last two staying down, I found myself once again making the rounds of various pubs the rest of that day and night. I didn't know where I went or what I did, but whatever horrors were experienced that day, Ray only recorded: "Nov. 29th — another try-and-forget-it day. Nov. 30th — this day was even worse."

The whole rest of that week was a total blackout. Drunk and incoherent the entire time, I continued to go into places, create scenes, and be asked to leave, to be found later, either on the way back to the camper or at the camper on the street, passed out. The trip to Morocco, after which we would part, was postponed for some reason. I was mildly interested in Morocco, but didn't care whether I went or not. Drugs like hashish frightened me, and I had heard that the stuff over there was very strong. I trusted alcohol, sure of the feelings accompanying it, but with a mind that was already crazy, mind-altering drugs did not hold that much fascination for me. That was not enough to keep me from drugs, especially if booze wasn't available. It didn't matter to me what I did or mixed now, to get away from myself. And no longer was there any escape, not even in total intoxication — because then unknown fears and that damnable power that ordered me to do things, lurked heavily over my shoulders, around street corners and in barrooms, waiting, always waiting to show me new frightening and ghoulish horrors.

At the end of that week, on Saturday morning, I lost all control and became completely hysterical. Shrill, loud screaming and insane babbling ended with Ray slapping me and throwing me out, and me winding up just two feet away, because I was now too sick to go any place that required walking. As I sat there on the ground, blubbering, to my surprise into my mind came the first lucid thought I'd had all week — a clear picture of the past Sunday morning in church. I saw the preacher's face in the picture. Without thinking what I was doing, I decided to go back there. Typically, the decision turned into a compulsion, as if I'd been swimming and swimming, and going there meant to shore. I couldn't walk and had no other way of going, and so once again, I made some slobbering plea to Ray, for him to drive me to the church.

For some reason, Ray looked at me without his usual look of disgust. On the contrary, he looked frightened, as though it was only a matter of time before I completely flipped out for good — and that the time might be very soon. His sudden fear prompted him to get into the front seat of the camper and drive me there, almost thankful that there was a place to drop me. At the end of his rope, he was afraid of some horrible, macabre or sick scene that he would not be able to handle. And there were times when he began to wonder about his own sanity; anyone who would put up with something like me for as long as he had, must be "off" somewhere.

Before I knew it, we were in front of the church. In a maudlin state of melancholy, I told Ray to wait there for me, and promised not to be long.

"Why are you going in there?" he asked me.

"I don't know. I honestly don't know. I'm so sick, so very sick and this feeling came over me, to come here. What difference does it make anyway? At least, it's not a bar." And with that, I weaved across the street and through the door. Finding myself alone in the back, I looked at all the empty seats and then aisles, and turned my head in the direction of some music being played. Looking at the organ, I saw the same short, grey-haired man who had led me into church the previous Sunday. He looked up and saw me walking slowly down the aisle farthest from him, and he stopped playing. My jeans were even more soiled and my hair more matted and knotted — a disgusting sight, with eyes that were bloodshot and slitted, puffiness circling them.

Sensing that I didn't want him to come towards me, he stayed behind the organ and smiled. "Hello, my name is Robby. I remember you from last Sunday. Do you want to see the minister?"

"I don't know . . . I guess so."

"Well, walk straight ahead and then knock on that door in front of you. He's inside his office now."

"Thank you." My heart began to pound, as I barely walked the next few steps and knocked on the door.

"Come on in." Slowly I opened the door and peeked into the room, looking around until I focused on the man I had seen in my mind earlier that morning. "Oh hello," he said, apparently recognizing me. "I'm so glad you've come. I've been praying that you would." That statement completely stunned me.

And now he was up on his feet, his hand reaching mine, and leading me to a seat on the sofa opposite his desk. I thought for sure that I had made some horrible mistake. What on earth was he talking about — praying? "What do you mean, sir? Why did you think I should come, and for that matter, why did you even think about me?"

"Well, I'm a minister, a man of God, and I knew you were in great need. I believe I can help you."

No sooner were the words "help you" out of his mouth than I started to cry. "I don't know why I came here, but oh, do I need help! I need something. I'm sick, so sick. I am an uh . . . What I mean is I drink . . . I am an alcoholic." Why was it still so hard to get those words out? It was the first time I'd admitted to a stranger with as much awareness and honesty as was in me, that I was an alcoholic. I hated to say that word, loathed it and all that it stood for, but there it was.

He didn't seem shocked or even surprised, and just nodded his head knowingly. "Okay, we can start by you calling me Dan, if you don't mind. First, I'd like to talk with you, if I may, and then pray for you." I nodded and smiled through my tears. I was glad he said I could call him Dan, because I couldn't pronounce his last name, Del Vecchio. But pray for me? "What do you mean — pray? What do you do?"

I barely understood what he was saying, something about people having prayed for me since Sunday, which was partly why I was there, too, and then something about prayer going directly to God. Suspicious now of the whole situation, and very edgy, I practically freaked out when he mentioned Jesus Christ. "Oh no, sir, I mean, Dan; I don't believe in that stuff at all. I'm Jewish. I may not be religious and I don't even know about God, but I am Jewish."

His face lit up, as though he had just received the most fantastic news. Raising both his hands in the air with a big smile, he said something in what sounded like another language and then said "Praise the Lord!"

Oh brother, I thought. No wonder I'm here. This guy's nuts, and so is this place. "Look," I said rather bluntly, "you said something after church last Sunday, about some people meeting here who shared their alcohol problems. Can you give me a phone number? That's really all I want."

"Do you know," he chuckled, "that that was the first time I had mentioned that from the pulpit? I don't usually."

An eerie feeling came over me as I sat on the couch, shaking and shivering. "Look, I also need a doctor badly; I'm very sick. I've got to have something to steady me — nothing's helping any more, not even liquor."

"I will give you the name of a woman who lives a couple of

blocks from here. She has no phone, but if you catch her, she will see you. Her name is Anne Murray and she's American, retired here. I've heard that she hasn't had a drink in twenty years. Also, there is a doctor half a mile from here. How do you get around? Are you traveling alone?"

"No, I have a husband. We're on an extended camping trip. He's outside in the camper, waiting for me."

Once again he looked delighted, when I said extended camping trip. "Great! Then you'll be here for a while?"

"Yes — well, we'll be here for Christmas, but actually, our marriage is over." Choking up with tears, I now let down whatever guard I had left and sobbed about Ray and how much I loved him. The whole time I was crying, he seemed to be murmuring under his breath, in that foreign language he spoke.

With the information that I wanted written on a piece of paper, I wiped my eyes and said I was leaving.

"Please, let me pray for you. Je— I mean, God wants to help you, Barbara. Let Him."

Automatically I sat back down and watched Dan as he stood beside me and began to ask God to help me, and have mercy on me. When he said deliver me, and loose Satan's grip, or something crazy like that, he suddenly put both of his hands on top of my head.

I was petrified. If I was nuts, this guy was even nuttier, without booze! If Ray knew what was going on in here, he'd have me locked up here, in Spain. "Thank you, sir, uh Dan, for your help, but I should be going now," and with that, I leapt up and started for the door.

"All right," he said, smiling, "but please come back tomorrow to the Sunday service and bring your husband."

I turned back, on my way out. "My husband? He would never set foot in — I mean he's a Catholic, and an Italian," I concluded in confusion, not wanting to hurt this man who obviously meant well, and was only trying to help.

"So am I Italian."

"That's right, isn't it, some retired colonel came up to us on the beach and told us about you and this place, that's how I came to hear about it. He said you were also from New Jersey. How come you're here?" And without thinking, I came back into his office and sat down.

"Well, when I really came to know God through Jesus Christ, I began to go to Him with everything. He has led me everywhere, over much of Europe, and seven years ago He directed me to leave my home in New Jersey and come to Torremolinos and build this church."

"That sounds crazy. Are you a builder?"

"No, not at all, but when God directs, He also provides the essential tools and help and finances. That's never the problem; it's just finding out whether you're really in God's will or not." Enthralled with this amazing story, I was even more astonished when Dan told me that there was a devil called Satan, the opposite of God, and that he had had power over me, but that now God was trying to get in and wipe this Satan out.

"Well, thanks for everything, but now I really have got to go." Again I jumped to my feet, and yet, when he mentioned Satan and then power, while I couldn't believe such a wild thing, I couldn't help thinking about that horrible thing I had felt ordering me around. In fact, I had thought of it as some evil power, or presence . . . .

"Here, Barbara, let me give you this Bible before you leave," and grabbing a nearby pen, Dan hastily wrote something in the front page and then handed me the small paperback. I looked at it sadly, knowing that I would never read it, having been unable to sit still long enough to concentrate on anything for years, and tucked it under my arm. "That book will help you, even if you read just one line a day. It will tell you about God."

Closing the door behind me, I ran up the aisle, in a hurry to get out of there. Once outside, I opened the book he had given me, to see what he had written: "To Barbara, with confidence of complete freedom through Jesus. Your friend, Daniel Del Vecchio. Phone: 38-27-78." At the word friend, my eyes filled with tears. No one had wanted to be my friend in such a long time — but when I focused on that word "Jesus," I thought it brazen of him to slip that in there after I had told him I was Jewish.

"Raymond," I called out. "Wait till you hear what went on in there! Open the car door, hurry. Look what the preacher gave me, a Bible! Also, what do you know about Jesus? I don't know anything except that he's for Gentiles, not Jews. Anyway, this guy prayed for me and gave me a piece of paper with the name of a woman who could help me and a doctor."

"Oh brother," Ray replied. "Now it's religion! As if things weren't bad enough! Give me that piece of paper; where is this doctor?" After reading the note, Ray furiously started the car and drove off. Out of the corner of my eye, I saw that little guy Robby standing at the door, smiling.

As we drove, clouds came up, and rain fell. Ray's earlier fear had turned to hot anger. I was sick and had to have a drink, and there was nothing in the camper. Neither was there any way out in this wild rainstorm and Ray's furiously fast driving. My mind became filled with confusion about what had just happened. Evil power . . . Satan . . . "No, no!" I burst out. "I don't want bad power; I don't want it!"

"What are you talking about? You're flippy, again. That guy's made you worse!"

Saying nothing now, and focusing all my attention on keeping myself together until I could get some liquor, we found our way to the doctor's house. He took us reluctantly to his office in the next room. I insisted Ray wait outside. Once I was alone with the doctor, I told him that I had to have something for my nerves, "because he," pointing to the waiting room, "won't let me drink. I'm in terrible pain, terrible, and need something for my stomach."

He barely understood English, and I Spanish. The doctor wrote some prescription on a pad, saying that codeine would help the pain.

Just then, Ray, who had been listening behind the door to every word, barged in, furious. "Give me that paper! She's a drunk, doctor, can't you see? She's making up this pain. She just wants something, anything!"

Ripping up the piece of paper, Ray pushed the door open and, grabbing my arm, dragged me down the stairs and back into the camper. Shrieking my hatred at him, I tried to hit him and scratch him, but he ignored me and strapped me down tight in my seat belt. "I'm taking you to this woman, Anne, and if she'll have you, she can. I've had it with you!"

It had been too long since I'd gone without a drink. Objects, especially trees, were floating in front of me, threatening to come crashing through the windshield. I sat there, screaming as each tree approached, while Ray drove like a madman down the main street of Torremolinos. "Stop it, you crazy jerk!" he shouted. "There's nothing in front of you! There are no trees coming through the window!"

It didn't matter what he said, I saw them; they were real, and they were coming, one after another, some with leaves and some without. *"Help!* Duck, *help!* Here comes another!"

28

We finally arrived at this woman Anne's home. I wanted help, but I also wanted to drink, and so, when there was no answer at her apartment, I felt relieved and left Ray, and proceeded to spend the rest of that afternoon and evening drinking in various places that I don't remember. My drinking was done in total blackout now. But when I came to the next morning and left the camper to wash and fortify myself with more booze, I remembered that it was Sunday and decided to once again go to church. However transient, the hope that I had experienced the previous week was enough to bring new anticipation and a desire to go back.

Once again, I woke Ray, insisting that he drive me, only this time I asked him if he would please come with me. A battle royal ensued, but in the end he drove me to the church, and waited outside, reading the Sunday newspaper.

My foggy mind heard nothing that was said during the entire service, and I was aware only of the drawing of my emotions to the music. When it was over, anxious to get out in a hurry, I pushed through the crowds, even hoping to escape the minister's handshake. But Dan took my arm, as I tried to waik by him speedily, and asked me to "please wait a minute." And then, accompanied by his wife Rhoda, he insisted that Ray and I let them take us out to lunch. Before I could say anything, Dan was at the camper asking

Ray to come out. Before either of us realized what was happening, we found ourselves in the back seat of their car. Ray was snickering and whispering, "What's going on here? Did you put this guy up to this? I've got to get out of here!"

"Ray, don't make a scene!" I whispered back. "I never said a word. I don't want to be here any more than you do! But look, it'll be over with soon, and besides we're broke, and you're getting a free lunch."

The next thing I remember happening was Dan asking Ray to wait a moment, as he started to eat. "What am I waiting for?" Ray asked.

"Grace — I'm going to say grace."

Ray dropped his fork, and I wasn't even sure I knew what saying grace meant. Dan began softly by thanking God for the day and then for us. Can you imagine? He actually thanked God for our being there! Already suspecting he was completely off his rocker, I became convinced beyond a shadow of a doubt when to my amazement, he then raised his hands to the sky. He suddenly and enthusiastically started praising God.

I felt frightened and Ray looked frenzied, and kicked me in the shin under the table. Oh, how I craved a drink! How I ever got through that lunch without one was beyond my imagination. Rhoda's face lit up every time she talked about God, as though she knew Him intimately and loved Him. She made it sound so personal — too personal; it couldn't possibly be that real. As for Jesus Christ, well, every time that name came up, and it seemed to be more frequently, I winced and shuddered, trying not to hear it.

Dan seemed to sense this, as well as Ray's anger which was growing hotter every moment, and he adroitly changed the subject to something he thought Ray might enjoy talking about, like being Italian. Only Ray didn't want to talk about being Italian; the truth was, he had never wanted to be Italian in the first place. Politics was next, and when Ray discovered that Dan was not a Democrat, but one of "those Republicans," he became all the more furious.

At that moment, I didn't know which was worse: my desire for a drink, or my fear of the horrendous public scene that was only moments away. And then, to top off the whole luncheon, on the drive back to the camper, Dan had the audacity to tell us, looking directly at me, that we would be making a terrible mistake by going to Morocco. "Barbara, I'm concerned about you. I would like to help you, both of you. I have people praying for you everywhere. But if you really want help, if you want to stop drinking, you must *not* go to Morocco."

"*What?*" exclaimed Ray. "How can you tell us what to do like that?"

"Please, listen to me! I want to help you, to bring the reality of Jesus Christ, who's really your only hope and help left. Morocco is the pit of Hell itself. You'll only go backwards there."

Raymond was so incensed that he couldn't even speak. Dan and his wife warmly tried to embrace us, after we all got out of his car, but we were both rigid. "Please, why don't you come by the church tomorrow. We can visit together some more."

"No, thanks," Ray replied, "I'm grateful for the lunch, but we can't come there tomorrow at all, goodbye." I felt torn and pulled, after Ray said that, turning to look at them, feeling almost sad about leaving them as we walked off.

The rest of that day, and the next, and the next, were spent drinking. But Tuesday, at some time, somewhere, I suddenly remembered the church and that the preacher had said something about some people who had drinking problems gathering there on Tuesday evenings. I found Ray, or he found me, but in any case, we both ended up in the back room of the sanctuary, facing two people, one man and one woman. The woman introduced herself as Anne, the man as Dick, and I realized that must be the Anne whom the preacher had directed us to. Trying to look at least a little sober, I steadied myself, turned to Ray, and asked him to wait outside for me.

To my astonishment this woman, Anne, in a deep, strong voice told me to keep quiet, not to suggest that anyone do anything and sit down. Shocked at her command, I obeyed. Looking intently into Ray's eyes, she said, "Stay and sit down, boy, no secrets here." We sat there, I bit my nails and shook, as Anne didn't seem to notice or care how much I was suffering. She proceeded to tell me a little bit about her own life and how alcohol had just about killed her. The man did likewise. I must have said something about going to Morocco that week, because she told me I was absolutely insane to go to Morocco, just like the preacher. Only she added that I had no desire to stop drinking and that I was a liar. Too sick to feel insulted, I just cried. Then her voice softened a bit. "Look, kid, if you change your mind about Morocco, and if you really want help, you can come to my apartment any time. I'll help you dry out."

"Why?"

"Because someone helped me dry out. I know what you're going through, but I also know you've got one foot in the grave."

The day we were due to leave for Morocco, I swore up, down and sideways that I would prove them wrong about my going there and would use that two-week time to dry out. "Ray, I know I'll stop in Morocco. People don't drink there; I hear it's hard to get liquor. It'll be so easy; I'll have no choice! Please take me with you!"

Ray threw me on the boat as though I were excess baggage. My vow of sobriety lasted all of fifteen minutes after the boat got underway. There was a bar on board and of course, I was there. At Tangier, we were greeted by the rest of our traveling companions from Torremolinos with a guide they introduced as "Tangier Jimmy." We had repeatedly been warned not to get any guides in Morocco at all, but here was this guy Jimmy, and in his pockets and shoes were drugs. Oodles and oodles of kief — the most highly concentrated part of the marijuana plant, it had the most THC — producing with just one toke on a hash pipe the same narcotic reaction that resulted from smoking two or three full joints of marijuana.

I came out of my stupor long enough to get good and frightened, especially when veiled women and eerie-looking men seemed to watch and follow me with their dark, suspicious eyes. My own natural state of paranoia, coupled with this new and very real foreign intrigue, began to build in suspense and momentum after we checked into a hotel, smoked daringly on a hash pipe until we were stupefied, and then openly walked to a nearby cafe to drink mint tea. Suddenly, as if we were watching a movie, we found ourselves the star attractions, claiming all the limelight. Every passerby was gone. It was just our party — and the police and Tangier Jimmy coming towards our table. Jimmy pointed to us and then quickly disappeared around a corner. It didn't take us long to figure out that he did both the selling of drugs, and the informing to the police.

Absolutely panicked as the police approached us, and aware that Ray had some kief stashed inside his boot lining, I held my breath. But all the police did was ask us where we were staying and when we were leaving Tangier. "As soon as we can, sir," came the response of Ed and Ray simultaneously, "first thing in the morning."

The sinister-looking police left, after staring at us from head to toe for what seemed like a long time. Watching them head directly for our hotel, and believing that they were about to search our rooms and find the rest of the stuff hidden there, we sat at our tables speechless and frightened. But Ray didn't waste a minute. He jumped up and ran around the corner. In a second he was back. Leaning forwards, he whispered, "I just threw the kief down the street."

After waiting a good half-hour, we decided that since the police didn't return for us, perhaps they didn't find our drugs, or perhaps they were waiting for us in our rooms. Whichever, we walked back to our hotel. Everything seemed to be in order. We waited breathlessly another half-hour and then decided all was safe. Huddling together in one of the rooms amidst the dirt and cracked walls and crawling roaches, we shivered and waited till dawn, hoping to get out of Tangier as soon as possible, alive. We knew about Americans being arrested there, unable to get out of jails, we knew the heavy sentence for smuggling drugs, we knew we shouldn't have gotten a guide, let alone smoke pot in some sleazy hotel room, and now we vowed never to do it again — at least not until Marrakech.

The train trip to Rabat was long, tiring, and once again, eerie. Rabat at 2 o'clock in the morning, looking for an inexpensive place to stay, was like being in a movie. When we finally found a flophouse, and climbed the dark stairs to the "office," we were met by two men, all too eager to get our money, and we knew for sure that this "movie" was all too real. Ed, Evelyn, Ray and I marched obediently before them, as they took us to a room. We wanted to turn and run but fear kept us going. We were ushered into a dark room, heard a light switch click on and the door close behind us. It sounded as though the door was being locked from the outside.

Inside, we stood in the middle of the filthiest, most decrepit room I had ever been in. Low single cots with dirty sheets were on each side. One window with bars on the outside, and a single light bulb in the ceiling added quite fittingly to the hallucinations I was already having from lack of alcohol. Ray and I huddled together on one cot with our coats and boots on, freezing cold and now itching like crazy. Bed bugs and only God knows what else were swarming around us. "The preacher was right. We never should have come."

"Yeah, I'm not sure we're gonna get out of this place."

Afraid to talk above a whisper, we listened to the footsteps of people outside our room as they seemed to pace back and forth, back and forth. Drying out from booze was bad enough, but under surroundings like those, the double horrors were quite unbelievable. The night was one long, unendurable horror show, but eventually light came filtering through the bars on the window — morning! I was dripping wet, freezing cold, and unable to unclench my teeth or hands.

"Let's grab our gear and get the hell out of here." One by one, first very slowly and then more quickly, we got outside into the corridor, out to the office, and without looking down, back, sideways or forwards, we ran down the flight of stairs two steps at a time. Everyone else landed on their feet; I landed, as usual, face down in a dirty puddle. Then, with Ray pulling me along, we ran and ran and ran until we were well out of that neighborhood and unable to run any more.

As bad as Rabat was, Marrakech was worse. We rode there on a local bus with awful smells and chickens and women throwing up, traveling past palm trees, cacti, and flat land running to the foot of the Atlas mountains, where there were towering snow-capped peaks. I begged and begged for Ray to splurge and get a cab to a better section of town where the hotels had bathrooms that were decent and beds that were clean and showers and on and on and on. I wanted to die, but not slowly, being gnawed by vermin. I threw a fit in the middle of town, stamping my feet and crying for help and for my mother, like a baby. Ray, Ed and Evelyn actually walked off, leaving me. As soon as they started to turn the corner, and I saw three lecherous-looking Arabs come towards me, I took a deep breath of hot 105° air and ran after them, utterly hopeless. Ray was determined to live as the natives did in all lands, the poor natives, that is.

They found a room in a tenement hotel, completely dilapidated and roach-ridden, for fifty cents. It was a hotel haven of drugs, even the proprietor was a speed freak, running from room to room like an airplane zooming around. He talked faster than anything and was skinny and sleazy. Young American hippies, bearded and sandaled like Ed and Ray, and girls with long hair and no makeup like Ev and me, lay in drugged stupors on the roof and in their rooms, some even on the hall stairs. But it wasn't until we saw the cockroaches, big and black, come sauntering out of rooms and into the lobby that Ray began to grow pale for the first time, looking almost sick. A Japanese guy came running out screaming, his bare back covered with huge bites. "Get out of this place, quick! Look at me: you'll be eaten alive! Last night, I woke up to find one of them sitting on my face!"

Ray took my arm, turned and headed for the front door. He was even willing to part with the fifty cents he'd already paid.

Later that night we found a decent hotel with a private bathroom. Taking turns in the shower, we practically rubbed our skin off, trying to get rid of lice and whatever else we had. With a bag full of drugs that Ray had from somewhere, we spent the rest of our time in Marrakech in that hotel room stoned.

After two days without any booze and absolutely stoned on drugs, completely freaked out, I ventured out alone in search of a place that served at least wine. There was a cafe around the corner, and whenever Ray was occupied I ran over there and sat at the bar, the only woman in the place, with a bunch of seedy Arabs, downing one glass after another until I raised my alcohol level back up to where it had been. Now I was loaded not only on booze, but on drugs as well, and while I had always disliked the effects of drugs before, I now craved them more and more.

The day came when we returned to Spain. I must have traveled with the group, because one day I came to at a campsite in Fuengirola, twenty miles up the coast from Torremolinos. Ray either liked the campsite or wanted to make sure that the last of his days on the coast of Spain were far, far away from that Evangelical Church and that "preacher man."

I could no longer drown out the fears with alcohol or drugs. Hallucinations threw me into bizarre screaming fits, where I saw myself in hell, being devoured by ghoulish monsters. People sitting opposite me at pot-parties, even friends like Ed and Evelyn, became distorted-looking, their smiles plastic, their teeth decayed and falling from their mouths, blood trickling out of their eyes. In my mind's eye I saw women trying to seduce Ray, and I sat chained and bound to the sofa, hating to watch. I could see through people's flesh and into their bones. The wild, erotic music that was being played took on eerie sounds, even evil laughter. And through it all, there was the presence of that horrible power, the one that had been giving me orders for so long now. I couldn't see him, but he was there, laughing.

We spent all our days and evenings at the "compound" with this group, in this hell. I never drew one sober breath, nor ate one decent meal without throwing up and was repeatedly found by Ed or Evelyn or someone who was sent out to search the bars and track me down.

Ray never looked for me any more; he no longer cared.

Christmas was fast approaching. I overheard Ray and Ed talking one night. Ray was telling him of his plans to leave me after Christmas. The weather had cleared. I was to go home by plane from Malaga, and Ray would go on, and perhaps meet up with Ed and Evelyn later on in France. Grabbing my handbag, I knew the pills were still inside. I knew the inevitable was now soon at hand. Through physical and mental agony, I wandered on, mumbling and groaning, begging for drinks in and out of bars, and when I threw up, soon there was nothing left in my stomach but bile.

I twitched and shook, saw visions that weren't and screamed in the streets, as people turned and stared, not wanting to get near me.

Evelyn followed me and begged me to stop, and one day she even cried for me, until she, too, walked away from me as Ray would shortly do. There were times when, through my maze of drunkenness and insanity, I saw pictures of Meema and Peepa holding me, loving me, sheltering me, and I cried and cried and ached inside. I saw Mommy with her wide-brimmed picture hats, coming home from work in New York when we lived in Borough Park; I saw her arms held out wide to me as I ran to her, my long hair shiny, bobbing in the wind with bows and hands sticky from Turkish toffee. And I saw Ray when he looked at me as the girl he wanted to marry, with love and respect in his eyes, and I remembered the fond, warm way he used to call me Princess, and if I'd had the guts to grab a knife, I would have cut right through my heart and blotted out all those memories that would never be mine again. And I remembered the preacher and the little white church I had gone to, and something about God, and I said: "If You are there, hurry! Hurry and let me die!"

29

That Christmas Day of 1970 was supposed to be our last and most special festive farewell dinner with the whole group we had met and traveled with. Everyone would be going their separate ways early the next week. That included Raymond and me — his mind was made up: on Wednesday I was flying home, alone. This was Friday, and the fact that it was Christmas only intensified the lost and lonely feelings I'd always had on that day. Mother and I had always been alone, on the outside looking in, especially after Meema's death and our home split up. That happened when I was ten; I was twenty-eight now, and there had been many, many years where we cried together or separately.

"I've never gotten used to feeling alone and empty on Christmas, Ray. You'd think by this time, it would be easy. But what I dread more than anything in the whole world is to be left alone with myself." I looked over at him. "I wonder if you really know what I'm talking about?" Ray was at the wheel of the camper, and we were on our way to the "compound" for the big bash celebration. I'd been up since 5 a.m., searching the streets for a bar that was open. Even on Christmas, there were one or two that remained open, perhaps for people like me. Almost every other cafe would be closed that day, so I was eager to get to the party, my only source of liquor.

Raymond thought a moment about my question and said: "I don't know, I probably don't know the years of loneliness you're talking about, but I sure went through my own when I was at Deborah Sanatorium for eight months. And when my mother first became ill with TB, I was about six. She had to go away. Funny, I don't remember a thing about that then. I must have blocked it all out. As a matter of fact, I don't remember much about my childhood at all."

I loved it when Ray would talk and share with me, the way he used to. He hadn't for a long, long time. There wasn't much we had in common at all, except for our attraction to each other and what money could buy. And whatever it bought us, booze was always at the center. In the beginning of our relationship, it seemed to work for us, helping us to open up and relate to one another. If only things could have stayed that way, if only . . . .

My thoughts were interrupted when Ray pulled out a small box, beautifully wrapped with red and green bows. "Here, I almost forgot: this is for you. Merry Christmas, *Feliz Navidad.*" I didn't want to ruin the day by becoming emotional again, so I bit my lip and held back the tears. It would have been easier if Ray had given me nothing. It was unbearable, knowing that in five days we would be parting for good. As I fumbled to unwrap the bows and open the little white box underneath the wrapping, I thought of the pills in my handbag, the only way out of this heartbreaking torture. But as soon as I saw the pills in my mind and faced what I was going to do, I thought of my mother and how this would destroy her.

I couldn't help it any more; the tears just flowed down my cheeks when I saw the miniature chocolate, seven-layer Christmas cake that Ray had bought me. "It's scrumptious-looking! I'll save it for tonight, when we get back to the camper. I'll have it with a cup of tea or coffee."

How silly to say that! We both knew that I would never be sober enough to eat a piece of cake that evening, or any evening. And when was the last time I had had a cup of tea or coffee? But I had to pretend; it was the only way to get through the heartbreak. I had learned how important it was to lie to myself. It was hard to imagine what life would be like without rejection alongside daily, hourly. And ironically, masochistically, or whatever, it was so familiar that there was even a measure of security in it. But there was never anyone to really talk to about it. I didn't know for sure what it was I was feeling. If only there was someone who *really* understood, if only . . . .

One train of thought after another ended with "if only," until we finally reached our destination. All the shops were closed. Bells from somewhere were ringing, but hardly a soul was out walking. Inside the compound, our friends had gathered with food and bottles of brandy and wine and marijuana. Records were stacked in a corner, the long table was set with candles, and there were enough place settings for about fifteen of us. I held on to the little cake in the white box that Raymond had given me, as if it were the most precious gift I'd ever received. "What are you going to do with that?" he said, frowning. "Leave it in the camper, Barbara."

"No, please, let me take it with me. I want to look at it once in a while today." Ray shook his head in bewilderment. I could sense that he was anxious to get away from me and all this strange melancholia. Holding my cake under my arm, my shoulder bag over the other arm, and my bowl of rice, our contribution to the dinner, in both of my hands, I walked into the kitchen of someone's apartment. People were gathered round, preparing salads and different delicacies.

Putting down my bowl of rice on the counter, I looked up to see one of the fellows we knew, as he was putting down a bottle of bourbon. "I know what you want, Barb. Here, be my guest," and pushing the bottle towards me, he glanced at his watch. It was ten in the morning. I knew the time, and I knew what he was thinking. And I was hurt that he didn't offer me a cup or glass or even attempt to pour my drink. Funny I'd still be hurt about that; I'd never really gotten used to being what I was.

Ray was well liked. Everyone flocked to his side, greeting him with warm hello's. They liked his dry sense of humor and gentle manner. I stood in the kitchen, holding the bottle of bourbon in my hand, watching Ray smile and laugh and sit down in a corner of the living room near the record player. I looked around at the girls who were there and wondered if he was attracted to any of them.

Unable to stand the pain any longer, I got the bottle open and found a glass. It wasn't long before my mind became filled with maudlin thoughts and lonely anguish. The worse it got, the harder and faster I drank, hoping to wipe away what was happening. I was left alone. No one tried to stop me; no one cared. And so all that Christmas Day I drank. I left the compound sometime in the afternoon, found a couple of bars that had opened, talked to strangers about my life if anyone would listen, and then returned to the compound. I came in and went out again, until the last time, I went out very sick, very depressed and very drunk.

Through the blackouts and insane thinking, I met a tall man, a black African. He came up to me and said in a quiet, caring voice: "You are suffering. I can help you, heal you."

"Huh, what, help me? No, no one can."

"Yes, I have here a balm. It's a special balm. Let me put it on your forehead and in one hour, you will be free from that," he said, pointing to the glass of brandy in my hand.

"Okay, hurry, put it on." Maybe this is my help, I thought. This man who introduced himself as Rick the Candlemaker, rubbed some thick cream on my forehead. He told me to leave it alone and wait and expect to be cured. I waited. Oh, how I waited! One hour led into two, then three, and nothing happened. What a damned fool I've been! God, church, any hope of healing balms! My only hope is death.

Muttering to myself with intense feelings of bitterness and hate inside, and then suddenly hot tears of anguish, I went from bar to bar to bar, consuming unbelievable quantities of alcohol, and missing the Christmas dinner with everyone. "Goodbye Ray, goodbye Mommy, I love you. Oh Mommy, oh God, Mommy, I'm sorry for your life and mine." I was about to open the bottle of Librium that I was fingering in my handbag, intent on swallowing them, but couldn't bring myself to do it when my mother's face, full of undeserved sorrow, flashed before me. "I'll have to wait until there are no more thoughts. When will I be that drunk?" Somewhere between 9 and 12 that night, I was taken to a hospital emergency room. Suddenly finding myself on a table with several men in white standing over me, doctors, I assumed, I heard a baby crying. The crying became louder and louder. I began to believe there was a baby inside me. I started to cover my mouth, to throw up, to cry and hallucinate. "My baby is inside me. The baby wants to live." Louder in a state of hysteria, I screamed at the bewildered Spanish doctors who were standing there over me, now four of them. "Don't kill this baby. Don't kill my baby. I'm sorry, please. Oh God, I never wanted to kill the baby! Hurry, doctor, I'm in labor; the baby is coming!"

The doctors looked at me, and at one another. "Feliz Navidad, merry Christmas, the baby wants to live!" I kept repeating. One doctor tried to find out what month I was in. My stomach was so swollen from alcohol and lack of food, they assumed I was pregnant. I screamed and cried as they attempted to examine me. I heard someone say, "There is no baby; she is not pregnant."

"Nooo! The baby is dead; it's dead." I remember turning to one side, holding my face with my hands and sobbing uncontrollably.

Somehow once again I was either taken back or found near the compound. Ragged, bruised and torn apart in every way imaginable, I came in, and the people at the party looked at me and laid me down in a corner. I heard someone say, "Ray, your wife's here. We found her —"

"So? Just leave her there." I was unable to move or to even talk. Later that morning, three of the men carried me into the camper, and Ray drove us back to the campsite.

The next morning, I awoke in bed, fully dressed, with my shoes on, and sick, so very sick. I could hear the rain pounding on the camper. Trying to lift my head, I knew Ray was gone. I saw his book, his diary, and with one hand outstretched, I fumbled to the page that said Xmas, Dec. 25, 1970. It was blank, and I turned the page, to see Dec. 26th. "Today thus far has been — can't even write about this any longer. It was a mixed bag. Some good moments with the gang and music, all without B. who was on her own suicidal trip. Later I came down fast when news arrived of her return and her inevitable condition — the rest was more horror — Merry Xmas!"

Reading those words over and over again, I knew I had to put a stop to this madness called life. Groping for my handbag, I lifted it and put my hand inside, searching for the two bottles of pills that were there. But my bag, too, was a mess. Makeup had fallen out of its case, a lipstick was open, and I got it all over my fingers. I couldn't find the pills. Pulling the bag up to the bed, I looked inside. They were gone.

"Where are they?" I yelled, as if my only security left had just been taken away from me. And then I remembered the hospital, and the doctors. They must have found them in my bag, looking for my I.D. Damn it, they took those pills! And everything's closed this weekend, because of Christmas. What am I going to do? Now I have to wait till Monday. Sobbing, I stayed in bed, unable to move at all, even if I wanted to, until I fell asleep.

And then, in the midst of my usual horrors called dreams, I was back in Toledo, kneeling and looking up in the sky at a bright, illumined cross. And next I saw the little Evangelical Church, and I remembered looking up to the top, expecting to see the same illumined cross. It was there. I saw the preacher's face and his wife Rhoda. Their arms were outstretched to me. "We want to help you. God loves you, Barbara, He really loves you. God sent His Son to die on the cross for you." I didn't understand what they were talking about, but I felt a warm, safe feeling inside. How could they still want me? The light, airy scene left as quickly as it came, and the horrors returned.

I must have been screaming, because the next thing I awoke to was Raymond shaking me, and slapping my face, putting wet cloths on my forehead. Opening my eyes, I was aware of where I was, and I remembered something of that dream, but I didn't even know it was a dream. "Ray, who was just here? Were the preacher and his wife here?"

"Of course not. You've been out cold. It's afternoon now." My body was shivering, and no amount of blankets or sweaters helped. I shook and shook and shook. All I could feel was my heart, pounding faster than I'd ever heard it. It felt as though it was in my throat. My head throbbed, my eyes ached. I couldn't even get up to get to the ladies' room. My teeth clattered, and I don't know what Ray saw on my face, but he began taking my pulse and not letting go of my wrist.

Barely able to get the words out of my mouth, I looked at Ray, both eyes squinting and trying to mouth something. I clung to the remembrance of Toledo, the preacher, the bright illumined cross on top of the church, and hearing Rhoda's words in my ears: "Barbara, God really loves you. I know it. I promise you that's the truth, the only truth. He loves you." I asked Ray to somehow get me to that church.

"What? Please, Barbara, you're in no shape to go anywhere. I can't even lift you."

"Okay, okay." Then I thought of the woman Anne. I wanted to go to her. I had to get to her, that was all I knew. "Ray, I'll go to Anne. You must take me there, but please drive past that church, *please*. And let's stay here on the beach of Torremolinos another night or two instead of driving all the way back to our camp at Fuengirola. What difference does it make to you now? I'll be leaving in a few days."

With resignation in his manner, Ray just nodded. There was no fight, no argument, nothing. I lay in the back on the camper bed, unable to move, and Ray drove to the church. As he pulled alongside the curb, I lifted my head as high as I could, remembering the cross from the dream. There it was, and the outside door was open; obviously someone was inside.

"Ray, the door is open. Please help me inside." Ray said nothing, and his face was completely expressionless as he pulled and lifted me out of the bed to the ground. I leaned on him as he half-carried me across the street into the back of the church. With my eyes fixed on the door to the preacher's office, I pleaded with Ray to walk me down the aisle. Reluctantly he did, seeing that I couldn't make it on my own. When I was in front of the door, he left, walking quickly up the aisle and out the door. I knocked, trying to support myself with the doorknob. The door opened, and Dan stood there, looking at me.

"Oh my!" It was obvious that for a few moments he didn't know what to say. Then with both hands and a great assurance he helped me onto the couch inside. "When did you get back from Morocco? We've all been praying for you. I knew you'd be back though."

"Oh, quite a while ago. I'm very sick, very sick. I don't think I'll make it, Dan. I had to come here, and I want to go to Anne, too."

"Yes, okay. I won't keep you, but I'd like to pray for you, right now." Not about to take no for an answer, Dan gently rested both of his hands on my forehead, praying more earnestly than I'd ever heard him. Halfway through his prayer, as he pressed down on my head and said something about rebuking Satan, pleading some kind of blood over me and asking Jesus to keep me from alcohol, he suddenly said in a deep, firm voice: "You will not be able to take one drop of alcohol into your system today or tonight. You will be too sick to be able to swallow it, and if you do it will come right back up again." Abruptly Dan's voice became gentle again, as he closed his prayer. Then he looked at me, and there were tears in his eyes: "You are one of God's chosen people, a descendant of Abraham."

I couldn't understand what he meant. "Chosen" — how could that be? I was less than nothing, the scum of the earth. But at the name Abraham, I began to cry. "My grandfather's name was Abraham. I called him Peepa, but his name was Abraham."

"Barbara, tomorrow is Sunday. Please set your mind and will to come back here to church tomorrow morning. Promise me."

"But Ray won't come, he hates church and this place, and I'm sorry to say, he doesn't like you. He's leaving me Wednesday. He wants to send me back home on a plane from Malaga, and I don't want to go on living without him, alone this way."

"Listen to me! Listen, I say," and there was a note of strong command in his voice. "Don't think about Wednesday. Don't think about Monday. Get in that camper and get straight to Anne's house. Then concentrate on coming here tomorrow morning, without one drop of liquor in you. Do you hear me? If it gets rough, concentrate on God, and ask Him to help you. Jesus *will* heal you, believe me; I know it."

"Don't say Jesus to me. Don't say Jesus. You can say God, but don't say Jesus!"

"Okay, that can wait, but do what I tell you. I'll be praying for you. Others are going to pray for you. Don't think of Ray. You must do this for yourself. Ray will be okay. God will take care of him. He will not leave you, I promise. Now go, and may God pour out His mercy and blessings upon you. In Jesus' name. Hallelujah!''

I was annoyed that he had said Jesus again, but I nodded yes, just as if I actually was going to do that unbelievable thing and come back to church the next day without a drop of liquor in me. That was impossible, *impossible!* And yet, for that moment, in that office, facing Dan, I somehow believed that it was going to happen.

I closed the door behind me and hobbled to the first pew, where I supported myself from row to row until I got to the back of the church and out the door. It was raining so hard, I fell and stumbled. Ray came out of the camper to lift me up and get me inside. Saying nothing to him about what had happened, I asked him to take me to Anne's. Obligingly and in silence, he drove the van.

We found a parking space two blocks from Anne's apartment house, which meant we had to pass various cafes and bars along the way. I managed to get by three but when the fourth bar was directly adjacent to me, I ran in. The bar was lined up with the usual numerous glasses of common red and white table wine. That meant I didn't have to waste time ordering a drink. Grabbing a glass of red wine and drinking it down in one gulp, I was about to reach for another when I heard Ray's voice behind me: "C'mon, Barbara. Either we're going to this woman Anne's house or I'm leaving you here."

"Okay, leave me here, Ray. I can't go through with it, I . . . ."
But before I could finish my sentence my face flushed and I felt sick to my stomach. Barely making it to the ladies' room, I heaved up the entire glass of wine I had drunk, and while I hung over the toilet Dan's strong words came back to me: "You will not be able to take one drop of alcohol into your system today or tonight. You will be too sick to be able to swallow it, and if you do it will come right back up again." When there was nothing left to throw up, I darted out of the bar looking for Ray. I could see him walking in the direction of where the camper was parked. Running after him as

best I could and calling out his name, he finally stopped. "Ray," I said breathlessly, "no matter what I say or do, don't let go of me until we get to Anne's. There is no way I can stop drinking, but I'm going to try to get through this hour without a drink, so please help me, I beg you."

30

"Come right up," Anne said over the intercom. We took the elevator to the second floor. I was surprised there was an elevator; coming from New York with all its skyscrapers, I never felt that an elevator was necessary unless you lived higher than the fourth floor. But I sure was glad there was one; my legs couldn't have climbed a single step. Anne greeted us at the door, and I stood there, looking into her bright, well-decorated living room. Immediately my eye caught some bottles on a shelf. They were filled with gold and amber-colored liquid. My heart skipped a beat — liqueurs, perhaps? Galliano?

Anne caught my glance, and where my eyes finally rested. "Sorry to disappoint you, but it's just colored water. I don't keep booze around." She stood there, all of five feet two, a slim, white-haired lady in her early sixties. Instead of inviting us in right away, she told Ray to take me to the pharmacy up the street and get me some B-12 shots. "How can you get a shot at a drugstore?" Ray asked.

"They know how to do it there. Doctors are limited here; besides, she really belongs in a hospital, but I wouldn't send my worst enemy to one of these hospitals. They're not equipped to handle this sort of thing, and know nothing about alcoholism. They might lock her up and not let her out."

I became more and more frightened and less and less anxious to sober up, as the minutes ticked by and my body began demanding another drink. As we turned to leave, Anne spoke strongly and directly to Ray: "Make sure you get her the full B-12 complex and arrange to get back there for another at 6 p.m. And another thing: do not, under any circumstances, let go of her arm the whole time you're gone. In another half-hour, she'll try to break out." Ray nodded grimly and we left.

The drugstore was so crowded that I managed to convince Ray to wait for me by the door. I knew he wouldn't wait outside, but at least if he didn't go in the back room with me and the pharmacist, I could try to procure another bottle of Librium, just in case I needed them. Fortunately a different pharmacist waited on me, so I didn't have to worry about being remembered. After all, there probably weren't that many young American women coming in there buying large quantities of Librium and Darvon every few days.

After my shot, and once again with the death pills jiggling in my handbag, I took Ray's arm and we passed the many bars I frequented, until finally we reached Anne's apartment.

This is crazy; I can't do it, I thought. I've got to figure out a way to get a drink. Anne once again stood waiting at the door. This time she warmly invited us inside, motioning for me to lie down on the couch if I wanted to. The coffee table in front was filled with cakes and candies, cold cuts and cheeses and hot coffee. She looked with compassion on Ray. "This is for you, boy. You look pale and undernourished. You've been through hell, too, you know. Living with an alcoholic is not easy, not at all." Winking at him, she encouraged him to persevere. "Don't give up now you've come this far, now hang in there, boy, hang in."

That was the first time anything like that had been said to Ray. The "friends" we had made invariably felt sorry for him, urging him to get out of this mess. No one had ever said to hang in there. Ray made no reply, as he took a seat in the big easy chair in the corner of the room, facing the sofa. Every once in a while, he got up and took something to eat.

For the first fifteen minutes, I said nothing. My mind was working feverishly, trying to figure out a way to get out of that apartment. Perhaps when Anne is in the kitchen, or Ray in the bathroom, I'll run for the door. Oh God, I can't stand this! I've *got* to get a drink!

But when Anne asked me how I was doing, I said okay. She cocked an eyebrow at me, knowing full well that I was lying. My fingers were in my mouth, and my eyes were twitching.

An hour had not passed before I was heartily sorry that I had ever gone to the church, or anything. Anne even gave Ray my handbag. She began talking about her life there in Torremolinos and her life in the States, both when she was drinking and afterwards. I wished she'd shut up. She talked and talked and talked.

I couldn't stand it any longer, and made up my mind to leave the moment Ray went to the bathroom. But for the longest time he just sat there. Finally, he did leave the room. I gave him fifteen seconds, and then bolted out of the apartment and down the stairs, as fast as I could run. Up behind me, I could hear Anne yelling, "Raymond, hurry! She got out!"

I made it outside the building and ran into the first bar I found. Not caring that I didn't have any bag or money with me, I headed straight for the bar, calling loudly to the bartender who was busily mixing drinks: "Hurry! Give me some whiskey, a double, hurry, *please!*"

The bartender was taken aback, when he turned to see who was in such urgent need of a drink. Shaking violently, I waited an eternity for that damn drink to come. Just as the glass of whiskey was set before me, I felt a strong hand clamp down on my arm. *"No!!!"* I screamed and tugged. "Let go of me! Let go, do you hear? I've got to have that drink! I'll die if I don't get that drink!" I was creating a terrible, mortifying scene, but this time Ray didn't do what I was counting on. He didn't cringe with embarrassment and say the hell with you, and leave me. Instead, he pulled me from the bar. With all the strength that was left in my body, I pulled in the opposite direction. Everyone turned to watch, but no one stepped in to stop him. Finally, I realized that I was not strong enough to win the tug of war, and in desperation I began to shriek and cry, begging him to let me have one, just one to tide me over. He said nothing; his jaw was set, and he didn't even look at me as he took me out of there.

This time, when I arrived back at Anne's apartment, all facades were down. I sobbed and pleaded for a drink. Anne watched me sit down, get up, pace her apartment, hold my head in my lap, shove my fist in my mouth, go to the bathroom and throw up, and then scratch and scratch my skin, as if thousands of vermin were biting me.

Sometimes Anne would enthusiastically tell me that I'd been sober for two hours, sometimes she would tell me to just hang on for the next five minutes, depending on how bad I was. Hour after hour, my body went through the tortures of the damned, as I slipped in and out of blackouts and unreality. "I'll never make it!" I sobbed. "Somebody, *please, please,* get me a drink. Oh God, oh God, help me."

It was six o'clock. I had arrived at one that afternoon, or was it two? "How much longer will this go on?"

"Don't think about how much longer, Barbara. Just let's get through each moment, one at a time. You're doing fine." Ray sat in his chair. He looked worn and sick, tired and fed up. He watched Anne deal with me in a way that he had never dreamed possible. He even began to root for me, too, at times, when he forgot about the decision he'd made regarding us.

Finally, at about 11 o'clock that night, Anne suggested that Ray take me back to the camper for some sleep. Sleep, I thought, who can sleep? How can I pace the floor in that camper? "What'll I do, if she wants to go?"

"Don't let her, just don't let her. You could both stay here, but she's going to have to learn to fight alone, and better now than later." She stood up and saw us to the door. "Now go. I'll be praying for you, and I'll be here all day tomorrow."

Ray's eyes filled with tears, as he put out his hand to thank Anne for all that she had done. She reached up on her toes, pulled his head down, and gave him a kiss on the cheek. I could hear her whisper, "Hang in there, boy."

"I don't know if I can, any more, Anne, I've tried." Ray's voice completely choked, as he wiped the tears from his face and uttered a cry of help for himself. "I'm so tired, too; I've given up."

"No! Never give up. Never!" And with that, we went back to the pharmacy; it was time for another B-12 shot.

Afterwards we made our way back to the camper, past all the bars, restaurants and hotels. My mouth was dry and my body was shaking wet; I ached and ached for a drink. I muttered and murmured to myself, cursing and begging God to help me, both in the same breath. It seemed like such a long walk back to the camper by the beach. Rain gently fell, wetting our hair and clothes. It was some kind of distraction from the pain in my body, and it felt good. For a moment, I could actually enjoy the beauty of the night — the yellow lights of the street and the cantinas, reflected in the puddles, the warm, soft rain washing us, the sound of a distant guitar . . . . No longer fighting, and resigned to either dying at some point, or going mad, where I wouldn't know what was going on, I let Ray practically carry me. When we got in our van, Ray decided that we would stay right there on the beach in Torremolinos the next few days, instead of heading back to our camp. He was afraid that we would be too out of the way, in case of some catastrophe; also we had arranged with the druggist to give me another shot at 8:00 the following morning.

It was impossible for me to conceive of going through one whole night without a drink, totally and practically impossible. "Ray, I'm cold, freezing!" Those were the last words I remember saying. It became too difficult to talk, as my teeth clattered, and I shook. Chills coursed through my body, as Raymond covered me with the sleeping bag and anything else he could find. After boiling water and trying to get some tea in me which spilled down my mouth and chin, he put down the mug. "I don't know what else to do for you, Barb. Try to hang in there; I know it's rough."

Through the sirens that I heard in my head and all the other phantom noises and real aches, I wondered if I heard Ray correctly. Was he actually rooting for me? Or was it my mind playing tricks, more false hoping?

As the hours went by, and I lay in the blackness of night in the sleeping bag, I could hear Ray sleeping next to me. He was exhausted. I was, too, but I was too frightened to sleep, panic-stricken at the thought of being there alone with myself and my mind. My heart began pounding uncontrollably. Twisting and turning, I couldn't have gotten out of the camper if I had tried. And now, with Ray sleeping, it would have been so easy. The suffering now became more intense than it had been all day, and the ghoulish horrors on the walls and in the air around me were threatening and evil. I couldn't escape them. In desperation, I began to plead and beg God to help me. In my feverish mind, Dan stood before me, telling me that God loved me. He told me that I would find God through His Son.

Although that was something I didn't agree with or believe, at that moment I was willing to try anything. "Oh God, oh Christ, if there is, ever was, such a person, please help me. Either let me die or get me through this night. Get me through this next hour." And as the evening wore on, and one hour after another passed, and I still shook and ached and saw clowns mocking me and demons distorted with hate, I prayed and begged and then, to my astonishment, found myself asking God to keep me from a drink for the next hour. I had begun rooting for myself!

The dawn finally broke through, and I gasped tearfully at the first rays of daylight, with morning around the corner. How I hated the dark, and the long, terror-filled night! But now the night was finally over. With tears streaming down my face, I began to weep softly and to thank God for all these hours without a drink. And then I added: "And you, too, Christ, if you have had any part in this." Not knowing if I could stand, I knew I had to get to a ladies' room. The hotel across the street, I knew, had one. It also had a bar, and I also knew that I'd never make it past that bar without a drink. I fixed my mind on getting up first, then on finding my shoes.

Trying to do one thing at a time, standing up, I doubled over, practically vomiting on the floor, but after twenty minutes, I found myself standing outside the camper, leaning on the door. Ray was still sound asleep. I remembered his words last night — "Hang in there, Barb!" — and choked up. It must have been real, I thought, it must have. "Oh God, please, I beg you with all my might, don't let me stop at that bar, get me in and out of that ladies' room. Jesus Christ, if there are miracles, do it."

I was not aware of the change in my attitude from the day before, when I had broken out of Anne's apartment for a drink. Then I had been praying for a drink; now I was actually praying to stay away from one. And so, step by step, I walked over to the hotel. Sensing that the bartender knew who was coming, I kept my head down and bit into my lip so hard that the pain distracted me from the craving of my body. I made it and collapsed on the floor by the toilet. I don't know how long I sat there with the dry heaves, knowing full well what would relieve them, yet saying over and over one word: God. When the throwing up finally stopped, I began to make my way out, but this time it was harder. I stopped midway past the bar and turned to look at it, seeing myself in the mirror, swollen, straggly, sick, a pitiful sight. All the bottles were lined up, and there was so much of what I needed, so much.

I took a step towards the bar — and froze. "Nooo," I groaned. "God *is* helping me, noooo, not yet. I'll get through this next hour, just one more hour, and then later, I'll drink. I'll try to hang on. Oh God, do it again, I beg You and Christ together, do it again. Get me out of here fast, keep me away from alcohol."

Slowly my foot withdrew back to its original position. Again, I bit down hard, and slowly, but as fast as I could and feeling as though I were tied in the middle of a rope with forces pulling at either end, I made my way outside. With the easing of the rope, I walked more and more quickly back to the camper. Ray was still sleeping inside, but he turned and opened one eye, as I climbed back into the camper.

Sobbing uncontrollably, with breaks of laughter in between, I told him: "Ray, I did it. I got through the night, and I just came back from the bathroom in the hotel where I drink, and Ray, you're not going to believe it! It's a miracle, Ray. I prayed to God to keep me from drinking, and He did. I'm sick, so sick, but it's okay. Ray, for the first time, I walked away from a drink. Oh God, I can hardly believe it! It's a miracle!" And then, with a little more awareness and a little more unsure of myself, I added: "It's a miracle so far, Ray."

31

Uppermost in my mind was the desire to stay away from a drink, at least until I made it to church. The preacher's prayers and prophetic word about not drinking were being replayed over and over again as I recalled the glass of red wine I had drunk on my way over to Anne's. That was the last drink I had had yesterday afternoon, and what he said would happen had happened. It came right back up again. Anne's help and Ray's willingness to stay with me through it all were motivating and encouraging. However, I was also well aware of Ray's rapidly changing mood. He didn't have to say a word for me to see that he was not at all happy about driving me to church. In fact, the very idea of church was infuriating to him.

"Barbara, damn it, I never should have given into another one of your whims. I've changed my mind; I'm *not* going into that church! I'll wait for you in the camper."

"Ray, please, you said you would come with me, just this once. Look, I don't even know why I'm going back there myself, but Ray, it's the only way I can say thank you. Look: I've been sober for twenty-four hours! I know that Dan and his wife and that organ player Robby have been praying for me. I want to show them that I did it. Besides, Ray, it'll kill another hour and a half for me. Anything that helps pass the time makes it just a little easier; besides, what if God *is* God? I mean, what if He really is? If all that stuff is true, then wouldn't that be something! I mean, if God is God, then it's black or white, no grey areas. If He really is God, then He can do anything. And then God is the truth, the answer, the way out."

"C'mon, cut this Aimé Semple MacPherson crap out before you really go off the deep end! Look, I'm glad you're sober for twenty-four hours, but I'm not jumping up and down about it. It's happened before, and you've always fallen flat on your face. As far as I'm concerned, God is still dead." My jubilant mood came crashing down, and I cried and cried.

"Okay, okay! I'll go to this church with you, because I said I would. Only stop crying!"

I could not remember the last time I had bothered to put a skirt on, or pile my hair on top of my head in a bun. I wore the brown and beige checked wool suit that Aunt Mary had given me as a going-away outfit for our wedding, and with shaky hands I managed to get the knots out of my hair and cover up the circles under my eyes. I looked a lot different from my wedding day, about fifteen pounds of bloat heavier and a dozen years older, but at least it was better than the way I had looked the last time I had entered that church. Ray wore his old patched-up jeans but did put shoes on, instead of sandals. He didn't say anything, but I could tell he had trimmed his beard, and combed his hair.

As we drove up in our van, people who were filing into church turned to wave to us. We didn't know them, but they acted as if they knew us. "What are they waving for? They're not getting any money from me," Ray commented caustically. As soon as we got on line, Robby came rushing towards us, taking my arm and ushering us inside, ahead of all the other people. You'd have thought we were celebrities, instead of a couple of traveling bums. "Oh, brother, what the hell am I getting into?" Ray muttered loudly.

To our amazement, we were taken right down the middle aisle to the very first row and given the first two seats on the aisle directly off center. Ray slumped way down in his seat, and for some reason, I began hiccuping. After I got up enough courage to turn around, I saw people on all sides of the sanctuary smiling in our direction. Oh brother, I thought, God, please help me now. Don't let Ray turn around and see this, and don't let any of these people talk to us, and please God, keep Ray here in his seat and don't let him make a scene.

I was so busy asking God to help Raymond that without my realizing it, time was passing, and I was not preoccupied with the pains of alcohol withdrawal that my body was still going through. During all the customary churchly preliminaries, like missions and money and announcements and Bible studies, Ray looked furious, in a rage that he was where he was, listening to this "rubbish." I sensed he was about to walk back up the center aisle and out, when Dan's wife Rhoda began to sing a solo.

I didn't know anything about music, but her voice was clear, soft and beautiful. The song touched our hearts, and Ray's expression changed, as he relaxed back into his seat. Tears filled my eyes, when at the end of the song, Rhoda repeated it in sign language. I could hear other people crying and sniffing, some blowing their noses. It was enough to keep Ray sitting quietly through the sermon which followed. Dan told the story of the Prodigal Son from the Bible, and from time to time he glanced our way, sometimes looking as if he was going to break out in a big smile and a hand-raising "Hallelujah!"

I wasn't sure how I felt, but found myself listening intently at all times, identifying with the bad son who went out and got all dirty and did all the wrong things and then was taken back, and, can you imagine, he was still loved by God! He even had a party, a banquet given in his honor, because he was sorry for what he'd done and wanted to change and come home. I found myself thinking about what a real home like that must be like, what that warm safe feeling of security must be like, the kind I once had with Meema and Peepa. I found myself saying: "Oh God, how much I would like to feel that sense of belonging and acceptance again somewhere — but I know that's impossible for me." I cried for that son and how he must have felt. I was crying for myself and the yearning to have happen to me what had happened to him.

When it was time for us to leave, we waited silently until Ray voiced his annoyance about having to be last in line getting outside. Then, to our astonishment, people from everywhere turned around, broke through the line and came up to us. They grabbed our arms and hands and some even cried, telling us how God was answering their prayers by bringing us both into that church. One man looked at us and said, "We've even had friends praying for you two in England. Praise the Lord, He *is* faithful!" Stunned, bewildered and shaken, we just stood there. Within moments, Raymond regained his composure and shoved forward, saying, "This is crazy! I've got to get out of this place, got to get away from here!" But then Dan and Rhoda took his arm. They beamed and insisted that we go back to their house for lunch. Ray said "No!" curtly, but they kept on insisting, saying that we could leave as soon as we ate lunch, and that we would be doing them such a favor if we came.

"Oh come on, Ray, let's go. It'll pass more time. I'll have been sober another two hours, if we go, and then we can go back to Anne Murray's apartment after my B-12 shot. Maybe I'll have another whole day. Oh Ray, wouldn't that be fantastic? Two whole days without a drink? Oh my God, my God, I'll never believe it, if it happens." That same man who had said that people in England were praying for us, looked at me, smiled and said softly: "It *will* happen; believe it!"

Ray heard him and went nuts: "How does he know what's going to happen? These people are crazy! They've all been brainwashed by this lunatic, and I'm the craziest of all for even being here, because I know better."

As we followed in our camper behind Dan and Rhoda and their children to their house, my mind was racing. Let's see, first I ought to thank God that Ray somehow is still here regardless of how much he doesn't want to be. I just can't believe it! But no, first I really should ask Him for another two hours of sobriety... no, I think I'll make it three hours this time, maybe even four, why not? Then I ought to ask Him the biggest of all favors: to make some kind of sense out of all that is going on here. Because something is definitely happening; I can feel it. I'm excited about something for the first time in my life, and I'm not drinking. Am I crazy? Am I, too, being brainwashed, like Ray said? "God," I whispered to myself, "please listen to me: if You are who they say You are, and are keeping me sober, then tell me what's happening. I'm stupid in a lot of ways. I know nothing about the Bible or religion or heaven. I may know a little about hell, though. Give me some understanding of who and what You are. Amen." Then I had the feeling that I should add something before my "Amen". I had heard Dan close his prayer with "In Jesus' name, Amen." I didn't believe in Jesus, but just in case he was involved, I said, "In Jesus' name, Amen."

"Barbara," Ray exploded, "what *are* you doing? You look like you're off somewhere else, and you're muttering to yourself."

"I'm praying."

"*What?*"

"Yep! I know I really don't know how, so I'm kind of talking to God, the way I would to a friend or like when I used to write in my diary. I'm doing it this way, until I find out from Dan how to pray."

"Don't say things like that! I never should have asked you. I don't want to hear anything more about this nonsense; it's driving me nuts. It's stupid, for unintelligent people who need crutches. Can't you see what's happening? You're simply going from one crutch to another. When the bubble bursts, you'll be back on booze, and it'll be worse than ever."

I felt hurt, really hurt. Fear began to take hold again. The quivering in my body began to gnaw at me. I wanted a drink right then, desperately. "Ray," I said calmly, trying to keep the panic out of my voice, "would you please stop the car? I've got to go to the ladies' room."

"Can't you wait? We're almost at this guy's house."

"No, I can't. I'm going to be sick."

"All right, as soon as I find a place to stop. I'll have to signal them up ahead." Ray rolled down his window, honked his horn, and tried to signal Dan to stop, but Dan just waved back and continued driving.

"Raymond, stop this car now. I don't care what he does, or whether he stops or not. I'm getting out of here." With my hand on the door, I started to open it while we were still moving.

"What — are you crazy?" Reaching across me, Ray slammed the door shut, securing it. Then he looked at me quizzically, as if he had just remembered something. "I know what's going on: you're after a drink. Well, no dice, kiddo. If you're going to be sick, do it in this paper bag," and he reached behind his seat and pulled out a brown grocery bag.

I was furious and felt trapped. "Look, I've made a terrible mistake about this whole thing. You're right, this guy *is* a quack, and it's the last thing I need. I have no desire to stop drinking and never did have."

Realizing that what he had said had caused this change in me, Ray's whole manner changed. "Look, Barb, let's go to their house for lunch, as planned. We've got nothing to lose and nothing else to do. And you might just get another sober day out of it, after all."

"Well, I don't want one. I don't want anything from anyone. Remember, Ray, this is Sunday, and we're splitting up on Wednesday. You don't want to forget that, do you?"

"No, I don't."

"I didn't think so."

My changed mood was obvious to everyone, when we sat down to lunch. Rhoda had prepared a delicious hot chicken dinner, but I sat in sullen silence, my eyes darting everywhere for a bottle I could get my hands on. Dan sensed that I wasn't about to communicate with anyone, so he directed his conversation to Ray, but it wasn't about God. He laughed and joked with him about their similar Italian backgrounds. Ray even talked a bit about his Dad, and how he came over from Italy. Ray, too, seemed concerned about my anger and obvious intent.

After lunch, Rhoda took my arm and led me to the sofa. Her eyes sparkled and her dark, shiny hair looked so ladylike and refined, pulled back into the loveliest chignon, the way Mother used to wear her hair years ago. She began telling me how she had planned a career to become a professional opera singer, when she met Dan, and then how Christ had completely changed her life.

As soon as she got onto the subject of God, she was like a nonstop rollercoaster. She went on and on with indescribable joy, telling me how much God loves us and what He wanted to do for me and for Ray, too.

At first I was angry that I had to sit there and listen to that junk, then somehow her own joy became contagious, and I found myself once again lifted outside my own feelings of despondency, and hoping with all my might that what I was hearing was true. And yet I was so afraid to believe that it was, to trust and put my hope into something again.

As Rhoda talked, I thought of the hurt I had experienced when I had to leave my grandparents. It was excruciating; so much so that tears still came to my eyes at the recollection. And then there were the other hurts: the sense of unfairness and resentment I felt about my mother's life, her loneliness and mine, her drinking and mine. And the men, all the men, who had never cared and who I had so hoped would — my father, who wasn't even curious about seeing me; Jack Riley, I really believed he loved me; Roy, who had used me and thrown me away like tissue paper, again and again. And what was worse, I had taken it. I became used to that kind of treatment. How he had toyed with my emotions and taunted me! And Frank Maloney, a joining together of two sick, alcohol-dependent people. I almost married him. He left me waiting in a bar on our wedding day. And Raymond, my husband, the man in whom I had put all my faith and trust. Finally, the security that would take me out and away from the lonely hell I had known all my life. The one good thing that had ever come into my life, and I had destroyed it. Now I was going to end up in worse shape than I'd ever been in. I had tasted something fine and good and was going to lose it all, to be left alone with myself — and total destruction. How could I possibly be sitting here like this, so naive, so stupid, so hoping again? Haven't I learned my lesson, that there is no hope for me, short of death itself?

"Barbara, Barbara," Rhoda interrupted my train of thought. "Satan is trying to keep you from God. You must be aware of him and who he is, so that you can fight him. He doesn't have to have any power over you, anymore." As soon as she said "power," I leaned forward and asked her, "Rhoda, I *have* felt a power, some kind of evil power with me, for a long time. He's told me to do things I never wanted to do. He's been there gloating over my sufferings, in my dreams and unreal visions. He's just about convinced me that the only way out for me is suicide." I hadn't meant to go that far; it just came tumbling out.

Rhoda looked aghast. "No, no, Barbara! That's definitely Satan. That's not God talking. You have known only Satan. Please, please, give God a chance in your life. God gave His only Son, Jesus Christ, to die to be nailed to a cross for our sins — for you, for all that you've done and been through, so that you might really *live,* free from Satan and the torments of hell forever. Barbara, don't look at me like that! You must believe me! This is the truth; I know it with every fiber in me. Oh, how I wish I could make you see . . . ." and suddenly she began to cry. She was hurting for me, crying for me, and I didn't know what to do.

I felt pulled, torn, and then I put my hands to my face and cried, too: "Oh God, oh my God, I *want* to believe. Show me, show me, show me. And Jesus Christ? Rhoda? I am Jewish. I can't possibly understand who or what He is. Can't just God be enough for me?"

"Barbara, it is the most glorious thing in the whole world that you are Jewish; I don't even know where to begin about that. But Jesus was a Jew."

"What? I didn't know that!"

"Yes, He is the Messiah, the hope, the Savior. You don't have to take my word for it; ask Him to show you. Challenge Him. Do you have a Bible?" Reaching into my large handbag, I pulled out the New Testament that Dan had given me.

"When you go back to your campsite," she said, "open it and begin to read it, just one line at a time, from the beginning."

"But I haven't been able to read anything in years, because of my drinking. I can't sit still or concentrate."

"Just do it. I will be praying for you to understand what Jesus is saying."

"Rhoda, I don't know, I don't know . . . but, yes, I will try."

32

It was about 5 o'clock when we finally left Dan and Rhoda's home. My mood swings were now wide-scale, changing every half-hour it seemed, along with the constant desire for a drink. There were times when the smell and taste of alcohol would consume me, telling me that I had to have relief. Never had I thought so much, so long. There were times when the twitching and shakiness eased up, leaving me like an old, wet dishrag that had been wrung almost dry. Limp and exhausted, yet unable to doze, I counted my hours, my moments without a drink. Each additional half-hour became another triumph, but with it the constant worry of what would happen in the next half-hour. Would I be able to hold out? And if so, for how long?

"Damn it, Barbara, why did you tell Dan we'd come by his office tomorrow?"

"I don't know, I guess I didn't know what else to say. And after all, they've been so hospitable to us, feeding us and praying for us."

"Look, I never asked them to pray for us. They're great people, I'll admit that, and they make a nice family, in fact, a picture of what a family should be. But that kind of life could never be ours. Be realistic!"

"All right, we won't go tomorrow. Or we'll drop a note off saying that we can't keep the appointment."

"What did he want to talk about, anyhow? What else is there to say? He knows how we feel about God, let alone Jesus Christ!"

"He wanted me to hear a tape by some Jewish guy named Arthur something, how this guy searched and traveled like we're doing, and how as a Jew he came to find Jesus in Israel. He said that tape would say it all to me, and couldn't I spare one more hour out of my life? Actually, this is getting funny. 'Spare one more hour' to listen to some tape; I've certainly got enough hours to spare one, and they drag so. At least it's another hour away from a drink."

And then, all of a sudden, I laughed. "This is really crazy, you know. I never had any desire or intention of getting a Bible or going to church, even that first Sunday. All I wanted to do was go to a bar alone, so that you didn't have to watch me kill myself. What happened? I went to that church. Somehow, for some reason, I found hope there, something else, too, people who seemed to care about me as I was. They weren't disgusted with me, like you and everyone else at the compound."

I laughed again, ruefully this time. "Oh, I'm sure they will be soon, everyone is, and I know this God stuff is crazy, but *something* is keeping me sober, and it's been nearly a day and a half now." I looked at Ray. "Tell me something: what *is* keeping me away from a drink, every minute when my body is craving alcohol like crazy?"

Ray drove the camper in silence, as he sped along the Costa del Sol. "Where are we going in such a hurry?"

"To the compound. I want to see Evelyn and Ed. They're leaving tomorrow. We've done your thing all day, and now I'm going to be with my friends. You can come along, or should I drop you off in town?" I was afraid to go to the compound. I didn't want to see Ed and Evelyn and whoever else might be there. Booze would be plentiful, but I was even more afraid to be dropped in town. It was ironic to me that dry, I was afraid to be on the street alone, afraid of the dark, afraid of people I didn't know, and afraid of myself. Drunk, I was afraid of nothing, nothing.

When did I begin to lose my independence, I wondered. Tracing back through the years, my forehead leaning against the window of the camper, looking out at the ocean, I let my mind go, until pain, emotional pain began to take over, before I could even remember when. And when that pain came, so too did an over-powering feeling of anxiety and fear. I knew of no way to cope with those feelings, now that I wasn't drowning them with booze. What was I going to do?

I didn't want to think, I didn't want to feel, I didn't want to go on. I turned my head to look at Raymond. We thought we knew each other so well, and we really didn't know each other at all. In fact, I didn't even know myself — not sober, anyhow. I really didn't want to know that me. I saw myself as an awkward, unintelligent woman who was very lonely and uncomfortable with life as it was, for some reason. What was the reason, what had made me this way? I felt crippled. "Stop it, stop it!"

"What's the matter?" Ray was aware of another mood swing. Trying to stop the flood of thoughts and questions that poured through my mind, I shut my eyes and began to say "Stop it!" out loud.

"Nothing's wrong. I'm going with you to the compound, Raymond. I don't want to be dropped off in town, not now, not after sweating through 27 hours of sobriety! And if I make it through tonight, I'm going to the church tomorrow to hear that tape and if I make it through Tuesday night without a drink, then I'll be back at that church to see Anne and those people who drank the way I do. And if that happens, then maybe, maybe, there is a God after all."

And then, for the first time in weeks, I dared to look ahead to the possibility of our parting without recoiling in an agony of despair. "Wednesday's been a long time coming, Raymond. Maybe I won't let you put me on a plane and send me back to the States. Maybe I'll stay here by myself for a while, until I can get back on my feet, if I can do it a day at a time without a drink. Maybe God *is* up there, right over my head, looking and watching out for me, like Dan and Rhoda say. Maybe it's crazy, and maybe it isn't. I can decide what to do with my life, when you leave. To live or to die is my decision."

His eyes wide with surprise, Ray kept turning to look at me as he drove. He'd never seen me sober, really, especially talking the way I was, so firm and direct. He was used to my thousand-and-one "I'm sorry's," and sloppy tears.

He said nothing, but neither did he turn aside. He was going to the compound, and that was that. Okay, if God was God, then He was more than equal to it. If there was booze around, then I would just pray — as hard as necessary. But just to keep me steadier, I thought maybe one of those 10 mil Librium I had in my bag would help, so I took one.

Ed and Evelyn were all packed and ready to leave the next day. Raymond offered to drive them to the train or plane or whatever. He took down as much information as he could from Ed about where he and Evelyn were headed, and where they might be staying. Sensing that he was doing this so that he could join up with them once I was gone, my insecurity mounted and drove me into deafening silence. I could feel my heart pound with anxiety, and everything in me wanted to run. It began to overpower me.

I heard a voice, that old familiar voice that used to order me around, only now I remembered what Rhoda had said about Satan, and I recognized it for what — who — it was. As this power began to give me instructions, I nervously opened my handbag and pulled out my New Testament, holding it in my lap with both hands. Then I opened it, and my eyes rested on the comforting words Dan had written in the front: "To Barbara, with confidence of complete freedom through Jesus. Your friend, Daniel Del Vecchio." I read and re-read each word, but the word freedom leaped out. Freedom — and Jesus. I found myself hating, struggling with the name Jesus. Why did *He* have to be the answer to freedom? Why not just God? It didn't seem fair, not to me, to a Jew. I felt confused, torn and pulled. I was caught in the middle of a rope again, being pulled in two directions.

The strain I was under began to show. I could feel everyone's eyes on me, watching to see in which direction I was about to flee. In desperation, holding tightly to the Bible, trying not to make any decision but just sit where I was for the next few minutes, I said aloud: "Evelyn, Ed, I have not had a drink for twenty-eight hours now. I'm an alcoholic who can't stop drinking, but I'm trying to kick it." Lifting the Bible slightly with both my hands and looking at it, I told them: "This is a Bible, actually just the New Testament. I went to a small church near here a while back. There was something there. I don't know, but maybe there is a God. Anyway, I'm going to find out. Maybe I *am* crazy, I don't know, but I do know that I'm sober.''

Looking down at the small Bible, I thought to myself, what is this book? What is a Bible anyhow and who wrote it? Then I remembered Raymond writing, "God is dead" in the sand with a stick. It had bothered me, and I had brushed it out with my foot. Ray had tried to stop me. It had made him so angry that I wanted to rub that sentence out, and yet why had it bothered me?

Unaware of the time and the fact that Ed and Ev had long since stopped staring at me and resumed their conversation with Ray, I looked at my watch and was amazed to realize that I'd been lost in another train of thought about God for the last twenty minutes.

Twenty minutes had passed and I had not once thought about a drink. Incredible — could this be God's way of answering my prayer? Was He giving me new thoughts? Then I remembered what I had prayed: "God, if You are real, help me to understand who and what You are." Could He be doing some of that now?

But there's so much, how can I possibly get it? I felt a sudden sense of urgency and impatience, and then I remembered that Dan had said there was a Bible study Wednesday nights at that church. A Bible study? I couldn't imagine what that was like and what kind of people went to it. I dismissed the idea quickly, but decided to open the Bible to the first page that night and maybe even browse through the first few pages, to see if I could comprehend anything.

I became excited about the prospect of going back to the campsite now, even getting into my sleeping bag and having a cup of tea. This time I was going to ask Ray to stop at one of those yummy bakeries and get some pastries. The picture I had in my mind looked so warm, so inviting, that I jumped to my feet, smiling.

I could hear a distant "uh-oh," and saw Ray's untrusting glance. "Where are you off to?"

"Ray, let's go now. We've been here long enough. 'Bye, Ed and Evelyn, see you tomorrow. I want to get back and read, read this Bible.''

33

That night, as Ray began reading a new book he'd gotten by D.H. Lawrence, I opened the Bible. Several times I opened and closed the book, somehow trying to ready myself for this special occasion. I skimmed the first few pages, not taking in anything. Irritated, I kept turning page after page of the Gospel of Matthew. There were so many questions — like what does "Gospel" mean, and who is Matthew? Why did he write about Jesus? What are disciples? Then, as my eyes finally came to rest, it was on the Sermon on the Mount, and I read: "Blessed are the poor in spirit, for the kingdom of heaven is theirs." Well, I was certainly poor in spirit, and I grabbed on to that. Reading on, I knew I wasn't in mourning, but oh, how I wanted to be comforted!

"Blessed are those who hunger and thirst for righteousness, for they shall be completely satisfied," I read aloud, and burst out, "That's it! That's the answer! Raymond, listen, listen to this: I can't believe it."

"Oh no, you don't!" he replied emphatically. "Don't start bringing me into your reading. Read to yourself. It's enough that I went to church today and ended up at that guy's house; I am *not* getting involved in the Bible. I know what the Sermon on the Mount says. I went to parochial school and was an altar boy. But I don't want any more of it now, and so leave me out of it."

"Okay, okay, but listen anyway just to this one line." My enthusiasm about what I had read soared. I had to share this discovery, or I would explode. "Ray, if I hunger and thirst for righteousness, I will be satisfied. The word thirst — my thirst has never been satisfied. It's insatiable! Because I've been thirsting for the wrong thing. What if that's true? What if I become satisfied? And Ray, everything Jesus is saying here, everything we marched about against the Vietnam War, against violence, all the so-called love and flower children — this sermon is the answer. He tells us what we must do to achieve this kind of love and blessing, but it sounds like it's an individual thing; each one of us has to change direction. I would have to seek God, not a bottle, not more money, not travel or even you, Ray. I thought I'd find fulfillment in you, and then the drinking would stop, but it got worse instead."

Suddenly, I was struck by what an astounding key was here, for the whole world. "Ray, do people know about this? If we all lived just this way, it would work!"

He looked over at me and shook his head. "Look, that stuff has been around for centuries. Just because you're not well-read, and are just discovering something, doesn't mean it hasn't been discovered before — tried and failed at."

"Oh." Feeling very stupid and disillusioned, I went down like a popped balloon. But I kept turning pages, not understanding much of what I saw, until my eye caught a story about a woman who had suffered from hemorrhages for twelve years. Instantly, I thought of my alcoholism. I counted back through the years. I was twenty-nine now; ten years ago I was nineteen, and two more, I was seventeen years old and a senior in high school. That was when I had really begun drinking, on weekends, dating and going to fraternity parties. I saw myself at Columbia, New York University, and cafes in Greenwich Village and Germantown and I was the girl, the only girl, who finished all the beer and wanted more, all the drinks and wanted more.

This woman in the story had been to doctors, had sought help everywhere, and so had I. And now she knew that if she touched Jesus, she would be cured. And she was! I've tried everything . . . what if I believed this, what if this was true? "Oh my God,

Raymond, I can't believe this: listen to this story about this woman who —"

"Barbara, will you quit it? I can't take this anymore. You're driving me nuts, nuts!"

"Hey, I'm sober, remember?" But I did quiet down after that. And one question did not get answered that night: if Jesus was such a good guy, why didn't the Jews believe in Him?"

The next morning we said goodbye to Ed and Evelyn. I breathed a sigh of relief, after I watched them board the train, as though they were becoming a threat to us. "Well, Ray, that leaves you and me. The compound has broken up. Wednesday is in two days. I guess we'd better decide what we're going to do." It had now been two full days that I'd been without a drink, something incomprehensible to me, yet I still did not want to be left alone without Ray. I knew I was too weak to make it on my own, to even pursue this God I was beginning to find some hope in. My intentions were still to take my life as planned, by swallowing the Librium that I had procured when I received my first B-12 shot at the pharmacy. Since that time I had been taking ten milligrams of Librium every day, believing that even that small dose would steady me in case I really began to fall apart from nerves. Strangely though, I took the pill at different times, usually before a social situation such as going to church or visiting with Anne and her friends, or before going to sleep at night. I was not at all aware of the fact that I was using this one pill each day in the same way I had used alcohol in the beginning. And if Ray left me, I knew I would have no trouble whatsoever in getting another bottle of the same pills. I was still filled with my worst fear, being left alone and desolate, without Raymond.

"Well, Ray what are you planning to do?"

"I don't know yet, Barbara. I need some more time to think. Maybe we should stay here together for the rest of the winter and then decide. I guess another month or two won't matter. I really don't want to go to France in January anyway."

I couldn't believe what I had just heard from Ray's mouth. Inside, my heart leapt and melted; hot tears flowed down my cheeks. Not wanting Ray to see my reaction, and trying to maintain some kind of aloofness, I walked back to the camper ahead of him and wiped my eyes. Looking up to the clear blue sky, I said: "God, this must be Your doing. It's certainly not Ray's or mine. Oh thank You, thank You, thank You."

The whole ride back to Torremolinos from Malaga, I cried and worried and was completely bewildered. Now I became frightened. What if my hopes were raised up through this added time, and the crash was worse? I'd prepared myself for the end. What if I drank tomorrow or next week? I mean, how long could this last?

At the church, Ray intended to wait for me in the camper while I went inside to hear the tape, but Dan was just outside the door when we drove up, so Ray ended up getting out to say hello, and before he knew it, he, too, was led inside Dan's office. Dan didn't waste any time talking. He had us both sit on the couch, and then he immediately turned the tape on.

As soon as I heard the guy, Arthur Katz's voice, I knew he was Jewish. That alone gave me a kind of homey feeling, instead of the cynicism I usually had towards that sort of accent, even if it was well masked by intellect. Within moments I became involved, identifying like crazy with this fellow's search for something, although I could see more of Ray in him. This guy Katz didn't seem to have the obvious weakness I did. But as the tape went on, his feelings about Jesus as a Jew were like mine and the way in which he was gradually led to see Christ as the Messiah caused a strong response inside of me.

At the end of the tape, he was in Israel, of all places, and he found and gave his life to Jesus with assurance, excitement and tears. I broke down and cried. The tape switched off, and we sat in silence. I glanced at Ray, who was obviously deep in thought, the hostility gone from his face for a moment, and got up and walked to the door, thanking Dan for letting us hear it. He handed me two books. One was *The Cross and the Switchblade,* the other *Beyond Ourselves.* "Dan, I don't read. I have trouble concentrating."

"Try one page at a time, just try."

The next night at the church, seeing Anne Murray and some of her friends talking about the hell brought on by drinking, the pains of putting down that bottle, the fight for sobriety and then the continued maintenance of that constant battle one day at a time, I began to feel hopeless again. It's impossible, I thought, impossible to stay stopped. Then someone read something aloud: "There will come a time when no human power can keep you from that next drink. The only one is God. May you find Him now."

Over and over, those words confirmed what I was coming to believe, to grasp, to hope for — to want with all my heart.

The next evening was New Year's Eve. That was when Ray was to leave me, the time I had planned to take my life. But now, instead, it was the beginning of a new year. Ray and I were actually going out to dinner and that was all. No party to go to, no cocktails, no ending up someplace else with no memory of when or how I got there. No black-and-blue marks, no shakes, no nightmares, no ghoulish visions, no vomiting, just the soft sound of church bells at midnight, as we lay in the camper with the lights out, looking up at the sky. I was awake, alive and alert. Ray looked at me and whispered: "Happy New Year, Princess."

In my heart that night, as I waited to fall asleep, I felt so full, so satisfied. I had hungered and thirsted for righteousness, and God, oh God, You are satisfying me like You promised, and all in one week's time! How can I thank You! What can I do?

The name Jesus came into my mind. It was He who had given the Sermon on the Mount. It was through Him that I was becoming grateful to God. I shook my head. "Unbelievable!" I murmured. "My mother, my relatives — boy, oh boy, they'll never believe this!"

"What did you say?"

"Oh nothing, really, just thinking. Ray, I'm really wondering about Jesus now. I mean, really."

The greatest gift of the New Year was to wake up, turn over, and read Raymond's diary: "1/1/71 *Costa del Sol* — Last night was cold, windy — and warm."

Each day our time was spent walking through the markets of Fuengirola, deciding what to buy and cook for dinner. We visited a quaint town called Mijas; only the climb and walk were enough to tell me that my strength had far from returned. Still having two B-12 shots daily, I managed to stay away from a drink — sometimes by the skin of my teeth and always with a plea to God and Jesus for help. Ray even drove me to church to attend the Bible study, although he definitely refused to come inside and join in.

I read more and more of the Bible, still in the Gospel of Matthew, and I took everything as meant specifically for me. The Bible was giving me advice and telling me what to do and how to live. It was exciting, and somehow it and the prayers and God all seemed to be daily strengthening my resolve not to drink again. And so, night after night, I would read aloud one passage after another in the camper.

Raymond yelled, threw things and balked. And as time went on, he woke up sweating. In the morning, he told me that I had to stop this whole God stuff: he was beginning to have dreams of being pulled in two directions. He couldn't sleep well any more. In short, I was told to shut up from now on. And I did — until one morning I was in the middle of *The Cross and the Switchblade,* by David Wilkerson. This Wilkerson guy needed a huge sum of money to start a home for boys. There was no way he could get the amount of money he needed. He asked God to give him the money as a sign that he was, in fact, supposed to build such a place in New York and leave his comfortable suburban surroundings. When he got the money, all of it, I exclaimed, "This is absolutely ridiculous!"

Ray was outside, washing up some of the pots and pans, and we were about to head into Torremolinos, a twenty-mile ride along the windy coast. I had told Dan I'd stop by to say hello and let him know how I was doing, and we had errands to do and the American Express to stop at.

Disgusted all of a sudden with this totally irrational nonsense of asking God for signs and money, I threw the book on the floor. When I looked up, I saw a large, green praying mantis on the front window near my seat. Afraid that this hideous thing would fly into the camper, I froze where I was, staring at it, resting there on the window sill. How would I ever get it out of here?

Then I heard something gently go through my mind: "Ask Jesus to keep this praying mantis on the window, an impossibility, until you reach the church in Torremolinos."

"What for?" I wondered.

"As a sign that He alone performs miracles, and to show you that with God anything is possible."

"This is crazy," I yelled, "but okay, Jesus, I challenge You, here and now. If You are truly the Christ, the Messiah to the Jews, God's only begotten Son, then I ask You, as a sign of Your reality and truth, to keep this praying mantis on the window, just the way it is, until we reach the church in Torremolinos. Then it can fly away or whatever."

When Raymond returned to the camper about fifteen minutes later, I disregarded my challenge to God, not believing for a moment that such a ridiculously impossible thing could happen, and showed the insect to Ray, asking him to brush it off my window.

"Oh, just keep your window closed. Once the car gets going, it'll fly away or be blown off."

Raymond started the van, and we proceeded on our journey along the windy Costa del Sol this brisk, clear morning. Lost in conversation with Ray, I happened to glance out my side window — where, to my dumbfoundment, the praying mantis clung, hanging on to nothing. We were practically at the ocean, and gusts of wind were rocking the camper.

"What's with you; you look weird all of a sudden. Are you sick?"

"No," I managed to reply, "it's nothing. I just don't want to talk right now." I didn't dare to tell Ray about this, for fear he'd think I was joining the rest of the kooks who believed in miracles, this one being about the wildest. But my heart began to beat faster and faster as we drove, and I found myself rooting for this mantis to hang on.

"Hang on, hang on," I kept pleading to myself, as though it were meant for me, "hang on for dear life." If that insect could hang on, then so could I. I could hang on to life, trust God and Jesus. He must be real, God's Son. We have fifteen miles to go; it'll never make it. But what if — it does?

"Barbara, what the hell is going on with you? Your face is beet-red. You look shell-shocked or something."

"You'll never believe this," I said slowly and quietly, almost as if my voice might startle the insect, "but that praying mantis on the window — well, he's still there, and nothing's holding him. He's sitting or standing, or whatever they do, but he hasn't been blown away; in fact, he hasn't even moved. If he was dead, he'd fall off."

Ray glanced over. "Hey, that *is* something, isn't it!"

"Raymond, I challenged God. I asked Jesus to keep this thing on the window, the way I found it, after I read about a miracle in *The Cross and the Switchblade.* I did it this morning, while you were washing the pots. I said, if Jesus is really truth and not some myth or philosopher, He could keep this thing on my window as a sign, until we reached Dan's."

"I don't want to hear it, do you hear?" Ray exclaimed, and then added grimly, "I'll get rid of it."

"No!" I screamed. "Don't you touch it!"

"I won't have to. I'll go faster," and with that, he jammed his accelerator foot to the floor.

The camper gathered speed — soon we were hurtling along at 60 miles an hour, and rocking dangerously in the wind, which was howling past. The mantis still didn't budge. Tears began to stream down my face, and I found myself crying out: "Hang on, hang on! Oh God, Jesus, You are doing it! You *are* real!"

"Stop it, damn it, Barbara, *stop it!"* But I refused. Torremolinos loomed ahead, and Ray had to slow down at last. He screeched to a halt at the American Express, opened the door and slammed it hard, returning in a few moments with the mail. Getting back in, he again slammed his door, hoping to jostle the mantis off. I was obviously in some state, as if it were I out there, hanging on in the blowing wind, ready to fall off at any moment. As we turned the corner to the church, I could see Dan standing outside. I couldn't wait to run to him and tell him what had happened.

With half a block to go, half crying, half laughing, I promised the Lord in a loud voice: "Jesus, You are who You say You are. Thank You for showing me your supernatural power that defies all reason. I promise You, here and now, that with You supporting me, I am going to hang on. I'm going to fight for sobriety every day of my life, and I am going to give you my life." Hearing my words, Raymond came to a screeching halt, stunned himself at this whole impossible yet real miracle. He sat motionless, as the praying mantis flew away the moment he turned the ignition off.

Absolutely jubilant, unlike I had ever been in my life, I ran to Dan, tripping and hardly able to get the words out.

He stood there, questioning me and finally got up enough courage to say: "Barbara, have you been drinking?"

"Drinking? No, oh no, I've found Jesus Christ!" Without any continuity or ability to explain my miracle, I made a poor attempt, hoping that Dan would raise his hands high and praise the Lord. But he didn't; he just stood there quietly and told me to calm down. When I finally finished, he said, "That's wonderful," yet I sensed he was not sure what was wonderful.

Displaying the utmost of caution, especially with Raymond refusing to get out of the camper, just sitting there, white and silent, he said, "I am happy about this miracle, but I don't want you to get so excited that you can't calm down." I winced, hurt that this would be his response. Suddenly, I wanted to hurt him back.

"Dan, I'm not going to get excited about any of your miracles again." I felt crushed, but I still felt the rich, warm glow in my heart of knowing that I *could* trust God with my life.

That night, after spending an hour and a half coaxing Ray to come with me, he and I walked into the Wednesday night Bible study. Then, when Dan saw us, his hands went way up to the sky, and I could hear him shout loudly, "Hallelujah." The first thing on the agenda after we sang some songs and said some prayers, during all of which Ray sat while we all stood, Dan said that he was going to have a healing service and an altar call for those who wanted to make a real commitment to Jesus Christ, by asking Him openly to be their Lord and Savior.

As that moment approached, I could feel my body tense up, and I became frightened. The thought popped into my head: "Are you sure you know what you're doing? You've failed at everything before, what makes you think you're going to succeed at this?"

The Bible study room we were in was small and cozy, but I felt as though it was large and cold. I could hear Dan asking people to come forward to where he was standing by the blackboard. I sat glued to my seat, torn by the pull at the front of the room, and the hostility that was coming from Ray, as well as from this power, this evil power right over me, telling me that I was crazy, I was Jewish and that I would be making a fool of myself, plus that it wouldn't be long before I fell flat on my face again.

Dan looked at me, as though he knew the fierce struggle that was tearing me apart inside. I called out, "I want to, but I'm afraid. I'll never make it, Dan. I've failed at everything I've ever taken on. My whole life is a failure, and I'm so weak."

"Barbara, Jesus can, will and wants to take that spirit of fear away from you! He died for you. He loves you, the way no one ever has, and He knows your deepest need. He will give you life, not death, and He will give it to you abundantly. Jesus is your Messiah."

It took every ounce of effort for me to stand up, and take one step at a time, until I reached the front of the room. But what hurt and tore at me most of all was walking forward, away from Ray. I had never dreamed that I would be doing such a thing on my own.

Will Ray hate me for this, leave me? What is going to happen? Trembling, I murmured his name in the front of the room, quietly to Dan.

"Don't worry about Raymond. God has him in the palm of His hand, too. He's calling you now. Barbara, Christ died for you, do you know what that means? You don't have to take your life, to go on destroying yourself. He took on all your sin. You must repent, be willing to change and turn from darkness and the way you have been going, to light, to follow Him all the days of your life."

I felt woozy, as if I was going to pass out. "Oooh, that scares me. I can't do that."

"Do you want to?"

"Yes, but . . . ."

"By His grace you will."

"All right. I am willing to give my life to Jesus. I know what I am doing, but I still need much more understanding of who He is."

"It will be given to you."

Then, in the most sober of sober moments I had ever known, feeling calm but tingly, I asked Jesus Christ to take over my life completely, to teach me, guide and direct me. And then in a moment of great emotion, I cried and begged Him to keep me sober a day at a time and also to hold on tight to Ray and save our marriage. Dan laid both his hands on the top of my head and prayed for me.

And again with the greatest feeling of calmness I'd ever known, I turned smiling and wet-faced, to see Raymond sitting stiffly in his seat with his hands clenched, expressionless. My body felt light, clean and whole, and my mind free. That other power was gone, completely gone.

Going back and sitting down next to Ray, I took his hand and told him that I loved him so much and yearned for him to have walked up there with me, but that this was one thing I had to do alone. "It's funny, Ray, I feel good, like a young, innocent girl. Oh, how I hope this commitment works and lasts and is the answer I've been looking for all my life. I hope with all my heart that Jesus doesn't ever leave me alone, Ray."

34

During one of our many subsequent visits to the Evangelical Community Church, I asked Dan what it was like being a Christian, and most important, "What is going to be required of me?"

"To put it rather simply," he replied, smiling, "You no longer run the show. God will direct you, and you must follow Him. You already know a little about not drinking for one day at a time; well, that's how the Christian life should be lived as well — following Jesus each day. Right now, you're a baby Christian. You'll need to grow and mature. He will feed you, through His Word and through teaching, but when it comes to choosing, you will have free choice: His will or yours. And you've already seen where your will has gotten you, right?"

I nodded. "Yes, and I don't want to go back to that hell." I paused for a moment. "Does this mean I have to give up smoking marijuana? That's a natural element."

"Barbara, God's word says that your body is meant to be a holy temple for His purposes. Don't panic, but ask Jesus to help you give up the things that are not good for you, one at a time, and what you're not sure about, ask Him to show you the truth. He will."

I got up and paced, back and forth, stopping to look out the window at some children playing in the dirt. "Is it going to be boring to be a Christian, Dan?" I said at length. "I've been used to such a fast-paced, adventurous life .... How will I ever adapt to a quiet, spiritual, praying one, that might bore me to death?"

He shook his head and chuckled. "Barbara, Barbara, you're running way ahead of yourself and you're way off the track. You do need to slow down, at least enough to see all that you've been missing. But the Christian life is far from boring. You write to me from wherever you are, if it ever ceases to be an adventure."

I thanked him and got up to leave. But he held up his hand to keep me a moment longer. "Remember that now you have someone to look after you and really love you. All your life you've yearned for a father, haven't you?" Tears filled my eyes, as I nodded. "Well, now you have the perfect Father. God in His great love, mercy and wisdom, will keep you safe, in the palm of His hand. You will be protected."

I found great comfort in those words as I left; for once, I was not on the outside looking in, but on the inside, where it was warm and safe.

Most of my prayers were for Raymond now, as well as for each continued day of sobriety. Perhaps as a consequence, Ray and I began to get to know each other in many different ways. We found enjoyment in playing cards, shopping at outside supermarkets, reading aloud and talking about new discoveries I was making, which were new for me, but not for him. Alcohol had taken me away from so much that my lack of knowledge was overwhelming. There was so much to catch up on. About the only thing I knew was who was the current President.

Reading the Bible daily became a constant factor in my life. With enthusiasm, each day I looked for guidance and personal direction. When, for instance, I read that "it is a fine thing to abstain from eating meat or drinking wine, or doing anything which causes your brother's downfall," I was grateful beyond words that Ray had decided to stop drinking wine for a while, to make it easier for me. "You don't have to do that, Ray, just because I'm —"

"It doesn't mean that much to me, Princess. I can take it or leave it. So, if it helps you, why not leave it?"

I needed all the help I could get. Temptation to drink would strike when I least expected it, pulling the rug out from under me, and leaving me pleading for help and mercy at times when my mouth salivated at the thought of wine or whiskey. I could even smell aromas that weren't there. On my knees in the camper, I prayed in earnest, as though my life depended on the choice I made at that moment. And it did.

True concern for Ray's health and the fact that his tuberculosis lay just dormant, prompted me to urge him to stop smoking cigarettes. But unlike his ability to simply forego wine for my sake, I found that I could not simply give up cigarettes myself. And so I began to ask Jesus for the strength and desire. And one day it happened. As with drinking, I decided to stop smoking first for a half-hour, then an hour, then two, then one full day, and so on, until I had stopped for a whole week.

The greatest gift I received during that month was when I read in Ray's diary one morning: "It's incredible how we have become more communicative and how our desires for knowledge have increased. It's just strange." He was happy with me again! I just couldn't believe it, but the most thrilling of all was where he said, *"our* desires for knowledge."

With all of this, however, Ray did not feel that Jesus Christ was someone he needed in his own life at all. Obviously it was fine for me, but not him. Dan's religious fervor and structured life were not enough witness to Ray, even though he saw something beautiful inside the man and his family. So the Lord began to use another instrument to come against Ray's political and social arguments, and that was Robby, the organ-player.

A heathen like Ray, Robby was an ex-drunk and ex-owner of a brothel in Scotland, who had one day wandered into the church here, in search of a part-time job as an organ player. That was the beginning of Robby's conversion, and his enthusiasm and zeal now bubbled over for his new and changed life. Ray didn't feel inhibited in expressing himself with Robby, because occasionally Robby's old use of improper language emerged, letting Ray see the earthiness that still existed, making him all the more real.

Night after night in Robby's trailer, over tea and cakes, they talked, argued and fought about Jesus, until the wee hours of the morning, with Ray playing devil's advocate, yet always coming out on the short end after each session, always angrier, followed by tossing, sleepless nights. Sometimes he would jump up in the middle of the night in a cold sweat, questioning: "Is it true, or isn't it?" And in the morning he would be exhausted and weary.

"Raymond, I believe that Jesus is trying desperately to reach you. I think He wants to bring you to Himself before we go back to the States, even before we leave here. He knows how weak I am. It would be such a shame for me to walk alone."

And alone with Dan in the quiet of the church, I would cry and confess my fears and doubts about Ray ever coming to the Lord. But Dan never doubted, and eventually it became catching — so catching, in fact, that after reading about water baptism, I decided that whatever it was, I wanted it. "Dan, I want everything I read about in the Bible. I need it all. I want to leave the old me here and become baptized into new life with Jesus. Oh how I wish Ray would do it with me!"

But Dan did not respond the way I expected. "Barbara, you have got to let go of Raymond and leave him to God. I believe that Jesus will come into his life, but you are now demanding a timetable and trying to create situations so that it will come about. I agree that you should be baptized, but it involves you and Jesus alone, no one else."

Dropping my head, I despairingly said: "Okay, I'll give him up — again."

Dan smiled and added, "Keep on praying for him; that never hurts." All that day and all week I prayed up a storm for Ray, and he churned and churned, becoming furiously hateful with me, the church, Torremolinos, everything. After one harrowing argument with Robby, when I thought Ray would punch him for saying that Jesus was the only way so emphatically, I read in his diary: "This whole thing seems as though it's being directed. Miserable sleep — it's stuffy in camper, and the bags are too warm. I dreamt disturbingly again and was up half the night. This spiritual thing is tearing me up and becoming haunting. *I can't explain it to myself* — my rationality is not as sturdy — although it's easier when I'm awake. I'm in a quandary and am really going through hell. Ah well, we'll go into Torremolinos later and stay there for a couple of days. I dread it; that place is sickening. We were at Robby's trailer last night until 4 a.m., discussing the Bible; this is absurd!"

The happier and more exuberant Robby was, the angrier Ray became. He grew silent and sullen, counting the days until we were to travel on to Portugal. After a Bible study one Wednesday evening, we picked up Ray who was sitting outside alone in the dark in the camper, and insisted he join us at the English Tea House, a common hangout. Ray had nothing else to do, so he came along. He looked for any opportunity now to pick an argument with someone, anyone, about anything. Dan turned from conversing amiably with a parishioner and glared at Ray. It was the first time I had ever seen him angry.

"You are an angry person, Raymond. I believe it's your father whom you're angry at. And I remind you of him, don't I?" Raymond was stunned. And the moment Dan said it, I sensed that it was true, and that Ray knew it. But Dan didn't stop there.

"Not only do I want to see you become converted, Ray, but I want to see the two of you grow and become true Christians."

How could he say all that? He's going to ruin everything, I thought. Throughout that night, I was awakened by Raymond's groanings, and the next morning I began to feel sorry for him. Perhaps this is wrong; perhaps I'm too holier-than-thou. Heavens, I don't want to become a saint!

I wasn't aware of what was happening, but the moment I began to feel sorry for Ray, I let a whole stream of doubts in. I even became homesick, and when I focused in on that, I couldn't imagine what Mother and my family and friends would think about my becoming a Christian.

Convinced that I had suddenly become a realist, I found myself irritated with almost everything, and looking forward to nothing that day. Our trip and shopping excursion into Malaga was ruined by my annoyance and irritability. I found fault with everything and felt tired and empty. By the end of the day, I was in a state of anxiety and emptiness, not knowing how I got there.

It was obvious to Ray that something different had happened to me, and for the first time since my conversion, I saw him deeply concerned. He had every reason to be concerned, because I was unable to get out of where I was, and the only natural thing I knew to do when I was like this, ever, was to drink.

As we drove along looking for a place to have dinner, Ray attempted to converse; he even tried talking about God, but I turned to him and said, "Shut up. I'm through. I've made a dreadful mistake about this whole Jesus thing. I'm giving it up. You're right, and I'm wrong, as usual. God is dead."

"Barbara, what's with you? You can't throw away a whole month of sobriety. How do you know I'm right? I'm not even sure I am. Please — I'm afraid you'll drink if you stay like this."

Not only was I taken aback by the fact that Ray was questioning his own stand, but the truth of what he said about my drinking was all too visible, and it did seem to go hand in hand with my sudden desire to drink. I had gotten off the track somewhere, but couldn't recall when or where. I prayed for help, and then I saw clearly that it had happened that morning, when I had chosen to feel sorry for Ray instead of continuing to pray for him and to stand in Christ myself. I had stopped praying the moment I took on Ray's doubts and feelings. Suddenly, it didn't matter whether Christ was truth or not; what mattered was that with Him and leaning on Him, I was a different person, and I didn't drink. I had thrown Him out the window and tried to reason this whole thing through again, and look where it had gotten me. I was a mess.

"Oh Jesus, I'm sorry for throwing You out like this. Please come back. Help me, help me. What shall I do?" I cried out loud and then sobbed quietly to myself.

Raymond drove on, not knowing what was going on, but seemingly relieved that I was calling on Jesus again.

"I know what I've got to do, Ray. I'm in a bad way now. I let myself get there, and I need help from someone. I don't think I can handle dinner with wine on the table or drinking around me in a restaurant. Do you think we could get something and eat in the camper? Anne Murray gave me a telephone number of someone to call in Malaga if I needed help. I think I'd like to call that person. Jesus has given me practical help through Anne and so many others, Ray, even you. You helped me to see the light by what you just said to me. You know, God is showing you the truth, Raymond; He's bringing you closer to himself each day."

Raymond looked at me; his mind seemed burdened and confused. A desire to once again feel sorry for him and to fear the outcome of what would happen if he didn't give his life to Christ came over me, and I said, "Oh Jesus, please take Ray from me. I give him and his life to You right now. I don't even know how to pray for him any more. I want to be baptized, but I'm torn because I'm putting Ray before You. Help me right now!"

35

It was 6:30 P.M. Wednesday evening, February 17, 1971. Ray and I were getting ready to take the twenty-mile coastal ride we came to love so much from the campsite to the church. This was the night I was going to be baptized. Filled with excitement, and with anxiety periodically crashing through my thoughts, I would say to myself: "What on earth are you getting into now?"

I was still praying for Ray, moment by moment. He looked at me cautiously as we climbed into our seats in the front of the camper. Turning on the ignition, he said: "Here you go again, Princess, jumping into things; only this time you're going to jump into a fountain. I hope Preacher Man knows that you can't even float, let alone swim."

"Ray, please, he told me not to worry about that; he isn't going to let go of me. But that fountain sure looked deep, and it's awfully cold outside tonight. I am scared, I might as well admit it." I paused and looked at him. "Raymond, how I wish you would come with me. It would be so wonderful if you and I walked up the aisle together as baptized Christians, starting a new life together."

"Forget the movie script. I went up that aisle once, when we were married; that was enough."

My feelings were hurt. And the more I gave in to them and concentrated on wanting Ray to get baptized, the more I lost touch with Jesus and what He wanted to do for me. Tears and unbelief followed.

By the time we reached the church, I was a mess. Cars were everywhere. "What are all those people doing? Don't tell me half the church is here for my baptism? Oh my God, now I really am scared! What if I'm making a terrible mistake? How do I even know if I'm in my right mind, Ray?"

"You don't, but you're here and they're here, and you're going through with it. This isn't some kind of game, you dobo!"

His calling me that reminded me of a time during our travels, when I was miserably hung over, and Ray was utterly disgusted with me. We were on the road, and he noticed a big truck heading toward us. It said "Dobo" in big letters. "That's what you are, Barbara, nothing but a dobo, whatever that is."

Feeling like some kind of a monkey or baboon, I noticed that there was another truck directly behind the first, and it also had big letters on it, spelling "Dobo". "Look, Ray, there's another truck behind this one. That's you. There are *two* Dobo trucks — you'll be right behind me!"

"Yeah, sure, over my dead body!"

As soon as we entered the church, I looked for Dan, thinking that maybe I ought to reconsider what I was about to do, but he was nowhere in sight. Robby immediately took Ray away from me, ushering him to a seat up front. One of the women parishioners escorted me into an empty room, where she held out a lovely white robe. "Barbara, this is what you are to wear over your bathing suit."

I stood there looking at the white robe, so lovely, clean and pure-looking. "I'm going to wear that? I doesn't seem right for me to —"

"It is right, and it is for you. You're going to be cleansed white as snow. You are going to start all over with Jesus, this time. Your life is going to be different, a changed life."

Doing as I was told, and feeling suddenly light and feathery, I put on the white robe and then brushed my hair back over my shoulders. I felt almost as though I was getting married again. I tried to remember my wedding day, but could not even recall putting on my wedding gown. I had missed so much because of drinking, so much.

But now my mind was fresh and free to see and know exactly what I was doing, and for the first time I became instantly excited about the reality around me, grateful that I was sober and there in that church about to be baptized. And Raymond was still with me. God had not let him leave me. He must be holding him in the palm of His hand, like Dan said. Kneeling down alone before I left the room, I prayed with all my heart and soul for Raymond's salvation and for my mind to stay on Jesus, and not to doubt, or turn back or away, but always to remain on Him with renewed and deeper understanding, to hold me and keep me from straying. "I am so weak, Lord. You are so strong; lead me not into temptation, but deliver me from evil."

Walking down the side aisle, eager to take my seat next to Ray who was right in the second row, I saw everyone in the church waiting with eager expectation. My eyes filled up with tears when I saw Colonel Taylor there in the first row, and I remembered the day he had seen us on the beach and come up to us, telling us about this church and Dan. I shook my head. God must have had it all planned . . . so amazing, so beyond my understanding. We had planned to separate, I was going to take my life, and now I'm about to die to that life and be given new life, all because of Jesus Christ. To think that He really was born a Jew . . . and for me to have tested His power as the Messiah and know for myself that it is true. He is the One, the only One . . . . Why, it's all too much!

With these thoughts in my mind and the assurance of God Himself with me, I walked slowly up to the front where Dan was beckoning me. I fixed my eyes on the cross straight ahead of me. It was the cross I had seen back in Toledo when I was on my hands and knees outside that hotel bar. I remembered how dark I felt inside and hopeless. That cross, illumined in the sky, was a vision for me, a hope. Not even knowing what it was, I had pleaded for mercy before it, and crossed my chest with my right hand. And God has shown me that mercy, His incredible, miraculous mercy. Here I am before this cross, lights all around me. I don't have to squint. I don't have to cower. I haven't done anything today or yesterday that I'm ashamed of, at least not comparable to what I've done in the past. The ten-milligram Librium I took each day bothered me a little, but I rationalized that soon I would be emotionally strong enough not to need it any longer. I'm alive, bathed and clean....

My heart pounded with joy about who Jesus was, a joy that began to reach unmeasurable heights, as I climbed the few steps of the pulpit, taking Dan's hand, who was smiling broadly. Turning to face the large congregation, all of whom had been praying and rooting for me, for us, I spotted Anne Murray sitting in one of the back pews. I knew Anne had never been to this church, other than in the little room where we met Tuesday nights to help one another with alcoholism. I grinned; I had been secretly praying for Anne, too.

There was still much doubt in her mind, she had confided to me one day. She often told me that a spiritual awakening happens differently with different people, and that we are not all the same. With her, it had been a gradual coming to believe, where I was, for the most part, swept off my feet, as though God had to work quickly with me.

Dan whispered to me, as we stood side by side. "Before I baptize you, why don't you say a few words?"

"What? No, I'm petrified in front of these people." Knowing that I could never do such a thing without a drink, my head dropped.

Dan acted as though my answer meant nothing to him. "Barbara, Jesus will help you speak and say just the right thing. He's with you now, lean on Him, and you can do it."

Standing there numb for what seemed an eternity, I looked all around. My eyes wandered through the sanctuary, until I spotted Raymond. He looked different — the hard, cold expression that he had come in with was gone. And oh — could those be tears in his eyes? Love filled my heart, gratitude overflowed, and I found myself crying and groping for words. "I am here, because of God. I am here, because of Jesus Christ and because of the people He used to help me find Him and stay alive." I looked with blurred eyes at Dan and Rhoda, and then Robby, seated at the organ. "I don't know why God has chosen to save me and I don't understand it all. There are so many, so many who —" Tears choked my words. Clearing my throat, I added: "He found me, an alcoholic who wanted to die, and a Jew who had never known God. I am sober today, and I have found my Messiah." My voice sheepishly trailed off but Dan came booming in with shouts of "Praise the Lord!" and "Hallelujah!"

I was happy, too, but still so awe-struck at my being there, at being alive. I almost wondered if maybe I had, in fact, died, and this was all taking place in heaven. But before my imagination could take off on that one, I found myself walking before Dan, down some steps into a large, ominous-looking tank of water. "Oooh Dan, it's cold!" I whispered. "Don't forget. I can't swim."

Dan just chuckled a little, and within moments I felt his hands resting securely on top of my head. My body became stiff. I heard Dan praying for me, but I don't remember what he said. I was leaned backwards into the water, which I had always feared, from the time I had first got my head wet at age three or four, never again putting my head under, and watching all my friends learn how to swim. Dan prayed for my fear to leave, to be *rooted* out of me. And now the water felt warm, and with my head emerged and my eyes shut tight, I asked Jesus to help me and to continue helping me every day of my life, never ever to leave me alone with myself again.

When I came up for air and opened my eyes, Dan's arms were outstretched, raised high up to heaven. He was beaming, and so was I. No longer stiff, my body felt light, almost like a balloon, and I just bubbled joy all over, smiling and laughing and crying. Then, seeing Ray's face completely wet with tears, I whispered to myself: "Jesus, I'm leaving that old life here, right here. You died so that I might live. I just died so that you might live, in me. Have mercy upon me."

Running up the aisle and into the robing room, I hurriedly threw off my wet robe and got dressed. But when I returned to the sanctuary, looking to rejoin Ray, he was gone. I looked up at Robby, who was playing the organ, trying to question him by frowning at Ray's empty seat. Robby shrugged in bewilderment and nodded for me to sit down. Reluctantly I sat down, while the service continued, and Rhoda sang a song, a beautiful song about accepting Jesus once, and then letting Him rule forever, moment by moment.

When the service was over, people came from all directions to kiss me and hug me, many with tears still in their eyes. "But where's Raymond?" I asked everyone, until I saw Anne Murray in the distance. Hurrying over to her, I gave her a big hug and kiss and then asked her if she had seen Ray.

"Yes," she replied, "I was outside having a cigarette, when he came to have one too. I saw tears in his eyes. He came to me and sobbed and said that he needed help, too. You looked so different up there to him, so clean and beautiful, almost new. I told him that everyone had to throw in their own towel. We had a cigarette together, and he walked back into the church. I don't know where he is now, but Barbara, I am truly happy for you. I'm here if you ever need to talk. And don't stop praying for your sobriety, honey; remember, it's a daily thing. I've seen too many forget where they came from or get complacent about their sobriety, and that's dangerous. It's a gift to be cherished."

Anne's words were sobering and strong, putting my two feet back on the ground. "Anne, I don't know how to thank you for the way God has used you to help me, and I hope I don't ever take this gift for granted."

After I watched Anne walk out into the night, her white hair disappearing out of sight, I went back into the church, in search of Ray. One of the ushers took my arm. "Barbara, if you're wondering where Ray is, he's inside Dan's office. They're in there alone together."

"Yippee!" I shouted. "Robby, everyone, let's really pray right now for Ray." Pointing to Dan's office, I cried with glee: "He and Dan are in there alone with the Holy Spirit, and you know what that could mean, don't you?"

We prayed and prayed and prayed, until out of the corner of my eye, I saw the door open. Out came Ray, smiling. We looked at each other, and I knew that he had accepted Jesus. I just knew it, and I jumped up and down for a few moments and then we ran towards each other, throwing our arms around one another, new tears falling where old ones had dried.

These tears were different, so different. They were tears of joy, not sorrow, of new life, not death. "Raymond, Raymond, tell me how you feel, what happened in there? I can't wait until later, when we're alone, to hear all about it."

He grinned. "I accepted Jesus Christ as my Lord and Savior, Barbara, on my hands and knees. I wouldn't have gotten down on my knees, but Dan felt it would be good for me to do that before God. I feel exhausted and relieved. I've been through one hell of a struggle. But now I feel as though it has been done — and yet, just begun!"

36

Looking out the small windows of our camper, with the door swung wide open and the fresh air and morning sun lifting our spirits, we ate breakfast and chatted, something which we had never done together before. Raymond was glad that he had made the commitment to Jesus, but there were still many questions and doubts in his mind. He kept telling me that he felt and saw no sudden miraculous change in his life, certainly not like what he'd seen in mine.

"Well, Ray, maybe God is going to work differently with you. Don't forget, I had one foot in the grave, when it happened to me, and something drastic had to happen. Keep on believing; the emotional assurance will come eventually."

I encouraged Ray as much as I could. About the only thing I could ever really do, I believed, was to encourage someone towards the hope that I had found, Jesus Christ. And whenever I was doing that, it took my mind off myself, off my own body which still craved alcohol from time to time, even though the periods of temptation were now much further apart. But when they did come, they came on strong, and it still took a lot of prayer to stand against them.

This particular morning, however, I was still going over a dream I'd had during the night. It was so clear, even colorful, like slides being shown in my mind. Never able to keep anything to myself, I had to tell it to Ray, not only because it concerned him, but because it was still in my mind, making it difficult for me to concentrate on anything else. "Ray, now don't laugh at me and please listen. I've got to tell you about this dream I had last night. I know it'll sound crazy, but it was so real! And this morning I have the feeling that what I dreamt is going to happen one day."

Ray was still focused in on his bowl of cereal and his Danish, and didn't appear to have heard a word I said. "Ray, are you listening?" No answer. "Raymond Valentino Tamasi, are you *listening?*"

I knew that would get his attention; he didn't like his middle name bandied around the campsite or anywhere else for that matter. "Yeah, I hear you."

"Okay, then the least you could do is answer me. You could treat me with a little more respect; I'm not drunk, you know!" It bothered me terribly when Ray still treated me the way he had when I had been drinking.

Now that I had his undivided attention, I told him my dream. I saw myself in a house. It wasn't any ordinary house; it had three floors, and I was on the lowest floor which I'm pretty sure was below ground level. There were cubby holes and beds, rows and rows of beds. I was walking up and down the aisles, talking to some of the men who lay on these cots. Their arms were stretched out to me, as I walked by. Sometimes I had to hold back tears, because I felt so deeply for them. I was there to encourage them, to tell them how Jesus lifted me up out of my bed of anguish, so that I could walk amongst them and now tell them about Him."

I looked at Ray. "And you were there, too. You were busy up and down stairs; as a matter of fact, you were running the whole place. What I mean was, I had the distinct feeling that you were in charge and that was your job, your new field of work."

Before I could go on, Ray furiously interrupted me. "I don't want to hear any more! That's crazy! I would never, never do anything like that, especially as a vocation. I was a marketing man, an economics major; besides, I could never stand to be around alcoholics like that, let alone work with them."

"Okay, okay, it was just a dream. Why are you getting so angry?"

He put his head in his hands. "I don't know. It's you. You've always come up with new things, whether they're dreams or — oh, never mind. I guess I'm uptight about what I will be doing once we get back to the States. I'm kind of afraid to get back into the New York rat race. You know what I'd like to do? Have a little bookstore somewhere and write and be left alone."

"Yes, that sounds like you. Frankly, I'd hate that. I'd be scared to death to be doing anything alone. I think I'm going to need to have someone with me all my life. It even frightens me to think that you will have to go to work some day, and I'll be left alone. I'll never make it."

He chuckled. " Okay, then *you* work with the alcoholics and leave me out of your dreams."

"Fair enough, you go off somewhere, lock yourself up, and write your books." And with that, we both burst out laughing and proceeded to gather up the breakfast dishes.

Several more weeks passed, in which we continued with our very simple daily schedule of rest, shopping, long walks, church, Bible study on Wednesday nights, and meetings with Dan and Rhoda and Robby, who were giving us endless time and teaching. The most beautiful thing we had between us, though, was reading the Bible together. Starting from the beginning of Matthew, each morning and evening we would read as far as we wanted to, taking turns and taking in all we could, grabbing at each promise and hope. It was something we did together, and we intended to finish the whole New Testament by the time we left Europe. Raymond began keeping his diary more carefully, and I began mine again. Letter-writing became a daily duty that I knew I should do. I wrote letters to Mother about what had happened to me and Ray, even my baptism, all the while holding my breath, wondering what her reaction would be.

The only other person with whom I went into some detail was Clarence from Princeton. "Clarence, I want to apologize to you for the pain and ungratefulness I showed you. You were right and I was wrong, and I had to learn the hard way. You said that I was an alcoholic, my disease was progressive and I could not drink. But Clarence, I must tell you that I found Jesus here, when I was at the end of my rope. He pulled me up out of the pit and saved me, when I no longer could even choose not to drink. Clarence, I reached a horrible bottom, became a groveling animal in search of booze, but thank God, I'm free today! Ray and I don't know how to thank you for all the time and love you've given us and for your prayers. We can't wait to see you again. There have been times here when everything in me wants to drink, and I feel as though I'm hanging on by a thread, but somehow I pray and get the strength to hang on. Give my love to everyone, to Ed, Emily, Gurty, Jim and Sandy. I love you all and am praying for you too, remembering every bit of truth you spoke to me, especially in the times I needed it so desperately. Oh Clarence, I never would have believed it! I've now been sober almost two months."

As time went on, my faith grew, and I believed more and more in the power of prayer and that Jesus really was the Son of God. Often I'd count and recount the miracles He had performed in my life, starting with my sobriety. I still couldn't get over the praying mantis and how that small insect had hung on to our windshield. Then there was the fact that Raymond and I were still together, which was a surprise gift I thought I'd never forget, but even in that, there was more: Ray had become a Christian, our lives were taking on new meaning together, and the old life had been wiped away forever.

Often, as I walked around the campsite or gazed out our camper window, my spirit soared, as these miraculous events passed through my mind. Feeling so high, so way up there above the clouds, I found my arm taken by Ray one morning who said, "Let's take a long walk into town, Princess." Hand in hand, we strolled through the quaint streets and open markets in Fuengirola. Breathing in the fresh spring air, feeling the warm sunshine on my face, glorying in the fact that I was free — normal — I climbed right up to the sky within moments.

A man walked by me, stopped, turned and recognized my face but was not able to place me. I, too, looked hard at him. For a few moments while I was trying to place him, pictures of my past floated through my mind. Various bars that I drank at, parties, and then the oil company where I had worked. That was it. "I know you. We used to work for the same oil company?" When I heard his confirming reply in a deep British voice, I knew who it was for sure. "*Dick Budd!* For heaven's sake, what are you doing here?"

"Barbara Scheutz, right?"

"Yes, but now it's Barbara Tamasi, and this is my husband Raymond. We've been here camping for several months."

"Marvelous, my wife and I have a house here up in Mijas. We'll just have to get together for dinner."

"Yes, yes, we will." My soaring spirits crashed. I panicked. "No, I, uh, think maybe lunch would be better." At least lunch would be safer, I thought. Dick was part of that fast-living upper crust that I had so desired to become a part of. To him, a meal without wine would be like a hot corned beef sandwich on rye without a kosher pickle.

Dick wouldn't let us leave until we made a definite date. It was going to be this Saturday at noon for drinks and lunch at his villa. "Gee, that'll be a nice change of pace for us," Ray commented, as we walked away from him. "Hey," he said, looking at me, "you don't seem at all pleased about it."

"Raymond, what am I going to do? He drinks!"

"So what? So does everyone here. But you've been to restaurants, and wine has been on the table, and it hasn't bothered you."

"This is different. I don't know why, but it is . . . ." For the next three days, I imagined, projected and recollected parts of my life that I thought were dead, only to discover that the temptation to enter into them was still very much alive.

Not knowing how to handle this, let alone understand it, I worried myself into a frenzy by the time Saturday came. When we arrived at this magnificent mountain villa overlooking Mijas, my mouth watered for an extra dry martini, of the sort I recollected drinking in years past. We barely said hello, then Dick introduced us to his wife, and a rolling bar was steered into full view, with every mouth-watering, high quality alcoholic beverage available in the whole wide world. "Barbara, my dear girl, I know exactly what you'll have, an extra dry —"

"No, no, Dick. I'll, uh, have a coke."

"What? Just a coke? What about a rum and coke?"

"No, just coke, please." I spoke in hushed whispers, my voice shaking.

"Oh, Dickie darling, we don't have any coke."

"Oh, sorry, dear. I know what: how about some sherry, if you don't want anything too strong before lunch? Say, that's a good idea; think I'll have some myself. We've got a big bottle of champagne coming later."

Unable to talk now, I shook my head, no. Ray, seeing my distressed state, asked for ginger ale for me, or even club soda.

"Gee, I'm awfully sorry, Raymond," Dick's wife replied, "but we don't have any soft drinks at all, except for plain quinine water. All of our friends drink!"

I hated straight quinine water, and Ray knew that. My eyes filled with tears, as though I was going through a very great disappointment and humiliation. Self-pity took over, and I fled to the bathroom, where I bent down on the floor and cried, leaning my elbows on the bathtub. "Jesus, help me, please," I sobbed. "I want to drink more than anything. I'll never make it out there. I can see now, I'll never make it, period. Oh God, it's a mistake, I'll never change. I'll never be free from this bondage."

When I was all cried out, I returned to the living room, trying with all my might to smile and be sociable, yet wishing the time would fly, or I would get sick or something, anything to get out of this place. This was the first time we had been faced with a real social situation that was threatening. Raymond sat with a glass of quinine water beside him. Why, he could have had a drink, I thought.

Feeling disabled, crippled, I saw myself now as a noose around his neck. He just did that for me. He doesn't want that stinking old glass of quinine water. Obsessed with everyone's glass and what was in it, I found myself eyeing the cart with all the bottles, which was now out of full view. Automatically I began figuring out how I could get out of the living room or dining room, which was parallel, and grab a bottle, taking it into the bathroom and then returning it, while everyone was chatting. My old devious mind was at work, just as though it was yesterday that I used to plot and plan ways to get a bottle.

All this time, I thought, and yet I feel as if it were yesterday. "Jesus, oh Jesus, what does this mean? This shouldn't be. I'm a Christian now; why am I having this trouble? God, oh God, help me now or I'll have to drink."

Finally, finally, lunch was called. As wine was about to be poured into my glass, I put my hand over the top of it. Actually, it was as if my hand was put over the top of the glass for me.

"What, no wine?"

"No, nothing, nothing."

"I have just the drink for you, Barbara. Some tomato juice with Sherry Peppers."

"Okay, okay, give me that."

"Wait a minute," Ray interjected. "Does Sherry Peppers have sherry in it?"

"Well, yes, but just a little...."

I felt foolish, conspicuous, and so strange. Not even realizing or thinking about what I was going to say next, the words came tumbling out of my mouth. "Dick, I can't drink anything with any alcohol in it whatsoever."

"Oh, you're on the wagon, I see. Well, that's admirable. We should all do that now and then for a while."

"Dick, this is not just for a while. I'm an alcoholic. I can't drink." I am a leper, I am a leper. That was how I felt, as I watched Dick gulp hard and look from me to his wife to Ray and back to me again. And as though someone else was speaking through and for me, I broke the uncomfortable silence and proceeded to tell Dick and his wife a little bit about what alcohol had done to me, leaving out the gory parts, and then to my amazement, how I had found Jesus Christ. In the past, when I finally had the courage to speak whatever it was I thought to be the truth, I never had a leg to stand on, because I was drunk. But now, here I was doing something I had wanted to do all my life: have the guts to say how I felt about something important to me, without the aid of booze.

When I completely finished speaking, Dick got out of his chair and came over to me. His wife had tears in her eyes and both of them thanked me for sharing with them. "We're sorry we made it difficult for you, Barbara. It must be very hard for you to have to sit here and relive some of your —"

I hastened to put them at ease. "You know, it's funny; I can hardly believe I said what I did!"

Even Ray looked bewildered, and wondered how I had gotten the courage to say what I did. Later, after lunch, as we all sat in the living room with coffee and dessert, Dick and his wife began sharing some of the deeper, more personal experiences of their own lives and their feelings about God. Dick even asked me for the address of Dan's church. And on my way to the bathroom before we left, as I passed the cart with all the delectable bottles of liquor on it, I felt safe, as though a fence, the most beautiful fence I ever saw, decorated with small flowers filling in every opening, surrounded and protected me. Jesus really loves me! I couldn't believe how this whole lunch was taken care of and what had come out of my mouth.

But even though I got out of that house miraculously without a drink, I knew I had had a close call. When I suggested we see Anne that evening, Raymond was more than agreeable.

"I was frightened there for a few moments myself. I saw how much your being sober means to me, to our marriage and life together. I want to help you if I can. I want us to make it, Princess."

When I got to Anne's house I was higher than a kite, jubilant about my victory and the fact that I had witnessed as a Christian for the first time. Anne infuriated me, however; she didn't seem to share my joy at all. "Simmer down, girl. Get on an even keel. You just saw that not only is it one day at a time, but one minute at a time, when you least expect it. Besides you did nothing, not a damn thing; it was that God of yours, kid, just remember that."

When she left the room to make some coffee, I whispered to Ray: "She doesn't understand; she's not a Christian. We should have gone to Dan's house instead."

"Barbara, I think Anne understands more than you think. She's good for you, and doesn't let you get away with a thing. Besides, how do you know that she isn't a Christian? And even if she isn't, God may still want to use her in your life."

"Well, she sure doesn't let me forget where I was." But Ray was right, and so was Anne. I would take the credit to myself, rather than give it all to God, where it belonged.

Time began to move more rapidly for us, and with its passing came the fear of leaving Fuengirola and Torremolinos. Raymond began to wonder if maybe God intended us to stay there. Dan offered us a job. He had a vision about the church becoming a center, with a small community encircling it, and a coffee house. He saw people, especially those afflicted as I was, coming to this melting pot and vacation haven, searching for something more. He wanted us to be there to help him and to share what we had found. Torn, and in constant prayer about what God's will *was* for us, we didn't get any definite answer to stay or leave.

I was absolutely petrified about leaving. Fears of falling back, of not finding another church or minister in the States equal to what I had found here, haunted me. Even Anne and her friends, with their constant, stable support and practical help, I was sure would be unequaled. But then, when I thought that way, Clarence came to mind. I did miss him and others. But how could I go on without Dan?

I missed my mother terribly and couldn't bear the thought of not seeing her soon. She needed me, and now, I thought, maybe I had something to give her. It was the thoughts of Mother and worry about her that made me finally come to the decision to return to the States. Ray was still torn, inclining towards staying put.

Dan, in his wisdom, never pushed us one way or the other, believing always that Jesus would guide us and that he was just one of many instruments. "Barbara, remember it was that horrible, crippling spirit of fear I prayed for you to be released from. Don't give it ground again! God will lead you to a Christian church and leader. You will know by the Spirit if the teaching is true or not. We will always keep in touch. I believe one day you will come back here, even if just for a visit — a long one," he added, when he saw the tears streaming down my face, as we sat in his office for the last time. The next day was Sunday, the day of our last service in the little church which had come to mean so much to me. It meant my death and life. It meant Jesus.

Sitting in the front, listening to Rhoda sing one of my favorite hymns, "Jesus, I have promised to serve You to the end," we both wept. As Rhoda sang, I wanted to shake my head and say, "No, no, I can't do that. I can't serve Him or anyone to the end. I'm too weak, unstable . . . but Jesus, I feel so torn now, I hurt inside so much. I can't say goodbye. I can't take the pain of saying goodbye. I can't take it."

And as I began now to sob out loud, my shoulders shaking, people turned towards us, those who had come to love us and we them, and their eyes filled with tears, too.

37

Our first stop was Rota Air Force Base. We were given the names of some recovered alcoholics whom Anne knew. Anne Murray's parting words to me were, "Now don't wait until you think you need help. Remember: no matter how spiritual you think you are, you still can't think. Call as soon as you hit the base." And I did just that. I was celebrating sixty days of sobriety tomorrow, two whole months, and I made sure I was going to be in safe hands. It was February 23rd, and so hard to believe how much our lives had changed in two months. In some ways the time had seemed to fly by, and in others it had dragged and dragged. When I wanted to drink, getting through five minutes was like an hour.

We were exhausted from driving when we met Jim and his wife, but came alive quickly when we discovered that not only was he an alcoholic who had been sober five years, but that they had both found Jesus in Spain, as we had. Jim, as we learned over a quiet dinner at their home, had been "dry" for three years, but he sensed something was missing, something important, and he didn't know what. And when he found Jesus, he really found sobriety. "My cup runneth over. We are both truly filled now."

What a miracle that these two people, who invited us to stay in their home, believed in Jesus the same way we did. In bed that night, we couldn't get over the way God was leading us. This was such an encouraging sign that He *would* take care of us in each country that we were in, giving us more help, more of everything than we could imagine.

Quietly basking in the glory of God, I noticed an area of light on the door. Turning my head to see where this light was coming from, I looked carefully at each window, but the shades were fully drawn, and the room was in total darkness. Before I could say "Raymond," the light began to change shape and move around, looking like a white, bright, bouncy amoeba. My heart was pounding, and I could barely whisper "Ray, look quickly at the door."

"What? I don't see anything."

"Keep looking; you've got to see it. It's light. There is a light on the door."

"Barbara, we're in complete darkness in this room."

"I know, but I see a bright light shape, bouncing or dancing or vibrating. Am I going crazy?"

Becoming somewhat frightened now, wondering if perhaps my mind was finally gonzo, I was relieved when Ray exclaimed, "I see it! I see it! I see the light! Hallelujah, praise the Lord! It's a miracle!" Ray began praying and praising for all he was worth. I froze, and couldn't say a word. In awe, I stared and stared at this light and watched its shape keep changing, slowly and beautifully, always moving in the same pattern and repeating the same shapes. I wasn't in fear, but I wasn't deliriously happy like Raymond. I was stunned. What was this?

"Ray, what is this light? Is it the Holy Spirit?"

"I don't know. Light has come into darkness. Jesus has come into us. Let's not question it; just accept it and praise the Lord...." And he was off again. He finally fell asleep, murmuring thanks to his creator. I closed my eyes and opened them again every two minutes to see if the light was still there, and finally fell asleep also.

The next morning, we knew that it was Jesus, and that it was one tremendous miracle that would probably never happen again in our lifetime. It was a sign of His supreme power — supernatural, inexplicable and divine. "Ray, maybe it was also a sign that we were to be lights to those in darkness. Remember my dream about you working with alcoholics? The big, three-story house —"

"Barbara," Ray interrupted me, "you're getting carried away again. I told you I will never work with alcoholics, *never!*"

That experience stayed with us all the way to Portugal. But it wasn't enough to combat the terror we experienced when we were stopped by the Spanish Guardia Civil forty kilometres from the border because Ray was speeding. They didn't say a word as they carefully scrutinized us and our van. We prayed and prayed, as we sat stiffly in our seats, waiting, just waiting, for them to go in the back of the camper and find our hash pipes that were not at all cleaned out, and a rather large chunk of hash. Why on earth hadn't we thrown it all away?

We were asked to follow them to the police station. "This is it," I moaned. "Someone must have told the Spanish police that we had hashish and now they are going to arrest us before we cross the border. We'll be locked up and we'll never get out, like all the other American hippies caught here with pot and hash. Oh God, oh God, I'd rather die than be locked up."

"Barbara, will you shut up?" hissed Ray. "This is no time for hysterics." He thought aloud, as we drove.

"Let's just follow them as we were told, and trust Jesus," I said, and gave in to the emotions I was feeling, sobbing over and over, "I want to see my mother again!"

A little while later, we pulled up in front of the police station, where we were told to park the van and wait. An eternity later, one of the policemen came out, stern as ever, walked up to the camper and handed Ray a piece of paper.

Ray looked at it. "Sir," he said, "this says eight hundred pesetas, right? All I have to do is pay this?"

"This is your traffic ticket, sir, for speeding. You owe Spain eight hundred pesetas, and cannot leave here unless you pay it."

"Great, great," Ray said with relief. "I'll pay this eleven dollars right now, and then we can go over the border?"

"Yes, sir."

Ray took out his wallet and paid the ticket and we drove off praising the Lord, and very much relieved. "That was a close call, Raymond. Do you think Jesus was trying to tell us something, even though He saved us in the nick of time?"

"Like what?"

"Like we shouldn't carry hash anymore. Maybe we're supposed to stop smoking pot like Dan said."

But Ray didn't want to. "Pot is grass, and that's a natural element. It was here when Jesus was. He hasn't ruled that out. It doesn't do to you what booze does. Alcohol's lethal and a killer. This stuff is a natural high, man and besides, I'm taking those pipes back to the States."

"What, are you crazy?"

"Clean, dobo, they'll be clean as a whistle."

"All right, but I'm going to ask Jesus to show me the truth about it, whether He blesses our pot-smoking or not."

"You don't have to ask Him if He blesses it; just ask Him to show you if it's a horrible evil!"

As we continued on our journey, we made a stop in Portugal's beautiful village of Nazare, where we bought a fish to eat. It was a large fish, and a market woman, sensing our bewilderment as to how to cook it, took us into her home and cooked it for us. Nazare was absolutely beautiful, even though we did have several arguments. And when we left, I insisted Raymond stop in a luxury hotel, so that I could use the ladies' room. Once I was inside, I couldn't help but notice the rolls and rolls of American toilet paper stacked in a corner. Since that was an expensive item in Europe, and we needed it desperately, I saw nothing wrong with putting a roll under each arm of my ragged old trench coat.

Holding both my arms tightly to my side, I walked through the crowded lobby, outside and back into our camper. "Look what I've got, Raymond: two rolls of soft toilet paper! Isn't that great?"

"No!"

"No? Why not?"

"What do you think Jesus would say about that? You talk about pot-smoking being bad; what about stealing?"

"Raymond, how can you say such a thing? That's not stealing. I just took a couple of rolls of toilet paper from the ladies' room. That's hardly like going into a store deliberately."

"It's taking something that's not yours, and that's stealing."

"Well, I don't care, let's go."

We drove one block, when I looked at Ray and said, "Okay,

turn around. I'll have to take these two rolls back. Now I've got to march back into that lobby in front of everyone and return them."

"I didn't say you had to do that, Barbara."

"No, but the Holy Spirit won't let me rest until I do. From now on, I'm going to have to watch myself like a hawk on this stealing business. It's so subtle with me!"

It seemed like a lot of old sins were coming to the surface. I began to wonder — was this whole Christian life a mistake, after all? Or maybe we had been wrong to leave Spain and Dan? Returning to Monte Gordo where we had spent the first part of our glorious honeymoon, we found it had all the old allure and temptations. I couldn't bear to have dinner in a restaurant and not be able to have wine, and I became infuriated with jealousy and then self-pity when I saw other young couples having wine with their dinner. Wine now became the most important thing in my life; in fact, I couldn't see how I was ever going to go through life without it. I prayed hard in the beginning, but then when the desire to drink didn't leave, I gave up praying. It never entered my mind that I might have to pray even harder and longer on occasion. Up to now most of my experiences with the Lord were quick, direct answers and miracles. I was such an impatient person, I couldn't stand to suffer the irritation of even a hangnail, but would hastily pull it off and make it worse myself. And now I started to pout and argue with Ray.

"We never should have come back here. I'm not strong enough to be around memories, restaurants, romantic music, people, life, anything. I'll probably have to spend the rest of my life in church on my knees, and with other alcoholics who've stopped drinking always watching me and telling me what and what not to do. I'll have to listen to tapes and read Christian books and magazines. In short, my whole life will be spent in therapy!"

"Boy, are you being one hell of an ungrateful brat, Barbara!"

Since I obviously wasn't getting much sympathy from Raymond, I became a recluse at our campsite, insisting that I was not able to face the public at all. "Everyone drinks, everyone. I can't even go to the ladies' room in this campsite without coming across a group of people having wine or beer or brandy. Everyone's having fun but me." Fun — as if my misery had ever, ever been fun. But I didn't see that. I looked only at the tinkling ice in a glass and the color in a bottle and that initial warm glow — not at the non-stop drinking, the vomiting, the dry heaves, the blackouts, the loss of self-respect and the utter degradation. Nor did I do what Anne Murray had told me so specifically to do, when my "thinking became stinking": to follow through to where that lovely first drink would take me. And for me, it most certainly was the gutter. A BUD (building up to a drink) was exactly where I was, and it was getting worse. Ray left his diary open: "B. is not going anywhere. Stayed at camp all day. She is jittery and difficult. But with His help, we always manage to win out. *Praise Him!"*

The next day was worse. I began to feel queasy and shaky. We went in search of a hospital where I began a series of B-12 shots again. And as I watched the needle go in, I cried to myself as it pierced my arm: "Jesus, please, please, help me again. Forgive me for being so ungrateful. Lord, help me; I don't know how to be a Christian, to be good, to live in gratitude and a constant desire to stay sober. Even taking the toilet paper back was hard for me, and just yesterday I wanted to swipe some cheese from the camp store. Oh Jesus, this is why I never wanted to become a Christian. I told Dan I wouldn't make it. But Jesus, I want to make it for You. And Ray, he's never been so happy. Oh God, help me! Change me completely, do something with me."

The doctor interrupted my silent prayer. "Okay, miss, you may leave now. That bandaid can come off in an hour. Why are you crying? Did it hurt that much?"

"No, doctor."

But now he was curious. "Tell me: how did you get so run down?"

"I, uh, just didn't take care of myself. I guess I didn't care about living, or something like that."

"Well, you're on the right track now, young lady. Keep taking these shots."

My face beamed, when he said I was on the right track. I know I am, but it seems so hard to stay on that track, that's what I can't figure out. I wonder if I should write to Dan and tell him I'm having trouble, or ask for prayer, or ask him if this is unusual? No, I can't do that. I'll just disappoint him. He thinks I'm all healed, I'm sure. Other Christians probably don't get tempted like this, and if they do, it probably goes away quickly. I must be a hard case!

By the time we reached Sintra, on March 4th, and the Irish couple whose name Dan had given us, I was chafing at the bit. Stuffing in as many sweet chocolates as I could, I began to pound the seat of the camper and lock myself in, begging Jesus to keep me from a drink, and Ray not to let me out of his sight for one moment. I even thought of having him tie a leash around my waist when we went walking, for fear I'd escape into some bar, foaming at the mouth in search of alcohol.

The desire to drink was bad enough, but the anxiety attacks that followed made me think I was going to lose my mind. I began to itch all over, my back hurt, and even my gums ached. In short, I was a mess, and the last thing I wanted to do was see that Christian couple and hear them praise the Lord and shout Hallelujah. Even Ray was worried now. It began to seem that our glorious two-month second honeymoon was short-lived and over.

We were lost in Sintra, driving round and round. Having lost all interest in looking for this couple, we parked the camper in front of a shabby small apartment building. I was biting my nails furiously, while Ray was looking at a map for a camp near by. He was his old glum self, when the slip of paper that held the address of these people fell from his shirt pocket as he bent down to pick up his pen. Suddenly we realized that the number on the piece of paper was the same number as the building we were parked in front of. We looked from the paper to the building to each other. "Hey, we're here. This is it! We're parked in front of the building, and we didn't even know it."

"Hallelujah!" Ray shouted. "Jesus brought us here miraculously! It's meant for us to go in there, to see them. Princess, He's still with us, leading us. Hang on a little longer."

I cried and cried, smashing the cigarette that I was about to light, between my fingers. It had been six weeks since I'd had one, and one full month for Ray. Wiping my eyes and trying to get out of the van, I muttered, "Jesus, I don't understand so much. I thought I left the old me in Spain, in that fountain in church. How come it's still with me? But Lord, You're with me, anyhow. I can feel it and this, this miracle now is proof. Thank You, Jesus."

38

A pattern seemed to set in to our Christian life. After periods of intense struggle, where Ray and I even wondered if our conversion had "taken," we would experience great encouragement and joy, such as when we met Noel and Sandra in Sintra. The fact that their building was the very one we parked in front of to look for directions was only the beginning of a string of miracles that occurred during our stay with them. Although we couldn't understand the periods of lostness, arguing, and almost returning completely to our old selves, we struggled on in the Lord, not daring to discuss these times or bring them up with any of the fellow-Christians we met. Everyone always seemed so alive and enthusiastic, we were afraid to say that we were feeling depressed. "Ray, I think it will just take me longer to get healed. I was so sick from booze — maybe I'm a schizophrenic? How do I know that I'm not going crazy?"

"C'mon, Barbara, that is crazy! We've just got to keep our eyes on Jesus."

"But how do you do that twenty-four hours a day?"

Noel and Sandra knew the secret. They loved Jesus with a love that made them gladly give up everything they had to follow His call on their lives. Having left their native Ireland, Noel and Sandra and their little baby lived on next to nothing. After sharing their meal with us, which consisted of potatoes, they would pile Portuguese people from all over town into a broken-down van and take them to an out-of-the-way building, where they used the basement as a place to meet and worship Jesus. Since we had our new camper, it was a treat for all of them to drive with us.

Noel would lead the singing, praising the Lord, and directing Raymond through one of the poorest places we had visited. Yet the most heart-wrenching poverty that we saw couldn't take away the light that shone on the face of one of the young people, a girl who had spent nine months in the corner of a dark room in grave depression. This sixteen-year-old girl had been declared incurably mad six months before she found Jesus. I heard her sing out the most beautiful praises to the Lord — it was though an angel were singing. They began the meeting by singing and worshipping Jesus, praying for one another and sharing needs. How moving it was to see people so impoverished as these of Portugal, raising their hands over their heads and thanking Jesus for allowing them to be alive and there! When they thanked Jesus for Ray and me being brought into their kingdom, with tears in their eyes, it was all we could do to keep from weeping ourselves. I was so ashamed of my ingratitude, my bickering and questioning God....

Noel, the minister, asked Ray and me if we would stand on the platform up in front and give our testimony. "But Noel, we don't speak Portuguese or Spanish."

He chuckled. "It just so happens we have a translator here, whom God provided just the day before yesterday."

But I was terrified. "Noel, I'm sorry, but I could never talk before a large group of people. I've never done anything like that, except maybe to say one or two words when I was baptized in Spain. I just can't."

"Barbara," he said gently but firmly, "you're going to have to. God has a call on your life. This will be just one of many talks you will give. Trust Jesus with everything that is in you. Don't disappoint Him. Get up on that platform and tell them where you were and what Jesus has already done for you." He paused and looked at me. "How long have you been a Christian?"

"Two months."

"How long were you an alcoholic?"

"About ten years, I think."

"How long has it been since you've had a drink?"

"A little over two months."

"Okay, now get up there and share that. Jesus will do it in you. Believe me, I know."

I didn't doubt that Noel knew Jesus. He loved Him and was willing to starve, practically, in order to serve Him, in places where he really didn't want to be. And now he and this whole group here were praying and believing that God would give them a new truck to take them to their meetings. Ray and I had barely enough money to get back to the States, but we prayed and prayed that somehow, even though we couldn't do more than donate a little money towards the truck, somehow it would come.

With this on my mind, I stood up and immediately began to talk about how I had challenged Jesus to keep a praying mantis on our camper window during a twenty-mile coastal drive, as a sign that He was God. As Ray and I shared briefly about our lives, I shook and quivered, talking about where alcohol and serving my own desires had led me. I thought I would have an anxiety attack up there, as I watched the faces of these people, some of them who were now crying. Their tears touched me and I began to cry, too. I just stood there and cried and cried, until there were no more tears.

Then, as soon as I mentioned Jesus and how He intervened in my life, saving me from death, from probable suicide, there were shouts and people jumped to their feet and praised the Lord and shouted, "Hallelujah!"

"Noel, why are they doing this? Are they happy for me?"

"You bet they are!"

I began to laugh and cry and praise the Lord with them. And when everything was quiet again, Raymond picked up where I left off and finished our testimony.

Our stay was so real, warm and close with these people, it was as though we were related.

They offered us a home, our own house that would be given to us if we would remain with them. Again, our hearts were torn and pulled. Should we stay or should we go back to America? Back and forth, we pondered the question.

"Oh Ray, how will we ever know what God's will is?"

"Let's talk it over with Noel and Sandra tonight." That night, Noel said he didn't know what we should do. He needed help desperately, but said that the people in the States were poverty-stricken, too, "if not in the pocketbook, then truly in the soul. America is satiated and sin-sick. And it could be that God might want to use you there. Keep praying; He *will* speak."

In the meantime, Raymond, who had not been baptized in water, decided that he wanted to be. "Why not have the full course? I want all Jesus has to offer." And so, one cool day in March, Ray, along with several Portuguese, was baptized in the ocean by Noel. I froze as, with my jeans rolled up and my ankles in the icy water, I attempted to take pictures.

But Raymond wasn't cold at all. He emerged in his bathing suit with his hands raised and a big smile on his face: "My conversion is complete on formal levels; now all I need to do is stand firm in the faith!"

That was all I wanted to do, too: stand firm, for once in my life, in what I believed. Not to run or waver or hide, but to stand firm, and be able to speak up boldly for what I believed to be the truth, Jesus Christ, without a drink or pill to aid me.

"Raymond, do you really think we'll make it? Do you think we'll follow the Shepherd? Maybe you will, but I'm so afraid that I'm going to pull away, go off in another direction."

"Don't talk or even think that way. That fear is straight from the pit. Remember what Dan told us: your main problem was that spirit of fear. That's where Satan gets to you all the time. You're afraid you won't do this or that, or you'll fail, or — I don't know. Look: it *was* that way, but it's different now, with Jesus."

Our last night in Sintra we prayed up a storm to heaven, but still received no clear leading to stay or to go. It was the night of the prayer meeting; I watched and tried to listen for any sign I could see, hear or get. In fact, I was concentrating so hard on looking for signs that I missed what was being said and what was going on in the lives of the others at the meeting. An awareness of my self-centeredness quickened within me, and I saw myself with my arms folded about me, completely wrapped up in myself. I didn't know what to do with this feeling exactly, but knew that it wasn't at all pleasing to the Lord.

With everything in me, I got into the action of the room and what was going on. There were so many needs. And the problems of these people, who had to hide from the government to worship Jesus, were not just problems; they were tragedies.

For the first time, I saw my own life as not having been all that bad, and that I, like so many Americans, had been trapped within my own trappings.

As I was thinking about what seemed like so much to me, I noticed a tall, thin boy enter and take a seat at the back of the room. Somehow I sensed that this boy was sick inside, as I had been, tormented from within and couldn't get out of his own trappings. I stared at him across the room, unbinding him in the name of Jesus, praying for him and pleading for his soul, almost entering into a spiritual fight for him, though I didn't know what that meant.

Just about then, Noel asked for prayers aloud, for needs to be met. I waited until three other people had requested prayers for various concerns and then I jumped up, as though a surge of urgency had traveled through my body from head to toe. "I have a prayer request, Noel," I said quietly to him, not taking my eyes off the boy. "That boy in the back row must be saved, tonight." Shocked at myself, I sat down quickly and resumed praying for him.

Ray looked at me quizzically: "What are you doing? He's never been here before. How do you know it's safe?"

Stunned, I looked at him speechless; the thought had never entered my mind; nothing had, except that I knew he needed Jesus the way I did. Embarrassed now, and afraid to look up at the reaction of those around me, I kept my head down, praying. Then, before the service ended, Noel decided to have an altar call. People came forward, and many who had received the Lord went forward again. Then, when everyone else had sat down, and we were about to receive the closing benediction, the boy whom I was still praying for walked slowly forward to the platform. There was absolute silence in the room, as he stood there for the longest time, unable to say anything. Noel very gently whispered to him, but he didn't answer. Then Noel prayed for him, a few tears coursed down the boy's cheeks, and in Portuguese, he asked Jesus to come into his life.

I had gotten out of myself long enough to follow God's leading and pray for this soul. I was so grateful, I wanted to meet the boy I had prayed for. But the moment I took one step in his direction, I heard one word: *Stop.* Stopping right where I was, I looked at him. He seemed still somewhat confused by what he had done, wanting to shy away from all the hands that were coming his way. I sat back down in my seat and began praying for him again. This was my first experience with listening to God. I knew then that I would not meet the boy at all. I was to accept that, and continue to pray for him. And I did.

I was awestruck. I could hear God! It seemed impossible. It was impossible. But I had heard Him. And He wasn't finished. "Raymond, I think the Lord has told me that we should return to the United States as planned. It doesn't make much sense, but I think we can someday help those who are suffering inside, who are trapped and bound like that boy, by their own cravings, like booze and drugs, and maybe there's more, I don't know."

"You may be right about going back to the States; we're certainly not getting any definite leading or sign to stay here."

Later that night, just before we said our final goodbye to Noel and Sandra, and a few others of whom we had become especially fond, they all prayed for our journey and our life ahead in Christ. Noel was serious, more serious than I had ever seen him. Laying his hand on my head, he told us both to go back to the United States of America, where we were to serve our country. Surprised at what he was saying, he cried "Hallelujah!" and then, with more confidence, continued: "Grow and mature in Christ, children. Serve your country — and Barbara, tell the Jews who the Messiah is. You must tell them about Jesus of Nazareth!"

Chills went up and down my back. That was a key part of the reason why I was to go home, and I hadn't seen it. My excitement about hearing that lasted all of one minute; I thought of my family and Jewish friends — how could I ever tell them?

39

We left Sintra the following morning, feeling on top of the world. But by the time we reached Bordeaux country, where we spent Raymond's twenty-ninth birthday in the camper with a candle in a cupcake, both of us were down under the world. Bordeaux wine was always one of my favorites, even though any cheap whiskey, gin or sherry did just fine in the latter days.

Once again, I simply ignored that ugly truth and concentrated on the beautiful, dark, ruby red wine that looked so inviting and that the entire country of France was partaking of — everyone but poor little old me.

On our way to Paris, passing through Orleans and the beautiful chateaux country, I thought and thought about the Moulin Rouge and all the marvelous cafes and clubs I'd heard so much about all my life, and of course the champagne.

"I don't care about seeing the Eiffel Tower or the Arc de Triomphe or the Champs Elysees or anything else. I'm crippled for the rest of my life. I can't believe I'm actually in Paris and not able to drink wine! It's just incredible! Why, to any Frenchman, that's a sin!"

I wouldn't be cheered up, and so I stayed in my mess, until it got so bad I almost went into a bar and bought a bottle of anything. But by God's grace, at one point I murmured, "Jesus help me," and instead of finding a bar, I found a small piece of paper with a man's name on it that the Christian couple at Rota had given me. I remembered them telling me that this man was a sober contact in Paris. "Call him right away! Don't wait!" But as usual, I waited, thinking that all I needed was myself and Jesus, and no outside help at all. Only the truth was, I hadn't called on Jesus, until it was almost too late. I finally began to see that I couldn't trust myself, and that I'd better use the number given to me, perhaps by the Lord.

We met our contact — a writer and journalist who had been sober for ten years — at a church in Paris. He spent nine hours with Ray and me, trying to get my thinking straight and my head glued back on. "You want to drink? Go ahead. But as you put that glass to your mouth, remember where the Lord found you, and what shape you were in. Because you'll be back there tomorrow! In fact, you're progressing there, kid, right now, even though you're not drinking. You'll be a hell of a lot worse, if you pick up that drink, than you were even two months ago. And next time, you may not get back. None of us knows for sure, if there really is one more chance left for us."

When the awful craving finally did subside, we found laughter in sharing with one another about our flaky lives. "Who ever wanted one cornflake anyway? Forget it, kid; what's one lousy drink to an alcoholic with a bottomless cup?" And so, at the end of our first day in Paris, I was free to see the sights and really enjoy the trip. We continued on with our Bible reading each night and were just about through with the New Testament, when we hit Amsterdam.

I felt *good* — so good, in fact that I forgot how needy I had been just a few days before. As we toured Amsterdam with its quaint canals and beautiful scenery, I longed for the sun to go down and the night to appear, with all its glittering cafes lined up one by one, next to each other. Even though the distinctive smell of booze was replaced by the sweet, pungent aroma of hashish, and the after-five attire of black cocktail dress, suit and tie was replaced by blue-jeans and a T-shirt, I still felt as though I was on familiar ground.

Hippies from every country, especially Germany, Scandinavia and America, packed into the smoke-filled rooms, slouched on low couches and walls, and listening to the loud, eerie sounds called music. Raymond really "dug" it, and the first person he met on a street corner who offered him hashish, he took it. For one week, we were stoned, stoned, stoned!

Refusing to listen to the nudge inside that later became a gnawing at my conscience, I blamed this entire week's "trip" on Ray. Because it was dope and not alcohol, I avoided the truth that a high was a high, and any escape would suit me just fine.

Late at night in our camper, there were still intervals when we would attempt a prayer, even ask God for forgiveness for our behavior. There were only a few more chapters to go before we would be finished with the New Testament, and yet each time we attempted to read any of the Bible, we were thrown into confusion. Finally, as a last resort we tried to take turns reading aloud to each other, only to find ourselves bursting out in hideous, uncontrollable laughter. Later, as I tossed and turned, trying desperately to fall asleep, I became aware of an old friend of mine — *fear*.

Our last night in Amsterdam, we went into a three-story nightclub, ironically called the Paradiso, filled with strange weirdos, like us. Drugs were everywhere. The entire building was decorated in the most grotesque fashion, with streams of toilet paper hanging from the walls. Bright orange and other colors that didn't blend at all, were slashed across the walls, ceiling and floor. There were people there dressed as animals, as creatures from the past and present, all looking deranged, sick and — full of Satan. I became terrified and had a horrible sense of doom all around me.

Abruptly, I remembered my prayer to the Lord back in Spain, where I had asked Him to show me if marijuana was wrong. I had pretended to myself that I never heard the answer to that prayer, never did know for sure that it was wrong. And now I had innocently fallen into this pit.

Except that this high — or any high — was something the Lord was trying to deliver me *from,* not lead me back into. There was no way to rationalize *any* escape from reality!

Yet even with this sudden awareness, I still accepted the pipe filled with kief that someone had taken from someone. Three drags of that stuff, and I was off into the torments of hell. Never had it taken so little to get me so freaked out! I began hallucinating uncontrollably, sensing that I was being lowered into hell itself for an experience, a reminder of what went on there. Only I didn't know if I would get out. "This is what you want? Here it is, all of it!"

I tried to leave by pushing through the crowds, falling up and down the stairs, in search of the second floor. The orange walls turned into fiery flames. The people around me were false; I saw their faces and mouths pulled back, taped to their cheeks creating a plastic or phony smile. They weren't happy; they were miserably doomed, having given themselves to their lusts, and now they were being devoured by these lusts, one by one. Some young people were skin over bones from lack of food; their teeth black an decayed. Some girls were stripped down to nothing, as they danced wildly around, having lost their minds and all ability to think or make a decision. Men turned into animals, eating human flesh. There were blown-up pictures of American movie stars on the walls, and there were cynical comments about America and its indescribable decay. "America, you are a joke! Don't you see how sick you are?" Banners held various statements all indicating that we were damned.

And then, as I reached the second floor, I literally saw through the flesh and bones of these people, as they paraded around like robots. Their hearts had shrunk; they were shriveled, dead, without feeling. "Oh my God!" I shrieked. "Get me out of here! Jesus, please help me! *Get me out of here!* I know what you're saying. I know where I am. I'll *never* do this again! Please take me back!"

Just then, Ray caught up with me. He was on his way to becoming one of them, I noticed, but his heart had not been touched yet. I could see through his chest; the arteries were filled and pulsating. "Ray, listen to me: we have got to get out of here — *now!* We are in hell now, because of what we are doing. It's *evil*, and the Lord is letting me see just how evil this is."

But Ray shrugged and patted me on the shoulder. "C'mon, relax and enjoy yourself. Your imagination is gonzo again."

"Ray, I'm leaving alone, then. I've got to get out of here; I'm suffocating." Unable to hold onto the bannister or walk by myself, I began to gasp for breath. Overwhelmed with fear, falling and drooling from the corners of my mouth, I began to crawl down the stairs. I saw some men dressed in black dinner jackets, looking at me. They smiled their hideous smiles, and their teeth fell out beside me on the floor.

Somehow, Raymond had followed me and now picked me up. "Okay, I'll find a way out of here, but after you get some fresh air, I'm coming back in."

All I could do was mutter the name of Jesus — but that was enough. Through drunken crowds, stepping over bodies, some passed out, some bruised and intertwined together, we made our way out of the Paradiso.

As soon as we were outside on the street, looking at the shills under the neon lights, beckoning people inside, I began to run. Breathing as deeply as I could, I kept gasping over and over, "Jesus, restore my mind and Raymond's," and I kept on running. Ray ran after me, yelling at me to slow down, but I kept on going faster and faster, until suddenly I found myself at a corner, where I could see our camper. Thanking God and screaming, I ran to it. Ray caught up with me, and then we were sitting inside the camper staring at one another.

"Ray! That was a nightmare!"

"Yeah! Where were we? I'm confused."

"Raymond, I believe Jesus showed us how He felt about drugs. They're Satan's kingdom. All I know is I can hardly believe I'm out of there. I'll never smoke anything again, never!"

Later we learned that the "stuff" we'd had that night had been mescaline mixed with hashish or kief.

I couldn't wait until we left for Brussels, for the reminder of my journey into hell was all around me. Each corner I turned, as we shopped for last-minute things, flashed another cafe and another horror picture with it. Sometimes I squeezed my eyes tightly shut, hoping to block out the mental memories of yesterday. Over and over again I asked Jesus to forgive me, and never, ever leave me. My stomach was in knots and I was still fearful until finally, late that night, our last night in Amsterdam, Ray and I began to finish reading the New Testament.

We both began to see that it was we who had left the Lord, because we wanted to indulge once again in the very thing that nearly destroyed us. We had rationalized over and over again, moving farther away from conviction and truth, as we told ourselves that pot was harmless, just a natural element to be used and enjoyed, like cigarettes. But seeing the fine line I was on, the brink of sanity versus sheer craziness, and black craziness at that, I vowed never to take drugs again.

My tears and pleadings were finally hushed, as I re-read the very last paragraph in my Bible before Revelation, in the letter to Jude: "Now to the *One* who can keep you from falling and set you in the presence of his glory, jubilant and above reproach, to the only God our Savior, be glory and majesty, might and authority, through Jesus Christ our Lord, before all time, now, and for evermore. Amen."

"Ray, read this," I prodded, pointing to the paragraph. He had been more quiet than I, his mood still sullen. As he read, I watched his face change from a droopy, furrowed look to a clear, straightened one, with just a hint of a smile at the corners of his mouth.

"That's the answer," he said, closing the Bible. "He *is* the only *One* who can keep us from falling. Now, let's get back to Him and accept His forgiveness."

A little more suspicious of ourselves and of how easy it would be to get off the track we had found, we left Brussels for the airport — and the plane home. The odyssey was at last over. By the grace of God, we were still alive and together, and by His amazing grace, we were about to embark on a new odyssey — cleansed and forgiven. Only one more obstacle remained in our path, but it was a huge one, and it loomed right there outside the passenger gate. As we waited to board the ominous-looking airliner, Ray wrote the final entry in his trip diary, while I continued to nervously tear at my cuticles.

"Relax, princess. We're not traveling alone now."

"I know that Ray, but I can't help it. I'm scared to death of flying, especially without even one strong drink to steady my nerves." Leaning over to see what Raymond had written, I clasped my hand in his.

> We have come to the end of perhaps a turning-point in our lives, and we return, trying hard to take it a day at a time. If we can do that, it may work. If not, *the anticipations will* overrun us. Anyway, we shall pray daily, allow ourselves to be led by Him, and all will go well. It has been wonderful being alone this long with Barbara, and the experiences we have shared have drawn us closer than we've ever been. Our lives have become welded together these past 215 days, and this bond will help us in the States. It's hard to remember now, how I felt when we left to come over here, but it was uneasiness, vague hopes and dreams. But now, we have been away, alone in strange lands, and with God's help have solved problems, created problems, shared happiness, anger, highs (ha!), lows, everything.
>
> And we are better for it. Nothing will seem so impossible now, especially with God walking with us. So, I reluctantly write the last lines in this diary, which maybe we will go back to from time to time, to draw on for the strength we found in Europe. And — who knows — this may be just the first book in a volume — God willing. Finis.

As my eyes rested on those last words, Raymond took his hand from mine, getting to his feet, as the loud-speaker announced that it was time to board the plane.

"Oh no," I moaned. "I don't want to go. Ray, I'm not quite ready; can't we go tomorrow?"

"What? Of course not! Get ahold of yourself! We're going."

I tried to keep pace with Ray, who pulled me and our bags along. I kept saying, "Jesus help me," to the rhythm of my pounding heart, as we boarded the giant airplane that was to take us home.

"Do you want to sit by the window?" Ray asked lightly.

"No! Definitely no. I don't want to see a thing. I just hope we get there."

Raymond's smile vanished, as we settled into our seats. Looking at me seriously, he said: "Barbara, you have *got* to get ahold of yourself. Look at you: you're shaking. Talk to Jesus — and write your last words in your own diary; it will occupy your mind."

Reluctantly, I fumbled through my notebook for a clean page at the end.

> Jesus, please forgive me for my fear. Please guide us and direct us. Keep your hand on us, as you have. I pray that I can live this life in you and carry this message to others in need.
>
> We pray for Ray's parents, and my mother, Lord. Keep them safe and guide and direct them, Lord, as you have done with us, with love and compassion. I pray for the little church in Torremolinos and Dan and his wife Rhoda, and Robby, and the others. May your grace be upon them. Also Noel and Sandra in Portugal. Be with them too, always.

I stopped writing to look up at the stewardess who leaned over to tell me that she was sorry but they had just run out of soft drinks. And at that moment, she was interrupted by the loudspeaker system: *"Attention everyone: there is free champagne, as much as you want, on this flight back to America. Have fun!"*

Ray and I looked at each other — and burst out laughing.

"God has quite a sense of humor, doesn't he?" Ray gasped.

"Oh yes, this is a riot!" At this point, my mouth was so dry, I could have downed anything, but I did manage to chuckle a little, attempting to show Ray that I could see the humor in it all.

As the engine turned up and roared, I dug what was left of my fingernails into the palm of Ray's hand. We rolled down the runway, faster and faster, and then soared into the sky. My eyes were shut tight, and I kept pleading to the Lord to keep this plane safe. Then I added: "Lord, I don't want to die. I want to live. I want to go home to America. I don't feel the way I did when I left — about my country, my mother and Ray's parents. I want to make up to them and everyone else I hurt somehow. *Give me a chance to change, Lord. Help me, keep me and protect me.*"

I was interrupted by Ray's cheery words. "It's okay now, Princess, we're safely up in the air. Look at the sky; it's beginning to clear. C'mon, look!"

Still unable to look out the window, I opened my eyes and patted Ray's hand. "I'll look in a minute, Ray. Why don't you just enjoy it."

It wasn't long before Ray dozed off with a magazine in his lap. He looked so sweet and peaceful, my eyes began to fill with tears of gratitude for him and how Jesus saved our marriage.

"It is a miracle," I murmured to myself, "it truly is. I don't know how to ever thank you, Jesus."

Still feeling somewhat restless and jumpy, I opened my New Testament and read the words that Dan had written. "To Barbara, With confidence of *complete freedom through Jesus.*"

Very slowly, I peeked over Ray's shoulder to look out the window. Clouds that seemed to be made of huge wads of cotton gradually began to break apart from each other, and through them streamed the most beautiful golden light. Its brightness began to fill the sky, until every thread of cloud was far behind us. I felt bright, clean, and whole — like the sky. I was safe, free, and at peace. Eagerly now, I thumbed through the Bible, glancing up to look out the window, to make sure that none of the clouds had come back.

My eyes traveled from the window to page after page until they came to rest on Acts 26:16-18.

> I have appeared to you for a purpose: to appoint you my servant and witness, to testify both to what you have seen and to what you shall yet see of me. I will rescue you from this people and from the Gentiles to whom I am sending you. I send you to open their eyes and turn them from *darkness to light,* from the dominion of Satan to God, so that by trust in me, they may obtain forgiveness of sins, and a place with those whom God has made his own.

"Thank you, Jesus," I whispered, and closing my eyes, I nestled my head on Ray's shoulder.

Epilogue

God has done what I asked Him to do. He has helped me, kept me, and protected me. The first few years of sobriety brought highs and lows; after having spent such a long time anesthetized, to face life and learn about myself head on was (and still is at times) painful. Clouds did return in my life, and I have cried often, but *always* the Lord has been there, giving me a chance to choose Him and change. Eleven years have now passed since Jesus came into my life in that small church on the coast of Spain. Ray and I, our children, David, 9, and Christina, 6, now live in another coastal town. Ray is Director of the Alcoholism Detoxification Center on Cape Cod. We continue to learn of God's love and mercy and try, one day at a time, to live in obedience to His will.

"I see you walking hand in hand, going up a cobblestone path, tripping, and sometimes falling, but making it, together." This word of prophecy was given to Ray and me, on a weekend retreat in 1972. The prophecy has proved true, and by the grace of God, we are still making it, together.

If you or your church are interested in a presentation or a workshop on alcoholism, our address is:

>Box 873
>East Dennis
>Massachusetts 02641

Ray, Barbara, David and Christina

Acknowledgements

During the past ten years, the Lord has brought many people into my life to support, encourage and assist me in the writing of this book. I am grateful to them all.

I am especially thankful to my husband Raymond, without whose patience and love I could never have made it; to Cay and Judy, who have been used by God to encourage Ray and me; to Father Arthur Lane, whose insight helped me through my alcoholism and drug addiction. With all my heart, I thank God for giving me, in him, the father I never had.

Pastor Daniel Del Vecchio of the Evangelical Community Church in Torremolinos, Spain, who led me to Christ. To Rev. Peter Marshall, my former pastor, for his ministry in my life.

To Jill and David Elmer, Barbara Manuel, Helen and Hal Helms, Mary Jackson, and Camie Ford and many others at the Community of Jesus, for their support and encouragement. And to a close-knit group of friends at East Dennis who have shared so much of my spiritual pilgrimage for ten years.

And to my editor, David Manuel with gratitude for his perseverance in urging me to continue writing this book. His constant help, belief in Jesus Christ and reliance on prayer have been a bold and powerful example to me.

And finally to my mother, for all her patience and forbearance.